Empire, Global Coloniality and African Subjectivity

EMPIRE, GLOBAL COLONIALITY AND AFRICAN SUBJECTIVITY

Sabelo J. Ndlovu-Gatsheni

berghahn
NEW YORK · OXFORD
www.berghahnbooks.com

Published in 2013 by

Berghahn Books

www.berghahnbooks.com

Library of Congress Cataloging-in-Publication Data

Ndlovu-Gatsheni, Sabelo J.
 Empire, global coloniality and African subjectivity / Sabelo J.
Ndlovu-Gatsheni.
   p. cm.
 Includes bibliographical references.
   ISBN 978-0-85745-951-0 (hardback) -- ISBN 978-1-78238-193-8 (paper-
back) -- ISBN 978-0-85745-952-7 (ebook)
 1. Globalization--Political aspects--Africa. 2. Africa--Politics and
government--1960- 3. Africa--Economic conditions--1960- 4.
Nationalism--Africa. I. Title.
 JZ1318.N425 2013
 327.1096--dc23

                                                                    2012032901

British Library Cataloguing in Publication Data

A catalogue record for this book is available from the British Library

Printed on acid-free paper

ISBN: 978-0-85745-951-0 hardback
ISBN: 978-1-78238-193-8 paperback
ISBN: 978-0-85745-952-7 ebook

Contents

Preface

Humanity is today facing a stark reality of a modernity and civilization that is proving incapable of solving the problems it created. Modernity has created modern problems for which it has no modern solutions (Escobar 2004: 230). It is a modernity that is historically traceable to such Western processes as the Renaissance, Reformation, Enlightenment, French Revolution and Industrial Revolution, making it ontologically Western-centric. But read from a Western perspective, this modernity is sociologically credited with the creation of modern institutions such as the nation-state and basic features such as self-reflexivity as well as the disembedding of social life from local context (Giddens 1990). It is a modernity that is culturally credited with the substitution of folk knowledge by expert and techno-scientific knowledge (Habermas 1973, 1987). It is a modernity that is philosophically celebrated for creating the Cartesian subject as the fountain of all knowledge about the world.

I am here referring to Euro-American modernity that once promised humanity a brave modern world in which rationality and techno-scientific thought would be able to overcome all the obstacles standing in the way of human progress. This promise was only fulfilled to a minor extent, particularly if one interrogated the current state of the modern world order from the perspective of colonial difference and from Africa. Africa is an epistemic site where poverty has not yet been made history; where curable diseases still decimate human lives; where inequalities are still rife; where the legacies of Western racism and the dark side of modernity are still felt on a daily basis. This reality of a modernity and a civilization that was incapable of solving modern problems was clearly identified long ago by Aimé Césaire. He wrote that:

> A civilization that proves incapable of solving the problems it creates is a decadent civilization. A civilization that chooses to close its eyes to its most crucial problems is a stricken civilization. A civilization that uses its principles for trickery and deceit is a dying civilization. The fact is that the so-called European civilization – 'Western' civilization – as it has been shaped by two centuries of bourgeois rule, is incapable of

solving the two major problems to which its existence has given rise: the problem of the proletariat and the colonial problem; that Europe is unable to justify itself either before the bar of 'reason' or before the bar of 'conscience', and that, increasingly, it takes refuge in a hypocrisy which is all the more odious because it is less and less likely to deceive. *Europe is indefensible* ... What is serious is that 'Europe' is morally, spiritually indefensible. And today the indictment is brought against it not by the European masses alone, but on a world scale, by tens and tens of millions of men [and women] who, from the depth of slavery, set themselves up as judges. (Césaire 1972: 23, emphasis is in the original)

Césaire was writing during the heyday of direct colonialism. During this time colonialism was manifesting its DNA of violence, repression and exploitation. Today the problem is not colonialism but coloniality, which emerged from colonialism and has assumed global proportions to the extent of being best understood as global coloniality. This global coloniality is a leitmotif of the currently existing empire, that of the United States of America (U.S.A.). The present crisis of modernity was predicted by such theorists as Karl Marx, Vladimir Lenin, Samir Amin and many others. Today even those African theorists like Achille Mbembe (2012a: 34), who has been severely critical of nationalist-inspired discourses that were consistently opposed to empire and global coloniality, who instead favoured close integration of Africa into the global community that he considered to be open to cosmopolitanism, presenting the best global future that Africa must not resist; even he is now railing against the capitalist system and present modernity. He recently wrote a short piece about 'a planetary recording of situations of misery, debt and enforced idleness'. He elaborated that today capitalism is moving in two directions, the first is towards increasing exploitation of large parts of the world through the old strategy of primitive accumulation and the second towards 'squeezing of every last drop of value out of the planet'. At the centre of this is the reality of a 'labour that has ceased to be the great wellspring of wealth' (Mbembe 2012a: 34). This is possible because capitalist production could be increased using sophisticated machinery and technologies that do not need increasing quantities of labour (Mbembe 2012a: 34). The present-day economies operate like 'speculative bubbles of a finance industry constantly refining the arts of making money by buying and selling nothing but various forms of money' (Mbembe 2012a: 34).

The result of all this has been a global crisis. It is a crisis that is wrongly reduced to a financial crisis. In reality this is a crisis of modernity and its epistemology. It is a multi-layered and structural crisis. It is a crisis of methodologies, a failure to understand how to solve modern problems. It is a crisis of legitimacy for the current world order. It is a crisis of relevance for Euro-American epistemologies that have lost their redemptive potential. At the centre of all this is the intractable problem of the relationship of popular democracy and global capitalism. Popular democracy cannot be achieved without achievement of genuine decolonization that has the potential to empower the poor socially, politically and economically. But empowerment of the poor is seen in capitalist circles as a threat to private property and the freedom of market forces. Equitable redistribution of wealth is viewed as a threat to capitalism itself. Mbembe (2012a: 34) correctly observed that 'capital would rather abolish democracy to save capitalism from a majority dedicated to economic and social redistribution'. The fact that global capitalism and global popular struggles for popular democracy are at odds compounds and exacerbates the crisis of modernity.

It is this reality that sent me to work on two book projects beginning in 2010. This one is a sequel to my other forthcoming book entitled *Coloniality of Power in Postcolonial Africa* which deals with how coloniality made it impossible for a postcolonial African world to emerge as it disciplined forces of decolonization so that they ended up as reformist and emancipatory movements rather than liberatory ones. Reformist emancipatory movements do not question modernity per se. They operate as critics of modernity while using its terms of reference and their horizon shows democracy and human rights. Liberatory movements are expected to be qualitatively and ideologically superior to emancipatory movements in terms of seeking a radical decolonial turn that has the potential to create new humanity and genuine freedom accompanied by economic empowerment and cognitive justice.

The current book is as much about empire, global coloniality, and African subjectivity as it is about pan-Africanism and nationalism as part of African responses to global imperial designs and colonial matrices of power. Theoretically, this book is informed by decolonial epistemic perspective predicated on three core analytical concepts, namely coloniality of power, coloniality of knowledge and coloniality of being. These concepts enable not only systematic interrogation of power asymmetries, epistemological colonization, and pathologization as well as 'thingification'/objectification of what it means to be African, but also examination of the poverty of counter-hegemonic discourses evolved by Africans, such as Negritude and others that remained beholden to the immanent logic of colonialism and its racial articulation of human identities.

This book, however, does not dismiss African counter-hegemonic discourses as simply poor reverse discourses, but it rather captures their development and growth including revealing their complexities and ideological innovations and shifts in line with equally complex global imperial designs. African decolonial thought and resistance politics has never been fixed and frozen in time, but has always been complex, manifesting multiple genealogies and ideologies ranging widely from earlier versions such as Ethiopianism, Garveyism, Negritude, African Personality, Black Consciousness Movements, experimentation with African socialism(s) to African Renaissance and revival of pan-Africanism in the twenty-first century.

At the centre of African responses to global imperial designs has been the drive to engage and disengage, negotiate and fight, appropriate some aspects and resist others, and looking back and forward. Broadly speaking, the numerous African intellectual and academic productions have been basically about capturing the diverse aspects of African experience, about understanding and articulation of the African condition; and about searching for the absent centre of ontology. This is why Toyin Falola argued that scholarship on Africa inevitably carries anger and is polemical because it has been conditioned to respond to realities of alterity and emerges from a terrain saturated with '"others" statements, usually negative about its members and their continent' (Falola 2004: 17). This condition brought together intellectuals and political actors into an uneasy coalition on the necessity of decolonization. But when African leaders began to manifest crises of repetition without change, abusing juridical independence to enrich themselves while keeping workers and peasants in subjection, a majority of African intellectuals turned into severe critics of the postcolonial state and began to call for genuine independence. This struggle has been ongoing since the 1960s and is ranged against inept African leadership as well as against global coloniality.

The current book's point of departure is Michael Hardt and Antonio Negri's seminal study *Empire* (2000), which offers useful interventions on empire albeit from a Euro-American perspective. A Euro-American perspective and an African decolonial perspective on empire, global coloniality and African subjectivity, differ radically in the sense that the former departs from an epistemic site where the empire deposited its positive values and cultures of modernity, secularity, mass education, human rights, ethics, equality, development and democracy, whereas the latter emerges from an epistemic site where the darker aspects of empire that include mercantilism, the slave trade, imperialism, colonialism, forcible Christianization, apartheid, neo-colonialism, neo-liberalism, underdevelopment, 'hot wars', and structural adjustments, were the order of interactions. This is why Hardt and Negri could write of a 'phantasmagoric empire' that was decoupled from imperialism to the extent that such an empire became necessary to maintain global order.

The current book is not about this supposedly benevolent and magnanimous empire with a mission to maintain global order and enforce justice; it is about the 'actually existing empire' that is ontologically imperialist and colonialist, exploitative and violent, underpinned by hypocrisy and double standards. It is about an empire that is double-faced, hiding coloniality behind a rhetoric of spreading modernity, civilization, development, democracy and human rights. The book delves deeper into an analysis of global imperial designs and colonial matrices of power with a view to unmask this empire's leitmotif, coloniality. It is a book about an existing empire that is addicted to oil and is underpinned by a capitalist order whose nervous system is maintained by oil and other natural resources available in Africa in particular and the Global South in general. It is about an empire that is fully armed with weapons of mass destruction and does not hesitate in using/abusing multilateral and global institutions, including the United Nations (UN), to authorize its predatory interventions into Iraq, Afghanistan and Libya as long as these sites have natural gas and oil.

Its approach is historical and thematic. It situates the African experience and African struggles ranged against the empire and global coloniality within the context of the unfolding of global history since the dawn of modernity. The book's main proposition, which it shares with Latin American decolonial thinkers like Arturo Escobar, Walter D. Mignolo, Anibal Quijano, Ramón Grosfoguel, Enrique Dussel and Nelson Maldonado-Torres as well as with African scholars like Archie Mafeje, Bernard Magubane, Samir Amin, Issa G. Shivji, Bade Onimonde, Georges Nzongola-Ntalaja, Sam Moyo, Paul Tiyambe Zeleza, Tukumbi Lumumba-Kasongo, Thandika Mkandawire, Ibbo Mandaza, Carlos Lopes, Adebayo Olukoshi, Valentine Y. Mudimbe, Ngugi wa Thiong'o and many others, is that Africans in particular and peoples of the Global South in general continue to live under coloniality and as modern subjects they breathe coloniality on a daily basis.

Approached from a decolonial epistemic perspective, the current world order is best described as hierarchical, racialized, capitalist, hetero-normative, Christian-centric, Euro-American-centric, and asymmetrical (Grosfoguel 2007). At its apex are the U.S.A. and its North Atlantic Treaty Organization (NATO) partners. At the bottom is Africa and its people who are still struggling to liberate themselves from global imperial designs put in place at the time of conquest and colonial matrices of power that underpin ideologies and epistemologies of alterity.

Ideologies and epistemologies of alterity have combined to produce African subjectivity that is constituted by a perennial lack: lacking souls, lacking civilization, lacking writing, lacking responsibility, lacking development, lacking human rights and lacking democracy. It is an unending discourse that invents particular 'lacks' suitable for particular historical epochs so as to justify perpetuation of asymmetrical power relations and to authorize various forms of external interventions into Africa including military interventions. During the period of colonial encounters, explorers, adventurers, missionaries, colonial and imperialist ideologues like Lord Lugard, Cecil John Rhodes and Jan Smuts, and many others, including anthropologists, propagated ideologies and epistemologies of alterity. Today it is the Non-Governmental Organizations (NGOs) and the media that propagate these ideologies.

This book is written at a time when Western modernity, and its promises of a brave modern world in which rationality was expected to enable humanity to transcend every other obstacle to its chosen trajectory, has been hit by a severe crisis. This crisis of modernity is clearly exemplified by the ongoing global financial crisis. It is also a crisis of global leadership that is manifesting itself within the multilateral and global institutions that include the UN, the World Trade Organization (WTO) and many others, where consensus has broken down on pertinent issues like military interventions, strategies of mitigating climate change and trade regimes. The world is at a crossroads whereby modernity has created a plethora of problems like those of climate change, terrorism, proliferation of weapons of mass destruction, migration, and many others, to which modernity has no solutions. Euro-American epistemology is also in crisis, and this reality calls for mobilization and the harnessing of other knowledge.

It is within this context that this book joins the Latin American decolonial thinkers and African ones like Ngugi wa Thiong'o, Kwasi Wiredu, Archie Mafeje and many others: favouring a decolonial turn in the humanities and social sciences, with potential to legitimate and enable pluriversalism as opposed to the failing universalism predicated on Euro-American hegemonic epistemologies. What this decolonial turn entails is a recovery of that/those knowledge(s) that were displaced by triumphalist Euro-American epistemologies. The world can only be saved by a combination of ecologies of knowledge. This book must, therefore, be read as a modest call by a committed African scholar for another knowledge, another world, and another logic that is open to pluriversality.

Without the encouragement from members of the Africa Decolonial Research Network (ADERN), I would not have attempted to write this book. Informal and formal discussions with members of ADERN kept me motivated to write. I particularly want to thank Dr Finex Ndhlovu (University of New England in Australia), Morgan Ndlovu (University of South Africa and Monash University in Australia), Richard Eddie Plaatjie (University of South Africa), Sentime Kasay (University of South Africa and University of Stellenbosch), Tendayi Sithole (University of South Africa), Dr Wendy Willems (London School of Economics and Political Science), Pearl Dastile (University of South Africa), Dr Edith Phaswana (University of Johannesburg in South Africa), Monene Mogashoa (University of South Africa), and Eric Nyembezi Makoni (University of Johannesburg), with all of whom I spent a lot of time discussing the importance of decolonial epistemic perspective in understanding the structural predicament of postcolonial Africa. I must also thank numerous other colleagues who were opposed to decolonial thought and who always tried to get me to explain the value of decolonial thought during a time of increasing globalization, when, according to them, colonialism and imperialism had been defeated. Their challenging questions contributed a lot towards sharpening the conceptual part of this book. The more I faced opposition, the more I felt the need for this book.

Professor Ramón Grosfoguel (University of California, Berkeley) a leading decolonial thinker, made available to me useful information on decolonial thought produced by the Latin American Modernity/Coloniality Programme; Professor Valentine Y. Mudimbe (Duke University in the U.S.A.) read the whole of the first draft of the first volume to which this one is a sequel. His extensive and incisive comments helped me to organize the books into logical themes. I would also like to thank Professor Rosemary Moeketsi (Executive Dean of the College of Human Sciences, University of South Africa) for allowing me to toy with my ideas in decolonial thought and for giving me space to work with young academics to explore the merits and demerits of the decolonial epistemic perspective.

Professor Moeketsi supported our application as ADERN to participate in the Barcelona Summer School on Decolonizing Power and Knowledge, held in Spain from 9 to 19 July 2012, where I met like-minded academic colleagues who deepened my understanding of the importance of decolonizing knowledge and power as part of the struggle for liberation in the Global South. Professor Peter Stewart (Head of Department of Development Studies, University of South Africa) read and commented on Chapter Four of this book, as did Dr Siphamandla Zondi (Executive Director of the Institute of Global Dialogue) and Dr Sifiso Mxolisi Ndlovu (South African Democracy Trust-SADET).

I would also like to extend my thanks to my son Vulindlela Kings, whose love sustains me in all my academic endeavours. My young sister Sifiso was always available to remain with Vuli while I was away for research, despite her own demanding doctoral studies at the University of the Witwatersrand. Two anonymous reviewers identified by Berghahn Books, who carefully read the first version of this book manuscript and made comprehensive comments, enabled me to strengthen the central arguments of this book. Ann Przyzycki DeVita, the Associate Editor at Berghahn Books in New York, was a pleasure to work with throughout all the stages of the publication of this book. However, I remain entirely responsible for all the issues raised in this book.

Sabelo J. Ndlovu-Gatsheni
Pretoria, South Africa
August 2012

PART 1

GLOBAL IMPERIAL DESIGNS AND EMPIRE

CHAPTER 1

Empire and Global Coloniality
Towards a Decolonial Turn

The history of Africa is, of course, one of cultural oppression on a major scale. Nowhere else was the oppression so comprehensive, so savage. African history was denied or appropriated; African culture belittled; the status and standing of Africans as human beings was called into question.

(Pal Ahluwalia and Paul Nursery-Bray 1997: 2)

I am talking about societies drained of their essence, cultures trampled underfoot, institutions undermined, lands confiscated, religions smashed, magnificent artistic creations destroyed, extraordinary possibilities wiped out ... I am talking about millions of [women and] men torn from their gods, their land, their habits, their life – from life, from the dance, from wisdom.

I am talking about millions of [women and] men in whom fear has been cunningly instilled, who have been taught to have an inferiority complex, to tremble, kneel, despair, and behave like flunkies ...

I am talking about natural economies that have been destroyed – harmonious and viable economies – adapted to indigenous population – about food crops destroyed, malnutrition permanently introduced, agricultural development oriented solely toward the benefit of the metropolitan countries; about the looting of products, the looting of raw material.

(Aimé Césaire 1955: 5)

Contemporary Africans have a right to be angry, but they must also probe into the reasons for institutional failure, the roots of which lie in colonial past. They must question the inherited forms of government, economy, and relations between Africa and the West. They must situate the African condition in a global context: a poor continent supports the industrialised West with its labour, raw materials, markets, and service payments on debts, among other mechanisms that transfer wealth abroad. They must situate African politics in the context of colonialism: modern political institutions are derived more from the colonial past than the precolonial ... The postcolonial seeks its roots in the colonial, alienated from the precolonial and established local traditions. The modern country was modeled after the 'colonial country': black governors merely replaced the white ones ... We must also raise the issue of power and autonomy in the global context: to what extent can Africa self-develop? Africa was self-developing before the colonial intrusion. With violence, colonialism created new frontiers, developed new political and economic objectives, and ordered people around. When colonialism was over, Africa began to think about development in colonial, Western terms.

(Toyin Falola 2005: 4)

Empire, Global Coloniality and African Subjectivity is a study of global imperial designs, colonial matrices of power and technologies of subjection that produced African subjectivity as that of a being constituted by a catalogue of deficits and a series of 'lacks'. It is study of both global and African history as an inextricably intertwined narrative of production of both the 'Cartesian subject' (superior Western subject) and African subjectivity (inferior African beings). The analysis is situated within the broader unfolding of the current modern world order since the dawn of modernity and the unfolding of colonial encounters in the fifteenth century.

This book is organized into four broad parts, namely 'Part 1: Global Imperial Designs and Empire': 'Part 2: Subject, Subjection and Subjectivity;' 'Part 3: Coloniality, Knowledge and Nationalism'; and 'Part 4: Conclusion'. It is subdivided into nine chapters. The first chapter introduces the concepts of empire, global coloniality, coloniality of power, coloniality of knowledge, and coloniality of being. This chapter's point of departure is the ideas of empire articulated by Michael Hardt and Antonio Negri that are considered to be so complacent as to create an impression of a magnanimous empire that is decoupled from imperialism. Their approach is influenced by their reading of the empire from above, largely due to their location in Europe and America: at the centre of the empire. They were seduced by the rhetoric of modernity and the hypocrisies and double-standards of the empire, which blinded them to the coloniality subsisting at the base of 'really existing empire'. This chapter, therefore, shifts the lens of analysis towards reading empire from below and bringing back the geopolitics of knowledge from the margins of modernity and empire, where their dark aspects shaped the emergence of African subjectivity.

The second chapter provides details of the operations of global imperial designs and colonial matrices of power as well as showing how these have provoked the rise of pan-Africanism as a counter-hegemonic discourse responding to the experiences of slavery, racism, colonialism and apartheid. The emphasis in this chapter is on technologies of subjectivation and how they have worked to dilute pan-Africanism. The third chapter engages with discourses of development by treating them as part of global imperial technologies of subjectivation that resulted in the view that Africa in particular and the Global South in general was inhabited by human beings who were defined by catalogues of deficits and series of lacks, lacking history, lacking writing, lacking souls, lacking civilization, lacking responsibility, lacking development, lacking human rights and lacking democracy. The chapter also grapples with how the discourse of development, which began as part of the technologies of subjectivation, has been accepted by Africans and their governments as key to their realization of freedom and fulfillment of the absent centre of ontology, without much success.

The fourth chapter brings into dialogue the Western literature produced by such scholars as Jacques Lacan, Slavoj Žižek, Judith Butler, Chantal Mouffe and Enersto Laclau on the 'Cartesian subject' with the African literature produced by scholars and activists such as Léopold Sédar Senghor, Kwame Nkrumah, Kenneth Kaunda, Achille Mbembe, Paul Tiyambe Zeleza and others on the ticklish issues of the subject, subjection and subjectivity. The chapter's central argument is that discourses of subjection and development intersect tendentiously and inextricably in Africa to produce a particular African subjectivity defined by lacks and deficits. While the Western subject, here defined as the 'Cartesian subject', felt the void and doubted its being until René Descartes tried to fill it through the notion of 'cogito', the African subject is defined and told by the Western subject that it is lacking and deficient. These discourses unfolded during the colonial encounters as the 'Cartesian subject' pushed forward to master the world and other subjects, and through this process the 'Cartesian subject' claimed to be the only 'full' subject devoid of lacks. African scholarly productions since the time of colonial encounters have been preoccupied with refutations of discourses and epistemologies of alterity that have given birth to various notions of Africanity, ranging from Ethiopianism to African Renaissance.

The fifth and sixth chapters address the equally ticklish conundrums of the subject, subjection and subjectivity in South Africa and Zimbabwe. Here empirical data is deployed to explain the evolution of complex identitarian processes such as Bantucization, Anglicization, Afrikanerization and Africanization, in the case of South Africa, and how these culminated in the present-day notions of a 'rainbow nation' as a form of resolution of the politics of radical differences, which were imposed by imperialism, colonialism and apartheid. For Zimbabwe, the focus is on what is termed 'nationality of power', which captures how a nationalist political formation (ZANU-PF) has tried to create a national identity imbued with the spirit of patriotism from a people of different ethnic backgrounds. What is emphasized is how the nationalist movement, and the postcolonial state, evolved technologies of subjectivation that were underpinned by deployment of violence similar to those of the colonial state in its attempt to create national subjects. The ideology of *Chimurenga*, and the strategy of *Gukurahundi*, became the leitmotifs of ZANU-PF's technologies of subjectivation.

The seventh chapter is on the coloniality of knowledge and how it impinged on cultures of higher education in Africa, focusing first on Ghana, the first sub-Saharan African colony to gain independence in 1957 and the first to attempt the decolonization of knowledge and the transformation of higher education. The second focus is on South Africa, which is currently struggling to transform institutions of higher education to reflect their location in Africa, in terms of their African values and missions. The eighth chapter is on the pertinent theme of the African national project and the national questions that are crying out for re-consideration during the current crisis of modernity symbolized by the global financial crisis. Chapter Nine is the conclusion, pulling together the central arguments of the book to reflect on the global crisis and its impact on African imaginations of post-imperial and postcolonial futures.

Global coloniality, which today speaks to the existence of colonial situations and colonial power relations in the present epoch where direct colonial administrations have been dismantled as cogs of the modern capitalist world-system, is as old as modernity itself (Grosfoguel 2007: 219). The concept of global coloniality is useful in teasing out and revealing the mythology of a decolonized African world as well as unraveling the rhetoric of modernity. This book unmasks what has been obscured by celebrations of juridical freedom and reveals continuities between the colonial past and current racialized and hierarchical, modern and global world order. As noted by Ramón Grosfoguel (2011), at the apex of this global coloniality is the U.S.A., NATO, the Pentagon, and the International Monetary Fund (IMF) and the World Bank (WB) that ensure that Africa and other peripheral zones remained under colonial situation long after the end of direct colonial administration. About the state of this modern world order, Michael Hardt and Antonio Negri noted that:

> It is widely recognized that the notion of international order that European modernity continually proposed and reproposed, at least since the Peace of Westphalia, is now in crisis. It has in fact always been in crisis, and this crisis has been one of the motors that have continuously pushed towards Empire. Perhaps this notion of international order and its crisis should be dated from the time of the Napoleonic Wars ... or perhaps the origin should be located in the Congress of Vienna and the establishment of the Holy Alliance. In any case, there can be no doubt that by the time of the First World War and the birth of the League of Nations, a notion of international order along with its crisis had been definitively established. The birth of the United Nations at the end of the Second World War merely reinitiated, consolidated, and extended this developing juridical order that was first European but progressively became completely global. The United Nations, in effect, can be regarded as the culmination of the entire constitutive process, a culmination that both reveals the limitations of the notion of *international* order and points beyond it toward a new notion of *global* order. (Hardt and Negri 2000: 4, emphasis is in the original)

While Hardt and Negri are correct on the issue of a crisis-ridden world order, their attempts to locate its genealogy in major European events and peace settlements dealing with European conflicts ignore the importance of such processes as 'voyages of discovery' and mercantilism that resulted in the so-called 'discovery' of the New World in 1492 and the slave trade that culminated in the trans-Atlantic commercial circuit as epochal in the genealogy of the modern world order that survived on the logic of violence, politics of alterity and epistemicides. This reality is easily missed if the genealogy of the modern world order is analysed from the centre of the empire. What is not emphasized in Hardt and Negri's analysis is the importance of coloniality as the dark side of modernity, which has always been concealed by the rhetoric of modernity.

Global coloniality becomes most visible if one shifts geography of reason and geopolitics of knowledge from the centre of the empire into its borders. Despite its long contact with Europe and America, Africa remains peripheral and powerless in the face of global imperial designs. If looked at from the centre of empire, the modern capitalist system would be understood partially as produced by inter-imperial competition among European empires primarily over shorter routes to the East, which accidentally resulted in the discovery of the Americas and the Cape Colony (Grosfoguel 2007: 215). This rendition of the birth of the modern world capitalist system would cast it as a primarily economic system, driven by the logic of making profits and accumulation of capital on a world scale. This view was well expressed by Karl Marx and Fredrick Engels when they wrote that:

> The bourgeoisie has through its exploitation of the world market given a cosmopolitan character to production and consumption in every country. To the great chagrin of Reactionists, it has drawn from under the feet of industry the national ground on which it stood. All old-established national industries have been destroyed or are daily being destroyed. They are dislodged by new industries, whose introduction becomes a life and death question for all civilized nations, by industries that no longer work up indigenous raw material, but raw material drawn from the remotest zones; industries whose products are consumed, not only at home, but in every quarter of the globe. In the place of the old wants, satisfied by the production of the country, we find new wants, requiring for their satisfaction the products of distant lands and climes. In place of the old local and national seclusion and self-sufficiency, we have intercourse in every direction, universal inter-dependency of nations. And as in material, so also in intellectual, production. The intellectual creations of individual nations become common property. National one-sidedness and narrow-mindedness become more and more impossible, and from the numerous national and local literatures, there arises a world literature. The bourgeoisie, by the rapid improvement of all instruments of production, by the immensely facilitated means of communication, draws all, even the most barbarian, nations into civilization. The cheap prices of commodities are the heavy artillery with which it batters down all Chinese walls, with which it forces the barbarians' intensely obstinate hatred of foreigners to capitulate. It

> compels all nations, on pain of extinction, to adopt the bourgeois mode
> of production; it compels them to introduce what it calls civilization into
> their midst, i.e., to become bourgeois themselves. In one word, it creates a
> world after its own image. (Marx and Engels 1848: 6)

Marx and Engels were of course analysing the unfolding of Euro-American capitalist and hegemonic power from their location in Europe. Consequently, their Marxist-political economy perspective of the empire tells half the story which results in privileging of class analysis and structural transformations (Grosfoguel 2007: 215). What is often glossed over in African studies is how Karl Marx articulated a very Eurocentric view of global history in his analysis of colonial encounters. While critical of how Western powers violently invaded and colonized other parts of the world, he still believed that imperialism and colonialism had a double mission: to bring these societies into the ambit of Western modernity through destruction of precolonial social formations while at the same time creating a foundation for their modernization (Hardt and Negri 2000: 120). Like all European thinkers, Marx believed that non-Western societies could progress only through becoming like Western societies.

This Eurocentrism of Marx made his Marxist theory tell a partial narrative of the formation of the modern world order. To complete the story, there is a need to shift the locus of enunciation from the centre of the empire to the zones of 'colonial difference': zones of indigenous peoples and colonized subjects who experienced the dark side of modernity. Looked at from this locus of enunciation, it becomes clear that what was unleashed by modernity was not only 'an economic system of capital and labour for the production of commodities to be sold for profit in the world market' (Grosfoguel 2007: 215). What becomes clear is that what were bequeathed were an 'entangled package' and 'entangled power structure' underpinned by racial, sexual, ideological, epistemic, cultural, religious, aesthetic, military, and patriarchal dimensions that Anibal Quijano (2007) described as a 'colonial matrix of power'.

The entry point of this book is that imperialism, empire and global coloniality constitute an inseparable triad within global imperial designs in place since the dawn of colonial encounters. The book is, therefore, not about the 'phantasmagoric empire' depicted in Antonio Negri and Michael Hardt's influential book *Empire* (2000). The phantasmagoric empire is one which is assumed to be benign, ethical, and is said to be an empire without colonies that emerged at the end of imperialism. This supposedly benign empire is said to operate through the UN with the purpose of bringing order to the world (Hardt and Negri 2000: xi–xvii). But the reality is that such an empire exists only as a 'poetic and metaphysical construction' born out of neo-liberal mystifications of its substance and form (Boron 2005: 58).

The most depoliticized term used to describe this phantasmagoric empire is 'globalization' which is often simplistically articulated as 'uni-formization' of the world (Robertson 1992: 8). Zillah Eisenstein (2004: 183) correctly noted that if globalization is traced back to the time of the slave trade onwards, it unfolded as a 'systematic patriarchal structuring of racialised, sexualized, global exploitation'. This is not meant to totally dismiss globalization's other character of 'inexorable integration of markets, nation states and technologies' (Friedman 2000: 7). What is beyond doubt is that capital is moving very fast across boundaries while labour and technology are not. 'Hyper globalists' like Niall Ferguson, who in his *Empire: How Britain Made the Modern World* (2003) emphasized how 'Anglo-globalization' contributed to furthering the spread of liberal capitalism and opening up global markets, forgot to analyse global coloniality lurking within globalization, which is reproducing cultural oppression, economic exploitation, racial exclusions and inequalities.

This book is about 'real existing empire' rather than the 'phantasma-goric' one. The 'real existing empire' is underpinned by imperialism and remains vicious in its scramble for natural resources and markets. As noted by Barbara Bush (2006: 4) the existence of empires stretches back two thousand years and even before to embrace the Old Babylonian, Greek, Russian, Achaemenid, Byzantine, Roman, Ottoman Turkish, Spanish, Portuguese, Swedish, Dutch, Japanese, English and French Empires. The period after 1945 witnessed the rise of the Soviet and American empires. Today, the Chinese Empire is on the rise. The reality about empires is that they have 'waxed and waned, merged and dissolved for thousands of years, without such empires, there would be no "modern world"' (Bush 2006: 4). The 'really existing empire' is about power, territorial expansion, material resources, subordinating spaces and people, and securing hegemony. It was best described by Atilio B. Boron when he said:

> Today's imperialism is not the same as the one that existed thirty years ago; it has changed, and in some ways the change has been very important, but it has not changed into its opposite, as neo-liberal mystification suggests, giving rise to a 'global' economy in which we are all 'inter-dependent'. It still exists, and it still oppresses people and nations and creates pain, destruction and death. In spite of the changes, it still keeps its identity and structure, and it still plays the same historical role in the logic of the global accumulation of capital. Its mutations, its volatile and dangerous combinations of persistence and innovation, require the construction of a new framework that will allow us to capture its present nature. (Boron 2005: 3)

This 'really existing empire' just like 'the walls of Jericho', which 'did not collapse because of the sound of Joshua and the priests' trumpets', has not faded away because of the condemnations, fantasies of philosophers, and neo-liberal mystifications (Boron 2005: 4). The 'really existing empire' continues to operate through criminalization of social protest, militarization of international politics, and aggressive search for strategic resources. But Hardt and Negri (2000) seem to have fallen into the trap of empire's democracy and human rights rhetoric to the extent of justifying the new 'wars of pillage and territorial occupation' that befell countries like Iraq and Libya as 'altruistic operations of nation-building and the export of democracy' (Boron 2005: 21).

At the heart of the 'really existing empire' is a modern world order that is best described as racialized, colonial, capitalist, patriarchal, hierarchical, asymmetrical, imperial, hetero-normative, hegemonic, Christian-centric, neo-liberal and Euro-American-centric (Mignolo 1995; Mignolo 2000; Mignolo 2005a; Quijano 2000a; Grosfoguel 2007; Grosfoguel 2011; Ndlovu-Gatsheni 2012a). Within this empire, hierarchical and asymmetrical organizations of peoples, markets, states, and nations are under the hegemony of an international dominant bloc with the U.S.A. and its NATO partners at the apex. This global reality was clearly identified by Kwame Nkrumah (1965) who became very worried about the impact of neo-colonialism as a lever of global coloniality. Nkrumah described 'neo-colonialism' as the 'last stage of imperialism' and correctly noted that:

> In place of colonialism as that main instrument of imperialism we have today neo-colonialism ... Neo-colonialism, like colonialism, is an attempt to export the social conflicts of the capitalist countries ... The result of neo-colonialism is that foreign capital is used for the exploitation rather than for the development of the less developed parts of the world. Investment under neo-colonialism increases the gap between the rich and the poor countries rather than decreasing the gap between the rich and the poor countries of the world. (Nkrumah 1965: 8)

Nkrumah's *Neo-Colonialism: The Last Stage of Imperialism* (1965) remains the best work on the core dimension of neo-colonialism as a cog of global imperial designs. Nkrumah clearly understood that the essence of neo-colonialism was to produce seemingly and nominally independent African states, with outward trappings of international sovereignty, while their economic and political policies were directed from outside. The second feature that Nkrumah identified with neo-colonialism was that of creation of military bases in those zones where imperialist powers sought to maintain neo-colonial control. The current establishment of AFRICOM by the U.S.A. in Africa vindicates his diagnosis. He also correctly noted that 'A state in the grip of neo-colonialism is not master of its own destiny' (Nkrumah 1965: x). Nkrumah understood global coloniality as the 'tentacles of the Wall Street octopus' that were underpinned by what he termed 'the invisible government'. For a definition of the invisible government, Nkrumah drew directly from David Wise and Thomas B. Ross (1964):

> The Invisible Government ... is a loose amorphous grouping of individu-
> als and agencies drawn from many parts of the visible government. It is
> not limited to the Central Intelligence Agency, although the CIA is at its
> heart. Nor is it confined to the nine other agencies which comprise what
> is known as the intelligence community: the National Security Council,
> the Defense Intelligence Agency, the National Security Agency, Army
> intelligence, Navy Intelligence and Research, the Atomic Energy Commis-
> sion and the Federal Bureau of Investigation. The Invisible Government
> includes also many units and agencies, as well as individuals, that appear
> outwardly to be normal part of the conventional government. It even en-
> compasses business firms and institutions that are seemingly private ...
> An informed citizen might come to suspect that the foreign policy of the
> United States often works publicly in one direction and secretly through
> the Invisible Government in just the opposite direction. The Invisible Gov-
> ernment is a relatively new institution. It came into being as a result of two
> related factors: the rise of the United States after World War II to a position
> of pre-eminent world power, and the challenge to that power by Soviet
> Communism. (Wise and Ross quoted in Nkrumah 1965: 240)

The problem of neo-colonialism was also articulated by the Marxist revolutionary Che Guevara (1965: 10) when he said that 'As long as
imperialism exists it will, by definition, exert its domination over other
countries. Today that domination is called neo-colonialism.' The notion
of invisible government speaks directly of global imperial designs and
colonial matrices of power. It is not as new as David Wise and Thomas
B. Ross (1964) thought. It is not a postwar phenomenon. It has always
been at the centre of global imperial designs since the time of colonial
encounters. Such institutions as churches, schools and universities as
well as such disciplines as anthropology played a role in the invisible
government. Invisible government as a form of 'governmentality' is as
old as imperialism. The concept of governmentality is derived from the
work of the French theorist Michel Foucault and it refers to the 'particular modes of government and policy making, which work on the basis
of inculcating certain patterns of "mentality" in a broader population
such that it is possible for the ends of government to be attained with
decreasing levels of direct intervention and with a greater reliance on
the "self-government" of that population' (McEachern 1997: 111).

Early Marxist-inspired academics' political interrogations of the
African predicament, in which Nkrumah and others were involved, resulted in the emergence of the dependency theorists in the 1970s, who
were equally concerned to explain the African condition. The leading
Africanists were Walter Rodney and Samir Amin. Rodney's *How Europe
Underdeveloped Africa* (1973) boldly expressed how Africa was a victim
of deliberate exploitation and underdevelopment by European colonial
regimes. Rodney traced the roots of underdevelopment as far back as
the age of mercantilism. Two of his conclusions resonate with those

of Nkrumah. The first was that in the encounter between Africa and Europe, Africa lost power. He elaborated that:

> Power is the ultimate determinant in human society, being basic to relations within any group and between groups. It implies the ability to defend one's interests and if necessary to impose one's will by any means available. In relations between peoples, the question of power determines maneuverability in bargaining, the extent to which a people survive as a physical and cultural entity. When one society finds itself forced to relinquish power entirely to another society that in itself is a form of underdevelopment. (Rodney 1973: 45)

His other important conclusion was that the only path to human development and liberation lay in transformation of people's lives by the people themselves through consistent lifetime struggles to disengage from the neo-colonialism that shaped and dominated society, and prescribed modes of human of existence, within neocolonies of Africa (Rodney 1973: 67). After the murder of Rodney, Samir Amin became the most outspoken dependency theorist in Africa. Amin has written over thirty books and numerous articles in which he has consistently explored the structural origins of underdevelopment, the negative aspects of capitalist accumulation on a world scale, structural effects of the international integration of African economies in the evolving capitalist system, and the dangers of what he termed 'liberal virus' and 'empire of chaos' that bred nothing other than global disorder (Amin 1992).

What has distinguished Amin's interventions is his concern with the bigger picture of global politics. For instance, he is clear that the current global order is driven by five monopolies: over technology, finance, natural resources, communication and weapons of mass destruction. On the other hand, the peripheral social formations are characterized by predominance of agrarianism, dependent local bourgeoisie, bureaucratization, and incomplete proletarianization of the labour force (Amin 1998).

While it is not possible to review all Amin's work here, it is possible to comment on the value of two of them, namely *Delinking: Towards a Polycentric World* (1990a), and the most recent one, *Ending the Crisis of Capitalism or Ending Capitalism* (2010). The concept of delinking is one of Amin's keynote arguments throughout his analysis of imperialism and empire. He defined it this way:

> Delinking is the refusal to submit to the demands of the world-wide law of value, or the supposed 'rationality' of the system of world prices that embody the demands of reproduction of world capital. It, therefore, presupposes the society's capacity to define an alternative economic options, in short a 'law of value of national application'. (Amin 1990b: 70–71)

Writing soon after the end of the Cold War, Amin identified what he called an 'empire of chaos' that consisted of the U.S.A., Japan, and Germany, backed by a weakened Russia and the comprador classes of the Global South. The question is: what are the implications of the addition of China, and perhaps, to a minor extent, India and Brazil, to the growing 'empire of chaos'? It would seem that the new entrants into the league of empires are also prepared to stop at nothing in the campaign to protect and expand its capital markets (Amin 1992). Amin has consistently engaged with the problems of the empire, focusing on constraining aspects of neo-colonialism, globalization and neo-liberalism from a world-systems perspective (Amin 1989, 1991, 1997, 1998, 2000).

His 'delinking thesis' among his other various important critical intellectual interventions has raised a lot of debates and criticism, but Amin has been steadfast in his defence of delinking as an essential prerequisite and transitional strategy to socialism. This is how he justified delinking:

> First, the necessity of delinking is the logical political outcome of the unequal character of the development of capitalism ... Unequal development, in this sense, is the origin of essential social, political and ideological evolutions ... Second, delinking is a necessary condition of any socialist advance, in the North and in the South. This proposition is, in our view, essential for a reading of Marxism that genuinely takes into account the unequal character of capitalist development. Third, the potential advances that become available through delinking will not 'guarantee' certainty of further evolution towards a pre-defined 'socialism'. Socialism is a future that must be built. And fourth, the option for delinking must be discussed in political terms. This proposition derives from a reading according to which economic constraints are absolute only for those who accept the commodity alienation intrinsic to capitalism, and turn it into an historical system of eternal validity. (Amin 1990a: xiv)

The type of delinking suggested by Amin was a careful and strategic one taking the form of a transition during which underdeveloped countries adopted new market strategies and values different from northern developed nations. Delinking also meant a consistent refusal to bow to the dominant logic of the world capitalist system (Amin 2006a: 27; Amin 2006b). To Amin, delinking meant 'the pursuit of a system of rational criteria for economic options founded on a law of value on a national basis with popular relevance, independent of such criteria of economic rationality as flow from the dominance of capitalist law of value operating on a world scale' (Amin 1990a: 62). In short, delinking should involve less emphasis on comparative advantage, and more attention to the introduction of economic, social and political reforms in the national interests of the underdeveloped countries. It also entails seeking to create self-reliance in practice among peoples of the Global South including

South to South cooperation, particularly aimed at avoiding reproduction of relations of exploitation that currently exist between the capitalist centres and the peripheries.

But like all theorists that were converted to political economy and strongly believed in socialist future, Amin did not realize that socialism was and is just a form of opposition to capitalism, rather than an alternative. Looked at closely, socialism was in reality a project that tried to save Eurocentric modernity from a capitalism that operated through contradictions to the extent of portending a demise of Euro-American modernity. Another issue that remained vague within his delinking thesis was how a global problem like that of economic underdevelopment could be resolved through piecemeal national interventions. How can a global problem be solved through national or local solutions? But there is no doubt that Amin's broader interventions indicated his deeper understanding of global imperial designs and its technologies of subjectivation, which he correctly identified as 'five monopolies' used to keep Africa in a subaltern position (Amin 2000).

The challenge is and was that, if indeed Africa were trapped in this exploitative and dominating global monopolistic nexus, how could delinking premised at individual nations be a form of liberation? The examples of Tanzania under Julius Nyerere come to mind, as he tried to construct a self-reliant socialist state in one country but was disciplined by global matrices of power until he retired in 1985, lamenting how he underestimated the forces of neo-colonialism. As a scholar and activist, Amin (2009) continued to analyse the core aspects of the empire and he meticulously unpacked the phenomenon of Eurocentrism as a core component of the present world. He defined it as a world view fabricated by the domination of Western capitalism that claimed that European cultures reflected the unique and progressive manifestation of the metaphysical order of history. To Amin, Eurocentrism is nothing but an ideological distortion, and an incredible mythology as well as a historical and moral travesty based on appropriation of Greek rationality and Christianity to create, legitimize and justify the exploitative capitalist social order together with conquest of the non-Western world (Amin 2009: 160–175). Amin has revealed that 'Europe' is nothing but a relative culturalist-construction that masquerades as universal (Amin 2009: 165).

Consequently, Amin's analysis of Eurocentrism raised the challenge of how non-Europeans were reacting to it. The first reaction is the common navel-gazing attempts at returning to the ancient cultural roots that have informed some Islamic religious and African nationalist fundamentalisms. To Amin, this is a reactionary, blind and unprofitable rejection of the scientific view of the world and the progress made so far. The second response consists of attempts at projecting socio-economic diversities and pluralism as the basis of difference. To Amin, this response is inappropriate because its provincialism invites inevitable and insoluble conflicts among nations (Amin 2009).

Amin concluded his interrogation of Eurocentrism with a legitimate call for a 'Non-Eurocentric View of History and a Non-Eurocentric Social Theory' (Amin 2009). But what is problematic about Amin's analysis of possible solutions to Eurocentrism is that they fall into the same Eurocentric emancipatory option that includes a belief in the fact that in spite of its myriad of problems, capitalism reflected a certain universal rationality that must be accepted by the people of the Global South. Rationality is not just a product of Western civilization and the capitalist mode of production. The way he emphasized rationality indicated how he was also interpellated by Euro-American epistemologies and the rhetorics of modernity. What is needed is not uni-versal but pluri-versal rationality, where many worlds have a dignified space. Eurocentrism denies the co-presence of Africans and Europeans. This point is well expressed by Hardt and Negri (2000: 77) who stated that 'Eurocentrism was born as a reaction to the potentiality of a newfound human equality; it was the counterrevolution on a global scale.'

Amin's call for 'the socialist universalism', founded on a non-European, universal and rational paradigm of world order able to overcome the contradiction inherent in capitalist universalism, is informed by a form of political economy that is not totally freed from Western epistemology (Ndlovu-Gatsheni 2012a). The reality, which is often missed by those converted into socialism, is that it was nothing but another gift of Euro-American modernity to the world and that it was genealogically rooted in capitalism itself. This reality is further amplified by the fact that both capitalism and socialism produced two equally imperialist political formations: the Soviet Union (USSR) and the U.S.A. as they emerged after the end of the Second World War.

Amin seems to be concerned about how one can remove Eurocentrism from the modernity project. To him, the Modernist project is too spoiled by European culturalism for it to be a progressive universal project (Amin 2009: 17). What is not clear in Amin's analysis is what constitute universal values. He calls for what he termed 'modernity critical of modernity' (Amin 2009: 17). It is not clear whether this 'modernity critical of modernity' is a reformist agenda or a call for alternative modernity. But this critique of Amin's interventions is not meant to diminish his overall contribution to progressive thinking about how the Global South might free itself from the snares of global matrices of power. Amin remains one of the most consistent and unwavering critics of Euro-American domination over Africa in particular and the Global South in general.

Drawing from his long and painstaking analysis of capitalism, imperialism and empire, Amin has been prophetic. For instance in the 1990s he argued that 'Peoples peripherised by capitalist world expansion, and who seemed for a long time to accept their fate, have over the past 50 years ceased accepting it, and they will refuse to do so more and more in the future' (Amin 1997: 10). The outbreak of uprisings in North Africa and the ongoing 'Occupy Wall Street' movements vindicate Amin's predictions. In his *Ending of Capitalism or Ending Capitalism* (2010), Amin still pushed forward his delinking thesis and posed a number of fundamental questions that need scholarly attention. What are the relations between capital and labour in a globalized world? Which ruling groups conspire with an international capitalist system? How do nation-states generate an environment conducive for operations of empire and regulate conflicts between capital and labour? What strategies are necessary for working people in the peripheries to overthrow the capitalist order in their own locality as well as imperialist exploitation? What forms of solidarity are necessary between peoples of the North and South to overhaul capitalism and imperialism? (Amin 2010; Biney 2008a).

Indeed, one of the challenges of dealing with how empire and global coloniality continue to keep Africa as a dominated and exploitable site within global governance is to avoid creating an impression of a passive continent and passive people. This book does not in any way seek to perpetuate Coupland's myth of Africans as 'dumb actors' in their own history. In other words, the book is not about Africans as hapless objects of empire that were acted upon by major external protagonists. It is about imperial technologies of subjectivation and how these impacted on subjectivity, development, epistemology, and political practices of both the empire and the postcolony. It is a history book which is about the making of both the Euro-American world and the construction of the African condition and predicament. The book traces how particular human actions and historical processes produced the current world order through unleashing of mercantilism, the slave trade, imperialism, colonialism, apartheid, African nationalism, decolonization, neo-colonialism, underdevelopment, neo-liberalism and globalization.

The book is also a study of a two-faced modernity that was instrumental in the production of human subjectivity, notions of development, epistemology, and violence as well as the current global economic crisis. At one level, the 'rhetoric of modernity' highlights salvation, civilization, secularism, techno-scientific knowledge, progress, development, emancipation, freedom, and democracy. At the second level, 'the logic of coloniality' is always concealed by the rhetoric of modernity and consists of domination, oppression, epistemicides and exploitation (Mignolo 2005b: 111). The book is about the making of a particular double-faced world order and a particular racialized people. This particular world order is traceable to the dawn of modernity. About modernity, Santiago Castro-Gomez stated that:

> We can thus state that modernity is a project of governing the social world which emerged in the sixteenth century. Its constructions of power/

knowledge are anchored in a double coloniality: one directed *inward* by European and American nation-states in their effort to establish homogenous identities through politics of subjectification, the other directed *outward* by the hegemonic powers of the modern/colonial world-system in their attempt to ensure the flow of primary materials from the periphery to the center. Both processes are part of the same structural dynamic. (Castro-Gomez 2002: 277, emphasis in the original)

The people studied in this book are called modern subjects. Slavoj Žižek in *The Ticklish Subject: The Absent Centre of Political Ontology* (1999: 1) describes this subject as 'the Cartesian subject' whereas Jean-François Bayart in *Global Subjects: A Political Critique of Globalization* (2004) prefers to call them 'global subjects'. They are divided into two categories by what Boaventura de Sousa Santos termed abyssal thinking. Santos elaborated on abyssal thinking in this way:

Modern Western thinking is an abyssal thinking. It consists of a system of visible and invisible distinctions, the invisible ones being the foundation of the visible ones. The invisible distinctions are established through radical lines that divide social reality into two realms, the realm of 'this side of the line' and the realm of 'the other side of the line'. The division is such that the 'other side of the line' vanishes as reality, becomes nonexistent, and is indeed produced as nonexistent. Nonexistent means not existing in any relevant or comprehensive way of being. Whatever is produced as nonexistent is radically excluded because it lies beyond the realm of what the accepted conception of inclusion considers to be its other. What most fundamentally characterizes abyssal thinking is thus the impossibility of the copresence of the two sides of the line. (Santos 2007a: 45)

Abyssal lines separated the realm of the emergence of the Western subject as an independent actor from that of the African subject that was cast and reconstructed in the negative terms of a non-being. Within its Euro-American realm the Western subject managed to define itself to the extent of assuming the place of a 'master subject'. The Western subject created for itself the identity of a master subject as it grew from Rene Descartes's 'cogito ergo sum' (I think, therefore I am) to 'ergo conquistus' (I conquer, therefore I am) (Grosfoguel 2007: 215). This happened as the Western subject that had managed to master itself and conquer the spectre of doubt sought to further realize and consolidate itself through mastery of the world and other subjects. This process became vigorous from the fifteenth century onwards, when the Western subject began to move across oceans initiating what are known as colonial encounters. John L. Comaroff and Jean Comaroff argued that:

The colonial encounter also had the effect of reinforcing some features of indigenous lifeways, altering or effacing others, and leaving yet others unengaged. Along the way, too, new hybrids came into being: new aesthetic styles and material arrangements, new divisions of wealth and sense of identity, new notions of peoplehood, politics and history. (Comaroff and Comaroff 1997: 8–9)

The Comaroffs further argued that colonization was multifaceted from its beginning. It was as much a cultural as a political enterprise. It was as much about cartography and counting. It was as much about the practical logic of capitalism as about bodily regimes. It was also about the brute extraction of labour power 'as much as anything else about inscribing in the social world a new conception of space, new forms of personhood, and a new means of manufacturing the real' (Comaroff and Comaroff 1997: 16–17).

The African subject constitutes a second category of being, which emerged as the 'Other' within Western thought and colonial encounters. This is a point well articulated by Bill Ashcroft (1997: 13–14): 'The word "Africa" can never entirely escape its bondage to the idea of Africa in the European imagination.' Emerging within Western thought as available for colonization, the 'Other' assumed the identity of that subject that was incapable of mastering itself and was therefore described and represented by the 'master subject' as marked by deficits: lacking soul, lacking religion, lacking writing, lacking history, lacking rights, lacking development and lacking democracy (Grosfoguel 2007). This 'empty' subject experienced such historical and epochal processes as mercantilism, the slave trade, imperialism, colonialism, apartheid, neo-colonialism, neo-liberalism, globalization and other tentacles of imperial designs unleashed by modernity, as additions to its own epochal developments that included the Stone Age, migrations, the Iron Age, domestication of plants and animals, state formation and other internal changes. It is a subject that is caught within the nest of global imperial designs and colonial matrices of power that underpin the modern day 'empire'. This theme is fully treated in Chapter Four of this book. This introductory chapter introduces a series of conceptual tools that enable a construction of a new framework that will allow us to understand the present nature of the empire and the dynamics of global coloniality today.

Phantasmagoric versus real existing empire

The most influential, acclaimed, highly useful but also problematic study of empire and imperialism is Michael Hardt and Antonio Negri's *Empire* (2000). This book's importance lay not only in that it was written by seasoned authors from the centre of the empire and was published at the turn of the millennium, but also in that it is one of the most exhaustive historical studies of the constitution of the present. It is one of those important books that consolidated the paradigmatic retreat from orthodoxy Marxist and modernization analysis opening the way for new analysis of empire. Their paradigmatic shift can be depicted in these revealing words of John Comaroff: 'dialectics give way to dialogics, political economy to poetics, class conflict to consumption, the violence of the gun to the economy of the text, world-historical material processes to local struggles over signs and styles, European domination to post-Hegelian hybridity' (Comaroff 2002: 107).

But at the same time, Hardt and Negri's book cannot be easily read as underpinned by postmodernist and postcolonial theoretical frameworks because they criticize this body of thought as having been overtaken by new notions of power that underpin the present empire that has crystallized around American (U.S.) hegemony. It is a complex book that is ground-breaking at various levels while remaining problematic at other levels.

As such it has been open to both animated appraisals and severe criticism. *Empire* (2000) is a book that severely criticized the legacy of modernity as that of 'fratricidal wars, devastating "development," cruel "civilization," and previously unimagined violence' (Hardt and Negri 2000: 46) while at the same time being accused of adopting 'a complacent view of the empire' by Atilio B. Boron (2005: 14). Such controversial and convoluted arguments as 'Saying the Empire is good in itself, however, does not mean that it is good for itself. Although Empire may have played a role in putting an end to colonialism and imperialism, it nonetheless constructs its own relationships of power based on exploitation that are in many respects more brutal than those it destroyed' open *Empire* (2000: 43) to various critical interpretations. Here I offer one such reading and interpretation, informed by imperatives of decolonial epistemic perspective that do not see any positive aspects in the present empire despite its rhetoric of salvation, while at the same time accepting some of the trenchant argument of Hardt and Negri on the constitution of the present.

There are a number of standpoints in *Empire* (2000) that confirmed Hardt and Negri's complacent view of the empire. Boron mounted the most extended and systematic criticism of Hardt and Negri in *Empire and Imperialism: A Critical Reading of Michael Hardt and Antonio Negri* (2005). In the first place, Hardt and Negri's confidence in the democratic, emancipatory and liberatory quality of the post-Cold War multilateral world order forced them to fail to realize the reality of the appropriation of the UN system, and international law, by the international bloc headed by the U.S.A. to serve the interests of capital and empire. This led Hardt and Negri to interpret the military intervention of the empire's forces in Iraq, in particular, from a liberal perspective emphasizing the rhetoric of exporting human rights and democracy, while underplaying the empire's drive for strategic resources, particularly oil which constitutes 'the central nervous system of international capitalism' (Boron 2005: 13).

In the second place, Hardt and Negri overemphasized the reality of the obsolescence of the territorial nation-state in their endeavour to highlight the ubiquity of the empire, as though there were inherent anachronisms between the nation-state and empire. The nation-state has, up to today, remained the cornerstone of both imperialism and empire despite the rhetoric of a globalization that is said to have resulted in the de-territorialization and delegitimation of the nation-state. Their position on the obsolescence of the nation-state is to exaggerate the collapse of this entity, which emerged after the Treaty of Westphalia in 1648. Jean-François Bayart (2007) noted that while the empire, in its globalization phase, is establishing transnational solidarities and networks that overlap with the nation-states, it does not automatically undermine the nation-states system.

In the third place, Hardt and Negri seem to have been swayed by the empire's rhetoric of being a champion of global justice, human rights, and democracy to the extent that they became less critical of Washington's hegemonic drive across the world in search of strategic resources. To them, Washington is doing a good job of imposing international justice and legality. This is what they wrote about American post-Cold War military interventions:

> In the warning years and wake of the Cold War, the responsibility of exercising an international police power 'fell' squarely on the shoulders of the United States. The Gulf War was the first time the United States could exercise this power in its full form. Really, the war was an operation of repression of very little interest from the point of view of the objectives, the regional interests, and the political ideologies involved. We have seen many such wars conducted directly by the United States and its allies. Iraq was accused of having broken international law, and it thus had to be judged and punished. The importance of the Gulf War derives rather from the fact that it presented the United States as the only power able to manage international justice, *not as a function of its own motives but in the name of global right.* (Hardt and Negri 2000: 180, emphasis is in the original)

The impression one gets from reading Hardt and Negri's *Empire* from a decolonial epistemic perspective is that of the propagation of a magnanimous empire that is imbued with liberatory and emancipatory potentialities and possibilities (Boron 2005: 62).

In the fourth place, Hardt and Negri approached the subject of 'the political constitution of the present' in such a way that they viewed the empire as emerging without imperialism. To Hardt and Negri:

> The concept of the Empire is characterized fundamentally by a lack of boundaries: Empire's rule had no limits. First and foremost, then, the concept of Empire posits a regime that effectively encompasses the spatial totality, or really that rules over the entire 'civilized' world. No territorial boundaries limit its reign. Second, the concept of Empire presents itself not as a historical regime originating in conquest, but rather as an order

that effectively suspends history and thereby fixes the existing state of affairs for eternity … The Empire we are faced with wields enormous powers of oppression and destruction, but that fact should not make us nostalgic in any way for old forms of domination. The passage to Empire and its globalization offer new possibilities to forces of liberation. (Hardt and Negri 2000: xv)

To decouple imperialism and conquest from empire is problematic because these remain the leitmotif of empire. What can change can only be the means of conquest as weaker nations rarely volunteer to be under the imperial rule. Hardt and Negri also articulated the emergence of the empire as a product of capital's response against contemporary forms of domination and oppression nurtured by 'the multitude's desire for liberation' (Hardt and Negri 2000: 21–24). But in reality empire is the creation of a world capitalist coalition under American bourgeois hegemony. It would seem that Hardt and Negri partly misread not only the political constitution of the empire but also its global mission, when they wrote that:

With the end of the cold war, the United States was called to serve the role of guaranteeing and adding juridical efficacy to this complex process of the formation of a new supranational right. Just as in the first century of the Christian era the Roman senators asked Augustus to assume imperial powers of the administration for the public good, so too today the international monetary organizations (the United Nations, the international organizations, and even the humanitarian organizations) ask the United States to assume the central role in a new world order. (Hardt and Negri 2000: 181)

In reality, no one ever asked the U.S.A. to assume the role of the world's guardian of international law and order. If one needs to understand American hegemony and the considerations that drive it, one must abandon Hardt and Negri's *Empire* and read the work of Samuel P. Huntington who clearly mapped out American imperialist logic as:

To press other countries to adopt American values and practices on such issues such as human rights and democracy; to prevent that third countries acquire military capacities susceptible of interfering with American military superiority; to have the American legislation applied in other societies; to qualify third countries with regard to their adhesion to American standards on human rights, drugs, terrorism, nuclear and missile proliferation and, now, religious freedom; to apply sanctions against the countries that do not conform to the American standards on these issues; to promote the corporate American interests under the slogans of free trade and open markets and to shape the politics of the IMF and World Bank to serve those same interests … to force the other countries to adopt social and political policies that benefit the American economic interests, to promote the sale of American weapons and prevent that other countries do the same ... to categorize certain countries as 'pariah states' or criminal states and exclude them from the global institutions because they refused to prostrate themselves before the American wishes. (Huntington 1999: 48)

It would seem that Hardt and Negri really were misled by modernity's rhetoric of salvation, democracy, progress, and development to the extent of underestimating modernity's logic of coloniality, both of which are operational at the heart of the U.S. empire. Walter Mignolo argued that 'Modernity is a three-headed hydra, even though it only reveals one head: the rhetoric of salvation and progress. Coloniality, one of whose facets is poverty and propagation of AIDS in Africa, does not appear in the rhetoric of modernity as its necessary counterpart, but rather as something that emanates from it' (Mignolo 2011a: 46). Because Hardt and Negri bought into what Mignolo (2011a: 46) depicted as 'fairy tales of the rhetoric of modernity', they eventually misread the U.S.A.'s rhetoric as a global standard for its judgement of other states, not recognizing the presence of double standards. As articulated by Boron (2005: 75): 'One standard is used to evaluate the sovereignty of friends and allies of the United States; another, very different, is used to judge the sovereignty of neutral countries and its enemies. The national sovereignty of the former must be preserved and strengthened, the latter's should be weakened and violated without scruples or false regrets'.

Perhaps because of their complacent view of the empire, in Hardt and Negri's response to the question of how to break out of the domination of the empire, they introduced the concept of the 'multitude'. They defined the multitude as the totality of the creative and productive subjectivities that 'express, nourish, and develop positively their own constituent projects, creating constellations of powerful singularities' (Hardt and Negri 2000: 61). It is not clear what ideologies inform the multitudes as agent of change. At the end of the day, Hardt and Negri end up idealizing and romanticizing the desperate migrant who migrates to the centre of the empire as the hero of the struggles to transcend the domination of the empire. Their other hero of the struggle is Francis of Assisi who railed against poverty.

This is nothing but degeneration into unproductive idealism at a time when the world order is in crisis, and needs new imaginations of the future beyond the present phenomenology of uncertainty. Hardt and Negri added to the disillusionment when they argued that revolutionary thought has become incommunicable. While it is, to some extent, true that a new language of liberation beyond the rhetoric of neo-liberal democracy and human rights is still in the making and that both the democratic project and decolonial projects have suffered some levels of paralysis to the extent of remaining as unfinished business, there are many initiatives taking place across the globe that are pushing the emancipatory and liberatory struggle forward.

These range widely from anti-globalization protestors, such as the Global Justice Movement and the World Social Forum, to peasant movements, such as the Zapatistas of Mexico, that fought for the rights of peasants in impoverished rural areas, and the *Third Chimurenga* and its fast-track land reform in Zimbabwe that sought to redress racist heritage in an ex-settler heartland where land had remained in the hands of the minority white settlers, to First Nation struggles for recognition in such places as Australia, South Africa, Siberia, Amazonia, South-east Asia, North and South America, Northern Norway, Sweden and Finland (Bush 2006: 205–206). The Arab Spring that rocked North Africa, parts of the Middle East, and the ignition of similar activities inside the centre of the empire and in parts of sub-Saharan Africa, generated some hope that the world was indeed entering 'the end of the end of history', with the formerly repressed masses flexing their muscles and deploying their agency by continuing to make history.

But it is clear from Hardt and Negri's *Empire* that theirs was a complacent reading of empire from above, from 'its dominant strata', resulting in their views being 'trapped in the ideological nets of dominant classes' (Boron 2005: 23–24). My book departs from Hardt and Negri's work by reading the empire by examining imperialism in Africa in particular and in the Global South in general, as privileged epistemic sites. Following the work of Mignolo (1995; 2000) this book does not in any way seek to understand empire and imperialism from 'inside itself': rather the reading is from 'colonial difference', as an epistemic space, to 'where coloniality is enacted' (Mignolo 2000: ix). As further articulated by Mignolo:

> It is also the space where the restitution of subaltern knowledge is taking place and where border thinking is emerging. The colonial difference is the space where local histories inventing and implementing global designs meet local histories, the space in which global designs have to be adapted, adopted, rejected, integrated, or ignored. The colonial difference is finally, the physical as well as imaginary location where the coloniality of power is at work in the confrontation of two kinds of local histories displayed in different spaces and times across the planet. (Mignolo 2000: ix)

If empire and imperialism were read from the vantage point of 'colonial difference' a complacent view is avoided from the beginning. What is distinctive about my book is its locus of enunciation, that is, 'the geo-political and body-political location of the subject that speaks' (Grosfoguel 2011: 4). The premise of locus of enunciation is that 'Nobody escapes the class, sexual, gender, spiritual, linguistic, geographical, and racial hierarchies of 'modern/colonial/capitalist/patriarchal world-system' (Grosfoguel 2007: 213). Africa as a locus of enunciation enables appreciation of empire's materiality rather than its neo-liberal mystification. I speak from the Global South in general and Africa in particular as privileged epistemic sites that have not yet fully recovered from the negatives of modernity.

What is today termed the Global South (formerly the Third World) received the darker side of modernity and has since the time of colonial encounters struggled to achieve decolonization. The decolonization struggles, whose genealogy can be traced to as far back as the slave revolts and such early protest writings as Ottobah Cugoano's *Thoughts and Sentiments on the Evils and Wicked Traffic of the Slavery and Commerce of the Human Species, Humbly Submitted to the Inhabitants of Great Britain, by Ottobah Cugoano, a Native of Africa* (1787), involved revealing the dark side of modernity. Cugoano was originally from Ghana and was sold as a slave to European merchants at the age of thirteen.

Cugoano became part of the cohort of runaway slaves who benefited from the Mansfield Decision of 1772 that enabled the ex-slaves to stay in England. Having learnt to speak and write in English, Cugoano mounted a severe criticism of the excesses of modernity that resulted in the brutal slave trade. Cugoano used Christian ideas to indict Western Christians, who became accomplices in the slave trade. According to Mignolo (2011a), Cugoano's work must be read as part of the earliest treatise in decolonial thought. This approach immediately called into question the very idea of human progress as emanating from Europe, as the centre of the world that 'ignored how deeply this history was entwined with overseas conquest, and rejecting the consignment of "non-Europe" to static backwardness regardless of how those regions' fate were shaped by interaction with Europe' (Cooper 2005: 6). The slave trade stands as one of the most remembered indictments of Euro-American modernity. Since that time, Europe and America could not stand on a higher moral pedestal despite their claim to be advancing human emancipation and liberation. Taken together, the various works of such thinkers as Molefi Kete Asante, Frantz Fanon, Nkrumah, Albert Memmi, Amin, Rodney, and others from Latin America, whose ideas inform this book, have contributed to the body of thought that made it possible for the decolonial turn to emerge as a liberatory epistemology.

Towards a decolonial turn

While the imperial vision seeks to impose, reproduce and maintain dominant Euro-American hegemony over the world, 'the decolonial paradigm struggles to bring into intervening existence an-other interpretation that brings forward, on the one hand, a silenced view of the event and, on the other, shows the limits of imperial ideology disguised as the true (total) interpretation of the events' (Mignolo 1995). The decolonial turn is a product of the combination of colonial difference and locus of enunciation, which results in what Mignolo terms 'border gnosis' or 'border thinking' as a new way of looking into the modern world order from sites such as Africa, Latin America, Asia, and the Caribbean where the darker or underside of modernity was received (Mignolo 2000: 3–9).

Ramón Grosfoguel defined border gnosis as the epistemic response of the subaltern to the Eurocentric project of modernity, not in the direction of rejecting modernity but in the redefinition of emancipatory rhetoric of modernity from the cosmologies and epistemologies of the subaltern. The subalterns are defined as those people who were located on the oppressed side of colonial difference (Grosfoguel 2011: 23). Border gnosis inaugurates a redefinition of knowledge, citizenship, democracy, human rights, humanity, and economic relations beyond the narrow confines imposed by European modernity (Grosfoguel 2011: 23).

The darker or underside of modernity included the slave trade, fratricidal colonial wars of conquest, negative development, violent civilizing missions, forcible Christianization, material dispossessions and other forms of violence. The brighter side of modernity included the flowering of individual liberties, universal suffrage, mass democracy, secularization and emancipation of the masses from the tyranny of tradition and religion, rationality and scientific spirit, popular education, technology and many other accomplishments (Boron 2005: 32). But for one to experience the darker or brighter aspects of modernity depended on which side of the abyssal lines one was located as well as the racial category into which one was classified.

The 'decolonial turn' first of all challenges the mythology of the West as the only epistemic site from which the 'rest of the world is described, conceptualized, and ranked' (Mignolo 1995: 35). It therefore encapsulates the locus of enunciation, colonial difference, and border gnosis as useful conceptual tools to fight an epistemological struggle. It does not simply conceptualize the liberation of Africans as cascading from the end of formal colonial relations but as continuing confrontation with the empire and its racial, gendered, and sexual hierarchies, rooted in modernity. The decolonial turn provides an ideal entry point to capture core contours of the 'really existing empire'. It marks an important departure point from such previous turns as the 'cultural turn', the 'linguistic turn', and the 'historical turn'. These 'turns' revolved within a discursive, historical, and structural world order enabled and authorized by modernity. They never inaugurated or imagined an alternative to modernity simply because they operated within a 'chronological history or archaeology of European ideas' (Mignolo 2011a: 46). A decolonial turn is distinctive in that it is informed by epistemic disobedience, which forms a departure point from modernity and its Euro-American epistemology.

A decolonial turn is genealogically traceable to various responses and resistance(s) to such inimical processes as the slave trade, imperialism, colonialism, apartheid, neo-colonialism, neo-liberalism and even globalization. A decolonial turn inaugurates a new thinking about strategies and tactics of opposing coloniality of power, coloniality of knowledge, and coloniality of being that are constitutive of global imperial designs in place since the colonial encounters of the fifteenth century. Mignolo (2011a: 48) noted that *'The decolonial turn is the opening and the freedom from the thinking and the forms of living (economies-other, political theories-other), the cleansing of the coloniality of being and of knowledge; the de-linking from the spell of the rhetoric of modernity, from its imperial imaginary articulated in the rhetoric of democracy'* (emphasis in the original text).

On the other hand, Nelson Maldonado-Torres (2007: 261) articulated the decolonial turn as introducing 'questions about the effects of colonization in modern subjectivities, modern forms of life as well as contributions of racialized and colonized subjectivities to the production of knowledge and critical thinking'. It is also 'about making visible the invisible and about analyzing the mechanisms that produce such invisibility or distorted visibility in light of a large stock of ideas that must necessarily include the critical reflections of the "invisible" people themselves' (Maldonado-Torres 2007: 262).

What is also distinctive about the decolonial turn is its horizon. It envisages a pluri-versal rather than uni-versal world. 'Pluri' means many and 'uni' means one. Therefore, a pluri-versal world is one in which 'many worlds fit' (Mignolo 2011a: 48). Its core metaphor is that 'another world is possible'. Boaventura de Sousa Santos's *Another Knowledge Is Possible: Beyond Northern Epistemologies* (2007b) captures the horizon of the decolonial turn. It is the opposite of the TINA mode (There Is No Alternative) that dominated the 1990s, resulting in Francis Fukuyama's (1992) thesis of 'The End of History and the Last Man'. The decolonial turn easily reveals the myths of decolonization. The important point here is that new studies of empire and global coloniality should deliberately aim at transcending both the rhetorics of modernity and myths of decolonization. While grappling with the myths of decolonization, Mignolo argued that:

> One of the reasons for the 'failure' of the decolonization movements is that, as in socialism/communism, they changed the content but not the terms of the conversation, and maintained the very idea of the state within a global capitalist economy. The appropriation of the state by native elites in Asia and in Africa … remained linked to and dependent from global imperial politics and economy. So much so that in certain cases, the decolonial states followed the same rules of the liberal game, as in India; in other cases, they attempted an approximation towards Marxism … The enormous contribution of decolonization (or independence), as much in the first wave from 1776 to 1830 in the Americas as in the second in Asia and Africa, has been to plant the flag of decolonial pluri-versality against the flag and the tanks of imperial uni-versality. The limits of all these movements were those of not having found an opening and a free-

dom of an other thinking: that is, of a decolonization that would carry them... towards a world that would fit many worlds (e.g., pluri-versality), that would reaffirm the conviction that another world is possible in the World Social Forum. (Mignolo 2011a: 50–51)

The African nationalist movements that spearheaded the decolonization processes were formulated, defined and interpreted within the 'revolutionary' logic of modernity whose templates were the Glorious Revolution in England, the French Revolution, the Chinese Revolution, and the Bolshevik Revolution in Russia. In short, decolonization processes either borrowed from liberal bourgeois revolutions or from the socialist revolutions (Mignolo 2011a: 52). During the liberation struggles in Africa, the Russian and Chinese Revolutions were misunderstood as 'alternatives' portending another future. But the work of Madina V. Tlostanova and Walter D. Mignolo (2009) has indicated that Euro-American modernity culminated in 'two modernities', that is, liberal-capitalist on the one hand and socialist-communist on the other.

Tlostanova and Mignolo (2009: 136) argued that the unfolding of modernity followed 'a serpentine and not a vector trajectory'. In broad terms, the trajectory went from the fifteenth and sixteenth centuries dominated by the Spanish and Portuguese empires as well as by theology and conversion to Christianity. This was followed by a secular and commercial language predicated on plantation economies in the seventeenth and eighteenth centuries, unleashed by the industrial revolution but worked by slave labour. The nineteenth century was dominated by civilizing missions and by colonialism led by Great Britain and France, which survived up to the 1950s. The postwar period witnessed the rise of the U.S.A. and the USSR as global powers. The world after 1945 was also marked by the developmental and modernizing mission that branched into two versions: capitalism and socialism (Tlostanova and Mignolo 2009: 134–135).

Besides being dominated by developmentalism and a modernizing mission, the period after 1945 also witnessed the celebrated decolonization process and the drive by African leaders like Kwame Nkrumah of Ghana and Patrice Lumumba of the Democratic Republic of Congo for institutionalization of pan-Africanism. African celebrations of political independence became short-lived as the period between 1970 and 2000 witnessed the entry of neo-liberal policies backed up by the Washington Consensus, which in turn enabled Structural Adjustment Programmes (SAPs) while, at the same time, intensifying capitalist competition against what was considered to be an evil form of socialism.

With the collapse of the USSR in 1989, the neo-liberal agenda became triumphant. Soviet modernity simply fought to refashion the rhetoric of modernity in the language of socialization of capital. It was also equally imperialist and colonial to the extent of producing what the West considered to be a 'red' and 'evil empire' that engulfed central Europe, central

Asia, parts of Latin America, and parts of Africa such as Ethiopia under Haile Mariam Mangistu. But as noted by Tlostanova and Mignolo (2009), the Soviet modernity became nothing other than an opposition rather than an alternative to Euro-American modernity. This was inevitable because its ideological basis which was Marxism-Leninism did not call for a total break from modernity but was a critique of modernity within modernity just like present postmodernism and post-structuralism.

The current world-system is perhaps best described as a polycentric world order in which the U.S.A. as the sole superpower struggles to contain the rise of competing powers like China, India and Brazil. Tlostanova and Mignolo (2009: 138) postulated that today: 'Regardless of how great were the Western contributions to world history in the past half a millennia, the West does not have any global authority any more to pressurize the rest of the world into acting like Western Europe and the U.S.A.' Today the discourse of war on terror has been added into the old standing rhetoric of modernity to camouflage the new scrambles for natural resources. What has remained constant is the colonial matrix of power that underpins global coloniality. This reality led Tlostanova and Mignolo to conclude that:

> Yet, the colonial matrix of power is not going away. Coloniality will remain as long as the final horizon of human life is guided by the desire to accumulate capital. The control of authority will continue, disguised by a rhetoric of progress, happiness, development and the end of poverty, and will justify the huge amounts of energy and money spent on the conflicts between the centres ruled by the capitalist economy. (Tlostanova and Mignolo 2009: 139)

What is happening today in the absence of socialist modernity is a neoliberal future that is fighting for its life and the slowly emerging decolonial future, within a context where the ideas of a revolution are dead. What is dominant is what Tlostanova and Mignolo (2009: 140) termed 'colonial revolution' or 'the revolution of coloniality'. This one has been in motion since the time of colonial encounters. But this very revolution inadvertently generated critical dimensions from within that encouraged germination of the 'seeds of decolonial consciousness' (Tlostanova and Mignolo 2009: 146).

The decolonial turn is part of the maturation of the seeds of decolonial consciousness and remains the ideal option, enabling a deeper interrogation of the workings of the present-day empire and revealing the inner logic of global coloniality because it privileges robust intellectual interventions at the level of power, knowledge, and being. It is Maldonado-Torres (2007: 262) who elaborated that the decolonial turn is opposed to the 'paradigm of war which has driven modernity for more than five hundred years'. It is also opposed to the imposition of Westernization.

Meic Pearse's *Why the Rest Hates the West: Understanding the Roots of Global Rage* (2004) details how Westernization provoked anger from the non-Western world. He argues that everything the non-Western world held dear and even sacred was crushed by the Euro-American economic and cultural juggernaut. This anger is manifest in President Hugo Chavez of Venezuela's speech to the UN, where he railed against U.S. hegemony:

> We have to look directly at the terrifying reality of the world we live in. It is necessary to ask a series of questions on the basis of the risks and threats we face: Why is the United States the only country that scatters the planet with military bases? What is it afraid of to allocate such a staggering budget for increasing its military power? Why has it unleashed so many wars, violating the sovereignty of other nations which have the same rights on their own fates? How can international law be enforced against its insensible aspiration to military hegemonizing the world in order to ensure energy sources to sustain their predatory and consumer model? Why does the UN do nothing to stop Washington? If we answer these questions sincerely we would understand that the empire has awarded itself the role of judge of the world, without being granted this responsibility by anyone, and, therefore, imperialist war threatens us all. Washington knows that a multipolar world is already an irreversible reality. Its strategy consist of stopping, at any price, the sustained rise of a group of emerging countries, by negotiating great interests with its partners and followers in order to guide multipolarity along the path the empire wants. What is more, the goal is to configure the world so it is based on Yankee military hegemony. Mankind is facing the very real threat of a permanent war. The empire is ready to create political conditions for triggering a war anywhere, and the case of Libya proves it. Within the imperial view of the world, the well-known Clausewitz's axiom is being reversed: politics is the continuation of war by other means. (Chavez's Speech to the UN, 26 September 2011)

Without a clear understanding of the form and substance of the empire, the present African condition cannot be fully articulated. In an attempt to describe the convoluted postcolonial condition, Gayatri Chakravorti Spivak (1990: 166) used the term 'post-colonial neo-colonized world'. While the term 'postcolonial neo-colonial world' might sound vague, it captures very well a complex and convoluted situation of truncated African liberatory projects that gave birth to a problematic and fragile postcolony (Ndlovu-Gatsheni 2012a). Achille Mbembe (2001a) defined postcolony as an age that enclosed 'multiple duress made up of discontinuities, reversals, inertias, and swings that overlay one another, interpenetrate one another, and envelop one another'. He elaborated that in the postcolony, a 'before' and an 'after' of colonization constituted an entanglement made up of several temporalities and concluded that:

> African social formations are not necessarily converging towards a single point, trend or cycle. They harbour the possibility of a variety of tra-

jectories neither convergent nor divergent but interlocked, paradoxically. More philosophically, it may be supposed that the present as *experience of a time* is precisely that moment when different forms of absence become mixed together: absence of those presence that are no longer so and that one remembers (the past), and absence of those others that are yet to come and are anticipated (the future). (Mbembe 2001a: 16)

The various African initiatives including Negritude, African Human-ism, African Socialism, African Consciencism, African Personality, Black Consciousness, and African Renaissance that envisaged a new African decolonized world and a new African humanity could not successfully break the strong snares and bonds of global neo-colonial imperatives that disciplined the African liberatory process into emancipatory re-formism (Ndlovu-Gatsheni 2012a: 1–2). But Afro-enthusiasm that failed to take into account coloniality as a pervasive terrain of continuation of colonialism resulted in disillusionment and despair. What needs to be clearly understood are the core matrices of power underpinning global coloniality, particularly the levers that have kept it going since the fif-teenth century. The first important concept to understand is coloniality. Anibal Quijano defines it this way:

> Coloniality is one of the specific and constitutive elements of global model of capitalist power. It is based on the imposition of a racial/ethnic classification of the global population as the cornerstone of that model of power, and it operates on every level, in every arena and dimension (both material and subjective) of everyday social existence, and does so on a societal scale. (Quijano 2000b: 342)

Coloniality must not be confused with colonialism because the latter de-noted a direct political and economic order in which the sovereignty of a nation and peoples rested on the power of the colonizing power, which made the colonized nation part of an empire. Maldonado-Torres (2007: 243) articulated coloniality as referring to the longstanding patterns of power that emerged as a result of colonialism but that transcended colo-nialism to be constituted in culture, labour, intersubjective relations, and knowledge production. In Maldonado-Torres's words:

> Thus, coloniality survives colonialism. It is maintained alive in books, in the criteria for academic performance, in cultural patterns, in common sense, in the self-image of peoples, in aspirations of self, and so many other aspects of our modern experience. In a way, as modern subjects we breathe coloniality all the time and everyday. (Maldonado-Torres 2007: 243)

Today's empire is sustained by coloniality rather than colonialism. Colo-niality is itself informed by what Quijano (2007) articulated as colonial-ity of power. Both coloniality and coloniality of power capture the dark side of modernity. While coloniality enables a deeper understanding of the continuity of colonial forms of domination through production of colonial cultures and structures, coloniality of power refers to a crucial structuring process that subordinates peripheral societies to global imperial designs (Grosfoguel 2011).

The first point is that coloniality of power is in turn underpinned by colonial matrices of power that enable empire to take control of African economies including land expropriations, exploitation of labour and natural resources. The second point is that it enabled usurpation and control of African kingly and chiefly authority and power as well as reducing present-day African presidents and prime ministers to a subordinate status in global governance, receiving orders from Washington, London, Rome, Paris and other Western capitals. Therefore, the process not only entailed the reduction of defeated African chiefs into the lowest ranking colonial officials responsible for supervision of Africans as providers of cheap labour during colonial encounters, but continues to make present-day African leaders work as supervisors and foremen of the processes of production of primary products needed in Europe and America. The third point is that it enabled control of gender and sexuality while at the same time affecting the structures of African families and forms of African education by presenting Western bourgeois forms as an ideal template. Finally, it enabled control of subjectivity and knowledge, including the imposition of Euro-American epistemology and the shaping of formative processes of development of black subjectivity.

Coloniality of power, therefore, articulated and still articulates continuities of colonial mentalities, psychologies, and worldviews within the so-called 'postcolonial era', highlighting the social hierarchical relationships of exploitation and domination between Westerners and Africans, rooted in centuries of European colonial expansion but currently embedded in cultural, social and political power relations (Quijano 2007; Grosfoguel 2007). The concept helps to understand heterogeneous structural processes unleashed by global imperial designs in its multiple relations that impinged on culture, politics, and economy in Africa and other ex-colonized zones. Grosfoguel (2007: 217) defined 'coloniality of power' as an entanglement of multiple and heterogeneous global hierarchies and hetararchies of sexual, political, epistemic, economic, spiritual, linguistic and racial forms of domination and exploitation where the racial/ethnic hierarchy of the European/non-European divide transversally reconfigured all of the global power structures. Grosfoguel's argument is also expressed by Abiola Irene (1991: 58) who argued that the West has exerted so much pressure on the African experience to the extent that 'it is no exaggeration to say that all forms of modern African expression have been conditioned by it'.

Grosfoguel (2007: 216) distilled nine contours of coloniality of power that underpin the current Western-dominated world. The first contour is the formation of a particular global class formation where a diversity of forms of labour ranging from slavery, serfdom, wage labour to petty-commodity production and many others, were co-existing and being organized by capital as a source of production of surplus value through the selling of commodities for profit in the world market. The second contour was the international division of labour of the core and periphery where in the periphery coercion and authoritarian forms predominated. The third contour was the creation of an inter-state system of politico-military organizations manned by European and American males and ready to discipline deviant states like Iraq and others (Grosfoguel 2007: 216).

The fourth contour was an elaborate global racial/ethnic hierarchy that privileges Western people over non-Western people. The fifth strand is an equally elaborate global gender hierarchy that privileges males over females and Western patriarchy over other forms of gender relations (Spivak 1988). This strand is related to the next one of a sexual hierarchy that privileged heterosexuals over homosexuals and lesbians, invariably feeding into the politics of homophobic ideologies. The seventh contour is that of privileging Christianity over all other non-Christian/non-Western spiritualities.

The eighth contour is an epistemic hegemony that privileges Western knowledge and cosmology over non-Western knowledge and cosmologies that is evident in universities across the world. The final contour highlights the present linguistic hierarchy whereby Western languages (English, French, Portuguese, Spanish, Italian, and others) enjoy global outreach above non-Western ones, leading to the pushing of African languages to the barbarian margins of folklores (Grosfoguel 2007: 216–217). Therefore, the concept of coloniality of power is very useful as it enables ex-colonized peoples to understand why the present racial/ethnic hierarchy of the capitalist world-system continues to be constituted by a cultural criterion whose origins lie in colonial encounters and colonial relations. It enables historicization of why some human beings were at the bottom of the ethnic/racial hierarchy when the Anglo-Saxons remained dominant in the world. Quijano summarized the situation very well when he said:

> Racism and ethnicization were initially produced in the Americas and then expanded to the rest of the colonial world as the foundation of the specific power relations between Europe and the populations of the rest of the world. After five hundred years, they still are the basic components of power relations across the world. Once colonialism became extinct as a formal political system, social power is still constituted on criteria originated in colonial relations. In other words, coloniality has not ceased to be the central character of today's social power ... Since then, in the intersubjective relations and in the social practices of power, there emerged, on the one hand, the idea that non-Europeans have biological structure not only different from Europeans; but, above all, belonging to an 'inferi-

or' level or type. On the other hand, the idea that cultural differences are associated to such biological inequalities ... These ideas have configured a deep and persistent cultural formation, a matrix of ideas, images, values, attitudes, and social practices, that do not cease to be implicated in relationships among people, even when colonial political relations have been eradicated. (Quijano cited in Grosfoguel 2004: 326)

The next important concept is that of coloniality of knowledge. Coloniality of knowledge denotes a complex process of deployment of global imperial technologies of subjectivation taking the form of translating and re-writing other cultures, other knowledges, and other ways of being, and presuming commensurability through Western rationality. As noted by Mignolo (2007: 162), coloniality of knowledge worked actively in 'silencing or relegating other epistemologies to a barbarian margins, a primitive past or a communist or Muslim evil'. Therefore, coloniality of knowledge directly facilitates a critical interrogation of epistemological questions of how colonial modernity interfered with African modes of knowing, social meaning-making, imagining, seeing, and knowledge production and their replacement with Eurocentric epistemologies that assumed the character of objective, scientific, neutral, universal and only truthful knowledges (Escobar 2007).

Since the time of the European Renaissance and Enlightenment, agents of Euro-American modernity and hegemony such as classical philosophers, adventures, missionaries, colonialists, traders and anthropologists worked tirelessly to make their knowledge the only truthful and universal knowledge, ceaselessly spreading it through Christianity and other means across the world, in the process appropriating and displacing existing African knowledges. Western knowledge and imperial power worked together to inscribe coloniality across the African continent and other parts of the non-Western world. This way, Western domination and Eurocentrism assumed universality. Quijano clearly expressed the core logic of unfolding of coloniality of knowledge when he wrote that:

The repression fell, above all, over the modes of knowing, of producing knowledge, of producing perspectives, images and systems of images, symbols, modes of signification, over the resources, patterns, and instruments of formalized and objectivized expression, intellectual or visual. It was followed by the imposition of the use of the ruler's own patterns of expression, and of their beliefs and images with reference to the supernatural ... The colonisers also imposed a mystified image of their own patterns of producing knowledge and meaning. At first, they placed these patterns out of reach of the dominated. Later, they taught them in a partial and selective way, in order to co-opt some of the dominated into their own power institutions. Then European culture was made seductive: it gave access to power. After all, beyond repression, the main instrument of all power is its seduction ... European culture became a universal cultural model. The imaginary in the non-European cultures could hardly exist today and, above all, reproduce itself outside these relations. (Quijano 2007: 169)

The third important concept is that of coloniality of being. It is a useful analytical tool that helps to analyse the realities of dehumanization and depersonalization of colonized Africans and their reduction into *damnés* (the damned/condemned people, the wretched of the earth) (Fanon 1968; Maldonado 2007). Under colonialism, colonized Africans endured hellish life experiences informed by existing racialized hierarchies of power that prevented any mutually respectful relationships between black colonized Africans and white colonizers. The world of the colonized became a domain of violence, war, rape, diseases, death and mourning, as they were denied full humanity and reduced to non-beings who subsisted and lived within the underworld of coloniality (Mignolo 2007a; Mignolo 2007b; Quijano 2007; Grosfoguel 2007; Maldonado-Torres 2007; Escobar 2007). The life in the informal settlements (shacks) in South Africa provides a good picture of a hellish life as an underworld, a coloniality of being where human beings live in electrically unearthed shacks, unprotected from lightning. There are no sanitary toilets and no sources of clean water. Violence is endemic. Poverty has become an identity in itself. Social peace and human security is perpetually absent (Ndlovu-Gatsheni 2012b).

Jan Vansina in his *Being Colonized: The Kuba Experience in Rural Congo, 1880–1960* (2010) posed the question: what was it like to be colonized by foreigners? This is a fundamental question because a full answer to it leaves no doubt as to why Africa is in its current state of crisis, a crisis of development, a crisis of identity, and a crisis of mission. The concept of coloniality of being enables an analysis of being colonized from the victim's side. As argued by Maldonado-Torres (2004: 39): 'To be sure being colonized is not the result of the work of any one author or philosopher, but the very product of modernity/coloniality in its intimate relation with the coloniality of power, the coloniality of knowledge and the coloniality of being itself'. Frantz Fanon correctly rendered the state of being colonized as that of damnation in *The Wretched of the Earth* (1968). The wretched of the earth exist within what Maldonado-Torres (2004: 40) termed 'the wastelands of empires' as well as 'mega-cities which become small empires into themselves'.

Maldonado-Torres (2007) added that imperialism and colonialism were underpinned by a racist/imperial Manichean misanthropic scepticism as a type of imperial/colonial attitude that questioned the very humanity of colonized people and doubted whether they had souls. This imperial/colonial attitude was a deliberate strategy that opened the door to all forms of abuse including killing, enslaving and raping, and the use of various forms of violence that could not be inflicted on Western people. The colonized people experienced not only alienation but also depersonalization as they were stripped of humanity. Race played a central role to create what Frantz Fanon (1961) termed a *damné*, a conquered being deprived of humanity. Maldonado-Torres (2007: 255) had this to say on coloniality of being:

> Hellish existence in the colonial world carries with it both the racial and the gendered aspects of the naturalization of the no-ethics of war. *Indeed, coloniality of Being primarily refers to the normalization of the extraordinary events that take place in war.* While in war there is murder and rape, in the hell of the colonial world murder and rape become day to day occurrences and menaces. 'Killability' and 'rapeability' are inscribed into the images of the colonial bodies. Lacking real authority, colonized men are permanently feminized. (emphasis in the original)

What is emphasized here is that one of the core ideological life-springs of colonial conquest and colonial violence was the questioning of the very humanity of colonized people. Questioning the humanity of the colonized people authorized even slavery and other forms of abuse, repression, exploitation and domination of Africans. This reality led Bernard Magubane to produce *Race and the Construction of the Dispensable Other* (2007). This book articulated how colonized and racialized subjects whose humanity was questioned became the 'dispensable other'. For him, 'The ghastly deeds perpetrated in the name of race purity and white supremacy boggle the mind. In the scale of such atrocities, the African slave stands out as the classical expression of rabid racism in the West' (Magubane 2007: 1). Since the time of the slave trade, a Western conception of human history emerged which ascended from the 'state of nature' to Europe as the centre of world civilization, creator and exporter of modernity (Mignolo 1995; Quijano 2000a). Coloniality of being speaks to the unfolding of modern history in accordance with the logic of coloniality. This is why Maldonado-Torres posited that:

> I suggest that Being is to history and tradition, as coloniality of Being is to coloniality of power and colonial difference. The coloniality of Being refers to the process whereby common sense and tradition are marked by dynamics of power that are preferential in character: they discriminate people and target communities. The preferential character of violence can be spelled out by the coloniality of power, which links racism, capitalist exploitation, the control of sex and the monopoly of knowledge, and relate them to modern colonial history. (Maldonado-Torres 2004: 43)

The importance of coloniality of being is that it is one way of theorizing 'the basic fundaments of the pathologies of imperial power and the persistence of coloniality' (Maldonado-Torres 2004: 44). Another important element that formed part of the core logics of coloniality was the notion of emptiness that was well captured by J.M. Blaut in these words:

> This proposition of emptiness makes a series of claims, each layered upon the others: (i) A non-European region is empty or nearly empty of people (hence settlement by Europeans does not displace any native peoples). (ii) The region is empty of settled population: the inhabitants are mobile, nomadic, wanderers (hence European settlement violates no political sovereignty, since wanderers make no claim to territory). (iii) The cultures of this region do not possess any understanding of private property – that is, the region is empty of property rights and claims (hence colonial occupiers can freely give land to settlers since no one owns it). The final layer, applied to all of the Outside sector, is an emptiness of intellectual creativity and spiritual values, sometimes described by Europeans as an absence of 'rationality'. (Blaut 1993: 15)

The key challenge that this book grapples with is that of why after some fifty years of decolonization and the supposed end of colonial empires, the continent remains in a subaltern position within the global power hierarchy. Part of my response is that a postcolonial African world has not yet been fully realized because of the continued entrapment of the continent and its people within global imperial designs. This is a point well articulated also in Ngugi wa Thiong'o's *Decolonizing Mind: The Politics of Language in African Literature* (1986: xii), where he stressed the point that:

> The present predicaments of Africa are often not a matter of personal choice: they arise from an historical situation. Their solutions are not so much a matter of personal decision as that of a fundamental social transformation of the structures of our societies starting with a real break with imperialism and its internal allies. Imperialism and its comprador alliances in Africa can never develop the continent.

The shifting geography of reason and the geopolitics of knowledge

In their recent book entitled *Theory from the South or How Euro-America Is Evolving Towards Africa* (2012), Jean Comaroff and John L. Comaroff posed the following challenge:

> Western Enlightenment thought has, from the first, posited itself as the wellspring of universal learning, of Science and Philosophy, uppercase; concomitantly, it has regarded the non-West – the variously known as the ancient world, the orient, the primitive world, the third world, the underdeveloped world, the developing world, and now the global south – primarily as a place of parochial wisdom, of antiquarian traditions, of exotic ways and means. Above all, of unprocessed data. These other worlds, in short, are treated less as sources of refined knowledge than as reservoirs of raw fact: of the historical, natural, and ethnographic minutiae from which Euromodernity might fashion its testable theories and

transcendent truths, its axioms and certitudes, its premises, postulates, and principles. Just as it has capitalized on non-Western 'raw materials' – materials at once human and physical, moral and medical, mineral and man-made, cultural and agricultural – by ostensibly adding value and refinement to them. In some measure, this continues to be the case. But what if, and here is the idea in interrogative form, we invert that order of things? What if we subvert the epistemic scaffolding on which it is erected? What if we posit that, in the present moment, it is the global south that affords privileged insight into the workings of the world at large? ... That, in probing what is at stake in it, we might move beyond the north-south binary, to lay bare the larger dialectical processes that have produced and sustained it ... Each is a reflection on the contemporary order of things approached from a primarily African vantage, one, as it turns out, that is full of surprises and counter-intuitives, one that invites us to see familiar things in different ways. (Comaroff and Comaroff 2012: 1–2)

The Comaroffs' argument encapsulates the central argument of this book, which is that of shifting the geography of reason and the geopolitics of knowledge within a context in which Euro-American epistemology is failing to offer modern solutions to modern problems. The work of such scholars such as Molefi Kete Asante, who is credited for originating Afrocentric philosophy and articulating it consistently over the last three decades, contributed to the need to shift the geography of reason and geopolitics of knowledge (2003). Asante defined Afrocentricity as a 'paradigmatic intellectual perspective that privileges the agency within the context of African history and culture transcontinentally and transgenerationally' (Asante 2007: 2).

Afrocentricity is genealogically traced to African ideas and African authors as they grappled with colonial encounters, colonial realities and postcolonial challenges such as Nkrumah's *Consciencism: Philosophy and Ideology of Decolonization* (1964) where he clearly posited that Africa has to come to terms with itself and create a scientific response to national and international issues based on African interests. Afrocentricity is a theory of human liberation and an intellectual critique of Eurocentrism, which fully accepts the agency of the 'African person as the basic unit of analysis of the social situations involving Africa-descended people' (Asante 2007: 109). This is how Asante elaborated on Afrocentricity as a liberatory theory:

The escape from the Western hegemony is not easy and, just as we have announced our escape; we recognize that the Fortress West is not going to let us leave the mental plantation without a struggle. Afrocentricity seeks to obliterate the mental, physical, cultural, and economic dislocation of African people by thrusting Africans as centred, healthy human beings in the context of African thought ... To be for oneself is not to be against others; this is the most authoritative lesson that can be learned from the Afrocentric school of thought. Only where there is an effective mass movement of Africans from the margins of Europe to the center of their own reality, in a self-conscious way, can there be a true revolution. This would, of course, mean the end of white hegemony. (Asante 2007: 120–121)

Africanity is related to Afrocentricity but speaks directly to issues of identity and being, embracing such intangibles as 'customs, traditions, and traits of people of Africa and the diaspora' (Asante 2007: 109).

Since the time of colonial encounters, Africans have been involved in 'creative negotiation' of the 'multiple encounters, influences and perspectives throughout their continent. Africans are actively modernizing their indegeneities and indigenizing their modernities' (Nyamnjoh 2006b: 393). But on top of this, there is the need to shift the locus of enunciation from a Western perspective to an African perspective of the world. This is important because one of the major limitations of a series of African struggles and initiatives aimed at extricating Africa from the snares of colonial matrices of power is that they were formulated within modernity, used Modernist techniques and tools to the extent that they became nothing other than a critique of modernity within modernity. Attempts at launching real alternatives to modernity have been a challenge.

Some of the few alternatives that were tried tended to be backward, looking to an ever-receding past. For example, the primary resistances of the late nineteenth century and early twentieth centuries sought to re-create the precolonial social order. When these failed, the initiatives that were launched such as the pan-Africanist congresses that began in 1900, Negritudist movements of the 1930s, anti-colonial liberation wars of the 1950s and 1960s, struggles for economic development of the 1970s and 1980s, such as the Lagos Plan of Action, the civil-society based struggles for democracy of the 1990s, right up to the revived pan-Africanist initiatives galvanized by the millennial African Renaissance, were constrained by their circulation within the worldview put in place by modernity. Commenting on the crisis on Third World nationalism that was ranged against colonialism, Kuan-Hsing Chen (1998: 14) noted that 'Shaped by the immanent logic of colonialism, Third World nationalism could not escape from reproducing racial and ethnic discrimination; a price to be paid by the colonizer as well as the colonised selves'.

The basic idea that lay behind the African initiatives and struggles for liberation and development was how to capture the positive aspects of modernity that accrued to the Euro-American world and were enjoyed by the minority of white citizens in Africa on the one hand, and how to rebut discourses and epistemologies of alterity on the other. Escaping the consequences of the dark side of modernity has become a lifetime struggle for Africans. At the centre of this struggle was the core aspiration of realizing a postcolonial life as new humanism that Fanon dreamt of. But Bill Ashcroft (1997) argued that the term 'post-colonial' was not a reference to 'after colonialism'. He posited that 'post-colonialism' began when the colonizers arrived and did not vanish when the colonialists rolled back direct colonial administrations after 1945. To him, postcolonial analysis examined the full range of responses to colonialism. The term described 'a society continuously responding in all its myriad ways to the experience of colonial contact' (Ashcroft 1997: 21). The crisis is exacerbated by those people who spend all their time responding to a world where they have been reduced to respondents rather than initiators, resulting in mimicry and compromised agency.

The decolonization process itself became overseen by the erstwhile colonial masters who were bent on channelling it into a neo-colonial direction rather than genuine liberation. For the 'Anglophone' African world, the Lancaster House in London became the political maternity ward for an African (re-)birth with the British and American powers acting as midwives. 'Decolonization' was less evident in the 'Francophone' African world, where a former colonial power (France) was embraced as an innocent father figure and where decolonization was interpreted in simplistic terms of 'democratization' under the tutelage of France.

The crisis of imagination of a new and brave African world order free from global matrices of power and global imperial designs was compounded by that fact that some of those Africans who were socially located on the oppressed side of power relations did not embrace a subaltern epistemology. Colonial interpellation and neo-colonial imperatives forced some Africans who were physically located on the oppressed side of abyssal lines to think and speak epistemically like ones on the dominant sides. Some of those who attempted to initiate alternatives fell into epistemic populism that was never translated into concrete liberatory projects. As noted by Bill Ashcroft (1997: 15) the most difficult challenge faced by Africans has been how to re-imagine themselves outside the thinking imposed by the Euro-American imagination and representation of Africans. Negritude was one example that demonstrated how Africans fell into the trap of racial binarism, imposed by imperialists and colonialists. This reality led Ngugi wa Thiong'o to pose the following soul-searching questions:

> Is an African renaissance possible when we keepers of memory have to work outside our own linguistic memory? And within the prison house of European linguistic memory? Often drawing from our own experiences and history to enrich the already very rich European memory? If we think of the intelligentsia as generals in the intellectual army of Africa including foot soldiers, can we expect this army to conquer when its generals are captured and held prisoner? And it is worse when they revel in their fate as captives. (Ngugi wa Thiong'o 2009: 92)

Mary Louise Pratt (1992) and Pal Ahluwalia (2001) introduced the notions of 'contact zones' and 'African inflections', respectively. Pratt's concept of 'contact zones' encapsulated the process of how people who were geographically and historically remote from each other came into contact with one another through such processes as navigation, migration, the slave trade, mercantilism, imperialism, colonialism and evangelism leading to a combination of peaceful co-existence, conquest, coercion and violence as well as blending and conflict. At the centre of contact zones exist 'radically asymmetrical relations of power' (Pratt 1992: 7). It is these radically asymmetrical power relations that developed during the colonial encounters of the fifteenth century that sustain global coloniality today.

The reality is that many features of the present world order still reflect the paradoxes and contradictions of the past mediated by '"universal truth" and "parochial cultures"', between a society founded on individual rights and one characterized by racial (dis)enfranchisement, between the world of the free citizen and that of the colonial subject. These tensions suffused the encounter between Africans and Europeans, animating histories that eluded easy control by their dramatis personae, histories carved out of the dialectics of exchange, appropriation, accommodation, struggle' (Comaroff and Comaroff 1997: xv). The results have been what Valentin Y. Mudimbe (1988: 2) described as 'the domination of physical space, the reformation of natives' minds, and the integration of local economic histories into Western perspective'.

While it is true that the present-day African problems cannot be reduced to what Mudimbe (1988: 6) termed the 'colonializing structure', African actions have also contributed to the exacerbation of the problems. Africans have exercised their agency not only to resist colonialism but also to create new forms of oppression and exploitation of one another. This point is well articulated by Toyin Falola:

> The current generation of Africans, born after the 'years of independence' in the 1960s, cannot help but blame the Africans in power for this mess. What contemporary Africans see are not the motives, manners and style of the European officers but the waste and greed of the African leaders. They see bad leadership, corruption, and a get-rich culture that trivializes the values of hard work and creativity. It is hard to defend the performance of a majority of African states and their leaders. Examples of political leaders who are interested more in their pockets than the people they govern are too numerous. Africans have contributed to the destruction of Africa in a myriad of ways: corruption, inept leadership, authoritarianism and tyranny, civil wars, endless political crises, and lack of concern for the poor. Critical reflections on the colonial state and its aftermath in no way exonerate the failure of leadership in contemporary Africa. (Falola 2005: 3–4)

But Ahluwalia's (2001) concept of 'African inflections' is important in that it provides a critical lens of reading how African societies have constructed and reconstructed themselves through engagement with Western and colonial modernity in creative ways including attempts at disrupting Euro-American hegemony. The concept of postcolonial inflections is meant to capture how 'post-colonial subjects confront their colonial legacy and define their post-colonial future' (Ahluwalia 2005: 152). Ahluwalia has persuasively argued for liberation of postcolonial theory from conflation with post-structuralism and postmodernism as part of articulating its liberatory content. To Ahluwalia, postcolonial theory is 'a counter-discourse which seeks to disrupt the cultural hegemony of the West, challenging imperialism in its various guises, whereas post-structuralism and postmodernism are counter-discourses against Modernism that emerge within Modernism itself' (Ahluwalia 2005: 140).

To elucidate the differences between postcolonial theory and post-structuralism as well as postmodernism, Ahluwalia delved into genealogies of French post-structuralism. His argument is that French post-structuralism has colonial roots if one understands the history of its formulators, such as Derrida who was a 'French Algerian' who suffered the crisis 'of belonging and not belonging in both French and Algerian culture, of occupying that in-between space' (Ahluwalia 2005: 140). Ahluwalia concluded that the some of the leading French post-structuralists and postmodernists, structuralists and psychoanalysts, namely Althusser, Bourdieu, Cixoux, Derrida, Fanon, Foucault, Loytard and Memmi, were 'Franco-Maghrebians who have sought to challenge the very epistemology of French colonialism and its ideas of cultural superiority. In the writings of these Franco-Maghrebians who had, or have, a foot firmly planted in Algeria, we see their impact on socialism, humanism, Marxism, post-structuralism, postmodernism, postcolonialism and the project of modernity itself. Above all, it is the spectre of Algeria that sharpens their focus and forces them to challenge the orthodoxy that sustained the cultural practices of the French imperial project' (Ahluwalia 2005: 152). The key point about this intervention is that it reinforces the importance of locus of enunciation in knowledge production and development of new theories. Ahluwalia does not use locus of enunciation but employs Edward Said's concept of 'worldliness'. On this he writes that:

> The materiality, the locatedness, the worldliness of the text is embedded in it as a function of its very being. It has a material presence, a cultural and social history, a political and even an economic being. (Ahluwalia 2005: 141)

Ahluwalia's intervention prompts a new thinking about postcolonial theory as part of initiatives towards decolonial turn that has been clouded by being conflated with post-structuralism and postmodernism.

How about the globalists and the future of Africa?

The present-day crisis is in fact a crisis of imagination of a different future. It is not simply an African crisis, it is a global crisis. Arturo Escobar (2004) described the crisis as the crisis of modernity, which is failing to provide modern solutions to modern problems. Military invasions of less powerful nations by the powerful nations are part of the 'Modernist attempt at combating the symptoms but not the cause of social, political and ecological crises of the times' (Escobar 2004: 209). The other attempt is to deploy 'Regimes of selective inclusion and hyper-exclusion' that result in 'heightened poverty for the many and skyrocketing wealth for the few' (Escobar 2004: 209). What are challenging are the means and ways of moving beyond the modernity that is in crisis. Does the current global crisis of modernity render the prognostications of globalists and cosmopolitanists obsolete?

Achille Mbembe has been one of the strong believers in the embracement of globalization as a solution to the African impasse. He is very critical of African discourses that concentrate on refutations of Western definition to the extent of creating a polemical relationship between the African continent and the world. To him, this results in nothing other than a cult of victimhood. To him, colonialism was a joint invention of Westerners and Africans. The future of Africa lies not in conceptions of 'identity as geography' and 'celebrations of autochthony' but in the embrace of universalism and cosmopolitanism (Mbembe 2002a: 271–273). But these enthusiasms for universalism and cosmopolitanism do not clearly express what is meant by universal and cosmopolitan.

Mbembe's thinking emerged from postmodernist and postcolonial thought. This body of thought's slogan is 'Long live difference! Down with essentialist binaries!' (Hardt and Negri 2000: 138). Postmodernists and postcolonialists railed against a modern world order that they understood as a Manichean world characterized by a series of binary oppositions of the 'Self' and the 'Other', white and black, 'inside and outside', dominated and dominant, as well as 'ruler and ruled' (Hardt and Negri 2000: 139). Postmodernists and postcolonial theorists directly attached to the modern world order 'meta-narratives', such as sexism, nationalism, patriarchy, imperialism, tribalism, ethnicity, colonialism and racism, which they saw as lying at the root of global conflicts and preventing co-presence. These binaries and vectors were said to be responsible for hierarchies and the fragmentation of humanity into 'white and black, masculine and feminine' (Hardt and Negri 2000: 141). According to Hardt and Negri (2000: 142–146), both postmodernists and post-structuralists have remained 'fixated on attacking an old form of power and propose a strategy of liberation that could be effective only on the old terrain' of colonialism. They have posited that postmodernists and postcolonial theorists' interventions have proven to be 'entirely insufficient for theorizing contemporary global power', which to them is no longer predicated on a Manichean conception of the world (Hardt and Negri 2000: 146). To Hardt and Negri:

> The ideology of the world market has always been the anti-foundational and anti-essentialist discourse par excellence. Circulation, mobility, diversity, and mixture are its very conditions of possibility. (Hardt and Negri 2000: 150)

Postmodernists and postcolonial theorists believed in the possibility of a harmonious universalism. But if uni-versal means one world, one universe, then Africans are invited to live in a village created and manned by disgraced Modernist guards and overseen by a naked Modernist king, hailing from a crisis-ridden Euro-American world. Cosmopolitanists always talk of tolerance rather than the equality of human beings. Africans do not want to be tolerated by anyone, to be treated as children. They need justice and equality. But it is necessary to analyse the option offered by globalists who argued for possibilities of re-imagining oneself into a world community. What can be gained by looking at 'Africa as part of a global system of capital, of profit and of exploitation?' (Ashcroft 1997: 17). What about considering the possibilities of abandoning a polemical view of Africa, and placing Africa at the centre of globalism, would that not resolve essentialist politics of nationalism, racialism and pan-Africanism? The short answer to these questions is that global coloniality makes it impossible to 'disrupt the idea of Africa inherited from the history of European imperialism' (Ashcroft 1997: 17). This is because 'Power is as much a part of our cultural life as the air we breathe' (Ashcroft 1997: 20).

This reality has made it impossible to really transcend Orientalism, which has remained in place since the time of conquest. Thandika Mkandawire (2009: 133) has noted that 'transcending nationalism does not necessarily always promise better things' as 'the many alternatives to nationalism have been disastrous – whether these take the form of ethnic sub-nationalism, idiosyncratic socialism or mimetic internationalism, religious particularism or neo-liberal globalism'. The notion of embracing globalization as a strategy of liberation for Africa is akin to arguing about a phantasmagoric empire rather than the really existing empire. In the really existing empire, the representations of Africa in binary terms play an important role in the really existing imperial project. The future that Africans should aspire for must not be a 'uni-versal' one but a 'pluri-versal' one, in which many worlds would fit without being imitations of another world. This book is basically about decolonization predicated on decolonial turn, which inaugurates a rewriting of history predicated on new canons of 'an-other logic', 'an-other language', and 'an-other thinking' (Mignolo 1995: xx).

The decolonial turn is towards the direction of Africanity as an assertion of African identity; Afrocentrism as a liberatory methodology; decolonial thought as a combative epistemology and pan-Africanism as a terrain of ongoing struggles for liberation. These agendas are imposed on Africans by history. Archie Mafeje explained the logic in these revealing words:

> ... we would not talk of freedom, if there was no prior condition in which this was denied; we would not be anti-racism if we had not been its victims; we would not proclaim Africanity, if it had not been denied or degraded; and we would not insist on Afrocentrism, if it had not been for Eurocentric negations ... Of necessity, under the determinate global conditions an African renaissance must entail a rebellion – a conscious rejection of past transgressions, a determined negation of negations. (Mafeje 2011: 31–32)

CHAPTER 2

Global Imperial Designs and Pan-Africanism

Introduction

Berlin represented an avaricious banquet at which gluttonous, corpulent European imperialists feasted on territories that clearly did not belong to them. They sought in the process to cloak the fraudulent scheme under patronizing and paternalistic moral principles of a mission civilisatrice (civilizing mission) that Africa's 'noble savages' had never agreed to. Berlin and its aftermath were akin to robbers forcibly breaking into a house and sharing out its possessions while the owners of the house – who had been tied up with thick ropes – were wide awake, but were powerless to prevent the burglary.

(Adekeye Adebajo 2010: 16)

We must leave our dreams and abandon our old beliefs and friendships of the time before life began. Let us waste no time in sterile litanies and nauseating mimicry. Leave this Europe where they are never done talking of Man, yet murder men everywhere they find them, at the corner of every one of their streets, in all the corners of the globe ... So, my brothers, how is it that we do not understand that we have better things to do than to follow that same Europe? Come, then, comrades, the European game has finally ended; we must find something different.

(Frantz Fanon 1968: 251)

In his seminal book *The Curse of Berlin: Africa after the Cold War* (2010) Adekeye Adebajo boldly traced the roots of the present-day African problems to the Berlin Conference of 1884 to 1885 that was hosted by Otto von Bismarck, the Chancellor of Germany from 1871 to 1890. He stated that 'Africa suffers from a curse invoked in Berlin' (Adebajo 2010: 2). He characterized Bismarck as 'the Grand Wizard of the Berlin Conference' and a 'German sorcerer' who assembled his 'European apprentices' while employing 'Western wizardry of the technology of the industrial revolution of the Victorian age' that included the use of the Maxim Gun 'to set the rules for the "Scramble for Africa"' (Adebajo 2010: 8). In convincing language, Adebajo, as a concerned African scholar, highlighted how one event within global imperial designs in one blow shaped the cartographic shape of the African continent. Whatever the apologists of imperialism and colonialism say in mitigation, the reality is that the Berlin Conference indeed galvanized the Scramble for Africa that resulted in the present boundaries of postcolonial African states. Ricardo René Leremont in *Borders, Nationalism, and the African State* (2005) argued that:

> The borders of African states were fixed by European colonialists during a narrow window of time (essentially from 1878 to 1914). In the immediate postcolonial period (beginning in the early 1960s), these borders were reified by independence leaders. From the 1960s until today the most ardent supporters of colonially inherited borders have been urbanized political elites who have most to gain by their maintenance. People in rural areas (where the majority of Africans still resides) consider borders – and often the state – irrelevant. (Leremont 2005: 2)

Leremont's intervention resonates with Adebajo's metaphor of a curse. The irony is that the curse has now been embraced as the norm by postcolonial leaders in the form of the maintenance and reification of colonially drawn borders. This reality impinges on the relationship of global imperial designs, territorial nationalism, and pan-Africanism, which is treated in this chapter. The important point that immediately springs up is that of how products of global imperial designs have been consumed by Africans in the process resulting in 're-instating of empire'. Commenting on the impact of the decisions taken at the Berlin Conference on Africa, Wole Soyinka said:

> One hundred years ago, at the Berlin Conference, the colonial powers that ruled Africa met to divvy up their interests into states, lumping various people and tribes together in some places, or slicing them apart in others like some demented tailor who paid no attention to the fabric, colour or pattern of the quilt he was patching together. One of the biggest disappointments of the OAU when it came into being more than 20 years ago was that it failed to address the issue. Instead, one of its cardinal principles was non-interference and the sacrosanctity of the boundaries inherited from the colonial situation. And now we see in Rwanda what that absence of African self-definition has wrought. If we fail to understand that all this stems from the colonial nation-state map imposed upon us, there will be little chance to correct the situation over the long-term. (Soyinka 1994: 31)

This chapter delves at once into some epistemological issues at the base of global imperial designs, nationalism and pan-Africanism as it tries to explicate the tortured trajectory of the African struggles for liberation and new humanism, and how these have been constrained by colonial matrices of power. At the epistemological level, the chapter focuses on understanding how Euro-American epistemology, which inaugurated rationality, progress, development, freedom and equality in the Western world, at the same time unleashed imperial technologies of subjectivation that enabled mercantilism, slavery, imperialism, colonialism, neo-colonialism, and apartheid on Africa as the dark side of modernity (Santos 2005: xviii). To further tease out the essence of global imperial designs, the chapter introduces the decolonial epistemic perspective as a counter-hegemonic intellectual thought questioning and challenging Euro-American epistemology's pretentions and claims to be the only mode of knowing that is neutral, objective, disembodied, truthful and universal (Grosfoguel 2007: 211–213). A decolonial epistemic perspective not only reveals epistemicides committed by the darker and underside of Euro-American epistemology, but also operates as an indispensable liberatory epistemology.

At the level of liberation discourse, this chapter focuses on pan-Africanism as a counter-force to the hegemonic global imperial designs in place since the time of conquest. As noted by Boaventura de Sousa Santos, the global imperial designs, in place since the fifteenth century, have 'many facets and assumed many names: discoveries, colonialism, evangelization, slavery, imperialism, development and underdevelopment, modernization and finally, globalization' (Santos 2005: xx). The chapter maps out three important issues that impinge on the pan-African agenda today. First, what are described as global imperial designs that unfolded in the fifteenth century? The point of departure is that modernity, defined as a process of submitting the entire world to the absolute control of Euro-American human reason, human knowledge, and human-made institutions, assumed two contrasting trajectories as it expanded out of Europe into other parts of the world (Wallerstein 1974; Amin 1989; Mignolo 1995; Dussel 1995a; Dussel 1995b; Dussel 1996; Mignolo 2000; Dussel 2000; Castro-Gomez 2002; Lander 2002; Ndlovu-Gatsheni 2011b). One trajectory was positive and enabled Europe and America to develop very fast. The other became negative and impeded Africa's development and unity.

A combination of global imperial designs and the curse of Berlin created the 'Kwame Nkrumah-Julius Nyerere curse' of the 1960s, which was partly invoked by issues of incompatibility between nationalism and pan-Africanism. It is important to visit these debates not only because they fragmented early postcolonial leaders into Casablanca, Monrovia and Brazzaville camps but also because it helps today's pan-Africanists to appreciate some of the nuanced and subtle issues that continue to hinder the full realization of pan-African unity. While previous scholars read and interpreted the Nkrumah-Nyerere debates as a simple case of contestations, pitting radicals against moderates, idealists against pragmatists, and 'immediatists' against 'gradualists', what they missed was the role of global imperial designs in causing all this confusion.

The imperial global designs enabled the decolonization of Africa to proceed without serious questioning of the Westphalian nation-state template that in turn enabled territorial nationalism that was antagonistic to pan-Africanism. Georges Nzongola-Ntalaja (1987: 48) argued that African founding fathers had three choices: to build postcolonial African states on the basis of a precolonial 'ethnic nation' whose development was arrested by colonialism; a colonially created 'territorial nation' that served global imperial designs; and a 'pan-African nation' that had to be created from scratch. Leaders like Chief Obafemi Awolowo (1947) of Nigeria defended the idea of building postcolonial Africa into multinational states based on a federation of precolonial ethnic nations. Nkrumah (1963) of Ghana advocated a pan-African entity and proposed the creation of a United States of Africa. But these two options had no strong social forces to advance them: most of the African petit-bourgeoisie reneged on pan-Africanism and embraced the colonial template for the postcolonial state (Nzongola-Ntalaja 1987: 49).

The current pan-African agenda is struggling to transcend not only the 'quilt of Africa' created at Berlin but also the Nkrumah-Nyerere curse of the 1960s. It is a curse because it diluted and dampened the spirit of pan-Africanism and opened the gates for the rehabilitation of imperialism in the 1970s. Africa is today finding it very difficult to re-emerge from the snares of neo-colonialism and neo-liberalism. But the ongoing crisis exposing and revealing the limits of a neo-liberal capitalist system is giving some space for Africa to intensify the institutionalization of pan-Africanism as a way of survival within a world dominated by the phenomenology of uncertainty. What is discomforting is that this crisis seems to be pushing the Euro-American world to resort to military means, and military invasions of resource-endowed countries of the Global South, as part of its strategies to survive the capitalist financial crisis (Zizek 2011).

What is often underplayed by pan-Africanists is the fact that invisible global imperial designs continue to cast a long shadow and surveillance over any initiatives aimed at implementing the overdue and urgent pan-African unity. Global imperial designs operate through colonial matrices of power that maintain Euro-American hegemony over the African continent in particular and the Global South in general. Divide and rule strategy constitutes one of the longstanding ways through which global imperial designs diluted, confused, and destroyed any counter-initiatives aimed at humanizing and democratizing the current unequal world order in favour of Africa (Ndlovu-Gatsheni 2011a; Ndlovu-Gatsheni 2012b). But what is even more dangerous is epistemic surveillance, subsisting on invasion of the imagination and the colonization of the minds of Africans, which makes it difficult for Africans to transcend the curse of Berlin so as to attain pan-African unity.

Since the emergence of pan-Africanism in the diaspora, it has been one of the most monitored initiatives from Africa, consistently put under

Euro-American surveillance because of its potential to produce a strong continent capable of defending its resources from external plunder. Global imperial designs are today hidden in institutions, contained and carried in seemingly noble discourses like those of development and democracy as well as epistemology that pretends to be neutral, objective, and universal while at the same time quietly facilitating epistemicides in Africa. The chapter elaborates on its core arguments through revisiting the 'Kwame Nkrumah-Julius Nyerere curse' of the 1960s that polarized the initiatives towards pan-Africanism into 'immediatists' and 'gradualists'. Up to today, this curse hangs over the minds of current pan-Africanists like a nightmare, with serious consequences for the pace of achieving pan-African unity.

The African reality is that since the time of colonial encounters, Africans have not yet been able to take full charge of their own fate although they are not completely at the mercy of global imperial designs, in place since the time of conquest. They have been at a crossroads since the time of colonial encounters in the fifteenth century. Going against the global imperial designs of domination, exploitation, and racism, has proven to be a lifetime struggle for Africans. The essence of the African struggles as articulated by Frantz Fanon (1968) has been to forge new categories of thought, construction of new subjectivities and creation of new modes of being and becoming. Such a vast struggle cannot be fought in one site (as if it were political theatre only) but in various domains and realms simultaneously, simply because global imperial designs and colonial matrices of power have permeated and infiltrated every institution and every social, political, economic, spiritual, aesthetic, and cognitive arena of African life (Maldonado-Torres 2007).

Global imperial designs and technologies of subjectivation

Global imperial designs refer to the core technologies of modernity that underpinned its expansion into the non-Western parts of the world from the fifteenth century onwards. Race and Euro-American epistemology, particularly its techno-scientific knowledge claims, were used to classify and name the world according to a Euro-Christian-Modernist imaginary (Mignolo 2005a; Mignolo 2011b). African peoples, and others whose cultures and ways of life were not informed by imperatives of Euro-Christian modernity, were deemed to be barbarians – a people who did not belong to history and had no history. Following Christian cosmology, the cartography of the world, divided into continents, had to be followed by assigning each part to one of the three sons of Noah: Europe to Japheth; Africa to Ham; and Asia to Shem, as shown in some of the early maps like that of Isidore (Mignolo 2005a: 24). Besides this mapping of the global geocultural identities into continents, a conception of humanity as divided according to race resulted in its division into inferior and superior, irrational and rational, primitive and civilized, traditional and modern (Quijano 2000a: 342; Quijano 2000b).

The idea of race was deployed to justify such inimical processes as the slave trade, mercantilism, imperialism, colonialism, apartheid as well as authoritarian and brutal colonial governance systems and styles. This constituted the ugly and dangerous face of modernity and these inimical processes were unleashed on the non-Western world. Race was also used as a fundamental criterion for distribution of the world population into ranks, places, and roles. Boaventura de Sousa Santos (2007a: 45) depicted the bifurcated face of modernity as informed by 'abyssal thinking'.

This thinking was constituted by 'visible and invisible distinctions, the invisible ones being the foundation of the visible ones' (Santos 2007a: 45). Abyssal thinking's invisible distinctions culminated in the division of global social reality into two realms – the realm of 'this side of the line' (Euro-American world) and the realm of 'the other side of the line' (Africa and other non-Western parts of the world). Ramón Grosfoguel clearly expressed how the logic of superiority-inferiority that informed 'this side' and the 'other side' also informed a particular rendition of human global experience:

> We went from the sixteenth-century characterization of 'people without writing' to the eighteenth and nineteenth-centuries characterization of 'people without history', to the twentieth-century characterization of 'people without development' and more recently, to the early twenty-first century of 'people without democracy'. (Grosfoguel 2007: 214)

This was a presentation of how the human trajectory on the 'other side' (the colonial zone) was assumed to have unfolded since the dawn of modernity. On 'this side of the line' (Euro-American zone), the trajectory was rendered this way: 'We went from the sixteenth century "rights of people" ... to the eighteenth century "rights of man" ... and to the late twentieth century "human rights"' (Grosfoguel 2007: 214).

The 'other side of the line' was imagined as incomprehensible and impossible to coexist harmoniously with 'this side of the line'. In short, the two sides were produced as characterized by 'impossibility of the copresence' (Santos 2007a: 45). This conception and division of the world into this side and that side authorized those from 'this side' to assume superiority and to arrogate order, civility, law and rights, to themselves, while denying the existence of the same on the 'other side'. Violence, lawlessness, primitivism, superstition, strange beliefs, and retrogressive knowledges distinguished the 'other side' (Santos 2007a: 47). This became the colonial zone where canons of ethics, law, rights, civility and other forms that underpinned human comfort in the Euro-American world were suspended, and war, violence, and appropriation constituted colonial governance (Fanon 1968; Santos 2007a; Maldonaldo-Torres 2004; Maldonado-Torres 2007).

With specific reference to Africa, Achille Mbembe (2000) categorized three colonial forms of violence. The first was foundational violence that authorized the right of conquest while simultaneously creating its very object (Africans) of violence. It had an instituting function. The second was legitimation violence: this became a form of colonial language and transformed foundational violence into an 'authorizing authority' (Mbembe 2000: 6–7). The third was maintenance violence and it ensured permanence of colonial sovereignty. Its function according to Mbembe was to 'ratify and reiterate' (Mbembe 2000: 7). Violence and race occupied a central place within global imperial designs.

Global imperial designs are shorthand for how 'It was from the West that the rest of the world is described, conceptualized, and ranked: that is, modernity is the self-description of Europe's role in history rather than an ontological historical process' (Mignolo 2005a: 35). Simply put, global imperial designs are those processes that drove the making of a capitalist, patriarchal, Euro-American-centric, Christian-centric, imperial, colonial, hetero-normative and modern world-system (Grosfoguel 2007; Grosfoguel 2011). A catalogue of identifiable historical processes that produced the current unequal world order includes the European Renaissance and Christianization in the fifteenth and sixteenth centuries.

This was followed by the Enlightenment, mercantilism and maritime trade in the sixteenth and seventeenth centuries. Industrialism, imperialism and colonialism commenced in the eighteenth and nineteenth centuries. This inaugurated modernization and the developmentalism discourses of the mid-twentieth century. Neo-colonialism, neo-liberalism, the Washington Consensus and the Structural Adjustment Programmes dominated in the late twentieth century. Today, American imperialism and NATO-driven imperial designs, hidden behind the mantras of humanitarian interventions, the fighting of global terrorism and discourses of exporting democracy and human rights dominate, at the beginning of the twenty-first century (Mignolo 1995; Mignolo 2000; Ndlovu-Gatsheni 2012a).

The key problem in Africa is that there is an illusion of freedom and myth of decolonization. There can be no freedom and decolonization as long as global imperial designs that have been in place since the time of conquest still shape and inform the character of the modern world-system. This point is well captured by Grosfoguel who argued that:

> One of the most powerful myths of the twentieth century was the notion that the elimination of colonial administrations amounted to the decolonization of the world. This led to the myth of a 'postcolonial' world. The heterogeneous and multiple global structures put in place over a period

of 450 years did not evaporate with the juridical-political decolonization of the periphery over the past 50 years. We continue to live under the same 'colonial power matrix'. With juridical-political decolonization we moved from a period of 'global colonialism' to the current period of 'global coloniality'. (Grosfoguel 2007: 219)

This critical analysis of the present condition of those people residing in a peripheral ex-colonized world is in no way meant to downplay the sacrifices they made towards the achievement of decolonization. While the decolonization period, as articulated by Paul Tiyambe Zeleza (2003: vi), indeed constituted the 'proudest moment' of African nationalism, Africans must not therefore relax and think that the struggle is over. The postcolonial states have remained operating like colonial states, unleashing violence on African people. African people are still often treated like subjects rather than citizens by their leaders. Juridical freedom has not been translated into popular freedom. Territorial nationalism informed by colonial matrices of power is proving difficult to convert into pan-Africanism and pan-African unity (Ndlovu-Gatsheni 2012b).

Ngugi wa Thiong'o (1986) not only recognized that colonization of the mind remained the most successful colonial realm, where colonialism had deeply inscribed itself, but also that colonialism is a vast process, requiring decolonization to assume the character of an equally vast process to respond and fight colonialism in its multifaceted forms. Decolonization has to assume global proportions for it to deal effectively with global imperial designs. Ngugi wa Thiong'o emphasized that imperialism is not just a slogan: 'It is real, it is palpable in content and form and in its methods and effects ... Imperialism is total: it has economic, political, military, cultural and psychological consequences for people of the world. It could even lead to holocaust' (Ngugi wa Thiong'o 1986: 2).

This is necessary because there are several forms of colonization such as colonization of consciousness, colonization of sexuality, colonization of gender, colonization of language, colonization of aesthetics, colonization of epistemology and other forms (Ngugi wa Thiong'o 1993). Decolonization must respond to all these forms of colonization if Africa is to be free. Decolonial epistemic perspective is therefore a necessary survival kit for understanding the need for continuation of the decolonization project in the present age of global coloniality, which is informed and underpinned by invisible colonial matrices of power. The agents of the decolonization process of the twenty-first century must thrust outwards, to democratize predatory postcolonial states and humanize the authoritarian leaders in Africa at one level and at another to push for democratization of global power structures, while at the same time consistently remaining vigilant against global imperial designs that are ever ready to dilute African struggles for freedom.

Today global imperial designs have assumed the form of neo-liberal imperialism imbued with latent discourses of re-colonization of Africa. At the centre of this neo-imperialism is the idea that 'beneficent nations' like the United Kingdom (U.K.), the U.S.A. and others should recruit local African leaders and guide them to embrace free markets, rule of law, and liberal democracy, to avoid affecting the smooth functioning of the global economic system (Mbeki 2012). These ideas were expressed openly by Robert Cooper, a British diplomat, former adviser to Prime Minister Tony Blair and current adviser to Baroness Catherine Ashton, current EU High Representative for Foreign Affairs and a strong advocate of new neo-liberal imperialism. This is how Cooper put it:

> What is needed then is a new kind of imperialism, one acceptable to a world of human rights and cosmopolitan values. We already discern its outline: an imperialism which, like all imperialism, aims to bring order and organization but which rests today on voluntary principle. (Cooper 2000: 8)

Hillary Clinton, the U.S. Secretary of State, also emphasized her country's preference for the use of 'smart power', which included deployment of democracy and human rights to disguise geo-strategic goals (Mbeki 2011). In short, democracy and human rights have been appropriated into levers of global imperial designs, leading some Africans to despise them as part of cultural imperialism.

Decolonial epistemic perspective and pan-Africanism

The decolonial epistemic perspective stands on three concepts that are introduced in Chapter One of this book. The first concept is coloniality of power, which is a description of how the current modern global coloniality and capitalist structure re-emerged, was organized, configured, and articulated according to the imperatives of global imperial designs. Coloniality of power points to coloniality as that broad but specific and constitutive element of the global model of capitalist order that continues to underpin global coloniality after the end of direct colonialism (Quijano 2000a: 342).

Coloniality of power describes modern global power as a network of relations of exploitation, domination, and control of labour, nature and its productive resources, gender and its reproductive species, subjectivity and its material and intersubjective products, as well as knowledge and authority (Quijano 2007). At the centre of the coloniality of power are technologies of domination, exploitation and violence, known as the 'colonial matrix of power', which affect all dimensions of social existence including sexuality, authority, subjectivity, politics, economy, spirituality, language and race (Quijano 2000a: 342–380). As articulated by Castro-Gomez:

> The concept of the 'coloniality of power' broadens and corrects the Foucualdian concept of 'disciplinary power' by demonstrating that the panoptic constructions erected by the modern state are inscribed in a wider structure of power/knowledge. This global structure is configured by the colonial relation between centre and periphery that is at the root of European expansion. (Castro-Gomez 2002: 276)

The importance of the concept of coloniality of power for present-day pan-Africanists is that it enables them to gain a deeper understanding of two crucial realities. The first is that achievement of political independence and the withdrawal of direct colonial administrations has enabled postcolonial nation-states to emerge and to exercise a modicum of juridical freedom; African people still live under global coloniality. Coloniality of power, therefore, allows pan-Africanists to understand the continuity of colonial forms of domination after the end of direct colonial administrations (Grosfoguel 2007: 219). The second is that it enables pan-Africanists to appreciate the challenges of confronting the strong hierarchies of the present modern global power structure, whereby at the apex is the U.S.A. and NATO partners and at the subaltern bottom is Africa and its people. This structure can only be changed if Africans fully embrace pan-Africanism not only as an ideological shield but also as an enabler of economic freedom.

The second concept on which decolonial epistemic perspective is built is called coloniality of knowledge. It is intimately tied to coloniality of power, as power and knowledge operate as inseparable twins within global imperial designs. But the coloniality of knowledge speaks directly to epistemological colonization whereby Euro-American techno-scientific knowledge managed to displace, discipline, destroy alternative knowledges that it found outside the Euro-American zones (colonies) while at the same time appropriating what it considered useful to global imperial designs. Combinations of natural and human sciences were used to back up racist theories and to rank and organize people according to binaries of inferior-superior relations (Castro-Gomez 2002: 271). Santos elaborated that in the name of introducing modern science, alternative knowledges and sciences found in Africa were destroyed and the social groups that relied on these systems to support their own autonomous path of development have been humiliated as epistemicides were being committed (Santos 2005: xviii).

Schools, churches and even universities contributed towards the invention of the 'other' as they operated as technologies of subjectivation that naturalized Euro-American epistemology as universal. But the same order of knowledge contributed to raising consciousness, among the early African educated elite, of the exploitative and repressive aspects of colonialism. But what ensued was the darkest aspect of coloniality of knowledge, 'epistemicides', which manifested in various ways: first in academic mimetism/intellectual mimicry, dominant in African scholarship; then the destruction of indigenous African knowledges; and a plethora of crises plaguing universities in Africa (crisis of identity, crisis of legitimacy, crisis of relevance, crisis of authority, epistemological crisis, crisis of student politics and crisis of historical mission) (Lebakeng et al. 2006: 70–87; Ndlovu-Gatsheni 2011b).

Coloniality of knowledge is very important because it speaks directly to the dilemmas of invasion of imagination and colonization of the minds of Africans, which constitutes epistemological colonization. This colonization of consciousness and modes of knowing is pervasive in discourses of development, technologies of organizing people into nations and states, as well as imaginations of the future.

The third pillar of decolonial epistemic perspective is coloniality of being. It directly addresses the physical and psychological predicament of colonized beings. It enables appreciation of the impact of colonial technologies of subjectivation on the lives, bodies, and minds of the colonized people. It speaks to the lived experiences of the colonized, which can be described as the phenomenology of subjectivity (Maldonado-Torres 2007: 242). Drawing on scientific racism thinking, colonialists doubted the very humanity of colonized people and doubted whether they had souls. This racist thinking informed politics of 'Othering' of the colonized people, which culminated in what Nelson Maldonado-Torres (2007: 245) termed 'imperial Manichean misanthropic skepticism' as a form of 'questioning the very humanity of colonized peoples'. The being of the colonized became that of a 'racialized self', open to all sorts of abuses and living a hellish life.

Slavery, war, conquest, violence, rape and even genocide constituted the ways in which the colonial conquerors related to the colonized. Ethics that governed human relations in Europe were suspended in Africa where Africans were designated as 'those outside the human oecumene' (Maldonado-Torres 2007: 247). Death itself was never an extraordinary affair among colonized and those racialized into non-beings. Death became a constitutive feature of their life. In short, the concept of coloniality of being is very useful because it links with the Fanonian concept of the wretched of the earth and the damned – the ideas of black people as condemned people whose being amounts to 'nothingness'. Maldonado-Torres (2007: 255) wrote that 'Indeed, coloniality of Being primarily refers to normalization of the extraordinary events that take place in war'. The list of 'extraordinary events' that have been normalized in Africa is endless, ranging from hunger, epidemics like HIV/AIDS, living in shacks (*imikhukhu* in South Africa and other parts of Africa), homelessness, political violence, communal violence, rape, to the risk of being killed by lightning in the rainy season (Ndlovu-Gatsheni 2012a).

Just like the coloniality of power and the coloniality of knowledge, the coloniality of being is very important for pan-Africanists because it facilitates a process of making visible the invisible. It also becomes a useful tool for deciphering the mechanisms that produce hellish conditions within which poor Africans are entrapped. Finally, the three concepts so far presented demonstrate the importance of pushing the unfinished agenda of decolonization forwards concurrently with the equally important and unfinished democratic agenda.

The decolonial epistemic perspective carries the totality of the above three concepts in its agenda to critique Euro-American epistemology that is currently in crisis. It inaugurates thinking that calls for opening up of plurality of epistemologies to enrich human experience from different vantage points. The decolonial epistemic perspective is a critical social theory encompassing the totality of critical thoughts emerging from the ex-colonized world, informed by imperatives of resisting colonialism and imperialism in their multifaceted forms. It contributes towards imagination and construction of a different future (Ribeiro 2011: 290).

Like all critical social theories of society, the decolonial epistemic perspective aims to critique and possibly overcome the epistemological injustices put in place by imperial global designs, and questions and challenges the longstanding claims of Euro-American epistemology to be universal, neutral, objective, disembodied, as well as being the only mode of knowing (Grosfoguel 2007; Mignolo 2007a). It is 'an-other thought' that seeks to inaugurate 'an-other logic', 'an-other language', and 'an-other thinking' that has the potential to liberate ex-colonized people's minds from Euro-American hegemony (Mignolo 2000; Mignolo 2005a: xx; Mignolo 2005b).

What distinguishes the decolonial epistemic perspective is its clear African and Global South locus of enunciation. A locus of enunciation is a reference to a particular location from which human beings speak within power structures. Its importance lies in capturing the fact that there is absolutely nobody who is able to escape the class, sexual, gender, spiritual, linguistic, geographical and racial hierarchies fashioned by the modern world-system (Grosfoguel 2007: 213). Unlike the Euro-American epistemology, it is not fundamentalist in its outlook as it concedes space for other knowledges emerging from different geo-historical sites and different human experiences. It does not even attempt to claim universality, neutrality, and singular truthfulness. It is decidedly and deliberately situated in Africa and privileges decolonial thinking as a form of liberation.

The decolonial epistemic perspective helps in unveiling epistemic silences, conspiracies, and epistemic violence hidden within Euro-American epistemology and helps to affirm the epistemic rights of the African people that enable them to transcend global imperial designs. Unless coloniality of power, coloniality of knowledge and coloniality of being are clearly understood as enabling the intellectual unveiling of colonial matrices of power and technologies of subjectivation that underpin the continued subalternization of Africa and its people since the time of colonial encounters, the pan-African agenda would not be pushed as vigorously and as urgently as it deserves.

Read from a decolonial epistemic perspective, pan-Africanism forms part of decolonial horizons involving Africans taking charge of their destiny and searching for new humanism. In this context pan-Africanism becomes a singular connector of a diversity of ex-colonized African people. This must begin with epistemic and cognitive freedom. It has become clear in recent years that the whole Euro-American structure of power in place since the fifteenth century has been undergoing a profound crisis of confidence. It failed even to predict the current financial crisis that is rocking the world. It has also become clear that what was universalized by global imperial designs as a universal science is in fact a Western particularism, which assumed power to define all rival forms of knowledge as particular, local, contextual and situational, while claiming universality (Santos 2005: xviii).

The decolonial epistemic perspective builds on this realization to inaugurate a 'decolonial turn' that calls for recognition of alternative knowledges and alternative ways of knowing, as part of re-opening vistas of liberation from global imperial designs and colonial matrices of power. The world in general, and Africa in particular, finds itself in a phase of paradigmatic shift that necessitates re-invention of the decolonial liberation agenda within a context in which Euro-American civilization is devouring not only its promises of progress, liberty, equality, non-discrimination and rationality, but is repudiating and criminalizing the very idea of struggle for these objectives (Santos 2005: xxi). It is, therefore, imperative to locate the place of pan-Africanism within modern international politics and global imperial designs.

Pan-Africanism and global imperial designs

Tukumbi Lumumba-Kasongo (1994: 109) described pan-Africanism as, above all, an international phenomenon that deals with power and interest, their dynamics in the international arena, international political forums, and international political economy. Understood from a decolonial epistemic perspective whose locus of enunciation of global politics is rooted in the Global South in general and Africa in particular, pan-Africanism is a counter-worldview to the hegemonic Eurocentric worldview. The current modern international system is a racial hierarchy, a patriarchal, imperial, colonial, hetero-normative and capitalist global social order (Mignolo 1995; Mignolo 2000; Grosfoguel 2007; Ndlovu-Gatsheni 2012b).

At the centre of this modern international system is coloniality defined as one of the key constitutive elements that lay at the root of imagination of a Eurocentric global social order that was constructed during the time of colonial encounters between Europe and Africa. Anibal Quijano defined and articulated coloniality as a Eurocentric project based on the imposition of a racial, ethnic and gender classification of the global population as the cornerstone and defining element of the modern international system (Quijano 2000a: 342). One of the main foundational events of global coloniality was the Berlin Conference of 1884 where the African continent was approached as a land of material and human opportunities for reaping and sharing among Europeans (Lumumba-Kasongo 1994: 42). According to the imperatives of the 'Berlin consensus', the African continent was nothing but 'a philosophical, historical, and cultural vacuum' and a 'dark continent' that had to be 'penetrated' and 'civilized' by white races (Lumumba-Kasongo 1994: 42–43).

The modern international system is, therefore, rooted in racial articulation of global social identities into white and black and geocultural demarcations of the world into Europe, America, Asia and Africa. This invention of the modern world that was permeated through and through by Eurocentrism was not only informed by a conception and division of humanity into 'inferior and superior, irrational and rational, primitive and civilized, traditional and modern' but also by capitalist imperatives that unleashed such 'darker' aspects of modernity as mercantilism, the slave trade, so-called 'legitimate trade', imperialism, colonialism, apartheid and globalization on the African world (Quijano 2000a: 343: Martin 2002).

Pan-Africanism emerged as a response to the manifestations of the 'darker' aspects of modernity, particularly the slave trade, which constituted one of the most inhumane elements in the unfolding and expansion of modernity into areas outside Europe and America. Locksley Edmondson argued that:

> Pan-Africanism, however articulated or conceptualized, whatever its functional scope or operational habitat, is by definition an international relations phenomenon. The essential aspect of pan-Africanism, indeed its distinctive characteristic within the complex of black racial expressions, is that it necessarily transcends territorial political boundaries. And when, in its most expansive manifestation, pan-Africanism embraces a range of transcontinental relations, international relations analysis necessarily bears profoundly on the elucidation of that phenomenon. (Edmondson 1986: 285)

The slave trade that adversely affected Africans was not an aberration of modernity as it assumed mercantile, imperial and colonial dimensions from the fifteenth century onwards. It was part of what Quijano has described as a 'colonial matrix of power' that entailed control over labour and its products; nature and its productive resources; gender and its products, including the reproduction of the species; subjectivity, including its material and intersubjective products such as knowledge; and authority and its instruments, including coercion (Quijano 2007: 168–178).

Epistemologically speaking, pan-Africanism can best be described as a subaltern world view that emerged as a rebellion against the inimical aspects of racial hierarchies, of the patriarchal, imperial, colonial and capitalist modern global social order that authorized and enabled the dominant powers of the West to enslave and colonize black races. The genealogy of pan-Africanism is located within the experience of oppression, which inevitably provoked resistance. Thus pan-Africanism is ontologically a resistance movement and a terrain of struggles for black human dignity and human rights, confirming Mahmood Mamdani's (1991: 236) analysis that 'without the fact of oppression, there can be no practice of resistance and no notion of rights'.

But what is surprising is that in mainstream studies of international relations (IR), pan-Africanism is not included as one of the important worldviews. Pan-Africanism, which arose as part of black racial consciousness, unfolded as a movement and worldview that questioned and indicted the dominant Eurocentric conceptions of the world, thus contributing towards making black identity visible as being dominated, oppressed, abused and exploited by white races. The issue of race as a core element used to justify black enslavement and colonization by white races provoked William Edward Burghardt Du Bois, one of the fathers of pan-Africanism, to articulate the contours of the human struggles of the twentieth century in this way: 'The problem of the twentieth century is the problem of colour-line – the relation of the darker to the lighter races of men in Asia and Africa, in America and islands of the sea' (Du Bois 1986: 666).

This ubiquity of race in the history of black oppression and exploitation, from which pan-Africanism emerged as a response, remains outside the core concerns of IR as an academic discipline that seeks to understand the international system. This absence of engagement with the question of identity provoked Albert J. Paolini to pose the following pertinent questions:

> Why is it that international relations, a discourse that sets out to explain the character of contemporary world politics and theorize the behaviour of states, makes so little space for questions of identity, subjectivity, and modernity, particularly as they apply to non-Western places such as Africa? Why do we need to make sense of world politics by referring to abstract concepts such as the state, sovereignty, order, and power than delving into the elementary human realm of culture and identity, which underpins the privileged categories of international relations? (Paolini 1999: 5)

A recent book edited by Martin Griffiths, entitled *International Relations Theory for the Twenty-First Century*, deals with nine worldviews that were considered to underpin IR and represent the world, but there is no mention of pan-Africanism as a worldview. Griffiths defines a worldview as 'a broad interpretation of the world and an application of this view to the way we judge and evaluate activities and structures that shape the world' (Griffiths 2007: 1). The nine worldviews analysed in Griffiths' book are Realism, Liberal Internationalism, Marxism, Critical Theory, Constructivism, The English School, Post-structuralism, Feminism and Postcolonialism (Griffiths 2007: 1–9). The absence of pan-Africanism as a worldview in this collection indicates how it is sidelined within studies of the international system.

There is no doubt that pan-Africanism qualifies as a worldview that played a major role in shaping the direction of global politics since the end of the nineteenth century. Of course, pan-Africanism is more than a simple worldview and there is a need to engage with its multifaceted meanings within global politics and its shifting character across time since 1900. Broadly speaking, pan-Africanism is about black race consciousness; self-determination of the black race; unity of the African people; economic development of African people; and finding a dignified niche for Africans within the international system.

To effectively deal with multifaceted and multi-layered essences and meanings of pan-Africanism, an ideal historical approach takes into account its key moments of development since 1900. Three moments, beginning with the phase of convening of Pan-African Congresses; the era of the Organization of African Unity (OAU); and the current phase of the African Union (AU) and its drive for regional integration and ultimately continental unity, deserve detailing. This approach is in tandem with Tim Murithi's (2008a: 3) idea of defining the unfolding and development of pan-Africanism in terms of what he termed 'stages in the institutionalization of pan-Africanism'.

The birth of pan-Africanism and the pan-African Congresses

Pan-Africanism is rooted in struggles against the racial hierarchies of the international system that encouraged the slave trade. The slave revolts in the so-called 'New World' and the literary works produced in the 'slave triangle' indirectly laid the foundations of pan-Africanism prior to Henry Sylvester-Williams' (a West Indian barrister) formation of the African Association in London in 1897, which encouraged pan-African unity throughout the British colonies, before he organized the first international Pan-African Congress in 1900 (Geiss 1969: 186).

The 1900 inaugural Pan-African Congress was very important because, for the first time, the black people who were on the receiving end of racism and colonialism gathered at the centre of a leading colonial power (Britain) to discuss such varied issues as the socio-political and economic conditions of blacks in the diaspora; the question of independent nations governed by people of African descent (Haiti, Liberia and Ethiopia); and the problem of slavery and imperialism and the impact of Christianity on the African continent (Adejumobi 2001; Killingray 2010).

The important result of this Pan-African Congress was the drafting of an address 'To the Nations of the World' by Du Bois that contained demands for the reform of the colonial system, including demands for the protection of the rights of people of African descent and guarantees for the respect for the integrity and independence of 'the free Negro States of Abyssinia, Liberia and Haiti' (Killingray 2010: 349). The report was signed and sent to Britain's Queen Victoria. For the first time, the term 'pan-African' was placed in the centre of the international system.

The baton of pan-Africanism was then carried forward by Du Bois, who subsequently hosted five Pan-African Congresses between 1919 and 1945. The hosting of Pan-African Congresses was well timed to coincide with major European events that impacted on black people or which might otherwise ignore African people's issues. For example, the 1919 Pan-African Congress held in Paris in France coincided with the gathering of European and American politicians for a Peace Conference in Versailles in France, marking the end of the First World War (1914–1918). The black representatives again demanded international protection of the black people of Africa from abuse, exploitation and violence; supervision of African colonies by the League of Nations to prevent further economic exploitation by foreign nations; abolition of slavery and capital punishment of colonial subjects; recognition of the rights of black people to education within colonies; and recognition of the rights of African people to participate in government (Adejumobi 2001: 458–478).

Another important and distinctive Pan-African Congress, among three others, was the one held in Manchester in the U.K. in 1945. Its first significance lay in the participation of African politicians from the African continent such as Kwame Nkrumah and Jomo Kenyatta. Before the 1945 Pan-African Congress, the Pan-African Movement was dominated by diaspora Africans. Its second was that the Manchester Pan-African Congress's resolutions abandoned the moderate position for radical demands, including calling for an end to colonialism. Colonized people were directly urged to unite and assert their rights to reject colonialism (Adejumobi 2001: 458–478).

But an exclusive focus on the Pan-African Congresses organized by Du Bois as the motivating forces of pan-Africanism tends to exclude the important contribution of Marcus Mosiah Garvey (a Jamaican) and his influential Universal Negro Improvement Association (UNIA). Unlike all those who pushed the idea of pan-Africanism through Pan-African Congresses, Garvey emphasized the issues of raising black racial consciousness and became popular for his 'back-to-Africa' movement and his radical slogan of 'African for Africans'. Uppermost in Garvey's activities was restoration of black people's consciousness and dignity, which slavery and colonialism had degraded. He also imagined a creation of 'a strong and powerful Negro nation in Africa' (Garvey 1970: 202; Dagnini 2008). Despite some of its contradictions and ambiguities, Garveyism had a lot of influence among black people across the world and inside Africa and contributed to the raising of black consciousness and the rise of movements such as the one that was led by Steve Bantu Biko in South Africa in 1970s.

At another level, even prior to the Pan-African Congresses, such African thinkers as Blyden and Horton from West Africa also propagated pan-African ideas (Geiss 1969: 188). This reality underlined the fact that pan-Africanism had various genealogies and was watered from various intellectual springs. The diverse genealogies contributed to pan-Africanism assuming an all-encompassing character: being concerned about the unity of black people; acknowledging black people's rights to self-determination in Africa; asserting the dignity of black people across the world; asserting the uniqueness of African identity; searching for equality of Africans with other races across the globe; and seeking self-government for the black peoples of Africa (Makinda and Okumu 2008: 18). Ali Mazrui identified three forms of pan-Africanism namely sub-Saharan pan-Africanism; trans-Saharan pan-Africanism and trans-Atlantic pan-Africanism. The first emphasized solidarity of black people of the African continent south of the Sahara Desert; the second emphasized African unity from Cape to Cairo; and the third emphasized the unity and solidarity of all black people, including those in the diaspora (Mazrui 1982: 25).

What is clear is that combinations of these pan-Africanisms contributed to the galvanization of the decolonization process in Africa because without decolonization it was impossible to realize any of these ideas. But the practicalities of institutionalization of pan-Africanism in Africa became a painstaking process largely due to incompatibilities of territorial nationalism and pan-Africanism. This problem resulted in what I have described as the 'Nkrumah-Nyerere curse', which continues to haunt the pan-African project today.

The curse of a divided African house: Kwame Nkrumah versus Julius Nyerere

Ideally, the pan-Africanist movement was a redemptive project that embodied ideals of freedom from slavery, freedom from racism, freedom from colonialism, equality of human beings, right of black races to unite under a pan-African nation, right of black races to own resources in Africa, self-determination of black races and the building of Africa into an economic and political giant capable of rivalling Europe and America. Pan-Africanism rose not only as part of humankind's quest for liberty, freedom, justice and liberation but also as a direct response to the historical reality of enslavement of black races (Geiss 1974; Shivji 2011).

Of direct relevance to Africa is the fact that the Pan-African Congress held on 15 October 1945 in Manchester brought together prominent black leaders like Kwame Nkrumah, Julius Nyerere, Jomo Kenyatta, Peter Abrahams and many others. It also brought together Anglophone and Francophone African leaders besides bringing together continental Africans and those from the diaspora. The involvement of continental Africans heralded the beginnings of the migration of hosting of the Pan-African Congress to African soil. But it was not until 1958 that the Fifth Pan-African Congress was held in Ghana. This congress marked the handing over of the leadership of the movement from William E.B. DuBois to Nkrumah (Abraham 2003: 27–28). But soon the pan-African movement under Nkrumah became affected by differing ideas on the best route and pace it should take to arrive at continental political unity. The problem began with Ghana pushing for a political union of Africa and Nigeria resisting such an approach. But later the disagreements took the form of Nkrumah against Nyerere, with ripple effects on other leaders, who had to choose sides.

The far-reaching tentacles of global imperial designs were becoming a hindrance to the realization of pan-African unity as early as 1960. Such newly independent countries as Nigeria, Tunisia, Kenya, Tanzania and the Francophone states preferred to maintain closer links with the West. Francophone states, with the exception of Guinea under Sékou Touré, had voted to remain under the tutelage of France (Martin 1995). Ghana, Guinea, Morocco, and Mali pushed for a political union of African states. They justified this move as a necessary shield against neo-colonialism (Abraham 2003: 49). But other African leaders saw maintenance of close ranks with the West as a redeeming move and a counter to infiltration of communism. But the danger of neo-colonialism soon took a concrete form in Congo under Patrice Lumumba. The Congo crisis became a complex mixture of Belgian interference to oust the pan-Africanist Lumumba, leading to secession by Katanga under Moise Tshombe and eventual assassination of Lumumba (Abraham 2003: 50).

The Congo crisis of 1960, just like the Libyan crisis of 2011, split African countries into rival camps of conflicting alliances. Some supported the founding father of Congo, Lumumba (first Prime Minister of Congo), who was facing secession and Western infiltration, others supported Kasavubu (the first President of Congo), and others the secessionist leader Tshombe. The divisions were exacerbated by Western interference in support of secessionist leader Moise Tshombe and Kasavubu who was considered to be pro-West. The pan-Africanist and pro-East Lumumba had to be isolated and then physically destroyed according to the logic of global imperial designs. Ghana, Mali, Guinea and Morocco formed the Casablanca bloc and vehemently denounced Western intervention in Congo. Those African states that were assumed to be moderate by the Western powers supported Kasavubu. They later met in Abidjan in October 1960 to form the Brazzaville bloc. A third grouping called the Monrovia bloc consisting of Côte d'Ivoire, Liberia and Senegal emerged, which tried to harmonize relations between the belligerent groups, but failed (Mazrui 1982; Martin 1995).

The early founding fathers of Africa's divisions symbolized a divided house that was destined to collapse under the weight of neo-colonial forces. The launch of the Organization of African Unity (OAU) in May 1963 occurred despite divisions among African leaders over what kind of union was to be formed. Nkrumah's book *Africa Must Unite* (1963), which he distributed widely to African leaders before the historic founding of the OAU, did not unite the divided African house. Nkrumah's book carried the message:

> We need the strength of our combined numbers as a resource to protect ourselves from the very positive dangers of returning colonialism in disguised forms. We need it to combat the entrenched forces dividing our continent and still holding back millions of our brothers. We need it to secure total African liberation ... At present most of the independent states are moving in directions which expose us to dangers of imperialism and neo-colonialism. (Nkrumah 1963: 217)

While the OAU was meant to institutionalize the principles of pan-Africanism, it did not fulfill the radical and maximalist vision of Kwame Nkrumah who wanted the establishment of an African Union Government straight away to lay the foundations of a United States of Africa. The OAU was launched within a context of tensions between forces of territorial nationalism with its proclivity towards national sovereignty and imperatives of pan-Africanism, which were considered by some sovereignty-obsessed African leaders as a threat to hard-won national-juridical sovereignties.

The leading personalities in the moderate bloc included Felix Houphouët-Boigny, Léopold Sédar Senghor, Hamani Diori and others, who were under the tutelage of the French leader Charles de Gaulle, who influenced them to dissociate with radical African leaders who wanted the political union of African states. The Brazzaville Group emphasized cooperation with France despite its neo-colonial 'Eurafrica' policy over solidarity with other African states (Martin 1995: 163–188). They feared most the radical Nkrumahist ideas of political union that was 'ideologically socialist and pan-Africanist at once' (Lumumba-Kasongo 1994: 132).

The Monrovia Group's position emphasized the absolute equality and sovereignty of African states, the right to existence of individual states and their freedom from annexation by another state, and the voluntary union of states. Their principles of non-interference in the domestic affairs of African states and prohibition of one state harbouring dissi-dents from another state won the day and informed the construction of the OAU (Lumumba-Kasongo 1994: 22). The OAU became the product of a compromise and did not push hard for realization of continental unity. Instead the OAU became actively in favour of the total decolonization of Africa, which went together with territorial nationalism.

It must be noted that the dreams of pan-African unity were further diluted by the imperatives of the Cold War (1945–1989), which contribut-ed to the fragmentation of postcolonial African states along ideological lines (socialist versus capitalist) (Laidi 1990). The middle-roaders pre-ferred non-alignment. On top of this, the erstwhile colonial powers also attracted former colonies into such organizations as the British Com-monwealth, which were not synchronized with the principles of pan-Af-ricanism. The late twentieth century was also dominated by discourses of a New World Order (NWO) that was expected to crystallize around the notions of world 'unipolarity', emphasizing cooperation and mainte-nance of global peace and security. Within this order, the U.S.A., which modelled itself as the leader of the so-called progressive and democratic nations, was expected to shift its foreign policy to support a democratic revolution in Africa (Ake 1992b). Such an expectation was informed by uncritical belief in the rhetoric of the empire about development, human rights and democracy, which were merely fig-leaves covering the mate-rial interests of the empire.

By this time of the NWO discourses, the OAU was pushing hard for the completion of the decolonization process while at the same time the other important issue was how to extricate African economies from the morass of underdevelopment. The Lagos Plan of Action of 1980 consti-tuted a centrepiece of African attempts to re-launch economic recovery of Africa informed by mobilization of indigenous resources and driven by Africans as opposed to the disastrous externally imposed Structural Adjustment Programmes that unfolded from the late 1970s onwards as a panacea for the problems of underdevelopment. In short, it was through the work of the OAU Liberation Committee that the decolonization of Africa was achieved. The transition from apartheid to democracy in South Africa in 1994 was perhaps the penultimate continental decoloni-zation project. While the decolonization of the continent remains one of the proudest moment in African history, under the OAU the pursuit of other goals of pan-Africanism, such as the political and economic unity of Africa, were postponed until the OAU was succeeded by the African Union in July 2002. As put by Kay Mathews:

> The OAU was more political than economic in its orientation. It was conceived primarily from a desire to safeguard and consolidate Africa's political independence, sovereignty and territorial integrity. (Mathews 2009: 32)

What emerges from this analysis is that Julius Nyerere was a reluctant pan-Africanist who emphasized dilemmas and problems that hindered pan-African unity while ignoring those positive factors that could be used to quicken the pace of realization of political continental unity. He criticized Nkrumah and all those who were pushing for political union of Africa as using this pan-African idea for the purpose of propaganda. He became concerned about the prospects of individual states surrendering their sovereignty. In 1966, he argued that:

> Indeed I believe that a real dilemma faces the pan-Africanist. One is the fact that pan-Africanism demands an African consciousness and an African loyalty; on the other hand is the fact that each pan-Africanist must also concern himself with the freedom and development of one of the nations of Africa. These things can conflict. Let us be honest and admit that they have already conflicted. (Nyerere 1966: 1)

While Nyerere was seen by others as a realist and pragmatist, he introduced a discourse of impossibility (rooted in Afro-pessimism) that culminated in criticism of Kwame Nkrumah, who wanted a quickened pace towards political continental unity as a survival mechanism, faced with vicious neo-colonial forces that worked against African progress (B'beri and Louw 2011: 335–345). The irony in Nyerere's thinking on development in Africa is that he urged Africans as 'late, late comers' to 'run while others walked', so as to catch up with the rest of the world. But when it came to the issue of pan-African unity, he suggested 'walking' (gradualism) and opposed Nkrumah who suggested 'running' (Mkandawire 2011: 1–36). The debates that ensued between Nkrumah and Nyerere over the pace to be taken towards realization of pan-African unity constituted 'a curse' because they have continued to haunt new generations of pan-Africanists in the twenty-first century, in their attempts to push forward Nkrumah's project of establishing political continental unity as an answer to threats of neo-colonialism.

Broadly speaking, Nkrumah and Nyerere's thoughts on nationalism and pan-Africanism provide a unique entry into understanding the complexities of implementing the national projects while pushing forward the pan-African agenda. Even when Nkrumah made efforts to explain what the structures and institutions of a political union would look like, Nyerere remained in a dismissive mood saying: 'To rule out a step-by-step progress towards African Unity is to hope that the Almighty will one day say "Let there be unity in Africa," and there shall be unity.' He even tried to dismiss the interference of imperialists by charging that 'to say that step-by-step method was invented by the imperialists is to reach the limits of absurdity' (Nyerere 1967: 302).

Despite Nyerere's attempt to dampen Nkrumah's spirit, he continued at the 1965 OAU Conference to urge his fellow African leaders to realize that the political and economic crises bedeviling Africa were a clear testimony of the dangers of neo-colonialism to pan-African unity (Biney 2008b: 139). There is no doubt that Nkrumah and Nyerere operated within a complex postcolonial terrain that exacerbated tensions among African leaders. The immediate postcolonial period was dominated by popular expectations that needed to be fulfilled and political turmoil emanating from outside that needed to be avoided. The question of regime survival in the midst of the Cold War impinged on national and social transformational agendas of the world's youngest states (Nkrumah 1965).

But Julius Ihonvbere has roundly blamed African founding fathers for numerous betrayals of the national project. He blamed them for failure to restructure the state; to empower Africans; to challenge foreign domination and exploitation of Africans; and to challenge the cultural bastardization in the continent (Ihonvbere 1994: 5). But Nkrumah's national project(s) embodied both a nationalist and a pan-African vision. To him, there were complementarities rather than tensions between nationalism and pan-Africanism. This vision was clearly expressed in three of his widely quoted statements: 'Seek ye first the political kingdom and all else shall be added unto it' (Mazrui 1999: 105). He also made it clear that 'The independence of Ghana is meaningless unless linked to the total liberation of the African continent'. He elaborated that 'The independence of Ghana was the first crack in the seemingly impregnable armour of imperialism in Africa. It created and furnished the bridgehead for organized assaults upon colonialism' (Nkrumah 1966: xiv).

Nkrumah interpreted the attainment of political independence by African states as a beginning of a political trajectory to real freedom predicated on pan-African unity. Territorial nationalism was for him a means to pan-Africanism. This is why he placed the independence of Ghana at the centre of the pan-African project, linking its sovereignty to the total liberation of the continent. Nkrumah identified two core problems that faced postcolonial Africa. The first was lack of pan-African unity. The second was the danger of neo-colonialism. His analysis of these problems was that no African country stood a chance of pursuing an independent national project(s) without inviting the wrath of neo-colonialism (Nkrumah 1965).

To Nkrumah, pan-African unity was a protective shield rather than a threat to sovereignty, as Nyerere insinuated when he said: 'It is some curious animal to which our individual states do not surrender sovereignty, and yet somehow becomes the strong instrument which we require to fulfill the purposes of modern states' (Nyerere 1967: 303). Nkrumah strongly believed that pan-African unity was the only real African protection from vulnerability to neo-colonialism. Pan-African unity was also an enabling factor for Africans to own their natural resources and pursue independent economic policies. Nkrumah concluded that

'The socio-economic development and progress of Africa will come only within the political kingdom not the other way round' (Nkrumah 1963a: 10).

Unfortunately, in 1966, Nkrumah had to prematurely exit the political stage as a consequence of a military coup. He was toppled just four months after the publication of his *Neo-Colonialism: The Last Stage of Imperialism* (October 1965). Its publication had elicited an immediate protest from the U.S. government, which promptly cancelled U.S. $35 million aid to Ghana (Shivji 2009: 152). One of the architects of the coup, Colonel A.A. Afrifa, wrote a revealing book about the coup, vilifying Nkrumah's pan-Africanism and support for the liberation movements. He stated that:

> At the attainment of independence, the British handed over to us a decent system of government in which everyone had a say ... Organization of African Unity or no Organization of African Unity, I will claim my citizenship of Ghana and the Commonwealth in any part of the world. I have been trained in the United Kingdom as a soldier, and I am ever prepared to fight alongside my friends in the United Kingdom in the same way as Canadians and Australians will do. (Afrifa 1966: 11)

This was a clear case of embracing the former colonial power as a friend rather than a neo-colonialist formation. By 1966 Nkrumah's dream of continental political unity had not materialized. His vision of turning Ghana into an economic paradise had not succeeded either. The coup removed from power a committed pan-Africanist, who had even predicted his political demise at the historic founding of the OAU in 1963. He told his fellow African leaders that:

> If we do not come together, if we do not unite, we shall all be thrown out, all of us one by one – and I also will go ... The OAU must face a choice now – we can either move forward to progress through our effective African Union or step backward into stagnation, instability and confusion – an easy prey for foreign intervention, interference and subversion. (Quoted in Batsa 1985: 30)

Nkrumah's foresight was confirmed by the fact that the second decade of independence became the age of military coups in Africa as well as rehabilitation of imperialism.

While Nyerere claimed that, like Nkrumah, he believed in the pan-Africanist project as the ultimate end of the African struggle for freedom, he did not push the pan-African agenda with the same zeal he pushed forward his Tanzanian national socialist project predicated on *Ujamaa* villages (Hyden 1980). He emphasized tensions between territorial nationalism and pan-Africanism, while in principle agreeing with Nkrumah that realization of an African continental government was 'our greatest dream of all'. He explained that:

For it was as Africans that we dreamed of freedom; and we thought of it for Africa. Our real ambition was African freedom and African government. The fact that we fought area by area was merely a tactical necessity. We organized ourselves into Convention People's Party, the Tanganyika African National Union, the United National Independence Party, and so on, simply because each local colonial government had to be dealt with separately. The question we now have to answer is whether Africa shall maintain this internal separation as we defeat colonialism, or whether our earlier proud boast – 'I am an African' – shall become a reality. (Nyerere 1966: 2)

Nyerere interpreted the dilemma of the pan-Africanist as that of how to deal with territorial nationalisms that were diverging and moving away from pan-Africanism. The divergences were driven by local realities such as promotion of nationhood to contain imperatives of disunity, economic imperatives that dictated inter-country competition over attracting foreign capital and investments, and promises to the people that needed to be fulfilled. He concluded that:

And the truth is that as each of us develops his own state we raise more and more barriers between ourselves. We entrench differences which we have inherited from the colonial periods and develop new ones. Most of all, we develop a national pride which could easily be inimical to the development of a pride in Africa. (Nyerere 1966: 2)

Unlike Nkrumah, Nyerere privileged the agenda of 'grappling with serious and urgent problems within our states' and dangers from outside over 'serious thinking about the way forward to pan-Africanism' partly because 'we are always assailed for "wasting money on conferences," or being "unrealistic" in our determination to build roads or railways to link our nations' (Nyerere 1966: 7).

Nyerere became one of the most eloquent exponents of the gradualist approach to continental political unity. He pushed forward for step-by-step progress towards pan-African unity, beginning with strengthening individual states' sovereignties and building of regional economic communities (Nyerere 1967: 300–306). His gradualist approach informed the formation of the OAU with a limited mandate of ensuring the total decolonization of Africa as the first step towards achievement of continental political unity.

It would seem that, unlike Nkrumah, Nyerere underestimated the colonial matrices of power that made it impossible for him to achieve self-reliance in one country. Nyerere had a tenuous relationship with the Bretton Woods institutions, critiquing their conditionalities and prescriptions, while seeking their funding. In 1997 at the Seventh Pan-African Congress that coincided with the fortieth anniversary of Ghana's independence, Nyerere confessed that:

Kwame Nkrumah was the state crusader for African unity. He wanted the Accra summit of 1965 to establish Union Government for the whole of independent Africa. But we failed. The one minor reason is that Kwame, like all great believers, underestimated the degree of suspicion and animosity, which his crusading passion had created among a substantial number of his fellow Heads of State. The major reason was linked to the first: already too many of us had a vested interest in keeping Africa divided. (Nyerere cited in Biney 2008b: 147)

Nyerere added that after Nkrumah, 'We of the first generation leaders of independent Africa have not pursued the objective of African Unity with vigour, commitment and sincerity that it deserves. Yet that does not mean that unity is now irrelevant' (Nyerere cited in Biney 2008b: 147). At retirement, Nyerere admitted his mistakes, including regretting why he even embarked on a nationalization programme that destroyed thriving enterprises, and urged his successors to adopt a free-market economy. He asked his successors to capitulate to the forces of neo-liberalism and to the Washington Consensus while at the same time lamenting the lack of pan-African unity.

The Nkrumah-Nyerere disagreements highlight the difficulties of pushing forward the pan-African agenda without consensus at the political level of leadership. It also magnifies, in the case of Nyerere, how those leaders who did not put pan-African unity first could torpedo the efforts of committed pan-Africanists and derail the whole project. Instead of present-day pan-Africanists degenerating into another Nkrumah-Nyerere-type cursed relationship, they must learn from it what not to do.

African Renaissance, the African Union (AU) and the revival of pan-African unity

The dawn of the twenty-first century witnessed the rise of the millennial African Renaissance as a revival of the Nkrumahist vision of a politically, ideologically and economically united African continent able to use its abundant economic wealth to benefit Africans. The mantle of pan-Africanism was now taken over by what Kay Mathews termed 'the new generation of pan-Africanists', leaders that included Thabo Mbeki of South Africa; Olusegun Obasanjo of Nigeria; Abdoulaye Wade of Senegal; Abdul-Aziz Bouteflika of Algeria; Joachim Chissano of Mozambique; and Alpha Oumar Konaré of Mali (Mathews 2009: 28). The 'new pan-Africanists' which Mathews (2009: 30) described as 'the renascent generation' engaged in 'revitalizing and remaking of a new Africa'. The revived philosophy of African Renaissance as re-articulated by Mbeki provided the overarching ideological framework for the new initiatives to re-build Africa into a strong and united pan-African entity.

The 'new pan-Africanists' pushed forward the agenda of pan-Africanism to the level of translation of the ideology and its claims into practical political and economic policies as well as the creation of living continental institutions capable of repositioning the African continent within global governance structures as a voice to be heard rather than a problem to the solved. Thus, since its formation in July 2002, the African Union (AU) tried to transcend the culture of being a mere 'talking forum' and engaged in the difficult task of creation and operationalization of new pan-African institutions. An array of new institutions emerged such as the pan-African Parliament (PAP); the Peace and Security Council (PSC); the African Standby Force (AFS); the New Partnership for African Development (NEPAD); the African Peer Review Mechanism (APRM: a mutually agreed instrument voluntarily launched in 2003), and others, as levers for the eventual creation of a Union Government for Africa (African Union 2006).

The 'new generation of pan-Africanists' are concerned about Africa's over-dependency on the external world economically and even in terms of technological know-how; Africa's failure to fully exploit its potential at national, regional and continental level with respect to trade, education and health; mobilization of the African diaspora to assist with economic development of the African continent; and reversing the asymmetrical global power relations that were installed by Western modernity whereby African is confined to a subaltern position in international relations (African Union 2006). According to the radical group of African leaders, particularly the late Colonel Muammar Gaddafi of Libya, these noble African concerns cannot be realized without achievement of political unity of the continent.

What is disappointing about the current discourses on the formation of a Union Government for Africa is that they seem to degenerate into the 1960s camps of what Delphine Lecoutre categorized as the 'maximalists' who advocated the immediate creation of a Union Government for Africa; the 'gradualists' who are stuck in the 'stage-by-stage' integration process taking place within Regional Economic Communities (RECs); and the 'sceptics' who are taking a middle position between the 'maximalists' and the 'gradualists' (Lecoutre 2008: 45–59). The fact that at the Accra Summit of African Heads of States and Governments in July 2007, held to decide on the path to be followed towards attainment of a Union Government for Africa, the 'gradualists' won the day, as they did in 1963 at the formation of the OAU, indicates a continuing challenge: when will the time be ripe to launch a United States of Africa? The next concomitant question is: have the gradualists not been given enough time to decide since the debate on a Union Government first emerged in the 1960s? (African Union 2007).

What is clear is that the Accra Summit failed to deliver a radical roadmap on the path to be followed towards the creation of a Union Government for Africa. But on 27 November 2007, the African Union Ministerial Committee on the Union Government met in Addis Ababa in Ethiopia to address some of the issues raised by the Accra Declaration. What can be highlighted about this meeting is that, while it was haunted by the fragmentations prominent at the Accra Summit, it managed to draw a timetable for the launch and operationalization of a Union Government for Africa although without a fixed date (Murithi 2008b: 183–189). It would seem that at this time of intensifying globalization, Africa can only succeed economically and be counted within global governance, if it is truly united on the basis of pan-Africanism to articulate a common position at the global high table.

The key challenge to the success of pan-Africanism as an alternative worldview that emerged from the unequal encounters between Europe and Africa is how to equalize the asymmetrical power relations created by Western modernity as it exported its darker/underside aspects to the non-Western world. Without direct engagement with global coloniality and the preparedness of the Euro-American world to unite with Africans in particular, and peoples of the Global South in general, it is difficult to fundamentally change the current racial hierarchies, the patriarchal, capitalist, hetero-normative, and hegemonic global social order, shot through by Eurocentrism, to create the space for realization of a United States of Africa that is truly postcolonial and independent, and the power to pursue an autonomous economic and political path unencumbered by the hidden colonial matrices of power remains minimal. The global capitalist imperatives that inform the 'new imperialism', orchestrated by the U.S.A., does not support a strong and united African continent within the current modern international system because such a new strong actor from the Global South will not tolerate the exploitative forays of Europe and the U.S.A., which leave Africans underdeveloped.

At another level, the pan-African project has suffered causalities with the exit from the political stage of such leaders as Mbeki and Obasanjo and the embattlement and murder of Gaddafi in 2011. Despite his political shortcomings, Gaddafi was one of those leaders who contributed towards the revival of the pan-African project and he had taken the space of Nkrumah pushing for realization of a Union Government for Africa in our time. One can only hope that other African leaders will emerge, who have the commitment to transcend the narrow nationalism that privileges individual and fragile state sovereignties at a time when even powerful and industrialized European states are and were maximizing the values of pan-Europeanism via the strengthening of the European Union (EU). What is clear is that pan-Africanism as a counter-hegemonic worldview must intensify the struggle for a just international system that does not interfere with the agenda of building a United States of Africa as a strong global economic and political actor, able to bargain effectively on behalf of the African people at such forums as the World

Trade Organization (WTO), International Monetary Fund (IMF), World Bank (WB) and United Nations.

Conclusions

There is no doubt that advances have been made on institutionalization of the pan-African agenda at the beginning of the new millennium. Since the launch of the African Union (AU) in July 2002, Africa seemed to be awakening from the crisis of pan-African ideas that dominated the period from the 1970s to the 1990s. It must be underlined that during the crisis years of pan-Africanism, the United Nations Economic Commission for Africa (UNECA) under the leadership of Adebayo Adedeji filled the gap and begun to produce plans that embodied pan-African thought. The case in point being the Lagos Plan of Action of 1980 which unfortunately was never implemented, partly because the realities on the ground were dominated by neo-liberal structural adjustment programmes (SAPs) that were hostile to pan-Africanism (Khadiagala 2010: 375–385). Credit must be given to the late Gaddafi of Libya, former presidents Mbeki of South Africa, Obasanjo of Nigeria, Abdul-Aziz Bouteflika of Algeria, and Abdoulaye Wade of Senegal – the 'African Renaissance coalition' – for reviving the pan-African agenda. Gilbert Khadiagala (2010: 382) noted that this coalition emerged 'at a vital historical juncture when a leadership vacuum had developed on continental issues'.

Taking advantage of the new millenarian optimism, the 'African Renaissance coalition', despite its differences, particularly with Gaddafi who wanted a United States of Africa to be declared immediately, initiated and shepherded an impressive process of building Pan-African institutions with the formulation of plans for Africa. The case of the most recently launched Pan-African University (PAU) in December 2011 is an interesting development that is aimed at dealing with epistemological issues, raised in this very chapter, that are very important as an underpinning of the pan-African agenda in the twenty-first century. The new pan-African agenda cannot be informed and predicated on a hostile and imperialistic Euro-American epistemology that drives global imperial designs.

Despite the fact that members of the 'African Renaissance coalition' had chequered domestic democratic credentials, they tried to bring into the new pan-African initiatives the importance of democracy and good governance. The APRM is a case in point, despite its lack of popularity among other African leaders, who have snubbed this initiative. What is most disappointing, though, are the ideas underpinning NEPAD, which seem to ignore Nkrumah's longstanding argument about neo-colonialism as a major threat to Africa's struggles to take charge of its own destiny. If Nkrumah's ideas are taken seriously, he never believed in a partnership between Africa and the Euro-American world while global imperial designs informed the current world order. But, as put by Adebayo Olukoshi and Yao Graham:

> If domestic SAPs in Africa tore up the post-colonial nationalist compact, NEPAD gutted the long-held belief that a pan-African economic strategy should promote *less* not *more* dependence on foreign capital. (Olukoshi and Graham 2006: xv)

This policy mistake that rehabilitates global imperial designs could have been averted if current pan-Africanists could have armed themselves with the armour of a decolonial epistemic perspective that is consistently alert to the snares of colonial matrices of power. More worrisome is the return of a cursed relationship, like that of Nkrumah-Nyerere, in the twenty-first century. Wade and Gaddafi appropriated the Nkrumah position and pushed for a fast-tracked Union Government that would be a precursor to the United States of Africa. Khadiagala (2010: 383–384) categorized their position as that of 'unionists/continentalists' as opposed to Mbeki, Obasanjo and others, who can be correctly labelled as disciples of Nyerere's gradualism. The return of this curse in the twenty-first century is a reminder that perhaps the graduation of nationalism into pan-Africanism is taking time to materialize, dictating the necessity for caution and gradualism, and it is not known when it will create a conducive atmosphere for a Union Government.

Finally, the politics that developed around the question of the invasion of Libya by NATO in 2011 that eventually culminated in the violent death of Gaddafi revealed another vacuum in pan-African leadership. The AU was ignored by the Euro-American world. Two of the sober-minded members of the 'African Renaissance coalition', namely Mbeki and Obasanjo, are no longer in office. Since their departure, once again, the crescendo of a new pan-African unity predicated on African Renaissance has gone silent. There is a need for another committed leadership to take over from where they left.

CHAPTER 3

Coloniality of Power and African Development

Introduction

I propose to speak of development as historically singular experience, the creation of a domain of thought and action, by analysing the characteristics and interrelations of the three axes that define it: the forms of knowledge that refer to it and through which it comes into being and is elaborated into objects, concepts, theories, and the like; the system of power that regulates its practice; and the forms of subjectivity fostered by this discourse, those through which people come to recognize themselves as developed or underdeveloped. The ensemble of forms found along these axes constitutes development as discursive formation, giving rise to an efficient apparatus that systematically relates to knowledge and techniques of power.

(Arturo Escobar 1995: 10)

What is 'development'? It is perhaps worth remembering just how recent a question this is. This question, which today is apt to strike us as so natural, so self-evidently necessary, would have made no sense even a century ago. It is a peculiarity of our historical era that the idea of 'development' is central to so much of our thinking about so much of the world. It seems to us today almost non-sensical to deny that there is such a thing as 'development', or to dismiss it as meaningless concept, just as it must have been virtually important to reject the concept 'civilization' in the nineteenth century, or the concept 'God' in the twelfth. Such central organising concepts are not readily discarded or rejected, for they form the very framework within which argumentation takes place ... Each of these central organizing concepts presupposes a central, unquestioned value, with respect to which the different legitimate positions may be arrayed, and in terms of which different world views can be articulated. 'Development' in our time is such a central value. Wars are fought and coups are launched in its name. Entire systems of government and philosophy are evaluated according to their ability to promote it. Indeed, it seems increasingly difficult to find any way to talk about large parts of the world except in these terms.

(James Ferguson 1990: xiii)

First, is water. It is the first thing needed to live. Without it, a plant, an animal or a baby dies. Second, is food. Without enough of it, life is miserable and short. Third, once water and food are won, is health – otherwise the human being becomes sick. Fourth, is education, once a human being has water, food and health, he/she needs to learn to open new horizons and unlock new possibilities. And there is a fifth – peace and order. Without these, none of the basic needs can be sustained.
(Anonymous Somali elder of Baidoa cited in Adebayo Adedeji 2007: 23)

It is not clear yet if development is really about human beings, not about things that professional economists call macroeconomic indicators or aggregates that serve no purpose other than to confuse the uninitiated (Adedeji 2007: 23). The anonymous Somali elder of Baidoa cited above revealed an excellent grasp of the essentials of human life that development is expected to fulfil. But since the Enlightenment's harping on human progress, and Harry Truman's inaugural address as the president of the U.S.A. on January 20, 1949, promised to 'make available to peace-loving peoples the benefits of our store of technical knowledge in order to help them realize their aspirations for a better life', poverty and inequalities have deepened (Truman 1949). The basic needs that were meticulously identified by the Somali elder remain elusive, particularly to the peoples of the Global South and Africa.

This failure of development to deliver on its promises has led to the rise of different sceptics such as Majid Rahnema, Arturo Escobar, James Ferguson and many others, who doubt the non-political intentions of development and its commitment to bettering the lives of human beings. In his influential article entitled 'Global Poverty: A Pauperizing Myth' (1991), Rahnema posited that:

The word 'poverty' is, no doubt, a key word of our times, extensively used and abused by everyone. Huge amounts of money are spent in the name of the poor. Thousands of books and expert advice continue to offer solutions to their problems. Strangely enough, however, nobody, including the proposed 'beneficiaries' of these activities, seem to have a clear, and commonly shared, view of poverty. For one reason, almost all the definitions given to the word are woven around the concept of 'lack' or 'deficiency'. This notion reflects only the basic relativity of the concept. What is necessary and to whom? And who is qualified to define all that? (Rahnema 1991: 45)

These questions have provoked the proliferation of literature that questions the value of approaching the issues of development and its presumed target of eradication of poverty from a 'depoliticized' perspective. Ferguson in his acclaimed book, *The Anti-Politics Machine: 'Development', Depoliticisation, and Bureaucratic Power in Lesotho* (1990), raised some fundamental and critical questions about the real meaning of development to the extent of arguing that 'development is the name not only for a value, but also for a dominant problematic or interpretative grid through which the impoverished regions of the world are known to us' (Ferguson 1990: xiii). He further argued that development institutions such as the World Bank and others generated their own form of discourse that constructed those places identified as needing development into particular kinds of objects of knowledge, in the process 'depoliticizing everything it touches, everywhere whisking political realities out of sight, all the while performing, almost unnoticed, its own pre-eminently political operation of expanding bureaucratic state power' (Ferguson 1990: xv). Eventually what is commonly marketed as a humanitarian attempt at overcoming poverty reveals its true meaning as 'an important instrument of imperial and class-based control' (Ferguson 1990: 13). Development becomes an apparatus within the arsenal of global imperial designs and a technology of subjectivation within the 'development industry'.

The arguments that Ferguson introduced were fully developed by Escobar in his seminal book *Encountering Development: The Making of the Third World* (1995). Escobar questioned how the industrialized nations of Europe and America came to occupy the place of being global models of development for Asian, Latin American, Caribbean and African nations. He interrogated how a postwar discourse of development actually created the so-called Third World. His take is that what was popularly marketed as concerns about development were actually technologies of subjectivation and mechanism of control that were just as pervasive and effective as their colonial counterparts, which used the discourse of 'civilization' to take control of Africa. Echoing what Ferguson noticed with specific reference to Lesotho, Escobar reiterated that the development apparatus generated categories powerful enough to shape the thinking even of its occasional critics while poverty and hunger became widespread (Escobar 1995). To Escobar, the so-called 'Third World has been produced by the discourses and practices of development since their inception in the early post-World War II period' through what he described as 'colonization of reality' that is 'reflected in an objectivist and empiricist stand that dictates that the Third World and its peoples exist "out there" to be known through theories and intervened upon from outside' (Escobar 1995: 6–8).

Development in Escobar's terms is one of those discourses that were produced under conditions of unequal power within the broader context of 'the colonialist move' and this move entailed 'specific constructions of the colonial/Third World subject in/through discourse in ways that allow the exercise of power over it' (Escobar 1995: 9). He therefore pointed to a fundamental flaw in development discourse, which is that it relies 'exclusively on one knowledge system namely, the modern Western one. The dominance of this knowledge system has dictated the marginalization and disqualification of non-Western knowledge systems' (Escobar 1995: 13). A fuller understanding of the discourse and practice of development requires a serious interrogation of the 'genealogy of the Western narrative of modernity and its dichotomizing representation of non-Western cultures and societies' (Mirsepassi 2000: 1). What has confused many analysts is how to penetrate beyond the rhetoric of modernity which promises openness and inclusive vision and coloniality that forecloses the possibilities of non-Western experiences from contributing to modernity.

This chapter builds on the above critiques of development and it highlights three related problems that impinge on the conception and practice of development in Africa. The first is that of weak historicization, which bred heavy empiricism/weak thought, resulting in the proliferation of consultancy cultures that continue to depoliticize development, hide global imperial designs, and displace rigorous diagnostic research in development studies. The second is timidity in dealing head-on with the question of coloniality of power and global imperial designs that prevent the emergence of alternative development options, free from Euro-American Modernist conceptions. The third is depoliticization and decontextualization of development from the African national project and the African condition, culminating in discourses that blame Africans for their underdevelopment. Without a clear understanding of these issues, the failure of development in postcolonial Africa will remain a puzzle. This chapter, therefore, is written following the tradition initiated by Ferguson and Escobar, so as to bring back politics into the discourse of development by recognizing that the discourse and practice of development is not innocent of power (Tripathy and Mohapatra 2011).

Development as conceived from the Modernist perspective cannot be ahistorically reduced to mere real-life problems of hunger, scarcity of water, diseases, malnutrition and poverty as though these were untouched and unshaped by the broader questions of power, epistemology, representation, and the historical unfolding of Euro-American modernity across the world, which gave birth to such negative processes as mercantilism, the slave trade, imperialism, colonialism, neo-colonialism, apartheid, globalization, and neo-liberalism. This is why this chapter deals both with invisible global designs and the African national project: the former has impinged negatively on the latter since the beginning of colonial encounters in the fifteenth century.

This discussion starts off with reinstatement of the epistemological and theoretical entry points informed by a decolonial epistemic perspective that facilitates deeper appreciation of the impact of global imperial designs and coloniality of power on African development and the African condition. It also enables a deeper understanding of how power, knowledge production, and representation shapes and impinges on discourses of development. The second section briefly sketches the current morphology of global power dynamics and how they provoke, entertain and tolerate 'weak thought', while annihilating any forms of radical thinking, particularly those not in tandem with the neo-liberal and capitalist hegemony. The third section examines African development as a political project that was deeply embedded in the African national project, which was unfortunately heavily curtailed by the forces of coloniality of power, which had underpinned global imperial designs since the time of conquest.

The fourth and final section engages with the character of the African postcolonial states as an actor in African development whose actions were heavily interpellated by the immanent logic of coloniality of power to the extent that it served Euro-American designs at the expense of African aspirations. It proceeds to articulate what should be done for Africans to realize development, and builds a case for the reconstitution of the postcolonial state, to make it serve the interests of the ordinary peoples of Africa.

Decolonial epistemic perspective on development

In the domain of development, the decolonial epistemic perspective privileges African colonial experiences as a point of departure and thinking for African subaltern groups, as the ideal locus of enunciation which enables and facilitates a deeper understanding of power, knowledge production, and representation as factors shaping discourses of development (Grosfoguel 2007; Grosfoguel 2011). It also draws insights from the literature on modernity and coloniality, which emphasized colonial difference and the borders of modernity as a locus of enunciation of the experiences of 'ex-colonized' peoples (Césaire 1972; Fanon 1968; Biko 1978; Mignolo 1995; Wiredu 1995; Wiredu 1996; Chinweizu 1975; Chinweizu 1987).

While colonial difference is a reference to those spaces, borders and peripheries of the empire that received the darker consequences of modernity (Mignolo 2000; Taiwo 2010; Osha 2005), coloniality of power addresses how the spread of Euro-American modernity into the non-Western world was largely through such negative processes as mercantilism, the slave trade, imperialism, colonialism, apartheid and others, which were mediated by social classification of human population according to invented racial categories of inferior and superior, developed and underdeveloped, primitive and civilized, rational and irrational, traditional and modern human species (Quijano 2000a; Quijano 2000b; Quijano 2007). This point is well captured by Ramón Grosfoguel, who put it this way:

> During the last 510 years of the 'Capitalist/Patriarchal Western-centric/ Christian-centric modern/Colonial World-System', we went from the 16th Century 'Christanize or I shoot you', to the 19th Century 'civilize or I shoot you', to 20th Century 'develop or I shoot you', to late 20th Century 'neo-liberalise or I shoot you', and to the early 21st Century 'democratize or I shoot you'. (Grosfoguel 2011: 28)

The concept of coloniality of power expresses and captures the processes of how the 'Eurocentrification' of the world was enacted, combining racial social classification of human population with cartography, privileging Euro-American epistemology while displacing African forms of knowledge and spirituality; and imposing Christianity, which was accompanied by the naming and shaming and various negative representations of those Africans who resisted the new religion (Delavignette 1964; Quijano 2007; Mignolo 1995; Mignolo 2000). As such, the concept of coloniality of power helps in understanding the logic and processes involved in construction of identities, cartographic formation of geo-historical places such as Africa and even the assignment of social roles according to race and gender. A systematic deployment of the concept of coloniality of power reveals how Europe and America constituted themselves as the centre of the capitalist world economy and how Africa was systematically pushed to the peripheries, if not the barbarian margins, to provide slave labour and raw materials that were used to consolidate Euro-American hegemony (Quijano 2000a; Mudimbe 1994; Mudimbe 1988). The process is still actively operational today.

Global imperial designs and African development

The current global order still remains Euro-American-centric but is undergoing troubled times with the fate of humanity being very uncertain. A devastating economic crisis, otherwise known as the 'credit crunch'/'capitalist crisis'/'financial crisis', has rocked the Global North, raising questions about the triumphalism of the capitalist mode of production as the only viable global economic system. The ripple effects of this crisis have also been felt in Africa and other parts of the world, simply because the capitalist system has assumed global proportions. In the midst of this, there is an intensive drive by the U.S.A. and its NATO partners towards military intervention in states such as Iraq, Afghanistan and Libya, under the cover of humanitarian intervention and the 'right to protect' people suffering from excesses of dictatorships and threats of acts of terrorism.

This has ignited new fears by weak peripheral states about what is termed the 'new imperialism'/'neo-liberal imperialism' hidden within the wave of globalization (Hardt and Negri 2000; Harvey 2003; Fine 2006; Harvey 2007; Negri 2008). Michael Hardt and Antonio Negri pointed out that the empire was alive and resurgent, carving a new economic, cultural and political globalized order (Hardt and Negri 2000; Bush 2006). Antonio Negri added that, today, empire no longer has an outer boundary and no longer tolerates any realities external to itself (Negri 2008). In short, a close look at the current dynamics of imperial global designs vis-à-vis Africa indicates a looming danger of 're-colonization', beginning with those African countries endowed with strategic resources such as oil, gas, and diamonds. The future dynamics of Libyan development will be a case in point: a popular internal rising was openly supported by NATO, inviting a closer analysis of Libya's likely future long-term developmental and political outcomes. The prospects of re-colonization for Africa are made concrete by a present-day 'new scramble for African natural resources'. Land grabbing and interventions in oil-rich countries are on the increase throughout Africa.

At another level, there is the increasing rise of Chinese imperialism, which its Chinese ideologues articulate as based on a 'win-win' approach compared to Western economic interventions that were predicated on a 'donor-recipient' relationship. But it is yet to be seen whether the Chinese economic drive across Africa will stimulate the needed economic development or if it will result in the underdevelopment of Africa, like the ongoing Euro-American colonial and postcolonial economic interventions. There are also newcomers like India and Brazil, increasing the tempo of the new scramble for African natural resources.

Ideologically speaking, the current world order does not entertain and tolerate any form of radical thinking that is not in tandem with Euro-American neo-liberal thought. Such radicalism is easily dismissed as sentimental, nostalgic, anti-systemic and, at worst, as terrorism (Ndlovu-Gatsheni 2012a). The radicalism of the twentieth century that gave birth to the socialist system as an oppositional modernity within modernity and launched Africans to physically fight against colonialism and apartheid has been reduced to support for the neo-liberal status quo where 'weak thought', which misses the bigger picture of coloniality of power and easily celebrates African agency without due consideration of structural constraints put in place by the dark side of modernity, is dominant. It is clear that today the development community has run out of 'big ideas' and 'strong thought'. This reality led David L. Lindauer and Lant Pritchett to argue that:

> Any push towards deepening market reforms will be seen as a continuation of the failed strategies of the present, while any strategy that calls for government intervention and leadership … will be seen as a reversion to the failed strategies of the past. What is of even deeper concern than the lack of an obvious dominant set of big ideas that command (near) universal acclaim is the scarcity of theory and evidence-based research on which to draw. (Lindauer and Pritchett 2002: 2)

What is driving development studies is a critical re-evaluation and consolidation of previous concepts and techniques as opposed to the formulation of new ideas per se. Eric Thorbecke noted that the 'important contribution to development doctrine in this decade is a technique rather than theory' (Thorbecke 2006: 26). What is lost is a clear understanding of the underlying structure of the system of relationships generating negative development outcomes in Africa (Mookherjee 2004).

The same 'weak thought' is predicated on a shallow understanding of global and local power dynamics to the extent that at times 'experts' from the developed North are still given space to deliver their 'pedagogy of development' on Africa in spite of the dismal failure of SAPs of the late 1970s and 1980s. What is often missed is John Henrik Clarke's warning that 'Powerful people will never educate powerless people on what it means to take power away from them' (Clarke n.d.). The truism is that: 'The aim of the powerful people is to stay powerful by any means necessary' (Clarke n.d.). This is as true for African dictators as it is for the 'experts' from the Global North, as well as for those who primitively accumulated wealth in Africa during the colonial and apartheid times. Developmental disparities are informed by deliberately constructed power asymmetries, which in turn underpin and maintain socially constructed hierarchies of superior West and inferior Africa.

Slavoj Žižek has railed against 'weak thought', which according to him has resulted in 'culturalization of politics', as it ignored broader historical, discursive and structural processes responsible for human developmental tragedies. He posed the question:

> Why are so many problems today perceived as problems of intolerance, rather than as problems of inequality, exploitation, or injustice? Why is the proposed remedy tolerance, rather than emancipation, political struggle, even armed struggle? (Žižek 2009: 119)

The field of development studies is terribly affected by what Žižek terms 'weak thought', as opposed to 'strong thought', privileging what he described as 'large-scale explanations' and 'true ideas', which are 'indestructible' and have the capacity to 'always return every time they are proclaimed dead' (Žižek 2008: 8). Weak thought has even blinded some academics and intellectuals to such an extent that they continue to uncritically believe in the innocence of development discourses and to defend wrong causes, when they masquerade as progressive and developmental and operate under such acceptable terms as democracy, reform, development, good governance, and humanitarian intervention without recognizing and sifting out the dangerous colonial matrices embedded in them. But the veteran journalist John Pilger has been able to unpack some of the dangers embedded in popular developmental concepts in this way:

> 'Democracy' is now the free market – a concept bereft of freedom. 'Reform' is now the denial of reform. 'Economics' is the relegation of most human endeavour to material value, a bottom line. Alternative models that relate to the needs of the majority of humanity end up in the memory

hole. And 'governance' – so fashionable these days, means an economic approval in Washington, Brussels and Davos. 'Foreign policy' is service to dominant power. Conquest is 'humanitarian intervention'. Invasion is 'nation-building'. Every day, we breathe the hot air of these pseudo ideas with their pseudo truths and pseudo experts. (Pilger 2008: 4)

For Pilger, discourses like development, democracy, humanitarian inter-vention, nation-building and others, which ideally sound like very noble concepts, have been manipulated into 'the most powerful illusions of our time' having been 'corporatized and given deceptive, perverse, even opposite meanings' (Pilger 2008: 5).

It was in the midst of this time of uncertainty that seventeen African states celebrated fifty years of decolonization in 2010. These celebrations have taken place against a bedrock of failed economic development and incomplete decolonization, and by continuing popular struggles repre-sented by what has been termed the 'Arab Spring', which are open in-dictments of the juridical freedom bequeathed on Africa by decoloniza-tion. Achille Mbembe (2011: 1) posed a crucial soul-searching question: 'Here we are in 2010, fifty years after decolonization. Is there anything at all to commemorate, or should one on the contrary start all over again?'

The answer came from Ali Mazrui (2011: 1), who argued that 'the fif-tieth anniversary provides a suitable occasion not only to evaluate what has happened to postcolonial Africa as a whole but also to estimate the impact of the colonial experience on the African peoples'. What is telling is that Mazrui decided to use the fiftieth anniversary of decolonization to judge '100 years of colonial rule'. Does this mean that the fifty years of decolonization is not worth judging? This question is addressed in this chapter through a critical evaluation of the trajectories of the African national project and the role of the postcolonial state in development since the dawn of decolonization.

Besides ideological questions there are also crucial epistemological conundrums that characterize these present times of uncertainty. The epistemological issues were clearly introduced and articulated by Mah-mood Mamdani, who identified the dominance of a 'corrosive culture of consultancy' as part of the epistemological crisis in Africa (Mamdani 2011). The pervasiveness of this 'consultancy culture' is manifesting it-self in many forms, including emphasis on training in descriptive and quantitative data-collection methods to enable efficient 'hunting and gathering' of raw data and the production of consultancy reports, which are eventually processed into theories and knowledge in Euro-American academies before being consumed in Africa as developmental knowl-edge. This 'consultancy culture' ends up turning Africans into pure 'na-tive informants' rather than authentic, rigorous and robust producers of knowledge, which can be used to drive African development (Mamdani 2011).

The pervasiveness of 'consultancy cultures' was also identified by Mamdani as manifesting itself in a tendency by academics to rely on what he termed 'corporate-style PowerPoint presentations', dominated by the parroting of buzz words at the expense of lively, engaged and rigorous intellectual debates. Finally, Mamdani singled out the crisis of reduction of academic research into a quick prescriptive exercise rather than long-range diagnostic enterprise (Mamdani 2011). It is within this context that 'weak thought' has occupied the centre stage of academia, leading to the glossing over of pertinent questions to do with the role of the empire and questions of identity that continue to ignite conflicts that hamper development in Africa.

It is also within this context that humanities and social sciences are viewed as irrelevant to development because development is conceived in simplistic and shallow terms of 'technicism' and 'innovation', or 'mortar and brick', terms where there is little space for debate and critique of knowledge-claims (Stewart 2007: 141; *Charter on Humanities and Social Sciences* 2011). This thinking has resulted in what Peter Stewart (2007: 141) has termed 'the current dominance of instrumental reason' resulting in knowledge being reduced to a 'polytechnic/technikon and industry mode of know-how'. All this is blamed on a combination of commodification, marketization and pervasive managerialism, which have invaded universities (Stewart 2007: 141).

In view of these difficult epistemological questions, it is instructive to take note of Immanuel Wallerstein's analysis and advice, which challenges academics to 'unthink' rather than always 'rethink' some issues. This is how he put it:

> It is quite normal for scholars and scientists to rethink issues. When important new evidence undermines old theories and predictions do not hold, we are pressed to rethink our premises. In that sense, much of nineteenth-century social science, in the form of specific hypotheses, is constantly being rethought. But, in addition to rethinking, which is 'normal', I believe we need to 'unthink' nineteenth-century social science, because many of its presumptions – which, in my view, are misleading and constrictive – still have far too strong a hold on our mentalities. These presumptions, once considered liberating of the spirit, serve today as the central intellectual barrier to useful analysis of the social world. (Wallerstein 1991: 3)

Wallerstein's radical intervention speaks directly to the problems of an intellectual and academic failure to escape the trap of reproducing Euro-American hegemonic ideas informing systems of oppression, domination and exploitation, as well as maintaining alien and alienating institutions during the search for alternatives to domination and oppression. Boaventura de Sousa Santos further amplified this epistemological entrapment when he said:

In search for alternatives to domination and oppression, how can we distinguish between alternatives to the system of oppression and domination and alternatives within the system or, more specifically, how do we
distinguish between alternatives to capitalism and alternatives within
capitalism? In sum, how do we fight against the abyssal lines using conceptual and political instruments that don't reproduce them? (Santos
2007a: 87–89)

Development studies is terribly affected by failure to distinguish between alternatives to the systems and structures that generate underdevelopment and alternatives within the same systems which lead to
dead-ends in development.

This is illustrated by Robert Calderisi, a long-time World Bank official, who wrote a book entitled *The Trouble with Africa* (2007), in which
he argued that most of the misfortunes that bedevil Africa are self-im-
posed. He linked the failures of development in Africa to kleptocratic
governments, mismanagement, anti-business behaviour, family values,
cultural fatalism, corruption, and tribalism. He called for what he termed
'new tough love' in dealing with Africa, involving halving foreign assistance and channelling the remainder to those countries that strictly and
obediently pursued neo-liberal democratic trajectories as dictated from
the West (Calderisi 2007).

Of course, Africans are not only victims of underdevelopment: they
have invariably contributed to some of the miseries. But problems like corruption are linked to the colonial logic of primitive accumulation, and the
fact that the postcolonial state was inherited from colonialism, which was
a grand corrupt system. Colonialism structured the state in such a way
that it did not serve the interests of the ordinary African people. What
must be noted is that Robert Calderisi worked for the World Bank for over
thirty years in various senior positions, including being the bank's international spokesperson for Africa. It means that he is aware of the havoc
wreaked on Africa by the SAPs that were imposed on Africa as part of
developmental salvation and he decides to ignore this fact.

In his book, Calderisi urges Africans not to point fingers at the West
and to blame themselves. It is this hypocrisy if not complicity in causing
African misery that a decolonial epistemic analysis seeks to reveal without necessarily degenerating into an analytical neurosis of victimhood.
The point is that the scale of African development challenges cannot be
clearly articulated outside a full and clear understanding of historical,
discursive and structural context of modernity, imperialism, colonialism, decolonization, neo-colonialism, neo-liberalism and globalization
(Appadurai 1996; Paolini 1999; Attwell 2005; Geshiere et al. 2008).

The pertinent question is: what did development mean within this
context? How was it defined? Who were the agents and objects of development? In the first place, understood from the empire as the locus of
enunciation, imperialism and colonialism, were grand 'civilising mis-

sions' (Conklin 1997; Stoler 2002). Europeans were agents of development and Africans were objects of development. Development in the context of imperial global designs meant opening up the African continent for economic exploitation and even the permanent settlement of white settlers on the continent. Development also meant defeating African resistance (read as pacification of barbarous tribes who were resisting modernity) to pave the way for constructions of colonial states (Asiwaju 1987). Development meant reorganization of land into the private property of white settlers in those areas of Africa that fell victim to settler colonialism, like South Africa, Algeria, Zimbabwe, Kenya and others (Edwards 1934; Magubane 1997; Magubane 1996). Development meant the rearrangement of African agrarian systems to make sure they produced cash crops that were needed in Europe and America.

Development meant the dispossession of Africans to force them off the land and transform them into peasants, workers and domestic servants. At the same time, acquired land was quickly transformed into plantations and farms owned by victorious white settlers. In other words, development in the colonial context meant pushing Africans out of their modes of life and production into the evolving capitalist one, where they participated mainly as providers of cheap labour. Achille Mbembe argued that 'in implementing its projects, the colonial state did not hesitate to resort to brute force in dealing with natives, to destroy the forms of social organization that previously existed, or even to co-opt these forms in the service of ends other than those to which they had been directed' (Mbembe 2000: 8).

In short, development meant the refashioning of and transformation of African society according to the needs, demands and imperatives of colonial regimes. As noted by Frederick Cooper, colonialism never provided a strong national economy to benefit African people because the colonial economies were 'externally oriented and the state's economic power remained concentrated at the gate between inside and outside' (Cooper 2002: 5). It was Cooper who described the colonial state as a 'gate-keeper state' that was not embedded in the society over which it presided, stood astride the intersection of colonial territory and the outside world, and drew revenue from duties on goods and taxing Africans (Cooper 2002: 88).

Socially, colonial development entailed reorganization and classification of colonial populations according to race. Mahmood Mamdani (1996) described the colonial states as bifurcated social formations inhabited by 'subjects' and 'citizens'. To prevent the coalescence of colonized peoples into nations, colonialists used cartography, census and law to classify the population into races and tribes, civilized and uncivilized people as well as citizens and subjects. The colonial state enforced political and legal identities via issuing of identity cards. Colonialism transformed fluid and accommodative precolonial cultural identities

into rigid, impermeable, singular, non-consensual and exclusionary political identities as part of technologies of colonial governance. In all this,
races were said to have a common future as citizens whereas tribes as
subjects were said to be lacking common futures. Colonial governments
went further to deny African people the space to coalesce into a majority
identity, through fracturing them into different and competing tribes
and minorities (Mamdani 2001b; Mamdani 2007).

Politically, colonial governance assumed the character of a hybrid-
mixed, military-civilian model where violence became a governmental
norm. Para-military authoritarianism was a core component of colonial
governance, with disciplining those categorized as natives as the order
of the day. Mbembe argued that 'the colonial state model was, in theory
as in practice, the exact opposite of the liberal model of discussion or
deliberation' (Mbembe 2000: 6). Three forms of violence underpinned
colonial governance: 'foundational violence', which was unilateral and
authorized the right of conquest and had an 'instituting function' of
creating Africans as its targets; 'legitimating violence', which was used
after conquest to construct colonial order and to routinize colonial reality; and 'maintenance violence', used to ensure permanence of colonialism and dispersed into colonial institutions and cultures (Mbembe
2000: 6–7). Nelson Maldonado-Torres argued that all sorts of colonial
violence against black people was justifiable under what he termed 'imperial Manichean misanthropic skepticism' that doubted the humanity
of black peoples and questioned whether they had souls in the first place
(Maldonado-Torres 2008).

Despite the fact that the colonial state was partly imagined along
Westphalian terms and the model of Eurocentric nation-states, citizenship rights for Africans became a scarce resource. Participation of Africans in elections also became scarce. By and large, the colonial state
became an institution of exploitation of black labour and of repression.
Coercion rather than consent formed the DNA of colonial governance.
Through its social, economic and political engineering processes it created a complex 'native-settler' question that was permeated by white
supremacist ideas and prevented the formation of multi-racial nation-
states from colonial encounters (Mamdani 1996: 12–17).

In countries like South Africa and Zimbabwe, with large populations
of white races, the resolution of the colonially created native-settler question has proven difficult and continues to impinge on nation-building
and development. Thinking about how this question could be resolved,
Mamdani located it within the politics of identity reconstruction and
asked how could 'a settler become a native?' (Mamdani 2001a). He elaborated on the intractability of the 'native-settler' question in these words:

> In the context of a former settler colony, a single citizenship for settlers and
> natives can only be the result of an overall metamorphosis whereby erst-

> while colonisers and colonized are politically reborn as equal members of
> a single political community. The word reconciliation cannot capture this
> metamorphosis ... This is about establishing for the first time, a political
> order based on consent and not conquest. It is about establishing a political
> community of equal and consenting citizens. (Mamdani 2001a: 67)

It is against this background that the decolonization process emerged
as a movement to reverse colonialism and inaugurate new African humanism underpinned by freedom, equality, social and economic justice
and human development. Decolonization was also expected to resolve
the 'native-settler' problem created by colonialism through construction
of nation-states of equal and consenting citizens. But the very idea of
people being organized into modern nation-states was itself a product
of modernity and the Westphalian consensus. African nationalists, as
they imagined postcolonial nation-states, accepted the Eurocentric template of the nation-state. The nation-states that were emerging from the
African soil informed by African histories, sociologies and psychologies,
were cut short by colonial encroachment and intervention. The geography of the modern African nation-state was shaped the Berlin Conference of 1884 to 1885 that formalized the scramble and partition of
Africa into European spheres of influence and into colonies (Gallagher
and Robinson 1968).

While conventional thought has been that colonialism brought about
a problematic modernity to Africa, Olufemi Taiwo challenges this wisdom. He argues that by the time of colonization, Africa was already becoming modern on its own terms and that colonialism disrupted those
indigenous initiatives through introduction of forms of indirect rule
that crippled African agency and impulses towards progress. Taiwo's
book entitled *How Colonialism Preempted Modernity in Africa* concluded
that 'colonialism was the bulwark against the implantation of modernity
in Africa' (Taiwo 2010: 237).

Taiwo's argument is that modernity in Africa predated colonialism.
Its ambiguities and contradictions, particularly those activities that drew
power from European modernity and African 'invented' traditions, adversely affected the development of African institutions as well as conceptions of development (Taiwo 2010; Ranger 1993). This ambivalence
led colonial ideologues and colonial officials to impose a static conception of African societies as traditional and unchanging in the midst of
considerable change. This way colonialism played a role in preempting
modernity by working towards the reproduction of social and cultural
differences that were informed by tensions between the imperative to
'civilize' and the proclivity to reproduce and invent 'traditions and customs' (Cooper 2002: 16–18; Mamdani 1996: 16–25). These ambiguities,
contradictions and ambivalences of colonialism had long-term impacts
on the African national project, the character of the postcolonial state,
and African conceptions of development.

Taiwo's argument on how colonialism preempted modernity in Africa is vindicated by the fact that those early members of African elites, like Edward Blyden, James Johnson, James Africanus Horton, Samuel Ajayi Crowther, Samuel Lewis, and others, who had trained and successfully completed advanced studies in missiology, medicine and law, among other professions, and were ardent Christians, who perceived colonization as a necessary evil for civilization, were despised by colonial regimes. These early African elites were enthusiastic about the benefits of British and French civilization. They were also excessively zealous to become as much like the Europeans as possible. Michael Onyebuchi Eze noted that:

> The civilized and educated blacks were frowned upon and ignored, among other reasons, for symbolizing and representing a threat to the colonial presence. They became obnoxious for they were equally modern in their demand for proactive participation in the colonial project ranging from 'parity of treatment' to 'equality of civil status'. (Eze 2010: 25)

The British in particular, for purposes of policy of 'indirect rule', expressed their preference for what Basil Davidson described as the 'uncorrupted child of nature' in contrast to the Western-educated elites. It would seem that acquisition of Western education ceased to be used as a standard of civilization. This action of colonial regimes revealed an inherent contradiction in the logic of colonial domination and its technologies of subjectivation at the time of establishing colonial governance structures in Africa.

Rethinking the African national project and development challenges

The national project(s) across the world are today threatened from three dimensions. From above, they are threatened by global economic change and imperatives of regionalism. From below, they are threatened by a re-assertion of sub-state identities and a coterie of new policy challenges with which they are often ill-equipped to deal. Laterally, they are threatened by the rise of new forms of collective identity, the advance of the market and individualized social relations. Despite these threats, national project(s) have remained an important terrain within which the successes and failures of development have to be understood (Keating 2000: 28). The fact is that development has remained an important component of the agendas of the African national project. The intimate connection between the national project(s) and development is well articulated by Arnold Rivkin who said:

> Nation-building and economic development [...] are twin goals and intimately related tasks, sharing many of the same problems, confronting

many of the same challenges; and interrelating at many levels of public policy and practice. (Rivkin 1969: 156)

The continuing relevance of national project(s) is partly explained by the fact that the state in Africa remains alive in all its diverse manifestations despite proclamations of its demise by advocates of transnationalism, cosmopolitanism, neo-liberalism and globalization. By 1993, even the Bretton Woods institutions conceded that the state still has a major role to play in development as it has done in East Asia. The reality in Africa is that the decolonization process that culminated in political independence was spearheaded by 'complex alliances of disparate social groups knit together by the emergent elites to resolve the "colonial question"' (Mkandawire 2012: 9).

The African national project in particular is a product of African nationalism that emerged as a response to colonialism. While colonialism brought about the Westphalian template of the nation-state into Africa, it consistently adjusted it to suit colonial imperatives of domination and exploitation. Like other earlier national project(s), the African one assumed from the beginning an omnibus-like character, seeking to carry too many burdens simultaneously. In the first place, it was concerned about forging common national consciousness out of people with racial, ethnic, class, gender, religious, and generational differences (otherwise known as nation-building). In the second place, it sought to construct, entrench, and consolidate African political power in terms of institution-building, monopolizing violence, and forging hegemony (otherwise known as state-building) (Olukoshi and Laakso 1996; Wamba-dia-Wamba 1991: 58–70).

In the third place, it set out, as its goal, to eradicate colonial autocracy and repression so as to build accountability, legitimacy, transparency and ensure the popular participation of ordinary citizens in governance (otherwise known as democratization). The eradication of poverty, ignorance, disease and promotion of economic growth so as to improve the standard of living of ex-colonized peoples (otherwise known as economic development) was another important burden of the African national project as well as how to reverse colonial dispossession through redistribution of national resources (otherwise known as economic decolonization/indigenization of economy). Finally, securing political independence from external threats (otherwise known as protection of sovereignty and territorial integrity) became a core component of the African national project (Hippler 2005; Ndlovu-Gatsheni 2009a; Mkandawire 2005).

It is clear that development occupied the heart of the African national project to the extent that on every door of the founding father of the postcolonial nation-state was an invisible sign reading 'silence: development in progress' and every African state was busy implementing some five-year development plan in one form or another (Nugent 2004). The topical question that cries out for a response is: why did the African national project not succeed in realizing its core objectives? Why has development eluded Africa? Julius Ihonvbere squarely blames African leaders and the African elite for the failures of the African national project and development. This is how he put it:

> Taken together, save for a few exceptions, the African elite and African leaders did little or nothing to restructure the distorted, disarticulated, dependent, and underdeveloped structures of the African social formation. They did little to empower the peoples of Africa. They did little to challenge foreign domination and imperialist penetration, domination and exploitation of Africa. They did almost nothing to challenge the cultural bastardization in the continent. They did nothing to strengthen or reconstitute the neo-colonial state. They confused the expansion of the armed forces, the importation of outdated military and security gadgets, and the establishment of violent security elements with the strengthening of the state. They foolishly confused the harassment of opposition elements, the asphyxiation of civil society, and criminal looting of treasury with power. They did very little to move Africa away from neo-colonial cultural, social, and political traditions and world-views imposed to serve the interests of the West. In short, this opportunistic, corrupt, decadent, irresponsible, largely unproductive, shamelessly subservient, and ideologically barren class ruined Africa and mortgaged the future of the vast majority to imperialist interests. (Ihonvbere 1994: 5)

Ihonvbere's explanation is familiar and is shared by some Africanists and African scholars such as George Ayittey, the author of *Africa Betrayed* (1994), who argued that it is naïve to blame Africa's misery on external factors because African leaders themselves betrayed both the aspirations of their people and Africa's indigenous political systems, which in no way endorsed tyranny (Ayittey 1994). Moeletsi Mbeki also reinforces Ihonvbere and Ayittey's explanations and identifies the African leaders and African elites as 'the architects of poverty' in Africa, who keep their fellow citizens poor while enriching themselves (Mbeki 2009). It is clear that African leaders and African elites are not blameless in squandering opportunities for development, betraying the objectives of the African national project and looting resources meant to help poor people.

But this analysis provides only part of the explanation and leaves a number of questions unanswered. For instance, why are African leaders prone to corruption and why are they failing to manage their states properly? Why are the African elites prone to looting, opulence and living to consume rather than production? Why is it that the African postcolonial state is best known for bad behaviour such as repression, brutality, corruption, inefficiency and failure to promote the collective well-being of its citizens? Some scholars have responded to these questions by articulating an 'African exceptionalism' thesis. For instance, Ulf

Engel and Gorm Rye Olsen, in their book entitled *The African Exception* (2005), have written that:

> In many respects Sub-Saharan Africa is an exception to the general pattern of 'development' in the South. Whereas many countries in Asia and Latin America have achieved some progress in economic growth and in the institutionalization of democracy, Africa's path into the 21st century is a different one. (Engel and Olsen 2005: 1)

The 'African exception' thesis degenerates into 'Orientalization' of Africa that was dealt with effectively by Edward Said (1978). It also privileges a static cultural relativist reading of the African condition and development. For instance, Patrick Chabal's and Jean-Pascal Daloz's book, *Africa Works: Disorder as Political Instrument* (1999), understands the African condition through the Weberian notions of state, state-society relations and citizenship, used as a global template for measuring African development. Their conclusions were that development in Africa is informed by a different logic from that which shaped the Western world; development in Africa is concerned with short-term consumption (politics of the belly); there is preference for reliance on outside resources instead of productive activities or proper savings; what appears as disorder to people from outside Africa is order to the African beholder; and, finally that the African state and its bureaucracy work differently from those of the classical Weberian interpretations (Chabal and Daloz 1999).

What this Orientalist thinking ignores is the role of coloniality of power in making it hard for sustainable development to take root in Africa. Because of the coloniality of power, Africa found itself at the interface between different value systems, different forms of logic: Western and African; urban and rural; patriarchal and matriarchal; religious and secular; nationalist and tribal/ethnic; modern and traditional; progressive and conservative; cultural and technical: the list is long. Up to today, Western values and concepts coexist uneasily with African concepts, partly because colonialism manipulated and deployed both Western and African concepts in its governance, simultaneously destroying some of the concepts and values that cascaded from precolonial Africa and reinventing some for colonial purposes. Western concepts were also introduced in a very measured way for colonial purposes. The result was that the colonial state and its successor were neither fully fledged replicas of the European state nor reflected African sociologies and histories.

The net effect of all this was the creation of African elites that dreamt in both Western and African languages: 'walking lies' to use Jean Paul Sartre's words. It is these African elites that produced African leadership. Colonialism created African elites that aspired to a capitalist lifestyle but had no capital. The black elites had seen how white colonialists used the colonial state to engage in primitive accumulation and experienced how colonial authoritarianism was used to silence African voices. They were never exposed to democracy under colonialism but were expected to run postcolonial governments along democratic lines. The reality led Kuan-Hsing Chen to argue that:

> Shaped by the immanent logic of colonialism, Third World nationalism could not escape from reproducing racial and ethnic discrimination; a price to be paid by the colonizer as well as the colonised selves. (Chen 1998: 14)

Emerging within this context, the African national project unfolded as a top-down enterprise informed by a form of pedagogical nationalism that was intolerant of questions and dissent. Development was to be delivered in a similar authoritarian fashion. The African state that drove the national project(s) was also authoritarian and intolerant of questions and divergent ideas. Single party and military regimes emerged from this context of intolerance of diversity, which informed the African national project. The postcolonial state became a monstrous hybrid, an inescapable combination of Hobbes' leviathan and Coleridge's albatross, weighing down upon, suffocating and/or disciplining any form of opposition. State legitimacy was questioned as development projects failed and authoritarianism deepened towards the end of the first decade of decolonization (Laakso and Olukoshi 1996).

When development initiatives of the 1960s were failing in the 1970s, numerous solutions were sought. During the 1960s and 1970s, African countries were pursuing two basic models of development. The first was the Western nationalist welfarist model informed by Keynesianism. The second was the Soviet and East European socialist model informed by Marxism and Leninism. During this period, state interventionism in the development process was accepted and financial support came from across the East-West ideological divide (Laakso and Olukoshi 1996: 15–17). Human rights discourse and questions of democracy were not yet dominant. States were, therefore, seen as unquestioned agents of development across the world until the economic stagnation of the 1970s provoked a new search for new approaches to development.

Structural adjustment programmes (SAPs) emerged within a context of economic stagnation in Africa and a global shift from Keynesianism to neo-liberalism, which privileged market forces over the role of the state. During this same time economic globalization was accelerating with enormous implications for the management of national economies. The World Bank and IMF began to play a leading role globally (Gibbon et al. 1992). SAPs came with anti-statist philosophies where the postcolonial state was seen as nothing but a 'giant theft machine' and this thinking inaugurated what Thandika Mkandawire described as 'wanton destruction of institutions and untrammeled experimentation with half-baked institutional ideas' (Mkandawire 2003: 10). The logic of neo-liberalism's anti-statist trajectory was unfolded in this way in Elliot Berg's report entitled *An Agenda for Accelerated Development in Africa* (1981): first, for Africa to develop it had to 'get prices right' and this implied allowing free rein of market forces with their laws of demand and supply. This logic did not result in any 'accelerated development' but as put by Mkandawire (2012: 2) led to 'maladjustment' and two 'Lost Decades'.

When this dismal failure raised critical voices within Africa, the Bretton Woods institutions did not give up their developmental pedagogy but shifted from the mantra of 'getting prices right' to that of 'getting governance right'. This mantra of dominance continues even today, resulting in debates on the trade-off between democracy and development. Mkandawire (2012: 3) noted that, besides the dominant mantra of 'getting governance right', the development industry had given two more 'decrees' to Africa, 'getting institutions right' and 'getting culture right', as it struggled to explain why development has not taken place under the SAPs that had been in place since the mid-1970s. The logic is simple: blame Africa for the failure of development.

There is no doubt that SAPs were a wrong remedy based on a wrong diagnosis of the causes of the failure of development in Africa. Pushing the state out of the development project was based on the assumption that the state per se was the culprit. What was wrong was the type of state that was tasked with promotion of development beneficial to the African people, without it having been fully decolonized to enable it to serve African interests. As noted by Fantu Cheru, the period of SAPs reinforced the imperial global designs' hold over African economies and African leaders lost the little remaining policy-making freedom they had enjoyed in the 1960s (Cheru 2009: 275–278).

Cheru concluded that 'What is normally accepted as "development" in Africa has been essentially an imperial project, derived and financed by the dominant Western powers to serve Western needs' (Cheru 2009: 275). He went further, to state that under SAPs 'policy making, an important aspect of sovereignty, has been wrenched out of the hands of the African state. This is colonization, not development' (Cheru 2009: 277). Africa has not yet recovered from this blow and the emerging consensus is that the state has to be reconstituted into a democratic institution and enabled to regain lost policy space so as to play a positive role in development.

There still strong belief among Western development agencies that the African state is not well positioned to deliver development in the same manner that the East Asian states did. Five main reasons are given. The first is that the postcolonial African state is not ideologically predisposed to imagine successful development. The second is that the postcolonial African state is manned by 'rent-seeking elites'. The postcolonial state is in fact captured by rent-seekers who channel its direction into pursuit of particularistic interests at the cost of the national interest (Mkandawire 2012: 4). The third reason is that the postcolonial state is an 'epicenter of neo-patrimonialism' that resulted in states that were crippled by a combination of tradition and modernity. Tradition is said to enable 'highly personalized reciprocity as the basis for exchange' while modernity 'is based on Weberian legal-rational order' (Mkandawire 2012: 4). The fourth argument is that postcolonial African states do not have the human resource capabilities, and technical capacities, with which to create successful developmental states. The final reason is that globalization has made it impossible for the state to play any meaningful interventionist role in national economies because economic activities are now globalized, making the role of the state irrelevant if not obsolete (Mkandawire 2012: 5). Mkandawire is very critical of the message contained in these arguments and his take is:

> I see no reason why Africa should be the exception, especially if one accepts that African states must radically and rapidly transform their economies, not only to address the known ills of poverty, ignorance and diseases, but also to deal with the new challenges of climate change and the ever present threat of external plunder. (Mkandawire 2012: 5)

The case for state reconstitution consensus

There is an emerging consensus not only on the 'return of the state' to play a central role in development but also on the nature of the state that is well positioned to spearhead development in Africa. This consensus is building on the rise of 'new institutionalism', the lessons gained from the rise of Asian Tigers, and the recent capitalist crisis, which has raised the possibility of pursuing autonomous development paths in the peripheries of the world economy (Moyo and Yeros 2011). The consensus was well captured by Pita Ogaba Agbese and George Klay Kieh (2007a: xii), who argued that the state does not need to retreat but instead needs to be reconstituted. Africa actually needs strong, democratic, and pro-people states that provide for the basic needs of the people as well as being capable of respecting and defending African people's fundamental individual and group rights, promoting gender equality, championing peaceful coexistence among various ethnic groups and religions, and defending the citizens from the exploitation and other vagaries of international finance capital.

Four compelling reasons inform the agenda of reconstitution of the state. The first is that the postcolonial state has not lost its colonial genealogy, which shaped it to serve external interests by facilitating the exploitation of African resources for external consumption. As such the state is not well positioned to advance the material well-being of

Africans. Decolonization did not automatically change the nature and essence of the African state. The second reason is that, in the past fifty years, the African state has failed to fulfill the most basic requirements of a modern state because of its colonial origins. The third reason is that the postcolonial state has been abused as a vehicle of private accumulation of wealth by African leaders, their cronies and clients. This has made struggles to control the state assume a life-and-death format in Africa. Fourth and finally, it has become clear that the state cannot be left alone to operate its politics and its economies in this distorted and unproductive fashion because this deepens underdevelopment and poverty in Africa (Agbese and Kieh 2007b: 12–14).

But how to practically and fundamentally restructure and reconstitute the postcolonial state, and reposition its missions and institutions to serve the ordinary African people, remains a big challenge. Agbese and Kieh provide four models. The first is the institutional reform model, which advocates elimination of inefficient state institutions: rebuilding of the social contract between the leaders and the citizens, establishment of independent judiciary, and reinforcement of accountability and transparency. The problem with this model is that it reads like a wish-list informed by neoliberal reformism that does not address the structural problem of coloniality of power in place since the time of colonial encounters.

The second model is the power-sharing arrangement. It is premised on the understanding that elite political antagonisms and conflicts over political power and control of the state have resulted in destruction of the state, if not its privatization, to serve cliques, cronies and clients of the dominant elites (Mukherjee 2006). Elite unity is seen as a fulcrum for a stable state. A number of problems are identifiable with this arrangement. In the first place, its focus is to unite the elites rather than the entirety of the ordinary people, who have not enjoyed any fruits of decolonization. At another level, power-sharing has proven to be nothing more than an armistice, usually of five years or less, rather than a durable resolution of elite conflicts. The examples of Zimbabwe and Kenya indicate the fragility of this model and the pervasive fear of elections as a moment of renewed intra- and inter-elite struggles that provoke communal violence that consumes the lives of ordinary citizens. What is also worrying is that democratic principles are often sacrificed for the sake of reaching a power-sharing deal in situations like Zimbabwe and Kenya where entrenched but unpopular elites refuse to leave power after losing elections (Cheeseman and Tendi 2010; LeVan 2011).

The third model is the constitutional reform model, which speaks to the need for good governance and strict adherence to constitutionalism. New people-driven constitutions are seen as providing a framework for resolving political conflicts and for addressing people's welfare. But again, case studies of countries like Zimbabwe have revealed that without a change of heart by the elites and a political paradigm shift, the constitution-making process can be nothing but a fig-leaf covering the nakedness of authoritarianism of entrenched elites. For constitutionalism to be a panacea to African problems there is a need for elite commitment to upholding the constitution (Shivji 1991).

The fourth model is that of state deconstruction, which calls for fundamental transformation of the neo-colonial state, including changing its proclivities to serve the interests of international capital, to serve the ordinary people of Africa. Mueni wa Muiu and Martin (2009: 191–210) proposed what they termed 'Fundi wa Africa' as a basis for radical deconstruction and reconstruction of the state. 'Fundi wa Africa' is a Swahili word referring to the tailoring of Africa. State-builders are seen as tailors engaged in fitting the state to suit African needs and demands (Mueni wa Muiu and Martin 2009: 191–210). As noted by Agbese and Kieh (2007b: 14–19), state reconstitution in Africa must be a holistic process rather than a superficial reformist process. Mueni wa Muiu and Martin (2009: 194–196) emphasized the re-anchoring of the state in African history, African values and traditions, and indigenous political systems, as part of its reconstitution. All this cannot happen without full decolonization of the state and a thorough decolonization of African minds to enable them to imagine alternatives.

Conclusion

The global current economic crisis raises anxieties, uncertainties, as well as opportunities to reflect and imagine alternative development paths. The important question is whether the current global crisis indicates the signs of the demise of the modern world order as constructed and reproduced since the dawn of modernity? Is the crisis just one of those recessions that have dogged capitalism since its rise in the seventeenth century? If indeed this crisis symbolizes a major crack in the capitalist edifice, are there alternatives to it? These are challenging questions because it seems that capitalism has ways of surviving these tectonic stresses. What is disappointing is that there seems to be a failure of thought, to think out alternative development paths.

The leftists are trying to take advantage of the capitalist crisis to rehabilitate the ideas of a socialism that failed with the fall of the Berlin Wall in 1989. Those scholars who still believe in the redemptive and liberatory potential of African nationalism are calling for revival of the dormant African national project as an anchor for development and for purposes of resolving the unfinished national question of how to achieve its goals (Moyo and Yeros 2011). This again is not a new thought as it does not take the form of a paradigm shift that could really inaugurate a decolonial turn whose horizon is a pluriversal world as opposed to the current drive towards universality.

Liberals still hold strong beliefs on the durability, suitability and viability of the capitalist system and why the system has already survived the credit crunch, while postmodern cosmopolitanists still believe that Africa is weighed down by a neurosis of victimhood which makes it fail to take advantage of the fruits of globalization to further the agenda of development. They totally ignore the structural barriers sustained by global coloniality that exist to prevent nations and states from the Global South in general, and Africa in particular, from enjoying the fruits of globalization.

This chapter deployed the concept of coloniality of power to critically assess the discourse of development in Africa. Its conclusion is that while Africa and Africans have been worked over by colonialism, global coloniality and empire, since the time of colonial encounters, the sustainable alternative is not to continue to seek solutions within the discursive terrain put in place by modernity, but to find creative ways of negotiating the continent out of the snares of colonial matrices of power. The first practical step is for Africans to speed the pace of pan-African unity, which will provide a shield against global coloniality during the current age of the new scramble for African natural resources.

The second step is for Africa to play an active role in strengthening South-South cooperation, as this presents a way of putting the African agenda on the table of global governance, and to directly confront the coloniality of power hidden in institutions like the IMF, WB and WTO. Deepening regional integration and pan-African unity is another way of minimizing the negative forces of coloniality of power over the continent. At the local national level of individual countries, local epistemologies and knowledges that reflect particularities of different African societies must be mobilized to enable a clear understanding of African social formations. Both decolonization and democratization must be taken to their logical conclusion, which is a pluriversal world into which many worlds fit, where equality is guaranteed and where ecologies of knowledges will be harnessed to enrich human life.

PART 2

SUBJECT, SUBJECTION AND SUBJECTIVITY

CHAPTER 4

The Ticklish Subject in Africa

Introduction

Identity is not something like a monument we have inherited from the past; it is not like a fate sent to us from either heaven or hell, nor like a trait of character that we can impossibly alter. No, identity is something we make ourselves and that continuously varies with what we do or do not do. Our identity is in our own hands.

(Frank Ankersmit 2010: xii)

Consequently, if we are to draw a resource from Africa's identities, we need first acknowledge that race, a shared glorious past or a metaphysical unity cannot be a source of that identity. Our identity must be derived from the vagaries of our present circumstances: 'we can choose, within broad limits set by ecological, political and economic realities, what it will mean to be African in the coming years'.

(Michael Onyebuchi Eze 2010: 193)

The vision of Negritude should never be underestimated or belittled ... In attempting to achieve this laudable goal, however, Negritude proceeded along the route of oversimplification. Its re-entrenchment of black values was not preceded by any profound effort to enter into the African system of values. It extolled the apparent. Its reference points took far too much colouring from European ideas. Negritude adopted the Manichean tradition of European thought and inflicted it on a culture which is most radically un-Manichean.

(Wole Soyinka 1976: 150)

The question of the subject, subjection and subjectivity has dominated African thought and struggles since the time of colonial encounters. The contours of the debate on African subjectivity revolve around how events and processes of slavery, imperialism, colonialism, and apartheid resulted in three-layered memories and the realities of the emergence of African subjectivity. The first layer is that of alienation of the African subject from the 'original Self' that led to 'a loss of familiarity with self' and the 'estrangement' of Africans from their ontological identities – relegating them to objecthood and nothingness (Mbembe 2002a: 241). The second is that of the dispossession of Africans, which has created a longstanding African grievance over property ownership, particularly in former settler colonies. The third is that of human suffering and human degradation that manifested itself in 'humiliation' and 'debasement', that has plunged the African subject into a 'zone of nonbeing and social death', 'denial of dignity, heavy damage, and the torment of exile' (Mbembe 2002a: 241–242).

In the West, the Slovenian philosopher Slavoj Žižek in *The Ticklish Subject: The Absent Centre of Ontology* (1999) informs us that the question of the subject is also haunting Europe to the extent that all academic powers have to be mobilized 'to exorcise' the 'spectre of the Cartesian Subject' (Žižek 1999: 1). Among those identified as deeply concerned and involved in the tasks of exorcising the 'spectre of the Cartesian subject' were the 'New Age obscurantists' who sought to supersede the 'Cartesian paradigm' so as to reach a new holistic one.

The second were 'postmodern deconstructivists' who doubted the substance of the Cartesian subject to the extent of labelling it a 'discursive fiction'. The third were Habermasian theorists of communication who pushed for transcendence beyond the 'Cartesian monological subjectivity' in favour of 'discursive intersubjectivity'. The fourth were the empirical cognitive scientists who sought to 'prove empirically that there is no unique scene of the Self', besides a 'pandemonium of competing forces'. The fifth were concerned ecologists, who squarely 'blame(s) Cartesian mechanicist materialism' that enabled massive and ruthless exploitation of nature. The sixth were post-Marxists who reduced the Cartesian subject to the 'bourgeois thinking subject rooted in class division'. The seventh were feminists who charged that the Cartesian subject 'is in fact a male patriarchal formation'. Finally, there were the Heideggerian proponents of Being, who stressed the need to interrogate the 'horizon of modern subjectivity' and whom Žižek pinpoints as producing 'current ravaging nihilism' (Žižek 1999: 1).

The Cartesian subject, which has dominated Western thought since the dawn of modernity, is being questioned and even disowned by those who are pushing the discourse of the 'death of the subject with a capital "S" and who strongly believe in the existence of multiple subjects suffixed by a small "s"'. Ernest Laclau has written that 'Perhaps the death of the Subject (with a capital 'S') has been the main precondition of this renewed interest in the question of subjectivity' (Laclau 1996: 20). What is, therefore, under critique within the Western academy is the existence of a transparent thinking subject whose intentions and actions were predictable.

The notion of a transparent thinking and transcendental subject is said to be obscuring the 'obverse, the excessive, unacknowledged kernel of the *cogito*, which is far from the pacifying image of the transparent Self' (Žižek 1999: 2). It ignores the existence of what Žižek terms 'a certain excessive moment of "madness" inherent to *cogito*' (Žižek 1999: 2). Excessive moments of madness are often realized during times of genocides such the Rwandan one of 1994 and in the practices of fascist politics whose examples include Benito Mussolini's regime in Italy, Adolf Hitler's regime in Germany, the apartheid regime in South Africa, Idi Dada Amin's regime in Uganda, and many others. What also made subjectivity the topic of animated debates was the 'structural impasse', born out of the increasing rejection of the transparent and transcendental Cartesian subject.

Ernesto Laclau and Chantal Mouffe (1985: 114–122) pushed the frontiers of knowledge of the subject beyond the 'structural impasse' when they argued that all identities were relational and were produced through articulatory practice, which actively worked to name and fix the meanings of social identities by linking them to such signifiers as 'industrial worker', 'African peasant' and others. According to Peter Hudson (2006: 301), articulatory practice worked to transform 'elements' into 'moments', 'floating signifiers' into 'determinant meanings' (see also Laclau and Mouffe 1985: 113). The debates on the subject within Western academy happened at a time when questions were being posed about the tyranny of meta-narratives and ideology.

In the African academy, however, the debate is not about the complex postmodernist, post-structuralist, Lacanian philosophies of subjectivity, and performative theories of subjectivity, espoused by Žižek, Laclau, and Judith Butler over questions of contingency, hegemony and universality (Laclau 1994; Žižek 1999; Butler, Laclau and Žižek 2000). The preoccupation of studies of the subject in Africa is about how coloniality constructed and represented African subjectivity, how the signifier of blackness has been used by the 'Other' to deny Africans a dignified space in the world, and how liberatory discourses ranging from Negritude to the African Renaissance have tried to facilitate and empower the African subject to 'find access to its soul, to its identity in order to discover the source of how it relates to itself and to the rest of the world' (Eze 2010: xi).

Therefore, this chapter delves into the African debates, building on the notions of the 'Cartesian subject' as a background to explore how the 'Western subject' came into being, how it matured into a 'master subject' (growing from *cogito ergo sum* to *ergo conquistus*, that is, from 'I think, therefore I am' to 'I conquer, therefore I am') in the fifteenth century. The focus of this chapter is on how the drive for self-mastery by the Cartesian subject (here read as the Western subject) grew into a desire to master the world and those 'Other' subjects that existed outside Western civilization, and the implications of this for African subjectivity.

The central proposition here is that one cannot fully understand the essence of African subjectivity without first of all gaining knowledge of the Western subject as it played an important role in the construction, naming, mapping, and representation of African subjectivity as the 'Other'. The attempts by Africans to construct, name, and represent themselves have remained hostage to invented colonial discourses, Western racial templates that were developed during the age of colonial encounters, and African counter-discourses that were finding it difficult to free their liberatory episteme from the immanent logic of colonial racism. This point is clearly articulated by Frantz Fanon, who raised the problem of pitfalls of consciousness and the crisis of repetition without change that resulted in an African trajectory of liberation developing and fossilizing in a strange manner: moving from 'nationalism' to 'ultra-nationalism', to 'chauvinism', and finally to 'racism' (Fanon 1968: 125).

As this circuitous trajectory unfolded, ideas of African unity suffered from fading 'quicker and quicker into the mists of oblivion' as a 'heart-breaking return to chauvinism in its most bitter and detestable form' occupied the centre of African politics (Fanon 1968: 157–158). Fanon's analysis is reinforced by the Asian scholar Kuan-Hsing Chen who argued that 'Shaped by the immanent logic of colonialism, Third World nationalism could not escape from reproducing racial and ethnic discrimination; a price to be paid by the colonizer as well as the colonized selves' (Chen 1998: 14).

African people's attempts to reinvent themselves as dignified subjects risk moral degeneration through the reproduction of racism and xenophobia. This tendency cannot be fully understood without delving deeper into how the human subject in general emerges as constituted by a void that generated a sense of doubt and lack. The African subject in particular emerges in Western thought as lacking substance, lacking being, lacking soul, lacking history, lacking writing, lacking rationality, lacking civilization, lacking development, lacking democracy, and lacking human rights. This negative representation of the African subject by the 'Other' as constituted by deficits lies at the root of African struggles that sought to reverse negative discourses and representations rooted in colonialism. During the current age of empire and global coloniality, one of the most enduring discourses promoting the idea of African subjectivity as lacking something is that of development, which today plays the role that the discourse of civilization did in the nineteenth century.

I therefore refer to identity and development as ticklish subjects in African Studies. The term ticklish captures the sensitivities generated by debates on African subjectivity and development that excite both pleasant and unpleasant sensations. The numerous adjectives used in the process of 'Othering' Africans as a child race, lacking knowledge, lacking learning, lacking civility, lacking common sense, as barbarians, as rude, silly, superstitious, nasty, dirty, dejected and lazy, to mention just a few, could tickle both laughter and anger, depending on which side of the power structures one is located.

In the nineteenth and twentieth centuries, negative representations of Africans were propagated by travellers, missionaries, colonialists and anthropologists, and today the non-governmental organizations (NGOs) and the media do the same job. Both discourses of identity and development continue to provoke some sensitive reactions as they touch on the supposedly 'absent centre of ontology' of the African subject, to borrow a term from Žižek. The negative representations of Africans as 'people without souls', 'people without intelligence', 'people without history', 'people without civilization', 'people without writing', 'people without development', 'people without democracy', and 'people without human rights' amount to consistent attempts to deny humanity to Africans.

The Latin American scholar Ramón Grosfoguel's work helps in understanding the unfolding of the trajectories of the representations of the Western subject's *alter ego* in epochal and polemic terms across the entire span of human history from the dawn of modernity to the present. The episteme of inferiorizing the 'Other' is consistent. This is how he put it:

> We went from the sixteenth-century characterization of 'people without writing' to the eighteenth century and nineteenth century of 'people without history', to the twentieth-century characterization of 'people without development' and more recently, to the early twenty-first century of 'people without democracy'. (Grosfoguel 2007: 214)

Today the Modernist grammar and logic of alterity is carried in development discourses and is hidden behind humanitarian pretensions and concerns about poverty. Theoretically speaking, Ernesto Laclau (2005: 65) wrote about subjectivity as an activity of 'constructing the "people"' and scholars like James Ferguson (1990) and Arturo Escobar (1995) articulated the idea of development as one of the Euro-American world's powerful technologies of subjectivation involving the cultural, social, and economic production of Africa in particular and the so-called Third World in general, as 'inventions'. Escobar elaborated that the notion of development must be understood historically as an idea emerging from the centre of Western thought informed by imperatives of power to name and construct human subjectivity in binary terms of developed and underdeveloped people and places (Escobar 1995: 10).

At the centre of notions of development are 'regimes of discourse and representation' that produce identities, making it exist as a discursive field carrying a particular epistemology that results in Orientalizing some people and their civilizations. If development is understood as a discourse, then it is indeed a process through which social reality is imagined and comes into being. It is a form of articulation of knowledge and power that cannot be simply depoliticized into mere life issues of poverty and depravity (Ferguson 1990; Escobar 1995).

Development discourses have been easily accepted by African governments to the extent that in the 1960s, every African leader's office had an unwritten sign that announced that the citizens had to be silent as development was taking place (Ki-Zebo cited in Mkandawire 2011: 15), and even today African governments are preoccupied by the issue of development, something which might indicate the dynamics of subjection. Here Judith Butler's harnessing of the Foucauldian notions of subjection to explain how subordinated individuals and communities ironically attached themselves to and came to be physically invested in their own subordination, becomes very useful. If development discourse emerged as part of the global imperial designs of subjectivation, as part of the articulation, construction and representation of African subjectivity as constituted by catalogues of deficits and a series of 'lacks', the emerging question is that of how and why Africans and their governments have fallen into the idea of Africa as an underdeveloped locale in global history.

In her book entitled *The Psychic Life of Power: Theories in Subjection* (1997), Butler sought to explain how conformity and attachment to subjection emerged. Butler's theory of subjection emerged within a context of a concern about how women, including those who had embraced feminist theories, had developed an 'attachment to pernicious and subordinating norms of femininity' that persist 'alongside a rational critique of those very norms in and on the same self' (Allen 2006: 200). It is a useful theory that explains the ways in which ambivalent processes of becoming a subject emerge in and through subjection to power structures and relations. It helps in explaining the emergence of interpellated subjecthood that is passionate about some of those technologies of subjection that it is expected to resist and defeat. There is no doubt that development discourse emerged from the centre of global imperial discourses of Enlightenment, modernity and coloniality that constructed African subjectivity as lacking something.

What has not been fully explained by Africanists and African scholars is why the same discourse of development, shot through by open 'Orientalist' and 'Westernizing' thinking, has become a main and legitimate preoccupation of African governments. Butler puts the question this way: how does a 'power that at first appears external, pressed upon the subject, pressing the subject into subordination, assume … a psychic form that constitutes the subject's self-identity?' (Butler 1997: 3). Her answer is that 'the subject is the effect of power in recoil', that is, the subordinated subject is formed by the power it is resisting to the extent that its identity becomes dependent upon the relations of power that shape it (Butler 1997: 6).

Consequently, any radical dismantlement of those power relations that shaped the subordinated subject's identity is experienced as threatening 'the subject's identity and sense of self' (Allen 2006: 201). Today, if one tells African people to abandon thinking about development, because it is one of the most enduring and seductive aspects of global imperial designs, they are quick to doubt your sanity simply because they have become prisoner to it despite its subordinating and Orientalizing undertones, which sustain the idea of African subjectivity as constituted by a lack. Butler elaborates that the subject is in fact 'a subject of power', meaning that it belongs to power and articulates its condition of formation and emergence – it is 'radically conditioned' by power to the extent of living and articulating it (Butler 1997: 14–15).

It would seem that the imprisonment of the African subject within the discourse of development that was initially imposed with the aim to 'Other' it, to explain the African subject's inferiority and prohibit it from entering the world with dignity equal to the Cartesian subject, and its present preoccupation with it, vindicates Butler's argument that a prohibition turns the subject on itself and against itself (Butler 1997: 202). Preoccupation with development in Africa has taken the form of a gesture of 'self-reproach', and 'self-beratement' as if African people's identity could not be complete without the achievement of development, which up to today is not easily defined beyond the discourse of 'catching up' with the Euro-American world. But Thandika Mkandawire, a leading intellectual voice on African development, articulated the idea of 'catching up' in this way:

> The idea of 'catching up' entails learning not only about ideas from abroad but also about one's capacities and weaknesses. 'Catching up' requires that countries know themselves and their own history that has set the 'initial conditions' for any future's progress. They need a deep understanding of their culture, not only for self-reaffirmation, but in order to capture the strong points of their culture and institutions that will see their societies through rapid social change ... The real issue about 'catching up' is not that of simply taking on every wretched instrument used by their pioneers to get what they have – wars, slave labour, child labour, colonialism, Gulags, concentration camps – but of finding more efficacious and morally acceptable ways of improving the life chances of millions of poor people.... There would be no point in investing so much in the study of history if it involved simply regurgitating scripts that countries must follow. (Mkandawire 2011: 13)

The development discourse including its articulation as 'catching up' or development as a 'good change', by Chambers (1995: 174) and more recently by Peter Stewart (2011: 38–47), is a notion that has been embraced by Africans and through it they seek recognition by those who depicted

them as a deficient people, as a backward people, and as incomplete subjects. Amy Allen has this to say about the subject:

> Subjects are the kinds of creatures who actively take up and enact their
> own position as subjects, who rearticulate and reiterate the norms to
> which they are subjected; thus, when disciplinary regimes produce sub-
> jects, they thereby also produce the possibility of their own subversion.
> (Allen 2006: 204)

The African logic is that if they attained development that was equivalent
to and even ahead of the Euro-American world, then they would be able
to stand up and articulate themselves with dignity. The predominance
of development discourse in Africa and its acceptance by African people
as a possibility is partly explained by the African people's struggles to
cover the void in their subjectivity. Casting the development discourse
in Althusserian terms, one can say that it is a term by which Africans
have been hailed by global imperial designs and they have responded
through acceptance of the terms by which they have been hailed (e.g.,
Hey, you there!) (Butler 1997: 108; Allen 2006: 204). What is often ignored
in this rush to embrace the discourse of development is that it carries
within it coloniality as an embedded logic that enforces control, domination, and exploitation, disguised in the language of salvation, progress,
modernization, and accompanied by myths of being good for every one
(Mignolo 2005a: 6).

   But to further interrogate the notion of void, lack and deficits as constitutive of the essence of the subject, the work of the French psychoana-
lyst Jacques Lacan becomes very important. It helps in understanding
the ontology of the subject as 'constitutively split' (miscognition of the
self and alienation) as well as constituted by a void (lacking a sense of
self) (Lacan 1966; Hook and Neill 2008: 248). In Lacanian thought on the
subject, 'lack' is 'a constant and inescapable condition' (Hook and Neill
2008: 248). The sense of 'lack' propels the subject into 'identificatory acts
which aim precisely to deliver a positive (symbolic-imaginary) identity
to that which has no positively defined essence' (Hook and Neill 2008:
248). What is important about the Lacanian perspective on subjectivities
is that it provides a clear and rational basis for why the Cartesian subject
embarked on various activities including voyages of discovery, imperialism, and colonialism, as part of its 'unceasing attempts to cover over its
constitutive lack' (Hook and Neill 2008: 248).

   In the process of seeking 'fullness' of essence, the subject conjures
up fantasies, which provides an imaginary means of attainment of the
'impossible ends' of cohesiveness and autonomy from dependency on
the socio-symbolic order (the material world of being and social norms)
(Lacan 1973; Hook and Neill 2008: 248). In short, Lacanian thinking on
the subject reveals it as ontologically precarious, operating 'in and be-

tween' different registers of the imaginary, the symbolic, fantasy, and the real. The imaginary speaks to one's 'sense of self' (ego-identity or self-image); the symbolic speaks to the discursive and socio-political and linguistic terrain of operation within which the subject gains significa-tion into such identities as black or white and African or European; and the real speaks to that difficult part of understanding subjectivity, that is, pre-subjectivity mode of being that is impervious to symbolization and naming (Glynos and Stavrakakis 2008: 256–274). The last useful La-canian concept is that of fantasy as the invention of the subject itself through its unconscious response to its sense of void and lack to try and capture *jouissance* (lost enjoyment and promises of fullness) that is thought of as lying beyond the socio-symbolic horizon (Glynos and Sta-vrakakis 2008: 262). A good example is the notions of heaven and para-dise in Christian thought.

It would seem that the Cartesian subject that Lacan has helped to un-mask appropriated the colonial encounters to continue its drive to attain *jouissance* and fullness, through a simple process of transferring its own doubt and sense of lack into the essence of the 'Other'. Through inven-tion of the 'Other' as deficient and constituted by 'lack', the Cartesian subject attained some sense of *jouissance* and fullness. No wonder that the invention of Africa became nothing but a by-product of the Western subject's imagination that concretely operated through invented dis-courses that portrayed a vision of African people as the 'Other side' of 'Western imaginary frontiers' (Eze 2010: 19).

The African subject immediately became Europe's alter ego, result-ing in what the celebrated Palestinian intellectual Edward Said (1978) termed 'Orientalism'. Said stated that by Orientalism he meant several things. At one level, 'Orientalism expresses and represents that part cul-turally and even ideologically as a mode of discourse with supporting institutions, vocabulary, scholarship, imagery, doctrines, even colonial bureaucracies and colonial styles' (Said 1978: 2). At another level, 'Orien-talism is a style of thought based upon an ontological and epistemologi-cal distinction made between "the Orient" and (most of the time) "the Occident"' (Said 1978: 2). At yet another, third level, '"Orientalism" is a Western style for dominating, restructuring, and having authority over the Orient' (Said 1978: 3).

In short, the concept of 'Orientalism' is useful for capturing the West's historical, cultural, and political perceptions of non-Westerners as the 'Other'. It is an important concept that reveals Western thought as 'abyssal thinking' that prevented the 'Other' from representing itself and preventing self-understanding. In this context, the African subject emerged as an 'offshoot of distilled historical forces of Western racialism and Negro activism (pan-isms)' (Eze 2010: 17). The difference between the Western subject and the African subject, in terms of their relationship to the notion of lack, is that the former felt it and the latter was represented by the former as lacking core ingredients of subjecthood.

So far Frantz Fanon provides the most comprehensive theory of African subjectivity in his *Black Skins, White Masks* (2008) [1952]. He presented colonialism as fundamentally a laboratory of construction of white citizens and black subjects. At the centre of colonialism was a powerful but contingent social relation, whereby being white became a radical difference from being black. Whiteness indicated possession of identity and sovereignty whereas blackness magnified lack of identity and lack of self-control. The second main feature of colonialism was 'asymmetry' in interdependence between white and black to the extent that whiteness became the master signifier that proclaimed the illusion of white self-sufficiency and full autonomy, which became so seductive to Africans that they craved being white. Eventually, Africans (blacks) became torn apart 'between two impossibles', these being 'to be white and to be black – the first barred and the second an impossibility in its own terms as there is no black being' (Hudson 2012: 3).

It is clear from Fanon's analysis that colonialism was constructed and managed in such a way that it left black people with nothing to hold onto. Peter Hudson (2012: 3) argued that the 'colonial symbolic is so constructed' that there is 'no orthopedic support for an identity [for blacks] – just a whiteness forever eluding him and a blackness that doesn't exist in any case'. This imposition of a crisis on the mind of black people was achieved through deployment of various colonial technologies of subjectivation which Fanon described as 'a constellation of postulates, a series of propositions that slowly and subtly work their way into one's mind and shape one's view of the world of the group to which one belongs' – 'a thousand details, anecdote stories' which were 'woven ' into 'prejudices, myths, the collective attitudes of a given group' (Fanon 2008 [1952]: 133).

No doubt the formation of African identities has been characterized by crises and conflicts. Deeply lodged within the discursive formation of African identities were complex historical processes and activities ranging from the politics of naming, physical cartography, religious demarcations, physical boundaries, cultural mapping, and linguistic classifications to ideological gerrymandering. Frederick Cooper (2002: 11) captured the complexity of the idea of Africa itself through the term 'many Africas'. He added that 'At any one moment, Africa appears as a mixture of diverse languages and diverse cultures; indeed, linguistically, it is the most varied continent on earth'. One of the key questions which preoccupied such scholars as Valentin Y. Mudimbe (1998) has been: how did the idea of Africa as the home of a people called Africans first emerge? Cooper has correctly noted that 'It is only by looking over time that "Africa" begins to appear' (Cooper 2002: 11).

Already Mudimbe (1988) has revealed that the idea of Africa was born out of multiple layers of inventions and constructions that commenced with explorations, 'voyages of discovery', missionary activities and colonial processes. What emerged were equally complex African identities that were not underpinned by any semblance of common cultures and languages, proving beyond doubt that Africa is a continent rather than a country. This means that extrapolations of 'African' culture, identity in the singular or plural remain quite slippery as the notions tended to swing unsteadily between the poles of essentialism and contingency (Zeleza 2006: 13). The discursive formation of African identities was permeated by complex externally generated discourses about the continent as well as by internally generated paradigms and politics through which the idea of Africa has been 'constructed and consumed, and sometimes celebrated and condemned' (Zeleza 2006: 14).

The making of the African continent itself as both an idea and cartographic reality cannot be understood outside a clear understanding of such identity-forming processes as Orientalism, Occidentalism, imperialism, colonialism, apartheid, and ideologies such as pan-Africanism, Garveyism, Negritude, African Personality, and the Black Consciousness Movement, right up to African Renaissance thought. These are some of the major discourses among others that established the world of thought in which African people conceived their identities (Mudimbe 1988). The encounters between Europe and Africa, often dated back to the fifteenth century, inaugurated the active imagining, naming and profiling of Africa in the West. To make meaning of what the explorers and missionaries encountered in a new environment, they had to mobilize their existing Western knowledge and then re-inscribe the new geographical spaces and inhabitants in European discourse (Ahluwalia 2001: 20). Mbembe noted that:

> It is now widely acknowledged that Africa as an idea, a concept, has historically served, and continues to serve, as a polemical argument for the West's desperate desire to assert its difference from the rest of the world. In several respects, Africa still constitutes one of the metaphors through which the West represents the origin of its own norms, develops a self-image, and integrates this image into the set of signifiers asserting what it supposes to be its identity. (Mbembe 2001a: 2)

But for the current age, Mbembe (2006a: 144) identified the dominant elements of current intellectual thinking on Africa as dominated by a concern with histories of freedom and modernities such as the nature of liberal democratic order mediated by complex politics of shifting and contested citizenship and identity; how to ensure ethical conditions of human peaceful coexistence that are sensitive to politics of recognition and inclusion across the globe; and questions of social justice in an unjust global economic, social, and political order. Politically explosive identities and the associated politics of difference, alterity, as well as resurgent discourses of nativism, xenophobia, and autochthony continue to impinge on definitions of belonging, citizenship and the broader politics of being African. But let us begin with how Europeans constructed global identities in general before focusing specifically on the making of African identities in particular.

The making of the modern social order

The modern world order is a product of Western imagination and this argument does not in any way mean to undermine or dismiss the agency and role of Africans in the making of history. It is meant to capture the over-determining role of global imperial designs in disciplining people and spaces on behalf of capital. Cartography led to the naming of what today are called continents, with their current reduction of importance so that they are now seen merely as the homes of various ethnic identities. The foundational technologies of the social classification of human populations according to race were rooted in Darwinian social evolutionism and dualism from within which Eurocentrism emerged. In this scheme of things, those people who were called Europeans deployed the benefits of Western modernity and techno-scientific knowledge to appropriate the course of human history so as to place themselves at its centre as its privileged agents. In this context, modernity becomes a name for the historical process within which Europe began its progress towards world hegemony, carrying within it a dark side called coloniality (Mignolo 2005: xiii).

Europe was promoted and represented as the centre of the world while other parts of the world were pushed towards the periphery (Quijano 2000b: 551). Most present-day social identities are traceable to the dawn of the period of the construction of the present-day power structures and colonial encounters. Geocultural identities like America, Africa, and Far East and Near East (Asia), as we know them today, were named and cartographically created by the Western subjects. Even though the West was not responsible for the settlement of different continents by different racial and ethnic groups, the logic that drove colonial encounters ensued from Europe and significantly changed the racial complexion and power configurations across the world.

In the first place, Iberians conquered, named and colonized Central and South America, which was dominated by different peoples such as the Aztecs, Mayas, Chimus, Aymaras, Incas, and Chibchas. Through colonization and naming, these people re-emerged with the singular identities of Indians and Latinos. In the second place, those peoples who were enslaved and taken out of their African homes bearing various ethnic names such as Ashanti and others were renamed as Negroes or blacks to distinguish them from Indians and Europeans (Quijano 2000b:

551–552). Africa emerges in all this as 'simultaneously a metaphor for otherness and a paradigm of difference' (Eze 2010: 20). During the same time, Western identities of being whites, Europeans and Americans emerged as superior beings when compared to others. This is how the Peruvian sociologist Anibal Quijano summarized the processes:

> The first resultant from the history of colonial power had, in terms of colonial perception, two decisive implications. The first is obvious: peoples were dispossessed of their own and singular historical identities. The second is perhaps less obvious: their new racial identity, colonial and negative, involved the plundering of their places in the history of the cultural production of humanity. From then on, there were inferior races, capable only of producing inferior cultures. The new identity also involved their relocation in the historical time constituted with America first and with Europe later: from then on they were the past ... At the other hand, America was the first modern and global geocultural identity. Europe was the second and was constituted as a consequence of America, not the inverse. The constitution of Europe as a new historic entity/identity was made possible, in the first place, through the free labour of American Indians, blacks, and mestizos ... It was on this foundation that a region was configured as the site of control of the Atlantic routes, which became in turn, and for this very reason, the decisive routes of world market ... So Europe and America mutually produced themselves as the historical and the first two new geocultural identities of the modern world. (Quijano 2000b: 522)

Three discursive processes were at play that created Eurocentrism: articulation of human differences into dualisms of capital/pre-capital, Europe/non-Europe, primitive/civilized, traditional/modern, all underpinned by a linear conception of human history from the state of nature to European society; the naturalization of the cultural differences between human groups by means of their codification by the idea of race; and the distorted-temporal relocation of all those differences into non-European identities that were represented as enclosed in an unchanging past (Quijano 2000b: 552–553). Nelson Maldonado-Torres wrote about the myth of continents as artificial creations of Western modernity. This is how he put it:

> In this sense it is possible to say that the 'myth of continents' is part of a larger racial myth in modernity formed in relation to imperial enterprises, in which continents denote not only space but also a well ordered hierarchy of customs, habits and potentials that are said to inhere in the people who live in them. Spaces thus become gendered and coloured, just as the forms of rationality, tastes, and capabilities of the peoples who occupy them. (Maldonado-Torres 2006: 3)

Even Christian imaginary was mobilized to reify the racialized imagination of the world. For instance, biblical narratives of Noah's three sons were assigned to each of the continents: Asia to Shem, Africa to Ham and Europe to Japheth (Mignolo 2005a: 24). What is clear is that the spatial, topological, and cartographic set-up of the world today is nothing but a product of European deployment of the coloniality of power (Lewis and Wigen 1997).

Negative perceptions of Africa as a home of inferior people and as a dark space emerged from this imperial scheme of things and African identities have continued to be reconstructed since that time into barbarians, primitives, natives, blacks, Negroes, Bantu, Africans and others, in typologies existing across time and space. The traceable trajectory of the development of African subjectivity, therefore, eventually proceeds like this: from barbarians to slaves, from slaves to colonial subjects, from colonial subjects to citizens. But we need to delve deeper into how this happened and capture the struggles involved and the discourses formulated by Africans in their attempts to reverse colonialism and its technologies of subjectivation.

The continent and its people

Michael Onyebuchi Eze (2010: 17) argues that contemporary Africa is a product of the 'distilled historical forces of Western racialism and African counter-discourses'. But its discursive formation is complex and has a chequered history. The name Africa is an external label. Its roots are traceable to Roman times when it was used with specific reference to North Africa before it was extended to the whole continent at the end of the first century before the current era. Zeleza (2006: 15) noted that the cartographic application was both gradual and contradictory as the idea of Africa became divorced from its original North African coding to be used with specific reference to sub-Saharan Africa. Gayatri Spivak had this to say:

> *Africa*, a Roman name for what the Greeks called 'Libya', itself perhaps a Latinization of the name of the Berber tribe Aourigha (perhaps pronounced 'Afarika'), is a metonym that points to a greater indeterminacy: the mysteriousness of the space upon which we are born. *Africa* is only a time-bound naming; like all proper names it is a mark with an arbitrary connection to its referent, a catachresis. The earth as temporary dwelling has no foundational name. (Spivak 1991: 170)

Inventions and ideas are always open to manipulation, re-constructions, representation and historical engineering. The idea of Africa has not been immune to these dialectics (Mudimbe 1988; Mudimbe 1994). The processes of 'invention' and 'construction' of Africa left the definition of an African open to contestation and appropriation just like all other identities. Such processes as the slave trade, imperialism and colonialism not only further complicated the picture but also actively played a role in the making of African identities. African nationalism and pan-Africanism emerged as antitheses to imperialism and colonialism but did not succeed in settling the question of who was an African. No wonder then that the question of who is or was an African has come to occupy not only scholars but also politicians in postcolonial Africa.

The safest way to define Africa is as a reality as well as a construct, 'whose boundaries – geographical, historical, cultural, and representational – have shifted according to the prevailing conceptions and configurations of global racial identities and power, and African nationalism, including, pan-Africanism' (Zeleza 2006: 15). Among key historical processes that contributed to the current identity complexion of Africa is the slave trade. Walter Rodney (1982), who studied how Europe underdeveloped Africa, identified the slave trade as one of the greatest forced migrations in history, which had and continues to have profound effects on the development of the African continent's identity complexion and meaning of Africanness.

The notion of blackness itself came from the experience of diaspora in the Caribbean and Americas, where it emerged as an essentialized marker of servitude and exposure to social death. Blackness as a key aspect of African subjectivity signified being open to enslavement, being an object, being a thing and being a commodity, within grand imperial designs. Blackness was also used to underscore the notion of apartness, that is, blacks seen as having no part in Western civilization, closed out of the world of human beings worthy of dignified treatment. William B. Du Bois elaborated on how enslavement impacted on black identity. This is what he wrote:

> In order to establish the righteousness of [African enslavement], science, religion, government and industry were wheeled into line. The word 'Negro' was used for the first time in world history to tie colour to race and blackness to slavery and degradation. The white race was pictured as 'pure' and superior; and the black race as dirty, stupid, and inevitably inferior; the yellow race as sharing, in deception and cowardice, much of this colour inferiority. Mixture of races was considered the prime cause of degradation and failure in civilization. (Du Bois 1965: 20)

But the slave trade not only led to the formation of a diaspora in the Americas and Caribbean but also to the formation of whole states composed of Africans transposed to other parts of the world such as Haiti and Jamaica. The formation of African diasporas led to the popularization of the name Africa and the increasing racialization of African identity (Zeleza 2006: 15). With this reality in mind, the definition of an African became even more complex and transnational. Jean-François Bayart (2000) wrote about racial mixing (miscegenation) that unfolded in tandem with the unfolding of trans-Atlantic commerce leading to the production of *assimilado* (mixed race) elites in the Angolan and Mozambican region as one of the legacies of the slave trade. The long presence of Arabs on the continent also impacted on race issues, particularly through their active role in the trans-Saharan slave trade that targeted black people.

External definition of Africa is not only attributed to white people. Rather, the slave trade contributed to the creation of a large black diaspora and these enslaved people began to think of themselves as Africans. The term 'African' was used interchangeably with the name 'Ethiopian', which was used mainly by those black people who had converted to Christianity. As argued by Cooper (2002: 12), the term Ethiopian 'evoked Biblical histories of King Solomon and the Queen of Sheba. "Ethiopia" or "Africa" marked their place in a universal history'. Cooper (2002: 12) added that 'The point is that "Africa" emerged as a diaspora asserted its place in the world'. At another level, a combination of mercantilism, imperialism, colonialism and other processes introduced whites, Indians and foreign diasporas such as that of the Lebanese, as well as other people, into the African continent from as far back as the fifteenth century and even before. Colonialism introduced race as a major factor in the definition of belonging and citizenship in Africa. Mahmood Mamdani (1996) argued that colonialism produced colonial states that were divided into citizens and subjects. What emerged out of the encounters between indigenous Africans and the colonizing whites was a complicated citizenship in which the white settlers tried to exclude the natives from full belonging. Mamdani (2001a) described this problem as 'the settler-native' question that has continued to haunt countries like South Africa and Zimbabwe which contained large populations of white settlers. Mamdani went further to argue that:

> In the context of a former settler colony, a single citizenship for settlers and natives can only be the result of an overall metamorphosis whereby erstwhile colonizers and colonized are politically reborn as equal members of a single political community. The word reconciliation cannot capture this metamorphosis ... This is about establishing, for the first time, a political order based on consent and not conquest. It is about establishing a political community of equal and consenting citizens. (Mamdani 2001a: 66)

Mamdani's intervention addressed three key questions in African studies. The first is about the structure of political power inherited from the colonial state that did not facilitate easy construction of a genuinely postcolonial African nation-state. The second is about the place of local African ethnic powers rooted in precolonial histories but also invented by colonialism within the postcolonial state that continued to function as a source of identity fragmentation. The third is about how African postcolonial states failed to transcend ethnic differences that sat uneasily with notions of civic conceptions of belonging and citizenship. But Mamdani's main point is that the 'native question' preoccupied and determined the form of rule which shaped colonial experience and postcolonial African governments are finding it hard to transcend this tradition (Mamdani 1996).

This preoccupation with the 'native question' made the African state differ from the European nation-state. Indirect rule as a key colonial system of administration impinged on identity formation to the extent that the postcolonial state had the task of de-racializing civil society, de-tribalizing native authority and developing the economy in the context of unequal international relations (Mamdani 1996: 287). But Pal Ahluwalia (2001: 104–105) criticized Mamdani for constructing a new set of binaries, of the citizen and subject, while he set out to demystify others. This criticism, however, does not diminish the force of Mamdani's argument on the pertinent issues of identity construction and power articulation in Africa.

Mamdani's analysis of colonial forms of governance and how they impinged on African identities is amplified by other scholars like Cooper (2002), who tackled the issue of re-tribalization of Africa as colonialists abandoned the rhetoric of 'civilizing mission'. On the other hand, African nationalism as a deeply interpellated phenomenon had no capacity to solve the 'settler-native' question. Rather it turned the scale upside down, putting the 'native' where the settler was and struggling to pull the settler down to where the native was. While colonial officials initially presented colonialism as a civilizing mission aimed at remaking Africans in the image of Europeans, Cooper (2002: 18) argued that by the 1920s colonial governments had realized the cost of such ventures and the limits of colonial power to govern directly using white personnel. Colonial polices shifted from the rhetoric of 'civilizing' Africans into attempts to invent African tradition.

As put by Cooper (2002: 18), the aim was to 'conserve African societies in a colonizer's image of sanitized tradition, slowly and selectively being led towards evolution, while the empire profited from peasants' crop production or the output of mines and settler farms'. It was during this period that the idea of Africans as tribes that were static and bounded gained importance. Those Africans who had imbibed Christianity and received Western education became identified as troublesome 'detribalized natives' who had lost their roots and traditions.

According to Eze (2010: 25), the civilized and educated Africans became frowned upon and ignored partly because they symbolized and represented a threat to the colonial presence and partly because of their unending demands for full participation in the colonial project, including claiming civil and political rights. The black educated elite were products of the contradictory logic of colonial domination. Sir Donald Cameron, a colonial official, explained the colonial logic of preferring to work through those Africans who were considered to be uncorrupted children of nature, in this way:

> If we set up merely a European form of administration, the day will come when the people of the *Territory* will demand that the British form of administration shall pass into their hands ... If we aim at indirect administration through the appropriate Native Authority ... founded on the people's own traditions and preserving their own organization, their own laws and customs purged of anything that is 'repugnant to justice and morality' we shall be ... capable of standing the shock which will inevitably come when the educated native seeks to gain the possession of the machinery of Government and to run it on Western lines. (Cited in Iliffe 1979: 322)

Another important contour in the debates on the identity of Africa and Africans is one that tries to reduce African identity to the 'phenotype'. As argued by Michael Neocosmos, in the attempts to define Africa at such institutions as the World Bank and even at the United Nations, there is the tendency to see North Africa as more part of the Middle East rather than Africa. In this case Africa is defined as 'Black Sub-Saharan Africa', largely inhabited by Bantu-speaking peoples (Neocosmos 2008: 7). The other colonially produced layer of identity in Africa is that which stressed the division of Africans into Francophone and Anglophone identities. All these identity-related complexities speak to the complexity of colonial discourse, its ambivalences, ambiguities and contradictions that impinged directly and indirectly on the emergence, constructions and representations of African subjectivity.

To Mbembe (2001b), African identities were a product of the combination of the 'the elsewhere' and 'the here' (*Eurozine* at www.eurozine. com). This is because even before the age of colonialism, Africa was already open to external influences that further complicated its identity. Bayart (2000: 217) has successfully challenged the Hegelian idea of an African continent that is 'cut off from all contacts with the rest of the world ... removed from the light of self-conscious history and wrapped in the dark mantle of the night'. Bayart argued that if the history of Africa is understood from the perspective of *longue durées*, the continent was never isolated from the rest of the world, in particular Europe, Asia and the Americas.

This was evidenced by early Christianity in Ethiopia, the spread of Islam on the coasts, the establishment of Austronesian colonies in Madagascar, and regular trade with China, India, the Persian Gulf and the Mediterranean. Due to these connections, the eastern and southern African parts were for centuries integrated into the premodern economic systems of the so-called Orient. According to Bayart (2000: 218), even the Sahara Desert was never an 'ocean of sand and desolation' that demarcated and cut off sub-Saharan Africa from external influences. A combination of all the processes outlined above reinforces Anthony Kwame Appiah's (1992) argument that Africa is not a primordial fixture but an invented reality.

But while it is true that Africans were not constructed from the same cultural clay, they have experienced some common historical processes that to a large extent justify their claim of a common identity. But the contingency of African identities should not be used to deny that we today have an identity called African. There is abundant evidence that numerous peoples and societies have carved out places of their own across the African continent, in the process creating their own 'little Africas, each laying their bricks across the huge and intricate cartographic, cognitive, and cultural construct, known as "Africa'" (Zeleza 2006: 18).

The flows of commodities, capital, ideas, and people have coalesced to create an African identity. Even the tragedies that have befallen the continent, including conflicts and underdevelopment, have indirectly provoked a consciousness of being African. In short, even negative interpretations of Africa that created a picture of Africa as 'possessing things and attributes' never 'properly part of human nature', contributes to the consciousness of being African (Mbembe 2001a: 1). The ongoing works of pan-Africanists informed by discourses of African Renaissance and the languages of unity used at meetings at the African Union and pan-African Parliament consistently build the idea of a pan-African identity.

Inevitably Africa is a continent that is ceaselessly seeking to free itself from the Eurocentric egoisms of singularities that continue to inform conventional and often insensitive notions of identities imposed on it and its people by external agents. Francis B. Nyamnjoh (2001: 25) noted that Africans continued to refuse to be defined by particular identity markers imposed on them from elsewhere, choosing instead to draw from the competing and different influences in their lives as individuals and communities. This is in line with the nature of identity as a relational concept that is always permeated through and through by imperatives of power and resistance, subjection and citizenship, action and reaction as well as by naming and controlling.

The idea of Africa emerged within a complex terrain of naming, conquering and controlling of weaker parts of the world by powerful ones. African politics of identity construction are permeated by complex desires for freedom and self-reconstitution after centuries of domination of the African continent and its people by the powerful nations of the North. Even the identity politics that dominated and haunted the post-Cold War world were partly informed by popular struggles for material redistribution and justice, autonomy, and desires for existential integrity and security in a context of collapsing and failing states and weakening regimes.

African nationalism and the making of Africans

The construction and reconstruction of African subjectivity in Western thought has been fraught with ambivalences. This ambivalence was well captured by Homi Bhabha, who informed us that Western subjects during the heyday of colonialism 'construed the colonized as a population of degenerate types on the basis of racial origin, in order to justify conquest' and the continuation of colonial rule (Bhabha 1994: 70). Building on Bhabha's analysis, Michael O. Eze has eloquently demonstrated the essence of ambivalence in these words:

> On the one hand, colonial discourse posits that the colonized subject is a strange creature whose peculiar and strange nature is a cause for curiosity and foreboding, and the 'other' who exists outside the Western parlance, that is, the inferior 'other' outside Western civilization. On the other hand, colonial discourses shift focus to and emphasize the attempt to civilize and domesticate colonized subjects and abolish their radical 'otherness' bringing them inside Western understanding through the Orientalist project of constructing knowledge about them ... In this way, the representation(s) and constructions of 'otherness' become split by the very ambiguous location of the colonized subject – simultaneously located in and out of Western epistemology. The colonized subject is at once a social reality that is an 'other' and at the same time wholly known and visible. The attempt to dilute the radical 'otherness' of the colonized subject is undermined by the continual fantasies imposed upon the colonized subjects. (Eze 2010: 30)

Therefore, African modes of self-writing inevitably carried the ambivalence of being inside and being outside the human oecumene as defined by the West. From this ambivalence, there emerged another option available to the Africans, which Albert Memmi captured in these words: 'The first ambition of the colonized is to become equal to that splendid model and to resemble him to the point of disappearing in him' (Memmi 1974: 164). This option was a result of the colonization of African minds resulting in an identity crisis that Fanon articulated in these words:

> I am no longer a subject, and I cannot define myself as a subject; I am an 'object' to be defined by the colonial paradigm. The only way to redeem my humanity is to embrace the dominating worldview, be like them in order that my humanity might be appreciated – to wear that mask of civilization. (Fanon 1968: 86)

There were indeed some Africans, particularly the early educated elite, who believed in the rhetoric of colonialism as introducing civilization and they tended to try to live out the promises of assimilation before realizing the hypocrisy and double standards embedded in this rhetoric. Toyin Falola noted that African thinkers became fragmented into many camps, ranging from 'traditionalists' who insisted that the old ways are better and that Western civilization should be avoided; 'assimilationists' who argued that change could come if Africans accepted Western civilization; to 'middle-roaders', who advocated embracing certain aspects of Western civilization while retaining many aspects of tradition (Falola 2001: 30). Examples included Blaise Diagne who was a typical example of an assimilationist, James Africanus Beale Horton who had a vision of a free and united Africa, Edward Blyden who is considered the father of the notion of 'African personality', Léopold Sédar Senghor who developed the notion of Negritude, and many others (Hensbroek 1999). This split consciousness became manifest in the nationalism that developed, reflecting a deep identity crisis, which led Robert W. July to conclude that:

> The crisis of identity was especially acute for the African intellectual. Each had received a Western education. All were cultural hybrids, recognizing the merits of both backgrounds, eager to bring them together in consonance in a modern Africa that was itself an amalgam of indigenous and Western institutions and values. Attracted to the West, they found they could not simply walk away from their Western heritage. The more they protested an African identity, the more it testified to the hold of the West. Could the Western demon be exorcised? Could African culture free itself to develop in un-self-conscious self-absorption? (July 1987: 220)

Leading African politicians like Léopold Sédar Senghor, Kwame Nkrumah, Kenneth Kaunda, Julius Nyerere and others contributed to the debates on the 'self-definition' of Africans. Negritude was one of the earliest examples of African attempts to respond to their definition by the 'other' as subjects characterized by deficits. Senghor, for instance, tried to respond to the Cartesian 'I think, therefore I am' essentialization of the Western subject by proclaiming that the African subject is defined by the dictum 'I feel, therefore I am'. Senghor also tried to define the African subject as a spiritual being compared to the Western subject that defined itself as a rational being. This is how Senghor articulated his theory of the African subject:

> Thus, the Negro-African sympathizes, abandons his personality to become identified with the other. He does not assimilate, he is assimilated. He lives a common life with the Other, he lives in a symbiosis ... 'I think, therefore I am', Descartes writes. The Negro-African could say 'I feel, I dance the other, I am'. At any rate Negro-African speech does not mould the object into rigid categories and concepts without touching it; it polishes things and restores their original colour, with their texture, sound and perfume; its innate humanity – it would be more accurate to speak of sub-reality. European reasoning is analytical, discursive by utilization; Negro-African reasoning is intuitive by participation. (Senghor 1998: 115–116)

Even those who are critical of Negritude, like Wole Soyinka, have emphasized that it should not be underestimated as an attempt to achieve the laudable goal of closing the discourse of an African subject that was marked by deficits, while at the same time pointing to its crisis of imitation and counter-factualization of European thought (Soyinka 1976: 150). Kwame Nkrumah also contributed to the elaboration of African being as a 'primarily a spiritual being, a being endowed originally with a certain inward dignity, integrity and value. It stands refreshingly opposed to the Christian idea of the original sin and degradation of man' (Nkrumah 1964: 86). He added that the African being was ontologically socialist. On the pertinent issue of intersubjectivity and interdependence of civilizations, Nkrumah was very clear that:

> With true independence regained, however, a new harmony needs to be forged, a harmony that will allow the combined presence of traditional Africa, Islamic Africa and Euro-Christian Africa, so that this presence is in tune with the original humanist principles underlying African society. Our society is not old society, but new society enlarged by Islamic and Euro-Christian influences. A new emergent ideology is therefore required, an ideology which can solidify in a philosophical statement, but at the same time an ideology which will not abandon the original humanist principles of Africa.
>
> Such a philosophical statement will be born out of the crisis of the African conscience confronted with three strands of present African society. Such a philosophical statement I propose to name philosophical consciencism, for it will give the theoretical basis for an ideology whose aim shall be to contain the African experience of Islamic and Euro-Christian presence as well as the experience of traditional African society, and, by gestation, employ them for the harmonious growth and development of that society. (Nkrumah 1964: 70)

Nkrumah elaborated that philosophical consciencism is a medium of enabling African society 'to digest the Western and the Islamic and the Euro-Christian elements in Africa, and develop them in such a way that they fit into the African personality' (Nkrumah 1964: 79). Unlike Senghor, Nkrumah did not advocate the assimilation of Africans into Western culture but the reverse, that is, the assimilation of Western cultures by African society. The predication of African subjectivity on humanism is also noticeable in Kenneth Kaunda's strong belief 'in the worth and possibilities of man and I expect him some day to achieve perfection' (Kaunda and Morris 1966: 19).

Kaunda believed that colonialism was a phase where humanity was devalued whereas nationalism 'restored our self-confidence, for it taught us what we could do together as men ... It was humanity in revolt that won us our freedom. I believe we triumphed not because we had the greater power, but because we occupied the superior moral position'

(Kaunda and Morris 1966: 21). Like Nkrumah and Senghor, Kaunda articulated African subjectivity as constituted by principles of humanity that included forgiveness. It would seem that some African leaders thought it to be their duty to restore humanity to the world and redeem both Africans and Europeans so as to transcend colonialism as a state of disgrace and fallen humanity.

But born out of a continent whose identity has remained hard to define, African nationalism was never a straightforward human affair. Its progenitor, pan-Africanism, was never a singular phenomenon. Pan-Africanism fell into six versions reflective of the complexities of historical experiences of the African people. These versions were: trans-Atlantic, Black Atlantic, continental, sub-Saharan, pan-Arab, and global. Zeleza (2003) summarized the core imaginations in each of the six pan-Africanisms as follows: proponents of the trans-Atlantic version imagined a pan-African world stretching from the continent right into the diaspora in the Americas; the Black Atlantic version preoccupied itself with the African diasporic community in the Americas and Europe, excluding continental Africans; the continental version was primarily focused on the unification of continental Africa; the sub-Saharan and pan-Arab versions restricted themselves to the peoples of the continent north and south of the Sahara, with pan-Arabism extending into Western Asia and the Middle East; the global version sought to reclaim African peoples dispersed to all corners of the world into one identity.

But it was continental pan-Africanism that became popular in Africa at the end of the Second World War. Its main achievement was the formation of the Organization of African Unity (OAU) in 1963. Continental pan-Africanism accepted the cartographic realities imposed by the Berlin Conference of 1884 to 1885 that resulted in the partition of Africa into various colonial states and protectorates. But again there was no consensus among African leaders on how to proceed concretely to create a union of African states. African leaders became fragmented into two broad camps, namely the Casablanca and the Monrovia groups. Led by Ghana under the charismatic Kwame Nkrumah, the Casablanca block wanted immediate formation of the United States of Africa. The Monrovia group, led by Nigeria, opted for the gradualist approach towards integration of the African continent into a single government (Adejumobi and Olukoshi 2008: 3–19). African nationalism had an ambiguous relationship with pan-Africanism. Sometimes it reinforced it and at other times subverted it due to issues of sovereignty. This tenuous relationship between pan-Africanism and nationalism was well expressed by Julius Nyerere when he said:

> Indeed I believe that a real dilemma faces the pan-Africanist. On the one hand is the fact that pan-Africanism demands an African consciousness and an African loyalty; on the other hand is the fact that each pan-Afri-

canist must also concern himself with the freedom and development of one of the nations of Africa. These things can conflict. Let us be honest and admit that they have already conflicted. (Nyerere 1967: 57)

This also reflected that African nationalism was itself a very complicated socio-political phenomenon. It was mediated by complex antinomies of black liberation thought and propelled and also constrained by ideological conundrums it sought to transcend (Ndlovu-Gatsheni 2008: 53–86). It was fuelled by a complex combination of ambiguous local struggles, diverse micro- and macro-histories and sociologies. Emerging within a colonial environment, it was already deeply interpellated by the immanent logic of colonialism including its racist and ethnic undertones, but was not completely disconnected from the fading precolonial past, myths, spiritualities, and memories.

African nationalism was also shaped from 'above', meaning its enunciations of Africanity remained open to continental and global ideologies, as they were seen as fitting and advancing local agendas. It is within this context that nationalism incorporated such external and diasporic ideologies as Garveyism, Negritude, Marxism, Ethiopianism, Christianity, pan-Africanism, Leninism, Maoism, Republicanism and liberalism, mixing these with indigenous resources such as land entitlement, for instance (Ndlovu-Gatsheni 2009b). African nationalism was basically a particular form of imagination of freedom. Decolonization was a popular term to define this imagined freedom. Five fundamental questions preoccupied African nationalists as active constructors of African subjectivity and prophets of freedom: how to forge national consciousness out of a multiplicity of racial and ethnic groups enclosed within the colonial state boundaries? How to fashion a suitable model of governance relevant to societies emerging from colonialism? What models of economic development were relevant for promotion of rapid economic growth to extricate postcolonial societies from underdevelopment? What role was the independent African postcolonial state to play in the economy and society? How might the new African political leaders promote popular democracy and mass justice that was denied by colonialism?

No African leader had clear answers to these complex questions. All nationalists embarked on trial and error backed by various grand theories of re-making African identity. Such early African ideologies of liberation and theories of African subjectivity as Negritude and African Personality emerged within this context. It is now common knowledge that Negritude first developed among African and Caribbean artist-intellectuals and emerged in Paris in the early 1930s. It was a complex reaction to the racism and alienation that was cloaked under the French colonial policy of assimilation. Its objective was to reverse the representations ascribed to the Africans, turning those negative identities into positive images. Léopold Sédar Senghor explained it this way:

In what circumstances did Aimé Césaire and I launch the word *negritude* between 1933 and 1935? At that time, along with several other black students we were plunged into a panic-stricken despair. The horizon was blocked. No reform was in sight and the colonizers were justifying our political and economic dependence by the theory of the *tabula rasa* ... In order to establish an effective revolution, our revolution, we had first to divest ourselves of our borrowed attire – that of assimilation – and assert our being; that is to say our *negritude*. (Cited in Ahluwalia 2003: 32)

At least five imaginations of community, citizenship, belonging and co-existence are discernible from the history of freedom and constructions of African subjectivity. Zeleza (2006: 14) identified these as the nativist, the liberal, the popular democratic, the theocratic, and the transnational prescriptive models. The nativist imagination of African freedom has elicited widespread condemnation for being backward-looking, navel-gazing and founded on false metaphysics of difference and alterity (Mbembe 2002b: 629). It is feared as the crucible of reverse racism and the nursery for xenophobia and even genocide. All these developments are taking place within a context in which a postcolonial world that Africans aspired for has remained elusive.

Even within the decolonization projects that were meant to create independent nations and sovereign states in Africa, as well as re-creating African subjectivity, there were some autochthonous and nativist forces functioning as hidden scripts that propped up parochial rather than broader pan-African identity. For instance, Benita Parry (2004: 40) revealed that, whenever intellectual considerations of the narratives of decolonization were taken, 'rhetorics in which nativism in one form or another are evident' was noticeable. But whenever these forces of nativism and xenophobia were noticed, scholars were quick to pull out the disciplining theoretical whip to dismiss these as catalogues of epistemological errors, masculinist dissent and as anti-racist racism. No one was bold enough to deploy the unsententious interrogation of such articulations as reflecting the problematic politics that were inherent in the development of the idea of Africa itself and construction of African identities (Namnjoh 2006b).

It is not surprising that as some African postcolonial states became weaker and others, such as Somalia, Liberia, Sierra Leone and the Democratic Republic of Congo (DRC), collapsed, identity politics became the dominant mode of mobilization further fragmenting the already weakened states and inflaming more conflicts. Contemporary postcolonial politics is dominated by such negative phenomena as xenophobia in South Africa, nativism in Ivory Coast and Zimbabwe, 'ethnic cleansing' in the DRC and the Sudan, and genocide in Rwanda. The idea of Africa and African identity is constantly reproduced within these conflict situations.

Zeleza (2008) linked African conflicts to the complex discursive constructions and conjunctures of Africa's political economies, social identities, and cultural ecologies as configured out of specific local, national,
and regional historical experiences and patterns of insertion into and
engagement with an ever-changing world-system. On the other hand,
Sara Dorman, Daniel Hammet and Paul Nugent (2007: 4) noted that 'It is
arguably in the nature of nationalism to distinguish insiders from outsiders'. The politics of 'Othering' and creation of strangers generated the
Rwandan genocide and fuels other conflicts across the continent as African identities continue to be defined and redefined for various purposes.
These examples vindicate the argument that the development of the idea
of Africa as it unfolded across various historical epochs ceaselessly generated conflicts and new crises.

Ivor Chipkin (2007: 2) argued that Africans across the continent
'emerged primarily in and through the process of nationalist resistance
to colonialism'. This is indeed a logical argument since nationalism was
and is basically a process of making people-as-nation and nation-as-state
(nation-building and state-building) through the homogenization of differences (Ndlovu-Gatsheni 2009a). African nationalism was therefore a
grand project and a process of making African citizens out of colonial
subjects.

The achievement of political independence did not result in full realization of the dream of transcending the distortions cascading from colonialism. Decolonization constituted the fantasy that propelled the African people towards *jouissance*. During the struggles for independence
the colonialists became framed as the 'evil Other' who prevented the
African societies from realizing enjoyment and full subjectivity called
citizenship. African nationalism embodied the fantasmatic narrative
that fostered solidarity among colonized peoples. The African nationalists indeed structured the social subjects' partial enjoyment through the
introduction of carnivals, commemorations, and festivals characterized
by consumption rituals. The narrative was that with the attainment of
political independence, the African subject had completed a 'long walk
to freedom' that ran like this: from barbarian to slave, from slave to colonial subject, from colonial subject to citizen (full being) (Eze 2010: 43).

But as noted by Grosfoguel, the decolonization process resulted in
'the myth of a postcolonial world'. The reality is that the 'heterogeneous
and multiple global structures put in place over a period of 450 years did
not evaporate with the juridical-political decolonization of the periphery over the past 50 years. We continue to live under the same "colonial
power matrix". With juridical-political decolonization we move from a
period of "global colonialism" to the current period of "global coloniality"' (Grosfoguel 2007: 219). Within present-day global coloniality, African subjectivity is still defined by deficits and lacks. This time, Africa
and Africans are no longer depicted as lacking civilization, lacking writ-

ing and lacking history. They are now said to be lacking development, lacking human rights, and lacking democracy.

Africanity: the course remains the same, but full steam ahead!

Robert W. July (1987) argued that the African as a human being who suffered multiple levels of alienation is in a struggle to regain his/her identity, that is, his Negritude, through a conscious existential effort. Even Fanon conceded that Negritude was a good start but did not go far enough. What lies ahead is whether the African will ever be able to define him or herself and be able to represent himself or herself beyond the straitjackets imposed on him or her by colonialism and global coloniality. Archie Mafeje argued that Africans were not going to talk about freedom if it were not denied at some point, about anti-racism if they had not experienced being victims of racism, proclaim Africanity if it had never been degraded and denied and about Afrocentrism if there were no Eurocentric negations (Mafeje 2011: 31–32).

For Mafeje, Africanity is a rebellion based on conscious rejection of past transgressions, and a form of negation of negation. He went further, to say: 'Africanity is an assertion of an identity that has been denied; it is a pan-Africanist revulsion against external imposition or refusal to be dictated to by others' (Mafeje 2011: 37). But the issue of Africanity becomes even more complicated in a context where resurgences of the complex politics of xenophobia and nativism are increasing concurrently the unfolding of Africa's drive for renewal and institutionalization of pan-African unity. This raises the question of who is an African. Ali Mazrui (2009) distinguished Africans into two categories: 'Africans of the blood' and 'Africans of the soil'. He went on to say:

> Africans of the blood are defined by racial and genealogical terms. They are identified with the black race. Africans of the soil, on the other hand, are defined in geographical terms. They are identified with the African continent in nationality and ancestral location. (Mazrui 2009: xi)

Among Africans of the soil, Mazrui included the light-complexioned Libyans, Egyptians and Tunisians, whose genealogical roots are traceable to somewhere else. Diasporic Africans, located in such places as Jamaica, Haiti, Brazil, the Caribbean and the U.S.A., are defined by Mazrui as Africans of the soil but not of the blood. Whites located in Africa, like Afrikaners and other such racial minorities as Arabs (Afrabians, to use Mazrui's term), Lebanese, Hellenes, Indians and others, were African of the soil too (Mazrui 2009: xi–xv). The intervention by Mazrui is one way of dealing with the question of who is an African. He concluded that 'Africans of the soil and Africans of the blood were converging into newer and more comprehensive identities' (Mazrui 2009: xv). The strength of Mazrui's intervention on this controversial and sensitive issue is that he adopts a non-xenophobic but historical definition of African-ness.

But there are other classificatory and definitional schemes that have been deployed to isolate one as an African, namely racial, geographical/ territorial, and consciousness/commitment to Africa (Adibe 2009: 16). The racial definition is found wanting in that it does not cater for those who were not black: it wrongly assumes that all black people were Africans. The geographical/territorial definition simplistically categorizes all those born in the continent of Africa as Africans (Prah 2009a). Its key weakness is that it excludes those Africans living in the diaspora who define themselves as Africans.

The definition of African-ness through consciousness of being African is one that was used by the former president of South Africa, Thabo Mbeki, in his famous 'I am an African' speech of 1996. It is pragmatic and politically loaded. But its weakness is that it is too fluid, to the extent of embracing 'anyone expressing any sort of interest in African affairs' (Adibe 2009: 22). Kwesi Kwaa Prah is also very critical of the definition of the African as anyone and anybody 'committed to Africa'. He sees it as a South African version of definition of 'African-ness' that is specific to the context of a former apartheid society (Prah 2009b: 57–60). His conclusion is that:

> It is important to remember that, the African identity (like all identities) is not a closed phenomenon cast in stone. It is a changing condition with evolving terms and conditions of reference. What remains the touchstone in this evolutionary process is that the emerging understanding of Africanness must be emancipatory for Africans and the rest of humanity. (Prah 2009b: 60)

Mohamed A. Eno and Omar A. Eno (2009: 63) have tried to synthesize the complex discourses of African identity to come up with six different typologies of Africanity drawing from the complex histories of Africa. The first is what they termed 'Africanity of accident of geography'. This category consists of those people who happened to be in Africa without their wish to be there. A good example can be that of Indians and Malays who came into Africa as indentured labour and slaves respectively. These individuals and groups found themselves living in the continent by virtue of circumstances beyond their control. The second category they termed 'Africanity by birth'. This refers to those people who were born in Africa regardless of their race or ethnic group, or even political ideology or cultural doctrine. They are the majority of the people populating the continent. The third category is designated as 'Africanity by settlership'. This category speak directly to citizens of colonial regimes who arrived in the continent from the time of colonial encounters onwards, forming settler communities under colonial governments and not leaving the continent after the end of colonialism.

The fourth category consists of 'Africanity by culture or acculturation'. Among these are people who may not be African by ethnicity but who have lived in the continent long enough to have adopted the way of life, culture and tradition of the average African. The fifth caters for 'Africanity by ideology': this category embraces people like Frantz Fanon, who was not an African by birth (although of part-African descent), but whose understanding and sympathy for Africanity was in no doubt and who contributed immensely to the development of theories of African liberation to the extent of being celebrated within the continent. The final category designates 'Africanity by pretension or circumstantial Africanity'. This group comprises individuals or societies who use African identity as and when it suits them for their specific purposes: in other words, circumstantial Africans. Members of this group are not pleased to be identified with blackness, be it by values, ideology, culture, ethnicity or any other quality except by 'the accident' of existing on the continent (Eno and Eno 2009: 63).

These various discourses on being African leave us with the message that African identity is complex, multi-layered and open to different interpretations. Both the idea of Africa and African identities were and are best understood as states of being and becoming that should be better studied as open-ended and as work-in-progress. What are disturbing are proclivities and tendencies towards the degeneration of identity politics into various antipathies that run counter to the broader pan-Africanist philosophy on unity and hopes for a prosperous postcolonial African world.

Conclusion

With reference to the whole universe, Ernesto Laclau (1996: 18–19) argued that people are today coming to terms with their finitude and with the political possibilities that it opens. He elaborated that at this point of crisis lies the potential for liberatory discourses. The Modernist promises of emancipation driven by the Cartesian subject have been exhausted and this opens the way for the beginning of freedom for those whom the Cartesian subject has been pushing to the peripheries of humanity. The idea is that the exorcization of the Cartesian subject and its dislocation is accepted as opening new vistas of freedom through acknowledgement of the existence of multiple subjects inhabiting many worlds. From a decolonial thought, this might be an opportunity for transcendence over universality into pluriversality.

What must be emphasized is that African identity is still in formation. It is still coming into existence, but within a modern world order that is dominated by anti-black sentiments and practices, put in place by colonial encounters. This chapter has, therefore, not brought Western discourses on subjection and subjectivity into dialogue with African discourses on the same issues: it has also mapped out in broad historical strokes the global and African terrain within which processes of subjection and subjectivity are unfolding. More importantly, it has underlined the fact that all those counter-discourses developed and fashioned by Africans since the time of colonial encounters, such as Ethiopianism, Garveyism, Negritude, pan-Africanism, African Personality, African socialism, African Renaissance and many others, constitute the African response to subjection and a consistent search for a dignified place in the world. They are also props, which seek to enable Africans to free themselves from the restrictions, inferiority and subjectivity constituted by catalogues of deficits and series of lacks. Because they emerge with the stomach of a racialized beast, they inevitably assume at various points what one would term 'anti-racist racism' to borrow a term from Jean-Paul Sartre (1976) and at other times what Gayatri Chakravorty Spivak termed 'strategic essentialism' (Spivak 1988a; Spivak 1988b).

The future of Africa requires an African Renaissance that consistently seeks to transcend the vicissitudes of histories of Orientalizing, inferiorizing, and Othering of African subjectivity. Such an African Renaissance should be informed by a deep knowledge of African history and global history that enables Africans to avoid being imprisoned by some global technologies of subjectivation, like development discourse, that repeat the rhetoric of modernity while perpetuating the idea of an African subjectivity that is constituted by a catalogue of deficits and lacks. The African subject must not remain imprisoned by those regimes of power set in motion by global imperial designs because such a reality risks degeneration of consciousness and crises of repetition without change. What is needed is an African subject who is able to rise above discourses of equilibrium to embrace those fluid identities in consonance with a rapidly changing world order, where the subject would be able to fight, negotiate and achieve its set liberatory goals. Such an African subject must be an active player rather than a spectator enclosed in the neurosis of victimhood.

In practical terms, the African subject of the twenty-first century must be imbued with the politics of fighting for a dignified place in the world through direct confrontation with the peripherizing and subalternizing technologies of global imperial technologies underpinning and reproducing the current racialized, patriarchal, Euro-American-centric, Christian-centric and asymmetrical organized world order together with its anti-black behaviours. This struggle cannot be won unless Africans are united so as to be able to bargain as a collectivity, one which has endured subordination and subjection to white power for centuries. The African subject of the twenty-first century must also be a confident one, capable of rejection of the discourses of deficits and lacks without degenerating into the celebration of mythical golden ages and also able to rise above the false belief in salvation and liberation coming from the West. It must be responsible, an African subject operating above discourses of impossibility and fully embracing the discourses of possibility informed by principled and consistent liberation struggles against clearly defined obstacles operating within the epistemological, institutional, economic and political realms wherein global coloniality is hiding.

CHAPTER 5

Subjection and Subjectivity in South Africa

Introduction

I owe my being to Khoi and the San ... I am formed of migrants who left Europe to find a new home on our native land ... In my veins courses the blood of the Malay slaves who came from the East. Their proud dignity informs my bearing, their culture a part of my essence ... I am the grandchild of the warrior men and women that Hintsa and Sekhukhune led, the patriots that Cetswayo and Mphephu took to battle, the soldiers Moshoeshoe and Ngungunyane taught never to dishonor the cause of freedom ... I am the grandchild who lays fresh flowers on the Boer graves at St Helena and the Bahamas ... I come from those who were transported from India and China ... Being part of all these people and in the knowledge that one dare contest that assertion, I shall claim that I am an African.

(Thabo Mbeki 1996: 31–36)

In the political catechism of the New South Africa, the primary enquiry remains the National Question. What is the post-apartheid nation? Who belongs or is excluded, and on what basis? How does a 'national identity gains its salience and power to transcend the particularities of ethnicity and race?

(Colin Bundy 2007: 79)

In contemporary South Africa, the issue of race continues to permeate every aspect of public life. Citizens are regularly required to indicate their race when filling out government or other official forms; race often plays a role in decision on whether a job application or the application for admission to certain university programmes are successful; in political debates the race of various protagonists are often noted when evaluating the merits of their contributions; and when judges are appointed to positions on the High Court, Supreme Court of Appeal or Constitutional Court, the race of the appointees are duly noted or commented upon and taken into account when considering the suitability of the candidate for appointment to the bench ... We cannot escape our own race. Even when we claim that we have escaped the perceived shackles of race, we are merely confirming its presence by our stated yearning for its absence. This is the paradox: while South Africa has emerged from a period in its history in which the race of very individual played a decisive role in determining their life chances, allocating social status and economic benefits on the basis of race in terms of a rigid hierarchical system according to which very person was classified by the apartheid state as either white, Indian, coloured or black and allocated a social status and economic and political benefits in accordance with this race, in the post-apartheid era the potency of race as a factor in allocation of social status and economic benefit has not fundamentally been diminished in our daily lives – despite a professed commitment to non-racialism contained in the South African Constitution, the founding document of our democracy.

(Pierre de Vos 2010: 2)

It is surely time … for historians to formulate detailed questions about how South Africa has been conceived and imagined, to analyse the different forms in which ideas about South Africa and South African societies have developed over time, and to trace the ways in which the South African 'problem' or predicament has been conceptualized. In order to do so, we should remember that the struggle for South Africa has long been, and continues to be, a struggle to become South African.

(Saul Dubow 2007: 72)

The post-apartheid South African Constitution that was officially adopted in 1996 re-constructed various ethnicities and races into non-racial citizens called South Africans. The erstwhile natives and citizens were expected to metamorphose quickly into equal citizens through constitutional interpellation and subjectivation. Blackness and whiteness had been badges of exclusion and inclusion that had to be removed and a badge of a 'New South Africa' had to be put on. The Truth and Reconciliation Commission (TRC) had been unrolled as a therapeutic means separating the dark days of apartheid from the birth of the bright days of the 'rainbow nation'. A new national consciousness of a South Africa being living in a democratic society in which both white and black people belonged as citizens was expected to develop as quickly as possible if the imaginary of a post-apartheid nation-state had to survive.

This chapter is written during the eighteenth year after the end of apartheid. The issues of subjection and subjectivity are still simmering. There is no clear trajectory. This chapter deals with three related issues of the subject, subjection and subjectivity. It is a historical study that explores how a geographical expression (South Africa) has undergone different translations into an identity of a people. The historical analysis slices right through the imperial and colonial encounters of the nineteenth and early twentieth centuries, right up to the present constructions of the 'rainbow nation'. What is clearly expressed is that South African national identity is very much a contested work-in-progress, which is open to different interpretations and trajectories. Racialized and ethnicized identities formed under imperialism, colonialism, and apartheid continue to hang like the memories of a nightmare over the body politic of the rainbow nation, refusing to go away, and continuing to throw up toxic questions around issues of the subject, subjection and subjectivity, that impinge on delicate issues of belonging, citizenship, entitlement, and ownership of resources like land and mines.

What is interrogated here are complex human experiences and subjectivities that developed from the time of colonial encounters to the present on the southern tip of the African continent that is today called South Africa. South Africa experienced the longest, most complicated, and most painful struggle for an inclusive South Africanness (subjectivity). Like all subjects, the South African subject is at once a product and agent of history as well as a site of experience and memory, an agent of knowing as much as an actional being, seeking liberation from domination and repression. Subjectivity, on the other hand, is not just the outcome of social control and subjection (domination), it is a domain through which subjects thought through their circumstances and made sense of their predicaments and contradictions (Biehl, Good and Kleinman 2007: 14). Subjectivity is definable as 'an awareness of oneself' that has no stable content, which at 'every moment brings different "self" to light' (Rorty 2007: 34). Read from the perspective of the subject, subjection and subjectivity, the history of South Africa reveals a painful and complex process of a people undergoing 'catharsis and reidentification' (Rorty 2007: 38). The history of black subjects is that of a 'people who are thrust to the outskirts of institutional power, regularly exposed to police violence, or battered by bureaucratic racism' (Kleinman and Fitz-Henry 2007: 54).

Broadly speaking, the history of South Africa might also be summarized as one characterized by four main discursive moments, namely those connected with the categorizations of Bantucization, Anglicization, Afrikanerization and Africanization, without ignoring the experiences of the San and the Khoisan whose painful experience is captured in Mohammed Adhikari's *The Anatomy of a South African Genocide: The Extermination of the Cape San Peoples* (2010). On Bantucization, Paul S. Landau (2010: xi) argued that the Bantu societies were 'historically well equipped to embrace and absorb strangers. Hybridity lay at the core of their subcontinental political traditions'. But Anglicization and Afrikanerization, which originated with the arrival of white people, brought ideas of radical difference if not fundamentalist ideas of racial differences. As put by Landau:

> Nineteenth-century European newcomers were different and attempted to repudiate mixing, politically and otherwise, albeit with only partial success. It was they who characterised, or mis-characterised, Africans as perennial tribesmen. (Landau 2010: xi)

This denial of co-presence was informed by Western 'abyssal thinking', predicated on racial hierarchies within the human species. The encounters between indigenous black people and Europeans marked the beginning of the construction of an unequal and racially divided society. What ensued from the encounter is what Thiven Reddy (2010) described as 'the construction of subaltern subjects in South Africa' informed by politics of 'radical difference'. This politics unfolded in terms of depiction of black people as 'savages'. This grew into the enslavement of indigenous black people, which 'enhanced and consolidated the importance of "colour" in the dominant discourse' (Reddy 2000: 11). Then white supremacy, through the politics of 'Othering', took the form of construction of whiteness as a moving 'frontier', carrying civilization by opening up 'tribal' communities that were closed within an ossified shell of tradition.

The notion of the 'frontier' conveyed a series of signifiers including representation of Afrikaners as active agents of historical change, as contrasted with agency-less Africans; and the establishment of fixed boundaries between white and black based on ideas of race and civilization, as well as victory of reason over 'unreason' (Reddy 2000: 33). Africanization is today one of those counter-discourses that emerged from various layers of resistance to the politics of radical difference to restore core aspects of *Bantucization*, those informed by traditions of embracing and absorbing strangers. This is why Nelson Mandela's reign was predicated on *ubuntu*. *Ubuntu* does not tolerate the politics of racial difference and the narcissism of minor differences.

On small events that otherwise matter

The Asian historian Sumit Sarkar argued that 'unimportant events of no obvious consequence which stick out and refuse to fit into any of the established patterns of historical reconstruction' are important as they 'afford oblique entry points into social history and can throw light upon dimensions obscured by dominant – all too often teleological – analytical frameworks' (Sarkar 1992: 3). One such dominant discursive framework is that, since 1994, various ethnic and racial groups of South Africa were coalescing into a new 'rainbow nation'. This thinking gained prominence during the reign of Mandela to the extent that competing and rival populist nationalisms that articulated issues of belonging, citizenship and ownership of resources from a nativist perspective were easily dismissed as anachronisms.

During this time, the rabid racists of the apartheid era were quickly re-inventing themselves into radical human rights activists whereas those who were considered to be dangerous communists and nationalist 'terrorists' were practically assuming a moderate position of committed builders of an inclusive nation-state and manifesting strong and genuine belief in true non-racialism. Nelson Mandela, who for over twenty-seven years was re-invented by the apartheid regime as a dangerous person who had to be banished to Robben Island, was fast assuming a new identity as father of the post-apartheid nation and an iconic symbol of reconciliation and unity. But beneath all this, the colonial and apartheid 'unconscious' provided a hidden script that lurked below the skin of the rainbow nation, occasionally coming into the open to remind the leaders of South Africa of the fragility of the national identity and emptiness of the notions of non-racialism imposed from above on 'former' racists who never apologised or repented for past racist sins.

The unconscious human beliefs about black and white that developed during the apartheid era continue to manifest themselves at times in the most detestable forms, threatening to tear apart the public imaginary of a rainbow nation. The most recent example has been the audacity of the artist Brett Murray (white) to artistically produce an offending portrait of President Jacob Zuma with his genitals exposed, the audacity of Goodman Gallery to publicly display such a piece of art and the audacity of the editors of *City Press* to place such a painting on their website. *The Spear*, as the painting is metaphorically titled, provoked heated debates about freedom of expression as enshrined in the South African constitution, and violation of dignity, the dignity of the president of the republic and of Zuma as president of the African National Congress (ANC), of Zuma as a person, and of Zuma as head of a family. It also offended black people in general. As a constitutional democracy, the contestations over the painting not only provoked public demonstrations but also judiciary intervention. But the best analysis so far about the implications of the painting for African subjectivity came from the theorist Peter Hudson. His analysis is worth quoting in *extenso* because it reveals what exactly is happening in South Africa and contextualizes everything meticulously. This is how Hudson explained it:

> The unconscious becomes transparent here – only the thinnest, most diaphanous of 'membranes' separates it from what is ordinarily and in which the unconscious is 'put' on display. Zapiro and Murray think they're telling us something about Zuma. No, they're telling us something about themselves and their audience. They're displaying the white unconscious, they're not telling us anything whatsoever about Zuma; they're enjoying their own unconscious fantasy even if, as they maintain, nothing could be further from their conscious intentions. They maintain they don't think about blacks in this way – but here it is, the white colonial image of the black, this just is – no two ways about it – it's a bit like the racist joke which isn't consciously planned but which just occurs to one, spontaneously one finds the word in one's mouth. And here it is, the black man and his penis, rather, the penis and the black man – once again. It's hard to believe in a way – that they could not see what they were doing while they were doing it – but what this shows is that this really is the white unconscious – they didn't think about it but this is what they've done ...
>
> If you take these objects out of the colonial frame – deprive them of their historic meaning – then what are they? Individual dignity eroded? Perhaps. But if you put them in their colonial frame, (as you have to),

then it isn't a matter of individual dignity – of any individual or of the individual, but it is a matter now of colonialism itself, i.e. the specifically black subject – as object – in the gaze of the white (self-possessed) master.

This is what liberalism, no matter how democratic, cannot appreciate: it cannot grasp what is at stake in these stagings of the colonial unconscious, because its very premises – an individualistic social ontology – won't allow it. On the other hand, the 'black' reaction has been I think, quite clear: a) they're seen as what they are, colonial objects, and b) 'something must be done' in response ...

From this black point of view what these objects show is precisely that colonialism is still with us – it isn't just 'structural inertia' combined with 'ANC corruption and mismanagement' that explains the ongoing racial distribution of life chances/assets in South Africa. Colonial identifications are still with us, and working silently to maintain the status quo. These objects discussed above are both revelatory of this and, at the same time, reinforce these identities. These objects stand out, however, because they're as close to not being silent, to being 'not silent' as the distinction between unconscious and conscious will allow. They're as close to being transparent to consciousness as it is possible to be, without being transparent to consciousness. Perhaps this explains something of the 'excess passion' that these objects have produced in the public space. (Hudson 2012: 9)

In the Žižekian sense, the *Spear* saga revealed the persistence of the 'white unconscious' that has always been embedded and present in social practice. Racism in South Africa is not expressed but realizable in various actions. It exists as part of an unconscious belief to the extent that white subjects behave in racist ways without being aware of doing so. The problem can be partly explained by the fact that the 1996 constitution simply 'prohibited' racism without dealing with structural issues that reproduce racism. The post-apartheid state became caught between a liberal democratic constitutional imperative that emphasized civil and political rights as indicators of freedom and the national democratic imperative informed by anti-colonialism that emphasized the need for transformation. Hudson (2012: 8) has correctly diagnosed that:

Liberal democracy doesn't recognize black experience – it says – this isn't the experience of colonialism – the struggle is over, we've got a liberal constitutional democracy – this kind of expression (colonialism – that is if liberal democracy even acknowledged its existence), isn't really colonialism – it's an *ersatz* colonialism, neutered by the very form of its expression – i.e. via freedom of expression in a liberal democracy. (Hudson 2012: 8)

Hudson's ideas on white political behaviour resonate with those of Achille Mbembe who articulates three discourses informing present-day white politics in South Africa and their attitude towards contemporary challenges facing South African society. The first is what he termed South 'self-absolution', whereby they wash their hands from any responsibility for the inequalities, poverty, and violence haunting post-apartheid South African society (Mbembe 2012b). They now apportion all the responsibility for these problems to the ineffective and inefficient government of the African National Congress (ANC), which they have dubbed as terribly corrupt. They also blame Africans for not working hard enough to pull themselves out of the quagmire of poverty. The scourge of violence is explained as a sign of African innate propensity for self-harming habits and by Afrophobia that the apartheid regime effectively dealt with through the policy of Bantustans that separated antagonistic tribes from each other.

The second trait that Mbembe identified is termed the 'Damascus Road' experience, which speaks of a biblical road that was travelled by those people, such as Saul, who persecuted Christians, only to be transformed by encountering the redemptive anger of God, which strikes Saul in the form of lightning, resulting in him becoming Paul, the renowned apostle. Mbembe used this argument to explain how the rabid white racists of yesterday (apartheid era) have been able to quickly turn themselves, soon after 1994, into radical democrats and defenders of the South African constitution and media freedom (Mbembe 2012b). Those who own large tracts of land, which they expropriated, gratis, in a typical colonial primitive style, whose land was accumulated from the Africans, are today the most vocal defenders of the ideals of inalienable property rights. The majority of them have organized themselves into the right-wing and neo-liberal-oriented Democratic Alliance (DA) that survives by using white-dominated courts and white-owned media to defend the status quo of inequalities and white supremacy. Others have organized themselves into AfriForum, which also uses the courts and media to sustain surveillance over black people and their black governing party. Through these means the white community has been able to claim a high ethical and moral ground and push the ANC into the corner where it is being seen as a threat to what they term 'our freedom' and democratic constitution.

The third strand characterizing white politics is what Mbembe (2012b) termed cries of 'reverse racism' and 'reverse victimhood', which is used to mask and hide real existing racism. Through this tactic the white community manages to escape from the shame and guilty conscience rooted in their construction of, complicity in and benefits gained from the apartheid regime. These three arguments provide an ideal entry point into analysis of the longstanding struggles and politics of becoming South African, which have remained highly contested and emotive. Hudson reinforced Mbembe's analysis when he elaborated that:

> The white colonial unconscious is a site of political struggle because its identificatory effects antagonize and subject the National Democratic

Revolution (NDR) – where a liberal democratic perspective implies tolerance and even silence, a national democratic state – because it is fundamentally challenged and put into question by this unconscious signifier
('Whiteness'), has 'to do something'. (Hudson 2012: 10)

The politics of racialization of ethnicities and ethnicization of races continues to raise its ugly head in a post-apartheid context where competition over resources, including jobs, invokes issues of who is an 'authentic' South African, entitled to resources. As recently as 15 February 2012,
Pieter Mulder, leader of Freedom Front Plus (FPP), could still reply to
President Jacob Zuma's State of the Nation Address of 9 February 2012,
which stressed the need for land reform, by saying:

> Sir, Africans in particular never in the past lived in the whole of South
> Africa. The Bantu-speaking people moved from the Equator down south
> while white people moved from the Cape to meet each other at the Kei
> River. There is sufficient proof that there were no Bantu-speaking people
> in the Western Cape and North-western Cape. These parts form 40 per
> cent of South Africa's land surface. (Mulder 2012)

Mulder harked back to the 'empty land' colonial invention, which was
used by the apartheid regime to deny that Afrikaners ever dispossessed
black people of their land. The 'empty land' thesis is also part of denying black people any claims to be 'authentic' subjects of the nation, who
are entitled to land. This revival of the debates on 'empty land', which
were corrected by historians (Marks 1980; Etherington 2010), confirms
the contestedness of South African national ideas today.

There are other numerous 'small events that matter' when understood within the context of the politics of the subject, subjection and
subjectivity. They include Thabo Mbeki's introduction and articulation
of the philosophy of African Renaissance that was easily interpreted as
a departure from Nelson Mandela's idea of a rainbow nation. Mbeki's
presidency became caricatured as a moment of re-racialization of identities (Glaser 2010: 3–40). The launch of the Native Club in April 2006 was
also interpreted as the brainchild of Mbeki's attempts to institutionalize the African Renaissance and exclude white races from the nation
(Ndlovu-Gatsheni 2007b; Ndlovu-Gatsheni 2008: 53–86).

Julius Malema's (the embattled and expelled ANC Youth League
leader) penchant for singing the liberation song 'Dubuli Bhunu/Shoot the
Boer' until he was taken to court over it, indicated, at the very least, a generational take on what was seen as the continuing liberation struggle, and
provided some evidence of a rising tide of black reverse racism. Further
to this, the ANC Youth League has, since 2010, pushed for nationalization
of the mines as a means of fulfilling ideals of economic emancipation.
The debate has incensed black neo-liberals and whites who own land and
mines as a threat to the private ownership of property, guaranteed by the

constitution and 1994 compromise. The compromise allowed 'colonists' to retain economic wealth in exchange for universal franchise and some form of redress (Planning Commission's Nation Building Diagnostic Document 2011: 2).

The *Mail and Guardian* of February 24 to March 2012 uncovered a 'Kommando Camp' run by a few right-wing Afrikaners located in a farm in Mpumalanga Province. Young Afrikaners were recruited and trained in Afrikaner commando-style military skills and were also indoctrinated with racist ideas to regard black people as their enemy (Gelder 2012: 24). Ideas of a separate Afrikaner nation were promoted as the young boys were urged to be ready for a day of bloodbath between blacks and whites. E. van Gelder discovered that the current South African flag was treated with utmost disdain and was used as a mat and a piece of cloth to clean the boots of the young recruits. The flag that was hoisted and revered was the pre-1994 apartheid one (Gelder 2012: 24). This is one case of denial of co-presence of Afrikaners and Africans as equal and consenting citizens of South Africa.

The net effect of racialization and ethnicization of identities on the southern tip of the continent is what Michael Neocosmos (2010) termed the invention of 'foreign natives' (Occidentalization of black people) on the one hand and 'native foreigners' (nativization of white races) on the other. This complex process proceeded in terms of two logics. The first was the logic of equivalence, which dissolved internal frontiers resulting in larger identities such as South Africans. The second is the logic of difference which dissolved the equivalences, creating internal frontiers, and highlighting internal antagonisms among both whites and blacks. Its well-known result was the fragmentation of black land areas into various Bantustans (Laclau 1994; Torfing 1999; Hudson 2006).

These recent events reflect how South Africa has for a long time existed as a contact zone where people of different ethnic and racial backgrounds converged, making it a cypher on whose terrain debates about belonging, identity, citizenship and national consciousness continue to mutate into different forms. This is a point that is captured in G.H. Calpin (1941), Anthony Marx (1998), Thiven Reddy (2000) and Ivor Chipkin (2007) where core issues that bedeviled the development of the idea of South Africa are interrogated. Calpin (1941: 9) posited that 'The worst of South Africa is that you never come across a South African'. Even how hard those who believe in the miracle of a rainbow nation can celebrate it, there is clear evidence that its future is not assured due to contestations over belonging, citizenship and resources.

The contestedness of national identity is amplified by three historians. Colin Bundy emphasized that the national question remained an important part of the political catechism of post-apartheid South Africa. It raises the questions of: 'What is the post-apartheid nation? Who belongs or is excluded, and on what basis? How does a "national identity" gain its salience and power to transcend the particularities of ethnicity and race?' (Bundy 2007: 79). Bundy is joined by Saul Dubow who urged historians to research into how South Africa has been conceived and imagined, interrogating the different forms in which ideas about South Africanism have developed over time, and tracing the ways in which the South African identity has been conceptualized. The continuing struggle is about 'becoming' South African (Dubow 2007: 72). Beyond the celebrated unity 'there remains the question of what is, and what is not, South Africa. Who are, and who are not, South Africans' (Ross 1999: 3).

The use of the 'rainbow' metaphor was an attempt to include various races and ethnicities into a single nation. It is a generous invitation to people of diverse cultures, languages, religions and races to unite under one nation. This is apparent in the country's coat of arms, which carries the message of 'Diverse People Unite'. But South Africa pushed the agenda of unity of diverse peoples at a time when other parts of the continent were experiencing narrowing conceptions of belonging and citizenship informed by what Peter Geshiere (2009) termed 'the return of the local' with its 'perils of belonging'. John L. Comaroff and Jean Comaroff (2009: 1) termed it 'Ethnicity, Inc.' (turning tribes into corporations) characterized by 'a lot of ethnic awareness, ethnic assertion, ethnic sentiment, ethno-talk; this despite the fact that it was supposed to wither away with the rise of modernity, with disenchantment, and with the incursion of the market'.

Indeed nowhere on the continent has the politics of identity been more prominent than in South Africa, during both the pre- and post-apartheid eras (Theron and Swart 2009: 153). South African leaders have not rested on their laurels to ignore the issue of identity and nation-building. The construction of a unique pan-South African nationalism that incorporated diverse ethnicities and races is ongoing and the challenging question is whether it will succeed in suturing and stabilizing this racialized and ethnicized society.

In his 'I am an African' speech, Mbeki (1998: 31–36) provided a historical and contextual definition of Africanness as something imposed by various histories ranging from voyages of discovery, to accidents on the Indian Ocean, imperialism, slavery, colonialism and various struggles and wars. To him, these histories and struggles were over 'being' and 'becoming' African. But despite Mbeki's efforts to define South African national identity as a historical production that is open for all to claim, the co-presence of 'whiteness' and 'Africanness' continues to raise sensitive aspects rooted in the intractable settler-native problem common to the majority of multi-racial societies born out of imperialism and colonialism (Friedman 2009: 79–83).

An appropriate historical approach is one that interrogates complex histories and unpacks ambiguous politics that coalesced towards the production and reproduction of South Africanism as a conflict-laden arena of claims and counter-claims to membership of the imagined and existing nation. Today one of the persistent popular quests in South Africa is for what Jean and John Comaroff (2003: 447) termed 'ID-ology'. This is a quest for 'a collective good, and sometimes goods, sanctioned by, and in the name of, a shared identity'. The term 'ID-ology' is also a reference to South Africa as a site within which various identities continue to struggle 'to express themselves in the politics of everyday life' (Comaroff and Comaroff 2003: 448).

But one of the negative manifestations of 'ID-ology' has been the upsurge of nativist and xenophobic politics that turned extremely violent in May 2008, claiming over sixty human lives (Nyamnjoh 2006; Neocosmos 2010). Within this xenophobic and nativist politics, possession of an ID (identity) book has become very important as a marker of being South African. The ID book, as part of the materialization of 'ID-ology', becomes useful as a basis of making claims on the state. Citizenship is confirmed through possession of an ID book. Employers have made possession of the ID book the essential pre-requisite for possible employment. This reality has forced immigrants from other parts of Africa to fight to acquire this document by fair or foul means. All this is a continuation of the struggles to 'become' South African.

Some theoretical issues

Eusebius McKaiser (2010: 187) argued that 'The notion of a common national South African identity is a conceptual migraine'. But Benedict Anderson's (1983) work on the social constructed-ness of nations and identities as products of imagination helps in gaining a deeper understanding of this 'conceptual migraine'. Anderson's work highlighted the role of print capitalism, vernacular language, the novel, education, and bilingual intelligentsia in facilitating the process through which people imagined their communities (Mueni wa Muiu 2008: 13; Hobsbawn and Ranger 1983).

The current debate on nations and identities is no longer about whether they are constructed or not, it is about the various specific and contextual mechanisms and technologies used in their construction. It is also about identifying the resources and prior identities from which new ones were constructed as well as the purpose for which particular identities served (Castells 1997: 6–7). This is important because social and political identities are products of identifiable acting and political subjects who constantly rework themselves, redefine their identities in relation to others.

For South Africa, colonial encounters provided identity markers with the necessary and visible 'other'. Within this context racial identity formation emerged in relation to the negative 'other'. Ted Lewellen (2002: 90) argued that identity was a 'matter of imaginative and creative rediscovery in which contemporary interpretation and needs fill in the gaps, recreate the past and bridge the discontinuities with new mythologies'. In this sense, identity was never 'an accomplished end point, of a people's history, but a constant process of becoming' that was 'always temporarily positioned within a particular context that needs to be imaginatively interpreted' (Lewellen 2002: 90). The point here is that identity has never existed as a primordial fixture, always out there, waiting to be embraced. It is a human construction that is very important because there are no 'people without names, no languages or cultures in which some manner of distinctions between self and other, we and they, are not made' (Calhoun 1994: 7).

Michel Foucault (1982: 212–221) argued that the processes through which reality was constructed and dissimulated were always acts of power and would always be resisted and contested. At the centre of contestations and resistance were 'political frontiers' as mechanisms through which social division was instituted, distinguishing 'insiders' from 'outsiders' (Norval 1996: 4–5). South African identities were formed through dissolution as well as the consolidation of political frontiers. The apartheid regime invented and recreated African ethnic fragmentations through legal codification, to prevent the possibilities of the coalescence of multiple ethnic African identities into a singular national identity. But such artificially constructed political frontiers provoked further imagined forms of African nationhood that resulted in the formation of such broader signifiers as 'Africans' as part of the resistance to the apartheid regime's divide and rule strategy.

Within this context, the logic of equivalence functioned through the homogenizing of otherwise heterogeneous peoples through undermining difference on one side of the frontier (Howarth and Stavrakakis 2000). The logic of equivalence resulted in two separate identities of whites as oppressors and blacks as victims. Empirically, Ivor Chipkin (2007) focused on how an 'African people', as a collectivity organized in pursuit of a political agenda, came into being and tended to confine analysis of the idea of South Africa to the period of the African nationalist struggle and the post-apartheid period although the idea emerged in the 1960s (Chipkin 2007). Chipkin's main concern was to correct a false but common idea within popular nationalist discourses whereby 'the people' were viewed as 'existing' prior to the period of the nationalist struggle (Chipkin 2007: 2).

Chipkin argued that South Africans emerged primarily in and through the process of nationalist resistance to colonialism. He distinguished between 'the people as datum' and 'the people as political subjects' (Chipkin 2007: 2). He was not interested in studying 'the people' as 'an empirical collectivity of individuals in a given geography', but 'the people' as 'a collectivity organized in pursuit of a political end' (Chipkin 2007: 1–2). To Chipkin, once the concept of the people was clarified as a political one, then it was possible to step up the argument to engage with the meaning of 'nation'. To him, a nation is 'not simply a cultural artefact' but is a political phenomenon. He defined the nation as: 'a political community whose form is given in relation to the pursuit of democracy and freedom' (Chipkin 2007: 2–3).

Chipkin's mistake was to believe that the nation preceded the state (Chipkin 2007: 2). Such generalization is not sustainable because for postcolonial Africa, leaders have inherited colonial states without nations. Eldred Masunungure argued that both nation-building and state-making were works of political art, by good political artists. He noted that African leaders have 'proven to be good state-building artists but poor nationbuilders' (Masunungure 2006: 3). But, crediting African leaders for being 'good state-building artists' ignores the fact that most of them inherited established colonial states. Their task was mainly to 'de-racialize' and 'Africanize' state structures. Because colonialism had prevented the coalescence of black people into stable nations, nation-building continues to be contentious works-in-progress across the African continent.

The historical record indicates that the idea of South Africa evolved as a complex continuum across different epochs. This is why the Foucualdian concept of genealogy becomes very useful to help unpack its origins, embeddedness, implicatedness in complex political histories and social struggles (Foucault 1977: 42; Norval 1996: 57).

On genealogy and historiography of the idea of South Africa

The late Kader Asmal presented the idea of South Africa as an invention of the ANC. This is how he put it:

> Here was born an idea, a South African idea, of moulding a people from diverse origins, cultural practices, languages, into one, within a framework democratic in character, that can absorb, accommodate and mediate conflicts and adversarial interests without oppression and injustice. (Asmal 2001: 1)

This rendition of South Africa ignores its long history, which goes back to the 1830s or even before. The idea emerged as a figurative expression describing the southern tip of the continent right up to the Zambezi River in the north. Shula Marks and Stanley Trapido (1987: 3) argued that by the 1870s South Africa was still a geographical expression characterized by pre-capitalist and capitalist modes of production existing side-by-side. They noted that 'there were two British colonies, two ostensibly politically independent republics and numerous still autonomous African polities' (Marks and Trapido 1987: 3).

Prior to 1902, there were no catch-all terms such as Africans and whites that existed as broad racial identities. African communities were identified by such ethnic names as the Ndwandwe, Mthethwa, Ngwane and others (Etherington 2001). Common identities were those of Zulu, Ndebele, Hurutshe, Hlubi, Xhosa and others that were created by an earlier discursive process that can be described as 'Bantucization/peopling of Southern Africa' (Inskeep 1987; Tobias 1978; Ndlovu-Gatsheni 2009d). The Bantu became active in state- and nation-building long before the arrival of whites and other races. Bantucization formed a strong background to the translation of the idea of South Africa into a people's identity. Bantu-speakers began to create larger identities like Sotho and Tswana. For Paul Landau (2010: xi) Bantu communities were historically well equipped to embrace and absorb strangers. Hybridity lay at the root of 'subcontinental political traditions'. But the colonial encounters brought European newcomers who were not predisposed to the habit and ideology of embracing and incorporation of black people. Whites resisted incorporation into black communities (Crais 1992).

Whites were scattered into Britons, Dutch, and others. Afrikaner identity was at its formative stage. Its nucleus was a handful of families living and travelling together under the leadership of a senior male. Proto-Afrikaner groups tended to be known by the name of their chiefs just like black people. Examples included the Cilliers Party, the Bronkhorts Party and the Potgieter Party (Etherington 2001: 244).

But colonial encounters were also a terrain of destruction and construction of identities. Black identity began to be used in opposition to white identity. White identity developed in relation to black identity. New identities emerged around 1910 when the state was being constructed as a single polity out of the British colonies, the conquered Afrikaner republics, and African kingdoms (Marks and Trapido 1987: 2).

An early liberal, Olive Schreiner Cronwright, dreamt of a rainbow nation before the 1920s. She was concerned about: 'How, of our divided peoples, can a great healthy, harmonious and desirable nation be formed?' (Schreiner 1976: 62). For her:

> For good or evil, the South African nation will be an absolutely new thing under the sun, perhaps, owing to its mixture of races, possessing that strange vitality and originality which appears to rise so often from the mixture of human varieties: perhaps, in general human advance, ranking higher than other societies more simply constructed; perhaps lower – according as we shall shape it: but this, certainly – will be a new social entity, with new problems, new gifts, new failings, new accomplishments. (Schreiner 1976: 370)

The colonial encounter also produced mixed-race communities such as the Griqua as well as Indians. These were additional identities to those of the Boers, Bantu, Britons, and others. Boers established the Boer Republics of Transvaal and the Orange Free State in the interior. In the 'British Zone' there existed not only the English-speaking British, but also Afrikaners and various Xhosa-speaking chiefdoms, San and the Khoisan as well as the Coloureds. In the Durban areas there were British of the Natal Colony living alongside such communities as the Zulu and others (Etherington 2001).

The term 'South Africa' was emerging as a colonial invention. It was used as a reference to the region extending northwards from the Cape to the Zambezi River. For P.A. Molteno it was 'the country bounded by the sea on all sides except the north, where the boundaries may roughly be said to be the Cunene towards the west and the Zambezi towards the east' (Molteno 1896: 39). For George Theal (1873), it was a collective term for the Cape Colony, Natal, Orange Free State, South African Republic, and all other territories south of the Zambezi. For Dubow it was 'an ideology of compromise' that 'developed out of a prior sense of colonial identity, namely, that which developed in the Cape from the early years of British occupation at the turn of the nineteenth century' (Dubow 2006: viii). Dubow was beginning to articulate the emerging identity of a people traceable to 'the institutions and associational life of Cape Town colonial culture, intellect, and politics' (Dubow 2006: viii). It is when the term 'South Africa' is approached as an identity that it becomes highly complex and open to contestation. Anthony Trollope argued that:

> South Africa is a country of black men – and not of white men. It has been so; it is so, and it will continue to be so. In this respect it is altogether unlike Australia, unlike the Canadas, and unlike New Zealand. (Trollope 1973: 454–455)

Trollope emphasized the fact that unlike the earlier British colonies of Australia, Canada, and New Zealand, where settlers were numerically superior to the indigenous people, in South Africa the numbers of indigenous black people far exceeded those of white settlers. While the British conceived of South Africa to be an expansion of the Cape Colony, an Afrikaner counter-imagination of South Africa, as constituted by independent Boer republics, was also developing, informed by emerging pan-Afrikaner identity (Lester 2001).

Anglicization as an identitarian process

By the late nineteenth century 'all the peoples of southern Africa existed to a greater or lesser extent under the hegemony of a mainly British merchant capitalism and a British imperialism' (Marks and Trapido 1987: 4). This omnipresence of British imperial power afforded any English-speaking settler some protection and power, drawn from the ties with a powerful metropolis and its political, technological, economic and ideological resources (Marks and Trapido 1987: 4).

The British Queen and the Union Flag (Union Jack) were symbols of national pride. English/British imaginations of a South African identity were predicated on a developing British superiority over other races and ethnicities. The adherence and loyalty of English-speaking settlers to Britain made them pursue an ambiguous national agenda divided between broader imperial mission and local colonial imperatives. Anglicization was also predicated on a contemptuous approach towards non-English-speakers, including Afrikaners who were considered an inferior race. No wonder then that, prior to 1902, a strong British jingoism locked horns with incipient Afrikaner republicanism leading to the Anglo-Boer/South African war of 1899 to 1902. During this period Lord Milner was the face of British racial patriotism (Marks and Trapido 1987: 7).

Four contending conceptions of national identity emerged from the centre of imperial and colonial tensions. One was a liberal trajectory that emphasized rational economic and social progress founded on principles of constitutionalism as well as ethnic and racial tolerance informed by the Cape liberal traditions. The second was the anti-liberal settler colonial version, informed by the upheavals of frontier life but still emphasizing freedom and autonomy as achievements of civilization and sacrifice (Dubow 2006: 152). The third strand emerged from the experiences of the 'Great Trek' as a heroic struggle for independence that informed Afrikaner republicanism as manifested in the existence of the two Boer republics of Transvaal and Orange Free State. The fourth strand emerged from the experiences of African people who endured the pain of being squeezed off their lands by both British and Afrikaners and being excluded from emerging white imaginations of the nation (Dubow 2006: 153).

Anglicization's template became the Cape Colony, where English language and other paraphernalia of British culture and ideology were in place. British colonial nationalism and British Crown imperialism tended to complement each other with some few areas of misunderstandings (Dubow 1997). In the Anglicization mind-map, the South African nation was to be nothing other than a 'greater Cape Colony' together with its institutions, replicated across South Africa.

But confrontation between the forces of Anglicization and Afrikanerization resulted in the Anglo-Boer/South African War of 1899 to 1902, which became a decider of the future imaginations of the idea of South Africa. The war was fought over possession of the country's riches on the one hand and on the other over what was meant by becoming South Africans (Dubow 2006: 158–159). According to Lord Milner, Anglicization was meant to construct a white self-governing polity comprising both British and Afrikaners but subsisting under the British Union Jack as a national symbol (Dubow 2006: 159).

Within this compromise, Africans were to feature as labourers. Therefore, the Treaty of Vereeniging of May 1902 brought about only a problematic peace. It was born out of conquest of the Boers and the exclusion of Africans from the nation. Both Afrikaners and Africans were resentful of British triumphalism. Africans had expected the British to practise liberalism, including incorporating them into the nation as rights-bearing citizens. Afrikaner nationalism had been deeply injured by the war.

Afrikanerization and apartheid

The Afrikaner vision of South Africanism was informed partly by their tradition of ethnic republicanism rooted in frontier life and by experiences of the Great Trek. Norval (1996: 12) argued that the specificity of Afrikaner nationalism and its re-emergence after the Act of Union of 1910 was a response to a catalogue of 'painful and conflict-ridden experiences'. After 1902, Anglicization policies, which were set to exclude Afrikaners from educational and administrative positions, galvanized Afrikaner republican nationalism.

Memories of the Great Trek provided the myth of foundation of Afrikaner nationhood. The Dutch Reformed Church provided an ideological anchor. Being surrounded by African communities and having to learn to adapt and distinguish themselves from other people, made Afrikaners panic over their identity. Afrikaans was not yet an acceptable and respected language. Isabel Hofmeyr (1987) has demonstrated empirically that Afrikaans was a twentieth-century invention. Afrikaans language began as a language of the poor and as a mixture of Dutch, Khoisan, San and Malayo-Portuguese languages spoken by slaves in the seventeenth- and eighteenth-century Cape Colony (Hofmeyr 1987: 95–123).

The development of Afrikaans as a language is one of the reflections of complex inter-racial and ethnic encounters of colonial modernity in a frontier region. But the upper and middle classes continued to speak Dutch while looking down at Afrikaans as either 'Hottentot language' or 'kitchen language' that was embarrassing (Hofmeyr 1987: 95–123). It had the status of a belittled vernacular language but eventually assumed a better status alongside the intensification of Afrikaner nationalism and its drive for 'nativization' of the Boers as South Africans.

At the centre of Afrikaner nationalism were perceptions and realities of the fragility of their identity within the context of the hostile and ever-shifting political and economic climate of the late nineteenth century and early twentieth century. Apartheid slogans emerged as powerful but empty signifiers promising the reconstruction of a lost unity (Norval 1996: 13). What the Afrikaners gained after Lord Milner's 1902 reconstruction dispensation was agreement with the British to reject the principle of equality between whites and blacks.

This was made apparent by the *Report of the South African Native Affairs Commission* (SANAC) chaired by Sir Godfrey Lagden, which inaugurated the policy of segregation of whites and blacks (Odendaal 1984: 65). The SANAC was the first drive by a combination of the English and the Afrikaners to begin to deal with what became known as the 'native question'. But the development of South Africa's capitalist-industrial revolution following the discovery of mineral wealth (diamonds and gold) was not favourable to Afrikaners, who were agriculturalists. Belinda Bozzoli argued that the early axis of intra- and inter-white conflicts in the late nineteenth and early twentieth centuries took the form of clashes between strong imperial 'mining and industrial' capital, which was represented by the British and weak 'agricultural domestic capital', represented by Afrikaners (Bozzoli 1981: 29–38).

The emergence of a bourgeois class crystallized around the economically powerful British mine-owners and industrialists who began to imagine the nation in capitalist terms. Strong economic interest-group associations such as the Transvaal Manufacturers' Association, the Colonial Industries Protectionist League and others, projected a concept of a nation founded on a uniform goal of capitalist development. The emerging bourgeoisie favoured a nation of English-speakers and Afrikaners and rejected the pre-war intra-white racialism of the late nineteenth century. For instance, 'manufacturing ideologists', as Bozzoli termed them, did not believe in the 'luxury of perpetuating the race feud, with all its sordid insincerities' and 'its internecine quarrels'. They viewed the Act of Union as inaugurating peace, progress and prosperity as well as 'new South African brotherhood' (Bozzoli 1981: 135).

The business elite even called for the formation of a new national party driven by national interests and representing a people united under one flag. But Africans had to be excluded from this white nation. What was envisioned was a 'South African, white, version of a bourgeois state' (Bozzoli 1978: 13). But this imagination of a homogenous white South African nation masked deep-seated intra- and inter-white divisions expressed through ethnic, class, ideological, as well as rural versus urban, cleavages. It was within this context that the powerful English business class was trying to mobilize and incorporate a defeated Afrikaner community that was already 'subordinated' into imperial hegemony.

Afrikaners began to form interest-group associations on top of the old Afrikaner Bond and the Federation of Afrikaans Cultural Association. These included the Economic Congress, National Youth League, Poor Welfare Council, and League for the Act of Rescue. These organizations began to push a common agenda for white Afrikaans-speaking people of economic, cultural, and political ascendancy. The push for improvement of the plight of poor white Afrikaners became entangled with the question of black natives, who were increasingly being proletarianized. Norval (1996: 19) argues that 'resolution of the Native question was thus central to the rectification of poor white problem, both socially and economically'.

Afrikaner nationalists feared rapid urbanization could lead to 'denationalization' of their community and destruction of their hard-constructed identity. They feared possibilities of miscegenation as poor Afrikaner women intermingled with Africans in the urban centres. Afrikaners called for a more rigid political and social frontier dividing white and black races, leading to the invention of natives as a homogenous identity. SANAC invented this category and stated that 'Native shall be taken to include an aboriginal inhabitant of Africa, south of the Equator and to include half-castes and their descendants by Natives' (Ashforth 1990: 33).

The roots of the National Party (NP) and its ideology of apartheid are traceable to the perception of dislocation of Afrikaner identity, provoked by the vicissitudes of industrialization and urbanization. Apartheid was formulated as part of a strategy to advance Afrikaners' socio-economic and cultural hegemony (Norval 1996: 52–55). By 1948 apartheid became officially institutionalized. It continued to live through 'negative operations' and drawing of frontiers as it tried to survive numerous dislocatory events and African resistance.

Apartheid's survival strategy consisted of four pillars. The first was restriction of franchise for Africans while monopolizing and centralizing state power in the hands of Afrikaners. The second was racial spatialization of cities, involving confining blacks to separate townships and homelands. The third included enforcing regulations that ensured a supply of cheap African labour to the mines, industries, farms and white domestic households. Finally, the apartheid state actively and directly intervened in spheres of employment, education, health and other human, daily life, activities in favour of the Afrikaner community (Cohen 1986: 7–10).

Ironically, the proponents of apartheid feared racial consciousnesses developing among Africans. They caricatured it as nothing but 'common hatred of whites' that was not sustainable and deep-rooted in a continent where people existed as different ethnic groups (Hugo 1988: 571). But apartheid's exclusion of blacks from citizenship and belonging constituted a strong internal limit. The international community could not tolerate it. Its multiple revisions and piecemeal reforms could not save it. Its survival techniques were not sustainable as they impinged negatively on the capitalist economic system itself. Trying to limit African entry to urban areas and trying to keep them in far-away Bantustans, did not correspond well to the labour needs of the capitalist system.

In the 1960s and 1970s, apartheid experienced a 'conjunctural crisis'. This developed into an 'organic crisis' in the 1980s. Towards the 1990s, it turned into a 'full-scale crisis of apartheid hegemony' (Norval 1996: 218–220). Apartheid precipitated the dislocation of identities, in the process enabling the emergence of a new search for new identity, a new imagination of South Africa and the formation of new myths to 're-suture the dislocated structure of the old, dying imaginary' (Norval 1996: 275). African nationalism provided a new imagination of South Africa and the ANC's 1955 articulation of a non-racial society was to become a pragmatic solution to the racialized and ethnicized national question.

African nationalism and the 'rainbow' nation

A political consciousness that could be called African took time to emerge from the fragmented ethnic identities rooted in precolonial history. Apartheid had kept and even invented rigid African identities as a strategy to prevent the emergence of African nationalism. As a result of this, even the early educated black elites were kept much more closely tied to their specific communities and home areas and towns (Odendaal 1984: xii). Moreover, the early educated elites were not fully opposed to colonial modernity as they had imbibed the Christian faith and Victorian ideas of liberalism and become committed to ideals of equality, non-racialism, and the enfranchisement of educated Africans.

Pan-African identity formation emerged concurrently with the intensification of scientific racism informed by Darwinist theories. These were increasingly used by imperialists and colonialists as powerful legitimating ideologies of domination and segregation in the early twentieth century (Marks and Trapido 1987: 6–7; Dubow 1987: 71–94). South Africanism increasingly became the overt imagination of a white nation. Racism became a key variable in the development of the idea of South Africa.

After 1902, the liberal incorporationist ideology was abandoned and a new segregationist policy was constructed by Lord Milner. The rationale of the ideology of segregation is that it spoke to the needs of the mining industry, serving white farmers who were demanding additional control over their tenants and labourers, and to white workers seeking protection from cheaper black labour, and it was an attractive solution for the white ruling class in the face of the rapid urbanization of poor whites and poor blacks (Marks and Trapido 1987: 8).

The Native Economic Commission (NEC) of 1930 to 1932 constrained black people by using 'Bantu-speaking people' as a proper name for them (Norval 1996: 31). Active colonialists were at work, deliberately creating new political frontiers between whites and blacks through discursive and symbolic processes that produced Bantu identity as if it were a natural species that deserved particular treatment and separate development, while justifying Bantu-speakers' exclusion from the nation and citizenship rights.

African imaginations of a South African nation were born within the context of resisting imperial, colonial and apartheid exclusivist imaginations. The first proto-African nationalist formation was the Native Educational Association (NEA), formed in 1882 as a vehicle for promoting African interest in modern education, social morality, and general welfare. This was followed in September 1882 by the earliest political organization known as *Imbumba Yaba Mnyama* formed in response to the growth of the Afrikaner Bond that was viewed as a threat to African people's interests. *Imbumba's* key aim was to unite Africans so as to enable them 'in fighting for national rights' (Odendaal 1984: 8). A construction of national African identity, by Africans themselves, had begun.

Odendaal (1984) provided excellent details of the proto-African political formations that arose as a response to particular exclusionary manoeuvres of the colonial state between the 1880s and 1912, the year of the formation of the South African Native National Congress (SANNC) as a black national political movement. Odendaal revealed how print media played a central role in the formation of black political consciousness and the imagination of a non-racial South Africa that accommodated them on an equal basis with whites. Independent newspapers with vernacular names such as *Ilanga lase Natal, Ipepa lo Hlanga* and many others propagated African issues and opinions on key national policies that segregated them.

Beginning with the SANNC, the African political organizations simultaneously contested racial discrimination while working to create national unity among Africans. Pixley Ka Isaka Seme's speech at the formation of SANNC emphasized that white people had formed the Union that excluded black people and that this action called for an African counter-union 'for the purpose of creating national unity and defending our rights and privileges' (Odendaal 1984: 273). African imaginations of the nation drew from a complex mixture of tradition of African resistance as well as from Modernist liberal traditions of progress and civilization.

The ANC and other African political formations emerged as successors and inheritors of an admixture of Modernist, emancipatory, revolutionary, and progressive strands, to become the grand synthesizers and mixers of various nationalisms. Following this logic, David Attwell argued that South Africa became postcolonial in 1910 with the Act of Union bringing about a coalition of Boer and Briton in a white colonial state. This was followed by 'a bleaker kind of postcoloniality' in 1948 that officialized apartheid. This was succeeded by 'a constitutionally defined, non-racial democracy' 'representing the point at which these various postcolonial histories have begun to coalesce, at least in the legal sense' (Attwell 2005: 2).

The situation of racial exclusion, political effacement and denial of citizenship rights to Africans inevitably provoked different responses. The first strand is the liberal tradition rooted in nineteenth-century Cape and Natal liberalism premised on the politics of inclusion of Africans within the body politic and the white nation. Colonial and apartheid intransigence and violence proved this strategy to be futile in the 1960s. The second strand was a radical Africanist one that stressed a common black identity rooted in Ethiopianist and Garveyist ideas of 'Africa for Africans' (Hill and Pirio 1987: 209–253). It was represented by the PAC which imagined a black republic called Azania. The idea was the deliverance of Africans from a white-dominated state rather than inclusion.

The founder president of the PAC, Robert Sobukwe, made it clear that the PAC did not claim Africa and South Africa for all people but for Africans. The national struggle was for complete overthrow of white domination. The third way of imagining the nation was represented by the ANC. The ANC has always been an umbrella political formation that began as an advocate of the 'Native Union' that Pixley Isaka kaSeme called for in 1911. Seme was an advocate of African regeneration, which looked towards activation and the galvanization of black race pride that was necessary for the birth of a proud African nation (Karis and Carter 1972).

Since 1912 the ANC underwent various ideological shifts. In the 1940s, the ANC Youth League became suspicious of mild liberalism and it shifted ideologically to embrace radical Africanism with Anton Lembede as the lead articulator. Lembede asserted that 'Africa is a black man's country' (Lembede 1946: 317). But by 1955, the ANC still projected a liberal-oriented, non-racial imagination of a multi-racial post-apartheid nation but without dropping the Garveyist slogan of 'I Afrika Mayi Buye' (Let Africa Be Restored to Us).

The ANC claimed South Africa for all those who lived in it, as articulated in the Freedom Charter. The imagination of a South African nation as a multi-racial and democratic political formation was a pragmatic solution for a society whose history was dominated by complex historical interactions and the coalescence of diverse people (Ndlovu-Gatsheni 2007a). The idea of a South Africa that belonged to all who lived in it made it difficult for apartheid government to develop a successful counter-discourse. The signifier of democracy was used to include all races and ethnicities, as well as classes, in a common imagination of the nation (Ramphalile 2011: 28–29).

But other imaginations of the nation, like those of the Inkatha Freedom Party (IFP), projected an ethno-cultural nationalism that defended the idea of a Zulu nation without necessarily ignoring broader nationalist politics. The Black Consciousness Movement (BCM) imagined a nation inhabited by mentally decolonized and proud black people. BCM frequently used the name Azania as part of its rejection of the colonially constructed name South Africa. BCM's conception and definition of black people included Indians and Coloureds (Biko 1978: 103–106). Blackness was expressed as an identity emerging from a common experience of racial oppression. But by stressing racial boundaries BCM inadvertently fell into the trap of the doctrine of separate development (Ramphalile 2011: 26).

At another level, the South African Communist Party (SACP) tried to construct a revolutionary subject from within the working class, as a cadre that was class-conscious but race-blind, and committed to a socialist society. In 1962, the SACP coined the concept of 'colonialism of a special type' to capture the complex situation wherein the independent state of 1910 was created not as a victory over imperialism and colonialism but as a nominally independent nation created through compromise between imperialism and colonialism. Within this set-up, a white nation was given power to internally colonize, dominate, and exploit black people (South African Communist Party 1962: 27).

The SACP also came up with the concept of a National Democratic Revolution (NDR), where workers were identified as a revolutionary force. Within the NDR, workerism and charterism coexisted tendentiously and uneasily, mediated by tensions over blending political interests of the 'people' and those of 'workers'. The NDR became an omnibus where the interests of all those opposed to apartheid across black, Coloured, Indian and white racial divisions, as well as class and ethnic cleavages, were accommodated (Ndlovu-Gatsheni 2008a).

The ANC became the biggest player in this complex coalition of interests. But over the years the discourse of NDR became more nationalist rather than workerist. These developments within the liberation movements indicated how difficult it was to define in precise terms the subject of liberation and by the same token pinpoint who was a South African beyond the rather elusive term of 'All who belongs to it' (Ndlovu-Gatsheni 2008a). The rainbow nation is underpinned by this inclusive ideology. But rival nationalisms and populisms of the past also continue to pulsate even within the ANC, reviving debates on whether South Africa is for black Africans first and others second.

Conclusion

This chapter analysed the intractable questions of the subject, subjection and subjectivity from a historical and theoretical vantage point, placing the complex events within a broader historical and political context of the genesis of the idea of South Africa and how it underwent various translations from being a geographical expression into an identity of a people. During translation, existing identities underwent racialization and ethnicization mediated by the logics of equivalence and difference as well as by the politics of nativity, power and resource ownership.

While Bantucization could have led to the creation of larger identities premised on its tradition of embracing and absorbing strangers, this process was cut short by the arrival of Europeans who operated according to the logic of an abyssal thinking that enabled projection of radical differences.

It was within this context that there arose the question of natives (native question), namely, how to use Africans as providers of cheap labour while at the same time maintaining separateness of races. This question preoccupied advocates of Anglicization in the same measure that it became a major issue in Afrikanerization. Apartheid emerged within this context as one possible way of maintaining an abyssal thinking that celebrated radical difference. Africanization might be interpreted as building from the inclusive ethos of Bantucization as it constituted itself a revolt against the politics of valorizing radical difference. The Freedom Charter of 1955 encapsulated this spirit of revolt against politics of radical difference.

The 1994 compromise was meant to reverse the politics of radical differences and to embrace the politics of inclusivity underpinned by *ubuntu*. But because of the residual aspects from the apartheid past, post-apartheid South Africa continues to be haunted by the spectre of racialized ethnicities and ethnicized races, which protrude into public discourse every time issues related to the equitable distribution of resources are debated. Rainbowism has not succeeded in banishing Africanist, nativist and other racist articulations of belonging, citizenship, and entitlement to resources. The connections between identity, allocation of resources, and access to power mean that, as long as economic and social justice is not achieved to the satisfaction of the majority, the black constituencies that experienced dispossession, the future of the rainbow nation will remain threatened from below. The celebration of different cultures and identities serves to disguise continuities of old animosities and reinforce the cancer of ethnicized races and racialized ethnicities. In short, South African national identity itself will remain a work in process whose success is dependent on resolution of economic inequalities.

CHAPTER 6

Nationality of Power in Zimbabwe

Introduction

Nationalism provides Eurocentric solutions to a Eurocentric global problem. It reproduces an internal coloniality of power within each nation-state and reifies the nation-state as the privileged location of social change. Struggles above and below the nation-state are not considered in nationalist political strategies. Moreover, nationalist responses to global capitalism reinforce the nation-state as the political institutional form par excellence of the modern/colonial/capitalist/patriarchal world-system. In this sense, nationalism is complicit with Eurocentric thinking and political structures.

(Ramón Grosfoguel 2011: 18)

Railing against the cultural hegemony of the West, the nativists are of its party without knowing it. Indeed the very arguments, the rhetoric of defiance, that our nationalist muster are … canonical, time tested … In their ideological inscription, the cultural nationalists remain in a position of counteridentification … which is to continue to participate in an institutional configuration – to be subjected to cultural identities they ostensibly decry … Time and time again, cultural nationalism has followed the route of alternate genealogizing. We end up always in the same place; the achievement is to have invented a different past for it.

(Kwame Anthony Appiah 1992: 56–60)

In Zimbabwe coloniality of power has given birth to nationality of power. Both 'powers' are colonizing and violent, perhaps indicating beyond doubt the salient point that 'a substantial part of the history of Homo Sapiens could be seen as the history of colonization and of its ideological, institutional and political legitimations' (Ribeiro 2011: 289). It is perhaps time for us to accept the idea pushed forward by Gustavo Lins Ribeiro (2011: 289) that 'Human beings could well be called the "colonizer animal"', an argument which is also articulated by Arif Dirlik (2002: 443), whose core thesis was that many of the national identities that today are accepted and taken for granted, were not only 'hybrid', but were the products of prior processes of colonizations, resistances, and encounters of various kinds, mediated by oppression, exploitation, and even forceful conversion. But these identities, which emerged out of these traumatic experiences, end up being embraced and celebrated as a form of historical emergence (Dirlik 2002: 443).

This chapter shifts analysis from coloniality of power to what Ribeiro (2011: 293) terms 'nationality of power', which seeks to understand how those who were fighting against the coloniality of power strove to create national identity through particular technologies of subjectivation that sought to create a 'nationalist state' and 'patriotic citizens' out of the (ex) colonized peoples of Africa. Nationality of power is not an opposite of coloniality of power because the technologies of subjection are the same, only perhaps differing slightly in the sense that coloniality of power was propelled through various forms of violence through and through. Nationality of power embraces persuasion and consent is sought without necessarily parking the machine of violence.

What is emphasized is that African nationalism was a productive discursive project that sought to inscribe nationalist power through the creation of a nationalist state that made visible the performance of a nationalist imaginary: beginning with changing the colonial names of the countries that were said to be independent and proceeding to the process of substitution of colonial names of streets with nationalist ones; introducing national anthems, independence days and various other commemorations of sacrifices made by the nationalist leaders; creating national currencies, some with the portrait of the founding father of the nation, and national postage stamps; continuing with the 'de-colonization' of national television and hanging the portrait of the executive president in every public office.

The case study of Zimbabwe is used to explain how the ideology of *Chimurenga* and strategy of *Gukurahundi* were deployed by the African nationalists who had organized themselves into the Zimbabwe African National Union-Patriotic Front (ZANU-PF) in the struggle not only to fight against colonialism but also to construct a Zimbabwean identity. This chapter is divided into five sections. The first section explains the politics behind the construction and use of the ideology of *Chimurenga* as a central pillar in ZANU-PF's re-construction of national history in partisan and Shona-oriented terms; and the imagination of the postcolonial nation as a successor to the precolonial Shona political formations (Mudenge 1988; Ndlovu-Gatsheni 2008b; Ndlovu-Gatsheni 2009d). The ideology of *Chimurenga* identified colonialism as the enemy of every black person and anti-colonialism as the rallying point of African unity and the basis for imagination of a postcolonial nation. Any black person who did not embrace the ideology of *Chimurenga* was, therefore, a legitimate target of violence. Zimbabweans are currently struggling to gain liberation from the ZANU-PF constructed monologue of the nation.

The second section traces the roots of the strategy of *Gukurahundi* as a central pillar of state-making and a tactic for maintaining regime security in Zimbabwe. *Gukurahundi* is defined here as a strategy of annihilating all those opposed to the ideology of *Chimurenga* and ZANU-PF hegemony. It is rooted in the exigencies of the armed liberation struggle, in which violence was embraced as a legitimate tool of resolving political questions and issues. The third section explains the changing and additional articulations of the nation by ZANU-PF under the changed political circumstances that existed after the millennium year. It added and intensified indigenist, nativist, racist and autochthonic, if not xenophobic, narrations of the nation. This shifting articulation of the nation happened concurrently with the process of ratcheting up the political language on the land reform, renewal of the ideology of *Chimurenga*, and intensification of the strategy of *Gukurahundi*, this time ranged against vocal civil society organizations and the popular opposition formation known as the Movement for Democratic Change (MDC) (Ndlovu-Gatsheni 2009a).

The fourth section focuses on the equally complex and ambivalent politics of counter-hegemonic initiatives. After the year 2000, political circumstances were dominated not only by the popularity of post-Cold War values of liberal democracy and human rights, but also by the revival of ideas of 'ethnic nations', and calls for national self-determination by those people who considered themselves to be written out of the nation and suffering economic marginalization and state-sanctioned violence (Ndlovu-Gatsheni 2008b; Ndlovu-Gatsheni 2009d). The final section is the conclusion, which assesses the impact of ZANU-PF nationalist monologues on the character of current national politics.

At another level, the celebrations of emergent national identities as artefacts of heroic struggles and sacrifices that also refer to Tony Bennett's (1995: 141) notions of 'nationing history' and 'historicizing the nation' become instructive. Modern Zimbabwean nationalism emerged as an anti-colonial force that not only contested colonially created African subjecthood but was pushed forward by active interlocutors of nationalism, who worked tirelessly to create and articulate an alternative national history that ran counter to colonial history. At the same time, the process of 'historicizing the nation' involved dominant nationalist movements trying ceaselessly to make their claims to be the sole progenitors of the nation acceptable to the general population, whilst blending their own hagiographies into the official history of the nation.

But it must also be made clear from the outset that ZANU-PF, which sought to weave its political hagiographies into a national and official history of Zimbabwe, was never, at any time, a monolithic political formation free from intra-party dissensions, conflicts and crises. This reality always limited its chances of achieving the hegemony that it so eagerly wanted. This point is captured by David Moore, who stated that:

If one goes back, into the history of the liberation war, there is also little unity of a hegemonic sort. The list of tensions is a long one: the split eventuating in ZANU emerging out of ZAPU; the March 11 Movement ... the Front for the Liberation of Zimbabwe (FROLIZI, or as some of its detractors called it the Front for the Liaison of Zezuru Intellectuals); the Nhari Rebellion – and centrally, the Chitepo Assassination ... the Zimbabwe People's Army and Vashandi Movement (wiped out with particular Machiavellian cold-hearts and ideological hypocrisy by the man these young radicals helped into power); the Hamadziripi-Gumbo 'coup' in 1978; and the mysterious death of Josiah Tongogara the day after he advised Robert Mugabe to go into the 1980 elections together with ZAPU, with which ZANU was ostensibly allied in the Patriotic Front. The closer one looks at the history of Zimbabwe, the more one wonders how anyone could 'imagine' a 'community' based on the nationalism exemplified by its political brokers. (Moore 2008: 32)

Taking note of this argument is very important for this chapter's approach, which can easily be misread as presenting an opposition between singular and plural, monologic and dialogic binaries in Zimbabwean political history, and thus falling into a kind of ahistoricity while it is concerned with the temporal processes of history itself. There is no attempt in this chapter to analyse *Chimurenga* and *Gukurahundi* in binary terms because they are the names of certain key historical dynamos, recurring occurrences and conflict-laden moments, within the chronology of the broader history of nationalism and the political journey of Zimbabwe from a colony to an independent state. But at the same time, the chapter argues that *Chimurenga* and *Gukurahundi* as ideology and strategy respectively are useful in understanding the dynamics of the temporal span of the Zimbabwean postcolony. At the same time, this is not an attempt to pick only two issues and then foreclose in advance the social and political complexities of each historical moment in Zimbabwe's political history.

The chapter is written at a moment when those who participated in the liberation struggle, and experienced postcolonial life, like Wilfred Mhanda, author of *Dzino: Memories of a Freedom Fighter* (2011), are detailing how *Gukurahundi* strategy was used widely within ZANU-PF itself, even in exile. Mhanda's thesis is amplified by another recent book by Zvakanyorwa Wilbert Sadomba (2011: 17), who clearly states that the Badza/Nhari rebellion was foiled by *Gukurahundi*: as he elaborates, 'the term has its roots in the liberation war, given to a force commanded by Dzinashe Machingura to quell the Nhari/Badza rebellion'.

Thomas Nhari and Simon Badza were young commanders of the Zimbabwe National Liberation Army (ZANLA), the armed wing of ZANU-PF. They became disgruntled with the lack of military supplies while they were operating in Rhodesia in 1974. This led them to withdraw from the front, to discipline those people responsible for military supplies, including General Josiah Tongogara, the commander of ZAN-LA. On arrival in Mozambique, they rounded up the military leadership of ZANLA and they proceeded to Zambia with the same mission. Their specific complaint was that those who remained in the headquarters were enjoying themselves and forgetting about the suffering freedom fighters inside Rhodesia. It is not clear what they wanted to do after arresting the leadership of ZANLA. Their plan was defeated by counter-military moves spearheaded by Tongogara and other military forces (Chung 2006; Mhanda 2011; Sadomba 2011). Nhari and Badza were captured and hanged for being rebellious. More details are given in the later sections of this chapter.

One of the main contributions of this chapter is to destroy the common conception of the term *Gukurahundi* as the name of an exclusive Korean-trained former ZANLA force otherwise known as the Fifth Brigade, which was deployed in Matabeleland and the Midlands regions in the period 1982 to 1987, leaving over 20,000 civilians dead (*Catholic Commission for Justice and Reconciliation and Legal Resources Report* 1997). This background is important to enable a clear appreciation of the contribution of this chapter to deepening an understanding of Zimbabwe's political history in general and genealogies of the cultures of violence in particular.

Therefore this chapter seeks to unpack how ZANU-PF government has used a combination of the ideology of *Chimurenga* and the strategy of *Gukurahundi* to build what Norma Kriger (2003: 72–76) termed a 'party-nation' and a 'party-state' as well as to maintain a hegemonic and mono-logic narrative of the nation. It begins by exploring how ZANU (before it became ZANU-PF in 1980) appropriated the history of African resistance to construct the ideology of *Chimurenga* and to eventually claim to be the divinely ordained heir to the nationalist revolutionary spirit running from the primary resistance of the 1890s to the mass nationalism of the 1960s and armed liberation struggle of the 1970s.

The ideology of *Chimurenga* is also used to claim primal political legitimacy by ZANU-PF that needs no renewal every five years via holding of free and fair elections, since the party received prior permanent oracular blessings from spirit mediums during the struggle for independence in the 1970s (Chitando 2005: 220–239). The official adoption of Marxism-Leninism-Maoism by ZANU, in the late 1970s, added another ideological resource that reinforced the notion of the party being the carrier of the 'burden of history' bequeathed on it by heroes of the 1896 to 1897 risings. The messianic role received a further boost from the notion of a vanguard political party, which led the masses from the front and knew what the people wanted (Chitando 2005: 223–225). It was this idea of ZANU-PF and President Robert Mugabe having a patriotic 'historic mission' that inspired Mugabe to arrogantly tell the electorate immediately before the 29 March 2008 elections that:

You can vote for them [MDC], but that would be a wasted vote. I am telling you. You would just be cheating yourself. There is no way we can allow them to rule this country. Never, ever. We have a job to do, to protect our heritage. The MDC will not rule this country. It will never, ever happen. We will never allow it. (Quoted in Solidarity Peace Trust 2008)

As will be clear in the later sections of this chapter, when ZANU-PF assumed state power in 1980, it quickly penetrated the state and nation, making sure the party was indistinguishable from the state and nation. This was done through selective deployment of history, memory and commemoration, to claim uncontested political legitimacy. The process involved the creative yoking of ZANU-PF's hagiography and national history, resulting in 'rule by historiography' (Ranger 2005b).

Political use of memorialization and commemoration dated back to the time of the liberation war and the Chinhoyi Battle of 1966 (when ZANLA cadres were killed by Rhodesian forces). The Chinhoyi Battle was celebrated as *Chimurenga Day*, marking the beginning of the armed liberation struggle (Ndlovu-Gatsheni and Willems 2009). ZANU-PF wanted to be remembered as the initiator of the armed struggle, acting before the Zimbabwe African People's Union (ZAPU and its armed wing the Zimbabwe People's Revolutionary Army-ZIPRA), from which ZANU emerged in 1963 as a splinter party. As well as this, the death of Leopold Takawira (the ZANU leader who died in detention, due to diabetes) was commemorated annually in Mozambique in the late 1970s. As articulated by Robert Mugabe, ZANU was the carrier of the 'burden of history', enjoying the oracular blessings of Nehanda and Kaguvi, spirit mediums who are claimed to have played an active role in the 1896 to 1897 uprisings (Mugabe 1978; Chitando 2002; Chitando 2005).

The fatal flaw, at the very heart of the African modern nation-state project in postcolonial Africa in general, was that of the idea of 'a tight correspondence between the nation and the state whereby each sovereign state was seen as a nation-state of people who shared a common language or culture' (Laakso and Olukoshi 1996: 11–12). The problem was that this notion of a monolithic nation-state contradicted the realities of African social existence, which was dominated by multi-culturalism, multi-lingualism, multiple religions and diverse ethnic and racial groups.

Zimbabwean nationalism was predicated on this assumption that diversity of ethnic and racial identities had to be homogenized into a singular national identity and that successful nation-building and state-making would culminate in the eradication of diverse identities and projection of the identity of the group that dominated state power. The ideology of *Chimurenga* became the nodal point around which imaginations of a monolithic nation-state had to crystallize.

The making of national history and national identity

The ideology of *Chimurenga* is a tale of the invention of a complex, politically usable, narrative by ZANU in its bid to construct a postcolonial nation, unite people, gain popularity, and assume political power at the end of settler colonial rule. It was and is premised on a doctrine of permanent nationalist revolution against imperialism and colonialism. This ideology constituted the leitmotif of ZANU-PF nationalism. The ideology of *Chimurenga* is deeply anti-colonialist. It began as part of nationalist innovation, involving the harnessing of precolonial and colonial historical moments to formulate an indigenous and vernacular conception of a nationalist revolution that linked the primary resistance of the 1890s to the nationalist struggles of the 1970s. The ideology of *Chimurenga* is constantly being renewed by leaders of ZANU-PF and it is today used to legitimize an increasingly unpopular regime that has presided over Zimbabwe since 1980.

The early historical work of the liberal British historian Terence Ranger, who was sympathetic to the cause of Zimbabwean nationalism, particularly his book *Revolt in Southern Rhodesia* (1967), provided a nationalist-compliant narrative of primary resistance that was quickly appropriated by the nationalists for ideological purposes (Ranger 1967). Ranger's central arguments were that the risings of 1896 to 1897 were informed by the creative strengths of Shona and Ndebele culture; that precolonial religious leaders, especially Shona spirit mediums (Mbuya Nehanda and Sekuru Kaguvi), led the uprisings; that these religious leaders provided prophetic and ideological inspiration; and that there were continuities and connections between the risings of 1896 and the mass nationalism of the 1960s (Ranger 1967; Ranger 1968; Ranger 1977).

Ranger's early academic work provided the historical raw materials for the nationalist reconstruction of the ideology of *Chimurenga*. But in 2002 Ranger lamented how his history books were being used to construct what he termed 'patriotic history'. He defined patriotic history as a populist proclamation of the continuity of the Zimbabwean revolutionary tradition as spearheaded by ZANU-PF cadres as patriots and the stigmatization of those not belonging to it as dangerous traitors. Such a populist history repudiated academic historiography's attempts to complicate and question the trajectories of nationalism. Its key trope was consistent anti-colonial rhetoric and anti-Western 'bogus universalism' (Ranger 2004: 215).

During the early development of the ideology of *Chimurenga*, it drew its power from 'nationalist historiography' which was different from the 'patriotic history' articulated by ZANU-PF in the period of the late 1990s and early years of the twenty-first century. Nationalist historiography conceived of the African nationalist movement as 'inclusive and even non-racial' and nationalism was celebrated as emancipatory (Ranger

2005a: 7–9). Nationalist historiography was also informed by universal ideas of human progress and modernity; hence it espoused projects of modernization, reform and even socialist egalitarianism (Ranger 2005: 8). Nationalist historiography matured into what Ranger termed 'historiography of nationalism': it embraced canons of critical social theory, which set it apart from uncritical intellectual commissariat-discourses of 'praising' nationalism rather than questioning it (Robins 1996; Ranger 2005a: 8).

The historiography of nationalism 'raised questions about the nature of nationalism and about the course of its development' (Ranger 2005a: 8). It also revealed 'struggles within the struggle', traced the roots of rural and urban nationalism, raised questions about nationalist violence, exclusionary tendencies and concerns about the *Chimurenga* monologue (Ranger 1999; Raftopoulos 1999; Msindo 2007; Ndlovu-Gatsheni 2009a). The revisionist interventions of David N. Beach and Julian Cobbing on the 1896 to 1897 risings can be said to have inaugurated a critical historiography of nationalism that ran counter to the populist pronouncements of the ideology of *Chimurenga* (Beach 1971; Beach 1986; Cobbing 1976; Cobbing 1977). Ranger has also been active in challenging his own early ideas on nationalism (Ranger 1999; Ranger 2003: 1–37).

On the abuse/use of his academic work by politicians, Ranger wrote that 'I recognized the outlines of many of my books but boiled down in the service of ZANU-PF' (Ranger 2002: 60). As early as 1975, the names of secular and religious leaders of the 1896 to 1897 risings that Ranger unearthed from the archives and oral sources were already being used by Reverend Ndabaningi Sithole, the founder president of ZANU and first Commander-in-Chief of ZANLA, to encourage them to continue the fight. In 1976 at the Geneva Conference, Bishop Abel Muzorewa, who led the moderate and internally based United African National Council (UANC), used the same list to connect the liberation struggle to primary resistance (Ranger 1977: 128).

Eventually Zimbabwe's national history was re-articulated by ZANU nationalists as constituted by a series of nationalist revolutions known as *Zvimurenga*. *Zvimurenga* is a plural of the term *Chimurenga*. It was used by Beach who challenged Ranger's thesis of a united Ndebele-Shona resistance to colonialism from 1896 to 1897 (Beach 1980: 107–112). Beach argued that the uprising was never 'simultaneous', it was not coordinated and there was no religious element that provided ideological unity. To him, the uprising followed the format of *chindunduma* (a Shona word he used to capture the nature of the uprising spreading with a ripple effect from area to area) (Beach 1979: 401–416).

Cobbing also challenged Ranger's thesis, arguing that a major theme of the risings was 'disunity and fragmentation', with the Ndebele disunited and even fighting a civil war while some Shonas even collaborated with the colonialists (Cobbing 1977: 84). Beach went further to deny that

Nehanda (whom ZANU projected as the divine inspiration of the liberation) played any instrumental role during the uprising of 1896 to 1897. Instead, Beach depicted her as an 'innocent woman' who was 'unjustly accused' (Beach 1998).

Despite the revisionist interventions of Beach and Cobbing, challenging Ranger's ideas of a united African resistance in 1896 to 1897, the notion of *Chimurenga* became very popular with ZANU nationalists in particular. The term was derived from Murenga, a name of a spirit medium that Ranger identified as actively involved in the 1896 to 1897 war of resistance, providing the desperately needed ideological support to the African fighting forces. Murenga is said to have administered some traditional war medicine to the African fighting forces that would make them invulnerable and immune to white forces' bullets (Ranger 1967: 217–220).

But the term *Chimurenga* began to be widely used in the 1970s by the nationalists, mainly within the ZANU and its fighting wing (ZANLA) as a vernacular name for the armed liberation struggle against the settler colonial state. It was also used as an ideological thread capturing the undying spirit of African resistance to colonialism, running from the primary resistance of the 1890s to the present controversy-ridden struggles for black economic empowerment, dominated and driven by an African elite, that began with the fast-track land reform programme christened as the *Third Chimurenga* (Mugabe 2001).

However it was in 1977 that the ideology of *Chimurenga* was re-defined from a radical Zimbabwe People's Army (ZIPA) perspective as denoting the ideas of total war against colonialism and capitalism, and as a call for total transformation of the future Zimbabwe's society and people (ZIPA 1977; on ZIPA see Moore 1995a; Moore 1995b). As they put it:

> The word drives its meaning from the national liberation war, fought by our fore-fathers in 1896–7 uprising in opposition to the British domination and occupation. The 1896–7 armed uprising by the entire Zimbabwe masses was one of the stiffest resistances registered by the African people in Southern Africa to colonial rule and imperial advance in the region … This was a total war to expel foreign capitalists and imperialists from the soil of Zimbabwe … This is a source of inspiration which guides us in our current struggle against the Smith regime … With the defeat of our forefathers in 1897 African resistance went underground up to the mid-fifties when African nationalism came to the fore. (Zimbabwe People's Army 1977; see also Ranger 1977)

In the ideology of *Chimurenga*, the nation was born as a result of the two violent *Zvimurenga* of the 1890s and 1970s. While in the 1970s the concept of *Chimurenga* had found a dignified niche within African nationalist revolutionary politics as an anti-imperial and anti-colonial ideology, by the beginning of 2000 it had been dented by ZANU-PF's use of violence against members of the MDC as a continuation of *Chimurenga*.

By 2000, the ideology of *Chimurenga* was being deployed to justify any form of nationalist violence, even against citizens of the postcolonial state. It was used to justify election-related violence beginning with the independence elections of 1980 as a means of defending national sovereignty (Kriger 2005). Every time ZANU-PF was cornered politically by the opposition forces, it tendentiously reminded people that 'Zimbabwe *ndeyeropa*' (Zimbabwe came after a violent war of liberation) and that it would go back to the bush to fight another *Chimurenga* if defeated in an election (Sithole and Makumbe 1997).

The ideology of *Chimurenga* was also mobilized to fragment the people of Zimbabwe into patriots, war veterans, puppets, traitors, sell-outs, born-frees and enemies of the nation. These political identities have resulted in polarization of the nation. The titles of patriots and veterans are reserved for those who participated in the liberation struggle (*Second Chimurenga*) in general and all members of ZANU-PF specifically. Members of MDC political formations are categorized as traitors, sell-outs and puppets, who deserve to die if the Zimbabwean nation is to live. By 2000, the white commercial farmers constituted the worst enemies of the nation as ZANU-PF used the unresolved land question as a political tool to prop up its waning popularity, especially among peasants and other landless constituencies (Ndlovu-Gatsheni and Muzondidya 2011; Ndlovu-Gatsheni 2011a).

In 2010, Blessings Miles Tendi, a young Zimbabwean academic, systematically unpacked the *Third Chimurenga* as a terrain of competing ideas and contestations over national history. He argued that 'patriotic history' as the motivating force of the *Third Chimurenga* was not just a 'fabrication' or a 'polemic' with little relevance to the interests of the people of Zimbabwe. To him, 'patriotic history' played on real grievances and its 'narrative must be taken seriously' (Tendi 2010: 2; Muzondidya 2007; Muzondidya 2010).

While the *Third Chimurenga* was popularly dubbed *Hondo Yeminda* (the war for land reclamation), President Mugabe articulated it broadly as 'conquest of conquest', marking the triumphalism of black sovereignty over white settlerism (Ndlovu-Gatsheni 2009b). This means that the *Third Chimurenga* was not only defined by the land question. In fact, the re-assertion of revolutionary nationalist tradition was premised on four other issues, namely: obsession with race; bifurcation of citizens into 'sell-outs' and 'patriots; anti-Western politics; and defence of the national sovereignty of Zimbabwe (Tendi 2010: 1).

One of the core objectives of the *Third Chimurenga* was to displace all other alternative political views that did not resonate with those of ZANU-PF. To achieve this objective, ZANU-PF mobilized what Tendi termed 'nationalist public intellectuals', trying to organize them into something like a priesthood of the *Third Chimurenga*, which articulated various aspects of patriotic history and facilitated such televised programmes as 'Nhaka Yedu' (our heritage and national ethos) as well as 'Living Traditions' (Tendi 2010: 11–42). At the apex of this priesthood were President Mugabe and Professor Jonathan Moyo (by then a ZANU-PF spin doctor and Minister of Information and Publicity). At the end of the day, ZANU-PF worked tirelessly to install a national political monologue rather than dialogue. Tendi argued that:

> *Nhaka Yedu, National Ethos* and *Living Traditions* were monologues, not dialogues, of ZANU-PF's cerebral praetorian guards, which attempted to legitimize violent land seizures and state-sponsored political violence against the MDC, divided Zimbabwean society along a good and evil distinction, and employed race essentialism. (Tendi 2010: 42)

The ideology of *Chimurenga* was underpinned by the strategy of *Gukurahundi* that authorized a culture of violence. The ideology of *Chimurenga* and violence were closely interwoven 'because it sees itself as a doctrine of revolution' (Ranger 2005a: 8).

Gukurahundi as a leitmotif of ZANU-PF hegemony

The term *Gukurahundi* was a colloquial expression, which in Shona language means 'the storm that destroys everything' (Sithole and Makumbe 1997: 133). This early storm often destroyed crops and weeds, huts and forests, people and animals, opening the way for a new ecological order. ZANU officially adopted *Gukurahundi* as a strategy in 1979 and that year was declared *Gore reGukurahundi* (The Year of the Storm) (Sithole and Makumbe 1997: 133). This storm was presented in revolutionary terms of destroying the white settler regime, the 'internal settlement puppets', the capitalist system and any other obstacles to ZANU ascendancy to power (Sithole and Makumbe 1997: 133; CCJP and LRF 1997). Sithole and Makumbe described *Gukurahundi* as a 'policy of annihilation; annihilating the opposition (black and white)' (1997: 133).

As part of official implementation of the strategy of *Gukurahundi*, Eddison Zvobgo (Information and Publicity Secretary of ZAN in the late 1970s) drew a 'hit enemies list' of the high-ranked personalities of the 'internal settlement' parties, who were singled out for killing (Sithole and Makumbe 1997: 133; Hudson 1981; Ndlovu-Gatsheni 2006). In 2004, ZANU-PF produced another list of traitors and sell-outs, who needed to be liquidated. The list included Archbishop Pius Ncube, a critic of Mugabe; Trevor Ncube, owner of critical independent newspapers; Geoffrey Nyarota, a journalist; leaders of the MDC including Morgan Tsvangirai, Welshman Ncube, Paul Themba Nyathi; Wilfred Mhanda, leader of Zimbabwe Liberators Platform that was opposed to the main association of war veterans who had been reduced to ZANU-PF storm-troopers; and critical public intellectuals, including Brian Raftopoulos, John Makumbe and Lovemore Madhuku (ZANU-PF Department of Information and Publicity 2004; Tendi 2010).

While the strategy of *Gukurahundi* was openly embraced as party policy in 1979, it had a long history in ZANU. It is traceable to the formation of ZANU in 1963. Its philosophy of confrontation entailed embracing violence as a legitimate political tool of fighting for independence and for destruction of opponents and enemies. Zvobgo wrote of the 'ZANU Idea' which he elaborated as the 'gun idea' that was foundational to the party's ideology of confrontation and violence (Zvobgo 1984: 23). Gerald C. Mazarire, who has been researching the issue of discipline and punishment in ZANLA, demonstrated how the gun was celebrated in ZANU as a tool of restoring order and 'cleaning up the rot' (Mazarire 2011: 571). The ZANU Departments of Defence and Commissariat promoted ideas of supremacy of the military within ZANU and enforced violent disciplinary measures that included outright elimination of those considered to be failing to adhere to the party line (Chung 2006).

The deployment of the strategy of *Gukurahundi* within ZANU was necessitated by internal crises of the 1970s such as the Nhari rebellion of 1974, which became the first major disciplinary case to be dealt with by the *Dare reChimurenga* and High Command (Mazarire 2011: 578). Thomas Nhari and his comrades were eliminated through execution, as disciplinary measures, on the orders of Josiah Tongogara and against the trial verdict passed by Herbert Chitepo who had recommended demotions and other forms of punishment rather than execution (Chung 2006: 88–95). On the logic of using execution as a form of discipline, Fay Chung argued that the ZANU High Command believed in the 'Old Testament version of justice of an eye for an eye, a death for death' (Chung 2006: 94).

By the 1970s the strategy of *Gukurahundi* leading to executions was entrenched within ZANU. It involved violent destruction of ZAPU structures inside Rhodesia (Ranger 1995: 203–210). It also took the form of punishing ZIPA cadres within ZANU. Mazarire argues that by the time of dealing with ZIPA cadres, 'a new order of discipline emerged under the idea of the "parade" called to order by "whistles"' (Mazarire 2011: 578). Camp authorities practised public displays as punishment, which included thorough beatings until those accused cadres soiled themselves (Mazarire 2011: 580).

Obsession with exposing sell-outs and counter-revolutionaries is a ZANU practice developed during the liberation struggle. Parades were used to identify traitors and sell-outs within the party. *Pungwes* (night vigils) were also used to do the same in the operational zones deep inside Rhodesia. Mazarire (2011: 580) identified what was termed *chikaribotso*, whereby pit structures were dug and built to keep prisoners underground. Some ZIPA cadres experienced this harsh treatment. Robert Mugabe, who took over as party president in 1977, celebrated the violent destruction of ZIPA in these words: 'We warned any person with a tendency to revolt that the ZANU axe would fall on their necks: *tino tema nedemo* ['we will axe you'] was the clear message' (quoted in Vambe 2008: 1).

Mugabe and his party were swept to power in 1980 by the use of the strategy of *Gukurahundi* (Sithole and Makumbe 1997: 134). The practice of dealing violently with the opposition was decided during the war of liberation. When ZANU-PF assumed state power in 1980, the state itself was used to unleash *Gukurahundi* style of violence on those who happened to be constructed as enemies of the state like PF-ZAPU and ex-ZIPRA cadres. Matabeleland and the Midlands regions became theatres of postcolonial practice of the strategy of *Gukurahundi* and an estimated 20,000 civilians lost their lives as ZANU-PF pushed for a one-party state. Joshua Nkomo, PF-ZAPU, ex-ZIPRA and all supporters of PF-ZAPU had to be annihilated as they stood in the way of ZANU-PF's assertion and consolidation of hegemony through imposition of a one-party state (Shaw 1986; Mandaza and Sachikonye 1991).

ZANU-PF has continued to use the strategy of *Gukurahundi* each time its hegemony is threatened. Such military-style operations as *Operation Murambatsvina* (Operation Urban Clean-Up) in 2005, *Operation Mavhoterapapi* (Where did you put your vote?) from April to August 2008, *Operation Chimumumu*, which involved abductions of opposition, civil society and other figures, testified to the consistent use of the strategy of *Gukurahundi* by ZANU-PF against those identified as threatening its hegemony (Ndlovu-Gatsheni 2009a). Stephen Chan argued that Mugabe was 'refusing to allow the Chimurenga to die' and interpreted this as a sign that Zimbabwe 'can never be cleansed because there cannot be an end to fighting and that for him [Mugabe] to fight is more important than to be cleansed' (Chan 2003: 183).

The revival of *Chimurenga* in the 2000s

When the ZANU-PF regime's popularity in the late 1990s, and early 2000s, reached its lowest ebb, it ratcheted up the ideology of *Chimurenga* and celebrated the strategy of *Gukurahundi*, boasting that the party and its leaders had 'degrees in violence' while at the same time trying to re-mobilize the populace around memories of the liberation struggle (Blair 2000). In the 1980s, ZANU-PF used the concepts of reconciliation and unity, development and nationalist rhetoric and symbolism to construct its hegemony. But in the late 1990s and early 2000s, the policy of reconciliation was repudiated, and the discourse of economic development, articulated in socialist transformative terms, no longer made sense as the party and the state had totally failed to deliver services to citizens. ZANU-PF increasingly resorted to cultural nationalism as a means of compensating for failure (Dorman 2001: 50; Ndlovu-Gatsheni and Willems 2009; Ndlovu-Gatsheni 2011a).

At another level, while the articulation of the nation in the 1980s assumed a partisan and ethnic character, with heroism attributed only to those who participated in the liberation struggle from the ZANU side, and the names of historical figures from Shona ethnic groups, such as Nehanda, were elevated into guardians of the nation, the nation after the year 2000 was defined in autochthonic and nativist terms, including attributing 'new meanings to concepts such as independence, heroes, and unity in the changed political context of the 2000s' (Ndlovu-Gatsheni and Willems 2009: 945). President Mugabe popularized the idea of 'Zimbabwe for Zimbabweans' including Occidentalizing white citizens, that is, framing them as Westerners who had to go back to the Euro-American world where they came from (Muchemwa 2010: 505; Ndlovu-Gatsheni 2009c).

It was in 2001 that 'galas' and 'biras' were introduced to celebrate the lives of Joshua Nkomo and Simon Muzenda, co-vice-presidents of Zimbabwe. After his death Nkomo, who in the 1980s was represented as the 'father of dissidents' and who was even forced into exile in 1983, finally gained the status of 'father of the nation'. A special form of commemoration of Nkomo known as 'Umdala Wethu Gala' (Our dear old man gala) was introduced in 2001. Its celebrations emphasized national unity as Nkomo was represented as a symbol of national unity because he signed the Unity Accord of 22 December 1987 which enabled ZANU-PF to swallow PF-ZAPU, making it possible for Mugabe to pursue the objective of establishing a one-party state unencumbered by any oppositional force. On the other hand, Muzenda was represented as the 'soul of the nation' and his life was celebrated under what became known as 'Mzee Bira' (Moore 2005c; Ndlovu-Gatsheni 2007a; Ndlovu-Gatsheni and Willems 2010).

Wendy Willems and I concluded that 'The national imaginary that was promoted through music gala was by no means an inclusive definition of the nation, but should be seen as the mediation of a "party nation"' (Ndlovu-Gatsheni and Willems 2009: 964). Moses Chikowero saw the galas as epitomizing 'the public construction and carnivalization of that nationalist project, utilizing the iconography of the country's departed and living patriarchs, matriarchs and heroes as well as the symbolisms of the 1987 Unity Accord and the achievement of independence in 1980' (Chikowero 2008: 323). On the other hand, Kizito Muchemwa (2010: 504) noted how the cemetery and place of death, particularly the National Heroes Acre, became 'the site from which the Zimbabwean polis is imagined and articulated' leading him to write of the process of 'necropolitan imagination' of the nation. ZANU-PF became engrossed in politics of using the death of the so-called 'patriots' to try and solicit sympathy from the populace and to re-narrate its contribution to the liberation of Zimbabwe from colonial rule.

What is also worth noting is that galas and *biras* were introduced at a time when the society was not at peace with itself: the economy was crumbling and ZANU-PF's political fortunes were declining. During galas and *biras*, modern music such as 'urban grooves' tunes were mixed with old *Chimurenga* songs so as to seduce the so-called 'born-frees' (all those born after the end of colonialism) into the nationalist project. ZANU-PF thought it was these 'born-frees' who supported and voted for the opposition MDC and therefore needed to be made into patriotic citizens (Ndlovu-Gatsheni and Willems 2009: 964).

This argument is further reinforced by the fact that all the galas and *biras* were staged in urban areas, where ZANU-PF had lost support to the opposition MDC; 'the galas migrate from one province to another', determined 'by pragmatic demands of the electoral moment, targeting those places where either electoral support is waning or there are party factional fights' (Muchemwa 2010: 512). Brian Raftopoulos argued that ZANU-PF attempted to 'naturalize the unity of the nation by concealing the internal ethnic tensions within the polity and the reality of Shona political dominance' (Raftopoulos 2007: 182). In short, memorialization and commemoration took the Stalinist form dominated by what Guy Debord described as 'the ruling order's non-stop discourse about itself, its never-ending monologue of self-praise, its self-portrait at the stage of totalitarian domination of all aspects of life' (Debord 2002: 8).

In short, by the year 2000, Zimbabweans were being taken back to the 1970s, a time when the ideology of *Chimurenga* had successfully established itself as the popular nodal point around which the anti-colonial struggle crystallized and the imagination of a postcolonial nation-state developed. But it was difficult for ZANU-PF to successfully wind the wheel of history backwards and to re-subjectivate and re-interpellate an angry and hungry populace that wanted food rather than doses of *Chimurenga*. The revival of the ideology of *Chimurenga* and the re-activation of the strategy of *Gukurahundi* on the changed political terrain of the 2000s provoked strong counter-hegemonic initiatives that could not be ignored.

Some counter-hegemonic articulations of the nation

Brian Raftopoulos's work on the labour movement unearthed tensions between nationalism and trade unionism as well as blending of the two. Nationalism's attempt to appropriate women's, church, peasant, student and labour movements, and subordinate them to the nationalist imperatives, was resisted by trade unionists such as Reuben Jamela and Charles Mzingeli, who wanted to maintain trade union autonomy without necessarily ditching the nationalist cause (Raftopoulos and Phimister 1997; Raftopoulos and Sachikonye 2001). The nationalists did not take this resistance from the labour unions lightly because it was an early challenge to their attempts to sow the seeds of hegemony. As noted by

Timothy Scarnecchia (2008), the nationalists began to unleash violence on trade unionists, who refused to subordinate themselves to the nationalist movements, justifying the violence by casting Mzingeli and Jamela as 'lackeys of imperialism and stooges'. This clash between nationalists and some labour trade unionists reveals one area of early contestation of the emerging nationalist hegemony.

But as noted in the opening part of this chapter, ZANU-PF was never free of internal dissensions and conflicts ever since its formation in 1963. After independence, the first signs of the decline of ZANU-PF's hegemonic monologism included the expulsion of the outspoken Secretary General of the party, Edgar Tekere in 1987, who eventually formed the Zimbabwe Unity Movement (ZUM) in 1989 opposing the one-party state agenda. The expulsion of internal critics also included Margaret Dongo in 1995, who went on to form the Zimbabwe Union of Democrats (ZUD), and Lawrence Mudehwe in 1996 (Sithole and Makumbe 1997: 135). The other internal critic of ZANU-PF was Eddison Zvobgo who in 1995 openly called for the democratization of Zimbabwe through cutting the powers of the Executive President (Zvobgo 1995).

The embers of counter-hegemonic articulations also occurred in internal party contestations that revolved around the definition and hierarchy of 'heroship' status and the concomitant material benefits. As noted by Norma Kriger (2006), there were tensions between elite nationalists who spearheaded the war from exile; those who actually handled the guns and operated inside Rhodesia against colonial forces; those who were incarcerated (ex-detainees, ex-prisoners and ex-restrictees) inside Zimbabwe; as well as those who were described as *mujibha* (male war collaborators) and *chimbwido* (female war collaborators). These contestations were over benefits and payments for the liberation war sacrifices.

What provoked questions was the open elevation of those nationalist leaders who were in exile (otherwise known as the old guard that included Mugabe) into what Muchemwa (2010: 509) terms 'Chimurenga aristocracy' who displayed 'vulgar opulence' and dominated the economic and political landscapes of the country, whereas other categories were languishing in poverty. Contestations within ZANU-PF were exacerbated by the fact that those who were buried at the National Heroes' Acre received less material benefits (Kriger 1995). At another level, throughout the 1980s, PF-ZAPU continuously protested against ZANU-PF's dominance in the selection of national heroes through boycotting heroes' celebrations (Werbner 1998; Kriger 1995; Brickhill 1995). This was a direct challenge to ZANU-PF's commemorative project by another former liberation movement until the time of the Unity Accord. PF-ZAPU and ex-ZIPRA initiated their own War Shrines Committee to identify and commemorate their fallen cadres (Brickhill 1995: 166).

The Heroes Acre, which was meant to be a powerful source of national unity and a strong source of legitimacy, has become a site of contestation with two veteran nationalists from Matebeleland, namely Welshman Mabhena and Thenjiwe Lesabe, indicating before their death that they did not want to be buried at the national shrine. Despite President Mugabe's glorifying words of condolence following the death of Mabhena, stating 'We have lost a true patriot par excellence', and the ZANU-PF subsequently declaring him a national hero, the Mabhena family stuck by his wish not to be buried at the national shrine (allafrica. com, 8 October 2010).

On the other hand, Lesabe was denied heroine status because she had left ZANU-PF to join the revived ZAPU (swradioafrica, 15 February 2011). The last case was the refusal of ZANU-PF to declare Gibson Sibanda, former deputy president of the MDC, a national hero despite a request by Morgan Tsvangirai for Mugabe to do so. Together, these events indicate that the National Heroes Acre was now exposed as a ZANU-PF shrine rather than a national shrine, one which some veteran nationalists find it repugnant to be associated with it.

The formation of the MDC, in 1999, led to the open declaration by its leader Morgan Tsvangirai in 2000 that nationalism was 'trapped in a time warp' and 'was an end in itself instead of a means to an end' (*Southern Africa Report* 2000). This was a direct attempt to depart from the ideology of *Chimurenga* as packaged by ZANU-PF. The MDC, as a political formation founded as a worker's party, tried to counter ZANU-PF rendition of *Chimurenga* in elitist terms by claiming that the liberation war was spearheaded by the working class and was then hijacked by nationalist elites (MDC 2000). But at the same time the MDC challenged the ideology of *Chimurenga* and the strategy of *Gukurahundi* as constituting gross violation of human rights as well as being anti-democracy.

As argued by Richard Werbner, 'memory as public practice' was 'increasingly in crisis' (Werbner 1998: 1). It was the MDC that encapsulated its vision of another Zimbabwe in the slogans of a 'New Zimbabwe' and 'New Beginning' that became very popular with young people and urban residents (MDC 2007). Thus, since its formation, the MDC has ceaselessly worked towards proving to the Zimbabweans, the Southern African Development Community (SADC), the African continent and the international community, that ZANU-PF has become nothing but an elitist project of wealth accumulation and has completely lost interest in pursuit of the emancipatory agenda, and that the MDC seeks to restore economic sanity, democracy and human rights.

The pulling-out of some members of ZANU-PF, like the former Minister of Home Affairs and veteran nationalist Dumiso Dabengwa, in an attempt to revive ZAPU, is another indication of new attempts and initiatives to move beyond the ZANU-PF monologue. ZAPU is partly trying to hark back to the pre-1963 period of nationalist unity and inclusive nationalism while at the same time partly working towards re-gaining its Matebeleland and Midlands constituencies through appealing to the

Ndebele-speaking people's grievances. ZAPU is also trying to pull the nationalist project away from ZANU-PF, which it accuses of having re-tribalized and regionalized the nation. ZAPU is also claiming its libera-tion credentials, which ZANU-PF tried to downplay and subordinate to those of ZANU-PF and ZANLA (ZAPU Manifesto 2010).

Finally, there are strong counter-messages from the Matebeleland region, adversely affected by postcolonial state-sanctioned violence that claimed the lives of an estimated 20,000 civilians under the pre-text of fighting so-called dissidents who were said to be supported by the minority Ndebele community in the 1980s (CCJP and LRF 1997; Al-exander, McGregor and Ranger 2000). The violence of the 1980s that is remembered in Matabeleland and Midlands regions as 'Gukurahundi genocide' has generated a radical politics of secession spearheaded by such diaspora-based political formations such as Mthwakazi People's Congress (MPC) and the Mthwakazi Liberation Front (MLF), fighting for restoration of the precolonial Ndebele nation, to be separate from the provinces of Mashonaland and Manicaland that they call Zimba-bwe (Ndlovu-Gatsheni 2008b; Ndlovu-Gatsheni 2009b). During the cel-ebrations of Independence Day on 18 April 2011, members of the MLF marched through Johannesburg and publicly burnt the Zimbabwean national flag as a symbolic statement of refusal to be part of Zimbabwe.

Those forces working for secession of Matebeleland have gone fur-ther, establishing a full-fledged virtual nation known as the United Mthwakazi Republic (UMR), complete with all the trappings of a na-tion-state including a radio station and national flag. Since 2000, ZANU-PF has been trying to ignore the rising tide of secessionist agitations simply because they were mainly exercised in cyberspace but in 2010 MLF launched itself inside Zimbabwe in Bulawayo and the government has acted by arresting some members of MLF, including a well-known politician, Paul Siwela. Members of MLF have also written a long letter to President Mugabe, dated 24 February 2011, stating that Mthwakazi's desire to exercise its self-determination as a free, independent and sov-ereign Republic of Mthwakazi is historical and that *Gukurahundi* massa-cres heightened the impetus for independence (Open Letter to Mugabe, 24 February 2011). There is no doubt that ZANU-PF hegemony entered a serious crisis at the beginning of 2000. As the crisis deepened, fac-tions within ZANU-PF, energized by the possibilities of Mugabe leaving power or dying from old age, have further weakened this once seem-ingly strong political formation.

Conclusion

Just like colonial technologies of subjectivation, African nationalist strat-egies and methods of creating nations, national histories and national subjects, generated opposition and counter-hegemonic discourses that revealed the limits of nationalist political engineering. The acceptance by ZANU-PF to share power with the MDC in September 2008, through signing the Global Political Agreement (GPA), and the installation of the inclusive government in February 2009, is a clear indication that President Mugabe and his colleagues have realized the limits of both the ideology of *Chimurenga* and the strategy of *Gukurahundi*. But within the inclusive government, the questions of ownership of the nation, control of the state, exercise of power, and lack of a unifying national narrative continue unabated. The nation remains polarized into patriots, puppets, sell-outs, war veterans, and born-frees as politicized identities, a clear testimony of ZANU-PF's survival through attempts to divide people rather than unite them. What is elusive in Zimbabwe, as elsewhere in postcolonial Africa, is a stable national identity underpinned by a common patriotism.

Therefore, the country has remained caught up in a Gramscian interregnum whereby the old ideology of *Chimurenga*, and the strategy of *Gukurahundi*, are taking time to die while the new politics, founded on values of tolerance, plurality, inclusivity, social peace and human security, are taking time to be born. In the interim, the old monsters continue to polarize the nation. This is a point that is well articulated by Raftopoulos (2011), who argued that the coming into being of the GPA and the installation of inclusive government, while it has not fully transformed the coercive base of ZANU-PF's support, has yet set on course a rhythm of change for a new set of political dynamics in Zimbabwe informed by what Gramsci termed the 'passive revolution'. But in ZANU-PF political parlance, all those people who are resisting its dominance and who are voting for the opposition are considered to be lacking nationalist subjectivation and have had to undergo national service training where they were exposed to nationalist catechisms. The prime targets for this were the unemployed youth upon whom ZANU-PF tried to reproduce its *Chimurenga* ideology, while at the same time subjecting the entire opposition fraternity to the *Gukurahundi* strategy.

PART 3

COLONIALITY, KNOWLEDGE AND NATIONALISM

CHAPTER 7

Coloniality of Knowledge and Higher Education

Introduction

Much better the African be tutored in his own history, languages, and customs, to hear his own songs and learn his own traditions, taught by Africans who knew and respected an indigenous culture so misunderstood and discounted by foreigners, studying at an inland university centre far removed from the deadly effects of alien influences.

(Robert W. July 1987: 158–159)

Most of the African Universities were founded by the colonial powers after the Second World War. They were based on European and American models. With the achievement of political independence, African governments were keen to indigenize these imported, although indispensable, institutions. Our first major task has, therefore, been, and still is, how to Africanize these institutions without undermining their identity as universities – i.e. as centres of independent thought and critical inquiry. We have tried to do this by Africanizing the staff and the curricula. The question still remains as to whether we have now localized these institutions sufficiently. Almost every week, we are attacked often by politicians, for being foreign islands in a sea of natives.

(Bethwell Allan Ogot 2002: 594)

The discourses of cultural transformation of higher education have a long pedigree in liberation history. At its centre is the quest for decolonization, not simply understood as political struggle ranged against formal colonial relations but as confrontation with the colonization of consciousness that inhibits African self-direction for the purpose of self-benefit (Maldonado-Torres 2007: 240–270). Western education emerged in Africa as one of the technologies of subjectivation. Instead of higher education becoming a medium to transfer the needed technological skills from the West into Africa, it became largely a laboratory for Westernization that produced Africans who were alienated from their societies and cultures.

Cultural imperialism has been identified as another key obstacle to independence and development. Therefore, what cultural transformation of higher education entails is the changing of the 'ideology of knowledge' as well as 'sociology of knowledge'. At the ideological level of knowledge, the aim is to repudiate the Eurocentric colonial paradigm that continues to reduce African people as objects rather than subjects of knowledge. At the sociological level of knowledge, the quest is to enable Africans themselves to take charge of academic life so as to produce knowledge that is relevant to Africa.

What is most detestable about higher education that was transplanted from Europe and America into Africa is the colonization of African minds. Colonization of the mind refers to a process of Western ideological intervention, and epistemological invasion of the mental sphere of the African, resulting in confused consciousness and identity crisis (Dascal 2009: 308; Chinweizu 1987). Jean Paul Sartre categorized Africans who have been exposed to mental colonization as a form of education as 'walking lies', that is, Africans who dreamt in both Western and African languages. While dreaming in two languages is not a big issue, what is problematic is the subjectivation/socialization of Africans through education into subjects who hated and belittled everything African to the extent of loving everything European and American.

The time has come for the establishment of African institutions for higher education that will produce African graduates who do not suffer from identity crises. An education that promotes and produces Africans who are nothing but copycats of Europeans and Americans needs to be culturally transformed. Such Africans are today popularly known as coconuts (Ndlovu-Gatsheni 2007b). They are white inside and black outside. They are physically located on the continent but epistemologically situated in Europe and America. They read and understand Africa from a European perspective. Cultural transformation of higher education is meant to change the character of institutions of higher education that continue to exist in Africa as factories for the production and reproduction of coconuts.

The cultural transformation of higher education is definable as an ideological and pragmatic exercise dealing with the problem of coloniality of being in Africa. Coloniality of being refers to the social, ideological, and epistemological process of reproduction of black people as a different human species, which is not worthy of treatment in an ethical way. Coloniality of being also highlights the colonial justifications of denial of any human rights to African people, including the right to life and culture (Maldonado-Torres 2007: 251–257). It is deeply embedded in global imperial designs that have been in place since the time of conquest. The roots of coloniality of being grow from the dark side of modernity, where articulation of civilization was through 'invention' of the African as the inferior 'other'.

The black inferior other was reproduced ideologically and represented socially as lacking soul, lacking history, lacking writing, lacking religion, lacking culture, lacking knowledge, lacking development, lacking human rights, and lacking democracy (Grosfoguel 2007: 211–223). Such a social construction of the black being as an 'empty being' became the basis for impositions of external knowledges and religions. The black being had to struggle to free and rescue itself from a situation of nothingness into subjectivity.

These struggles to challenge the representation of the African as an undefined 'empty' being have been ongoing since the time of colonial encounters. Frantz Fanon and Chinua Achebe understood the logic of the Africa struggles. Fanon said: 'The black must create his self-image to counter the image of the white man, define his existence from within, not permit that it be imposed from without' (Fanon 1968: 93). Achebe also captured the cultural contours of this struggle very well when he said:

> You have all heard of the African personality; of African democracy, of African way to socialism, of Negritude, and so on. They are all props we have fashioned at different times to help us get on our feet again. Once we are up we shall not need any of them anymore. But for the moment it is in the nature of things that we need to counter racism with what Jean-Paul Sartre has called an anti-racist racism, to announce not just that we are as good as the next man but that we are better. (Achebe cited in Moore-Gilbert 1997: 179)

In this context, culture is better interpreted in the Cabralian sense as a resource from which to launch struggles for political, economic, and epistemological freedom as well as cognitive justice. In this struggle, the black subject, who is still struggling to transcend the legacies and realities of colonialism and apartheid, becomes the primary agent of cultural transformation of higher education to take into account his or her historical experiences, aspirations, cultures and practical challenges. The discourses and actual initiatives to culturally transform higher education are part of the continuing liberation struggles. Amilcar Cabral defined national liberation as:

> [T]he phenomenon in which a given socio-economic whole rejects the negation of its historical process. In other words, the national liberation of a people is the regaining of the historical personality of that people, its return to history through the destruction of the imperialist domination to which it was subjected. (Cabral 1972: 102)

In this chapter, cultural transformation is understood to mean a package of transformations in teaching, research, epistemology, curriculum, pedagogy and institutional cultures, aimed at anchoring and repositioning higher education within Africa and the liberation trajectories of the

African people. Cultural transformation becomes an ideological and pragmatic exercise meant to underpin African renewal, with the objective to liberate knowledge from Euro-American hegemony, narrow class, technical, elitist, and Western-centric orientation (Nabudere 2011). What is envisaged as the end product of cultural transformation are institutions of higher education that privilege epistemologies, pedagogies, and curriculum that are consonant with specific African historical, cultural, and practical realities.

What is wanted is a higher education that does not lead to alienation of African people from their societies and communities. But cultural transformation does not mean the disconnection of Africans from the ambit of global human society and broader human problems (Olukoshi and Zeleza 2004: 1–18). It only implies that a confident African is one rooted in his or her society and whose locus of enunciation is African. Such an African would be able to formulate culturally friendly resolutions of the challenges facing the continent.

Practically speaking, cultural transformation, when creative, seeks ways of blending African and Euro-American epistemologies in an endeavour to advance and enrich the understanding of African experience, problems, and challenges. But it also entails a drive to decolonize knowledge, curriculum, epistemology, pedagogies, power, and institutional cultures. The point of departure for decolonization of higher education is that Africa remains entangled, woven, and trapped within the snares of colonial matrices of power in place since colonial encounters.

Such entrapment requires a decolonization therapy that is informed by the imperatives of a pluriversal epistemology of the future, which privileges a critique of Euro-American epistemological hegemony while arguing for other knowledges to be allowed into the academy. It is against the dominant idea of mono-epistemology and is pro-pluriversality of epistemologies (Mignolo 2007a: 159). In such a case, cultural transformation of higher education means decolonizing higher education and its institutional cultures through dealing with its Western orientation, symbols, rituals and cultures carried over from colonialism, apartheid and modernity. This exercise is necessitated by the realities of the existence of African universities, which are nothing other than universities in Africa that were and are finding it difficult to shed their historical emergence as Western transplants advancing Western interests and privileging Western ideas.

It is within this context that the agenda of cultural transformation of higher education becomes an urgent task. J. Teboho Lebakeng, M. Manthiba Phalane and Nase Dalindjebo argued that the university in Africa is besieged by a plethora of crises. These crises range from that of academic mimetism, which takes the form of failure to cut the intellectual umbilical cord from the Western epistemological paradigm, and those of borrowed discourses, crisis of legitimacy, crisis of identity, crisis of relevance, crisis of inappropriate epistemology, crisis of mission, to crisis of historical representations (Lebakeng et al. 2006: 75). The crises are attributed to what is described as epistemicide, which consisted of displacing African culture, pushing it to the margins of society, and unleashing epistemological violence against indigenous epistemology (Lebakeng et al. 2006: 70–72). Once this was done, academia became open to the free play of Euro-American epistemology.

The logic for pushing the discourse of cultural transformation of higher education in Africa in particular is that institutions of higher education have remained as purveyors and disseminators of atomized, racialized, Euro-American-centric, Christian-centric, hetero-normative, capitalist, neo-liberal and elitist epistemologies, pedagogies, and institutional cultures. The key question running in the minds of advocates of cultural transformations of higher education is how to establish the relevance of these pedagogies, epistemologies, and institutional cultures for the decolonization of minds, and advancement of African liberatory and developmental agendas.

If one has to take into cognisance the French theorist Michael Foucault's argument that Western education together with its social and human sciences emerged as products of historical and practical necessity and that knowledge and power are intrinsically intertwined, it becomes obvious that higher education in Africa must be driven by historical and practical agendas of Africans. On this Foucault wrote that:

> There can be no doubt, certainly, that the historical emergence of each of the human sciences was occasioned by a problem, a requirement, an obstacle of a theoretical or political order: the new norms imposed by industrial society upon individuals were certainly necessary before psychology, slowly, in the course of the nineteenth century, could constitute itself as a science; and the threats that, since the French Revolution, have weighed so heavily on the balance, and even on the equilibrium established by the bourgeoisie, were no doubt necessary before a reflection of sociology type could appear. (Foucault 1970: 344–345)

The most important point flowing from Foucault's argument is that each human civilization must develop its own education system informed by its contemporary historical and practical problems, challenges, requirements and realities. There is a strong feeling among many Africans that, from the first colonial encounters onwards, Africa lost control of its destiny as colonisers imposed their own agendas on the continent, including transplanting their religions and education as means to subjugate and subjectivate, dominate, and exploit Africans. The challenge in Africa is that the knowledge that was used to subjectivate, discipline and colonize was inherited in its institutional forms by the postcolonial states (L.T. Smith 1999).

Euro-American knowledge, which has been used to exclude, marginalize and deny any value to indigenous ways of knowing, cannot form the correct basis for African struggles for liberation, decolonization of the minds and development. The continued reliance on colonized Euro-American knowledge is manifest in the failure of universities in Africa to shift their attention from Europe and America in their search for models, epistemologies, pedagogies, theories and samples of curriculum development and innovations. The situation is poignant in South Africa, where at the dawn of democracy, instead of intensifying the transformation of apartheid-based education while working simultaneously with de-Westernized systems of education, they 'experimented with models of education derived from America, modified in Australia and then adapted for the South African situation in the form of Outcomes Based Education (OBE)' (Vambe 2009: 6). South Africa is not the only culprit in this. The case study of Ghana given in this chapter indicates the reluctance by some academics to cut the umbilical cord with the University of London, even after achievement of political independence.

But the cultural transformation of higher education must be done in a very careful manner that involves re-assessment of both the African and Western cultures and pasts. What must be avoided is an interpretation of cultural transformation to mean looking backwards, as with Negritude and ethnophilosophy, but without blindly embracing Westernization. Marcien Towa suggests a radical break with the African past and the creative and synthetic embrace of Western modes of thought:

> We must assert ourselves in the world of today... Naturally the decision to assert our selves, ... is at the same time a decision to assume with a sense of pride the validity of our past. Such a decision, however ... by introducing a radical change in our present condition, demands as well a similar break with a past that is at once responsible for that condition. The wish to be ourselves leads at once to a reassessment of the past since the essence of self comes from the past. Coldly and clearly scrutinized, the past attests that our present subservience is explained by the essence of self which is of the past. To change the present character of self means at the same time to change the essence of self, its particularities, original and unique, to enter into a negative relationship with the self. (Towa cited in July 1987: 223)

Towa's intervention raises the dangers of romanticizing African cultures and histories as Africans struggle to ground higher education within Africa and search for relevant knowledges that would enable them to extricate themselves from longstanding and evolving colonial matrices of power that have been in place since the colonial encounters of the fifteenth century. But Towa's encouragement of Africans to embrace Western thought is also problematic because Africans have already imbibed and embraced enough of Western culture and thought to be alienated from African cultures and histories. There is a strong case for Africans to fight for cognitive justice that involves decreasing the dose of Western thought and privileging African thought. Boaventura de Sousa Santos, João Arriscado Nunes and Maria Paula Meneses have argued that there cannot be social justice in the world without global cognitive justice. They noted that:

> The epistemological privilege granted to modern science from the seventeenth century onwards, which made possible the technological revolutions that consolidated Western supremacy, was also instrumental in suppressing other, non-scientific forms of knowledges and, at the same time, the subaltern social groups whose social practices were informed by such knowledges. (Santos et al. 2007b: xix)

Peter Crossman defined cultural transformation of higher education in terms of endogenization. By this he meant that the process of making African universities and their processes of knowledge production to be consistent with African cultural orientation and material contexts. These cultural and material contexts were acknowledged to be in a constant state of change as they appropriated and transformed external factors and influences to reinforce internal principles and priorities (Crossman 2004: 319–340). If indeed universities in Africa were able to appropriate and transform resources from Euro-American knowledge and education to reinforce local knowledges as they worked to resolve African developmental challenges, then there is hope for Africa to succeed. The reality however is that local epistemologies and cultures remain peripheral to the mission of universities in Africa. Cultural transformation itself is open to animated debates and controversies.

The third wave of higher education reform

The current endeavours to transform higher education in such a way that it deals with African challenges, problems and requirements is dubbed the third wave of reform (Pityana n.d: 39). Nyameko Barney Pityana defined this third wave of higher education reform with specific reference to South Africa. In the context of South Africa the driving force has since 1994 been as much to depart from the apartheid legacy as to assert the value of higher education institutions in a new milieu where values and principles of constitutional democracy prevail. The end product of such an education is not a decolonized subject but an active citizenry able to fulfil the human resource development of South Africa as a developing country (Pityana n.d.: 38). This sounds like a transformation informed by neo-liberal ideas rather than liberatory-decolonial imperatives. It does not go to the heart of the challenges that constrain higher education from being an agent of decolonial change in postcolonial and post-apartheid South Africa.

The discourses of cultural transformation of higher education must seek to address the soul of the African university. The soul of the African university must be open to embrace diversity of ways of knowing, alternative epistemologies and plurality of pedagogies. What will distinguish a truly culturally transformed African university would be its epistemic locus of enunciation. Its faculty and students must be epistemically located in Africa. Its motto would be 'I am where I think' (Mignolo 1999: 235–245). The issue of 'colonial difference' as a privileged epistemic site should be taken seriously as a launch pad to appreciate and understand how the darker aspects of modernity such as mercantilism, the slave trade, imperialism, colonialism, apartheid and neo-colonialism created the African condition and how it has mutated into global coloniality, where the Euro-American world remains at the apex and the African world at the subaltern bottom.

A truly culturally transformed African university would not be conservative but must even be open to experiment in 'epistemic disobedience' in its search for a new soul (Mignolo 2008: 1–23). Those epistemologies, cascading from the oppressed side of power and from subaltern epistemic locations, would form the mission of the culturally transformed university. This in simple terms means driving an education agenda in which ideas and intellectual production from the Global South in general and Africa in particular are given centre stage. This would be a moment of 'epistemic awakening' of Africa (Ndlovu-Gatsheni 2011b).

What must be said is that the cultural transformation of higher education across the African continent has largely skirted around the problem. The common route has been to re-name buildings, accompanied by increasing the numbers of women and black faculty. This might have addressed the culture of dominance of male and white faculty. But it does not get to the core issues of language and Eurocentrism. Worse still, increasing the numbers of black women and men does not in any way resolve the epistemological problems because the majority of black faculty have imbibed Euro-American cultures and epistemologies. Their blackness does not translate to shifting their locus of enunciation of knowledge. The same is true that being located in Africa physically does not prevent one from thinking epistemically as if one were in London, Washington or Brussels, for example. What is needed is a robust centre for decolonial thought to create a cohort of faculty and students who are epistemically located in Africa. But before this vision can materialize, a number of hurdles need to be transcended.

The first is that the issue of cultural transformation of higher education in Africa is itself engrossed in conceptual, ideological and pragmatic controversies. Culture as concept is open to various interpretations and meanings. As one pushes the agenda of cultural transformation of higher education, one dives straight into contestations between the forces of endogenization and the globalization of education. When one speaks of anchoring the African university in African culture, the question that arises is how students and faculty will deal with the cultural heterogeneity of the continent. Even within countries like South Africa, there is a cultural heterogeneity that defies easy definitions of African culture. If cultural transformation of higher education is a form of endogenization, the challenge is that endogenization is itself subject to various interpretations, including the insistence on the possibility of anchoring higher education in recovered African cultures. Worse still, Africa is becoming dominated by middle-class and elitist culture. Is this the correct culture in which to anchor the African university (Thaver 2009)?

It is easy for one to talk about the problems of Euro-American hegemonic epistemology but another to come up with practical strategies and tactics to transcend it. The challenge is compounded by the fact that Euro-American epistemology has deeply penetrated ontologies of human and social sciences, including the very idea of historicizing human phenomena, secular time, and ideas of sovereignty. Euro-American epistemology is not a singular body of thought and knowledge. It has its own diversities and pluralities that need to be carefully understood. It has its own contradictions and ambiguities that could be exploited by Africans as they strive to build an African university. But now Euro-American epistemology has permeated almost every institution and facet of modern society, including the African one, making it very hard to deal with or run away from. The ubiquity of Euro-American epistemology is well captured by the leading decolonial thinker Nelson Maldonado-Torres who argued that as a form of coloniality (carrier of colonial cultures):

> It is maintained alive in books, in the criteria for academic performance, in cultural patterns, in common sense, in the self-image of peoples, in aspirations of self, and so many other aspects of our modern experience. In a way, as modern subjects we breathe coloniality all the time and every day. (Maldonado-Torres 2007: 243)

Dipesh Chakrabarty's *Provincialising Europe: Postcolonial Thought and Historical Difference* (2000) provides part of a way out in dealing with Euro-American epistemological hegemony. His solution is that what the West has claimed as its modernity, epistemology, and civilization belongs to every human being and is a global human heritage. What is needed is for peripheralized societies to claim it from the margins (Chakrabarty 2000: 43). Instead of rejecting modernity and its liberal values, universals, science, reason, grand narratives, and totalizing explanations, there is a need to claim these as products of human history rather than European history. Chakrabarty gives the example of Third World nationalisms as modernizing ideologies that contributed to the making of the modern world of today (Chakrabarty 2000: 43).

If this route is taken, then cultural transformation of higher education would entail formulation of various ways of appropriating the fruits of modernity for the benefit of Africa. Francis Nyamnjoh (2006a: 393) wrote about what he described as the process of 'modernizing their indigeneities and indigenizing their modernities'. This African strategy has been in place since colonial days, with Africans engaging in creative negotiation of multiple encounters, influences and perspectives. As Nyamnjoh put it, these longstanding processes have not been 'always obvious to scholarly fascination with dichotomies' (Nyamnjoh 2006a: 393).

But this strategy has not worked successfully because it seeks epistemological redemption within the belly of Euro-American epistemology. Often it has reinforced and reproduced colonial matrices of power that are not predisposed to accommodate other knowledges that have a potential to threaten the assumed superiority of Western knowledge. The limit of this strategy is well captured by Boaventura de Sousa Santos in the form of a challenge:

> How can we identify the perspective of the oppressed in real-world interventions or in any resistance to them? How can we translate this perspective into knowledge practices? In search for alternatives to domination and oppression, how can we distinguish between alternatives to the system of oppression and domination and alternatives within the system or, more specifically, how do we distinguish between alternatives to capitalism and alternatives within capitalism? In sum, how do we fight against the abyssal lines using conceptual and political instruments that don't reproduce them? And finally, a question of special interest to educators: what would be the impact of postabyssal conception of knowledge (as an ecology of knowledges) upon our educational institutions and research centres? (Santos 2007a: 78)

For centuries African attempts to appropriate the fruits of modernity and even to resist in the form of nationalism have suffered from interpellation by the very forces they were trying to deal with. The consequence of this has been an African failure to imagine alternatives to what have been bequeathed on them by colonial modernity. Universities in Africa and the postcolonial state are two clear examples of institutions that were bequeathed to Africa by colonial modernity. The two institutions have proven very hard to transform into new institutions amenable to African interests, plans, agendas and aspirations. These institutions have successfully resisted indigenization and endogenization. Africans have also been reluctant to destroy these institutions and build their own.

Another issue which needs to be taken into account as Africans grapple with the cultural transformation of higher education is that a majority of African institutions of higher education remain anchored within the boundaries of the postcolonial nation-state, which makes sense for them to privilege, as a national duty, the primacy of carrying forward the national project(s) as well as the reflection of national cultures. But, at the same time, the new discourse of cultural transformation of higher education is taking place during an age of globalization, when imperatives of internationalization of education were emphasized. What this means is that there were emerging tensions between imperatives of endogenization and those of globalization that impacted on the mission, relevance, and identity of the university. This raises another challenge: how to make sure that the drive for the cultural transformation of higher education does not generate nativism and cultural relativism.

The key question is: what does cultural transformation of higher education mean in the context of globalization? The work of Achille Mbembe (2002a; 2002b) warns Africans about the dangers of degeneration into nativism as they fight to recover lost identity. Mbembe defined nativism as a discourse of rehabilitation, and a defence of the humanity of Africans, which is always underpinned by the claim that their race, traditions and customs make them a unique human species. In his words, Mbembe said:

> Well, I define 'nativism' as one of the culturalist responses Africans have given to the fact of denial of their humanity. It is a response which, while arguing that 'Africans are human beings like any other', nevertheless emphasizes the difference and uniqueness of their traditions or what they call their culture. (Mbembe 2006b: 6–7)

What Mbembe's intervention raises is: how different are discourses of cultural transformation of higher education from nativist discourses? Is the drive for cultural transformation of higher education not informed by what Mbembe termed 'African modes of self-writing?' (Mbembe 2002a: 239–273). According to Mbembe, nativist discourses are cultural in essence and they are watered from two springs, namely Afro-Marxism and African nationalism. These two ideologies are, according to Mbembe, very powerful and persuasive although they are philosophically false because they subsist on metaphysics of difference and grievance. Their end product is a neurosis of victimhood rather than redemption (Mbembe 2002b: 613–659).

While Mbembe's warnings are well taken, the attempts to dismiss African nationalism as a false philosophy and the African feeling of grievance as leading to a neurosis of victimhood is a form of caricaturing African resistance and African struggles to stand up after years of dehumanization by slavery, imperialism, colonialism, apartheid and neo-colonialism. What he calls nativism has material bases in histories of dispossession, colonization of the mind and racial exclusion. It is this history that informs present-day discourses of cultural transformation of higher education. Cultural transformation of higher education can be better read as a counter-discourse to the meta-discourses informed by global imperial designs. It is also a reverse-discourse aimed at reversing the ubiquity of Euro-American epistemological hegemony in higher education institutions. It seeks to reverse the cultures informed by androcentrism, whiteness, and Eurocentrism (Ndlovu-Gatsheni 2011b). It is therefore important to understand the various factors that inform the drive for cultural transformation of higher education in Africa.

Historical roots of epistemological alterity

At the time of decolonization the core emblems of a sovereign state were the national flag, national anthem, national currency, and national university, among others. This inclusion of the university among the emblems of national sovereignty speaks to the importance attached to higher education and the importance of knowledge production in the lives and development of Africans. However, for a university to play a critical role in the improvement of lives of Africans it must be rooted in Africa and draw its strengths and inspiration from the society it is located in while also borrowing, adapting, and innovating on the basis of external resources (Muzvidziwa 2008: 74–94).

Ideally, indigenous African knowledge systems should underpin the mission of the African university. Its primary mission should be to serve the needs of the people while at the same time contributing to global knowledge. But the fact that in this twenty-first century, the challenge is still to implement the cultural transformation of higher education, indicates the long-term impact on Africa of inheriting universities that originally existed as 'Western transplants advancing Western interests and privileging Western ideas' (Muzvidziwa 2008: 79). Once Western epistemology and worldviews were introduced, it became difficult for Africans to imagine alternatives, including re-rooting the inherited university in African cultures.

The debates on cultural transformation of higher education have a long history in Africa, beginning in the nineteenth century when early educated elites, like Africanus Horton and Edward Blyden, began to imagine and discuss the idea of an African university. Horton, who was trained as a medical doctor, became very critical of an unquestioning embrace of Western education. He argued for a marriage of indigenous and foreign wisdom as the best way to enable the African to find his or her way in the modern world. Horton argued that disciplines such as biology, chemistry, geology, and physics had to take into account the realities of the tropics if they were to facilitate the unlocking of the mysteries and riches of Africa (July 1987: 157–158). Horton was an early advocate of the cultural transformation of Western knowledge to take into account African histories, agendas, values, cultures and specific challenges.

Blyden was another pioneer, educated member of an African elite who understood the races of the world as complementary, with each possessing its own genius as well as its negative characteristics. For him, each race should be allowed to contribute to world civilization without interference. Blyden did not support the imposition of Western education in Africa because it would destroy the black race's special genius and talents. His vision of a university was one that was going to tutor African people in their own history, languages, and customs. The teaching had to be done by Africans who knew and respected indigenous cultures rather than by whites who misunderstood and deliberately discounted African epistemologies and cultures (July 1987: 58–59).

Unfortunately these early imaginations of an African university and the purpose of higher education never materialized. Africans became drawn into European domination and tutelage. As a consequence of colonialism, the African future did not grow directly from the seeds of their own cultures and histories unadulterated by colonization. As the nineteenth century came to a close, Africa became engrossed in intensified violent and ideological impositions of Western cultures. By 1914, only Ethiopia had survived direct colonization. The period from the 1920s to the 1930s was dominated by the routinization of colonialism. Christian missionaries played a role in codification and standardization of the spelling of African languages into teachable material. While in sub-Saharan Africa universities were a later introduction, they were still creations of colonialism meant to serve colonial and broader global imperial designs. It is these colonially created institutions that Africans inherited at the dawn of independence.

Postcolonial Africa possessed universities in Africa rather than African universities. This is a point confirmed by Robert W. July (1987: 56) who stated that 'The first universities in black Africa were imports, their purpose the indoctrination of a foreign culture'. The same is true of the postcolonial state itself. It was a state in Africa rather than an African state. This reality led Ira William Zartman to pose the following questions: 'Is there an African state now? Where is it headed? Is its trajectory similar to that on the other side of the Atlantic? And then, what is the alternative?' (Zartman 2007: 30). The same questions can be posed for the university as a producer of higher education in Africa. Where is it headed?

On the state, Pita O. Agbese and George Klay Kieh (2007a: xi) noted that 'There is a general consensus that the postcolonial state in Africa has failed to cater to the needs and aspirations of Africans. Consequently the state has become irrelevant and distant from its own citizens'. The universities, just like the postcolonial state, failed to cater to the needs and aspirations of Africans. Universities became rather irrelevant and distant from the people they were expected to serve. Neither the states nor the universities respected African cultures, values, ancestors, languages, knowledges, epistemologies, pedagogies and cosmologies. The reason was that the state and the universities were imposed from outside on African societies by colonialists. Even those universities that were built after colonialism became modelled on Western traditions. No attempts were made to imagine and invent new epistemologies, pedagogies and institutional cultures.

The colonial culture that was informed by what Wallerstein (1991) described as nineteenth-century social science continues to have far too strong a hold on African mentalities even today. The presumptions of Euro-American epistemology, which served Westerners very well, propelling them into the centre of the world, enabling them to develop and claim ethno-racial superiority over Africans, and ensuring the liberation of their spirit, could not do the same for Africa. Africa and its people received the darker side of modernity, characterized by the slave trade, imperialism, colonialism, apartheid, neo-colonialism and Christianization. Euro-American epistemology became more of a technology of subjectivation used to 'invent' Africans as the inferior other. It actually became a central intellectual barrier to useful analysis of the African social world and negatively impacted on African development as it concealed its Orientalizing purpose (Wallerstein 1991). The Peruvian sociologist Anibal Quijano explains the ways in which Euro-American epistemology as a handmaiden of colonialism displaced other knowledges and cultures:

> In the beginning colonialism was a product of a systematic repression, not only of the specific beliefs, ideas, images, symbols or knowledges that were not useful to global colonial domination, while at the same the colonisers were expropriating from the colonized their knowledge, especially in mining, agriculture, engineering, as well as their products and work. The repression fell, above all, over the modes of knowing, of producing knowledge, of producing perspectives, images and systems of images, symbols, modes of signification, over the resources, patterns, and instruments of formalised and objectivised expression, intellectual or visual ... The colonisers also imposed a mystified image of their own patterns of producing knowledge and meaning. At first, they placed these patterns far out of reach of the dominated. Later, they taught them in a partial and selective way, in order to co-opt some of the dominated into their own power institutions ... Cultural Europeanization was transformed into an aspiration ... The imaginary in the non-European cultures could hardly exist today and, above all, reproduce itself outside of these relations. (Quijano 2007: 169)

It became very hard for Africans to reverse this damage visited on them by colonialism. Cultural Europeanization remained a seductive aspiration even after decolonization. This became apparent in the propensity and proclivity of the members of African elites, including African nationalist leaders, to send their children to study in Europe and America.

The case of Ghana, the first country in sub-Saharan Africa to gain political independence, in 1957, reveals how the discourse of cultural transformation of higher education has been problematic from the time of decolonization.

The first wave of cultural transformation of higher education: the case study of Ghana

The University of Ghana emerged between 1946 and 1949 when Britain took steps to introduce higher education in its colonies of Sudan, Uganda, Nigeria and Ghana. These institutions of higher education were established as colleges of the University of London. This means that from birth, each of the offspring of the colonial university system reflected the predilections of its parentage (July 1987: 159). Linking these universities to one located in the metropolis was justified as ensuring the highest quality of education for a people that were being prepared for political independence. In reality the linkage was nothing but part of global imperial designs that emphasized control and tutelage over Africa.

From the start, under the pretext of ensuring academic quality, university colleges existed under close supervision of the University of London. The supervision took the form of checking, if not transplanting, syllabi, courses and examinations from London to Ghana. The University of London issued the degree certificate. The Asquith and Elliot Commissions were launched by the British government to develop the new universities in the colonies while mentioning the need for adaptation of higher education to local African contexts and meeting the new demands of non-Western societies, which also emphasized the need of these universities to emerge as 'facsimiles of British universities' (Ashby 1966: 190–235). Eric Ashby concluded that:

> No-one reading the reports is likely to come away with the impression that the long-term prospects of these universities depend upon their becoming indigenous, and that research, design of curriculum, pattern of government, should all contribute to this end. (Ashby 1966: 190)

The University College of the Gold Coast (now the University of Ghana in Legon) began to operate in 1949. The first principal was David Balme, 'a classics don from Cambridge', who strongly believed that 'the only consequential civilization in the modern world was the culture of the West as inherited from Mediterranean antiquity, a culture which therefore should dominate the curriculum of any university, quite apart from whatever culture obtained locally' (July 1987: 161–162). As part of introducing the culture and heritage of Greek and Latin civilizations, 'Balme took special pains to establish departments of classics and philosophy' (July 1987: 162). Western culture was indeed directly injected into the new institutions of higher education. Even the degree structure, of students pursuing three subjects at general level and concentrating on one subject at honours level, 'reflected academic preoccupations in Britain rather than the imperatives of African national development' (July 1987: 163).

The contestations over the cultural relevance of the education existed from the beginning with students complaining of entrance requirements designed expressly to fit postwar conditions in Britain, questioning the suitability of the London degree structure and the relevance of the curriculum as a whole. But the idea of maintaining standards was used to maintain inflexibility. Entering the university became very difficult for African students as they did not meet the entry requirements transplanted from London (Ashby 1966: 236–250). The crisis of the colonial universities in Africa was well captured by July, who said:

> It was one thing to insist that universities in Africa concern themselves with a Western culture to which Africa already had a deep commitment. It was something else, however, to compel an almost exclusive concentration on the heritage of the West, neglecting other bodies of knowledge, particularly those involving Africa. It was imperative that African universities address themselves to the study of the societies from which they had sprung. University graduates could scarcely serve their own people unless they understood and sympathised with indigenous social structure and political organization. Future teachers would never be able to reach their students without a firm grasp of aesthetic and philosophical principles that had guided Africa's peoples through ages. The future could only grow from the seeds of the past. (July 1987: 164)

When independence was achieved by Ghana in 1957, the first black leader of Ghana promised a university that was going to reflect African traditions and culture. Such a university was also going to play a constructive part in national political awakening and economic reconstruction (Nkrumah 1961). By the time of achievement of political independence, the University of Ghana was dominated by white expatriates who stuck to the idea of maintaining standards and did not buy into Nkrumah's transformative agenda. The university became the last institution to be decolonized.

Despite Nkrumah's pronouncements on the mission and identity of the university, he and his party became preoccupied with other political and economic issues to the extent of paying little attention to the transformation of the university. Thus, even after Ghana's achievement of independence, both white and black faculty at Legon continued to defend the special relationship with the University of London. Excellence was still understood and equated with a British degree and a Western curriculum. Students were 'fearful of the possible effect on their careers if they were graduated from an institution that did not bear the established label of the English university system' (July 1987: 167). Even within Nk-rumah's party and government, there were voices that were opposed to transformation.

When Balme left Ghana in 1957, Nkrumah did not take advantage to begin the transformation. Instead another white expatriate from England was appointed. The talk at the university was how to defend the university from political interference. It was only when Professor Kofi Busia left his post in sociology at the University of Ghana to pursue a new career as leader of the opposition that Nkrumah and his party began to view the university with a different eye (Curle 1962: 232–233).

From then on, the university became viewed as a seedbed for politically irrelevant elites. But Nkrumah had a vision of a university in Ghana that drew its 'inspiration from an African past, fusing ancient traditions with modern, chiefly Marxist ideas, and training peoples capable of working and living in the context of a new liberated Africa' (July 1987: 169). Such a university had to engage in intellectual decolonization, producing graduates who took a new look at the world, faculty researching in African history, culture and arts, in order to create a new kind of Ghanaian. Nkrumah had deep faith in the strength of Africa's civilizations. The university had to play ball (July 1987: 169).

The transformation of the University of Ghana was very slow. Nkrumah moved with moderation, searching for compromises and consensus. A special commission was created comprising educationists from Africa, Europe, the U.S.A. and the USSR. It convened in 1960 and produced its report in May 1960, which proposed keeping university autonomy while at the same time recommending that the university curriculum should be informed by the needs and aspirations of Ghanaians and furtherance of African unity. Increasingly, the government asserted that the university was a bastion of bourgeois mentalities in a country that was pursuing a socialist and pan-Africanist path. But the appointment of Nana Kobina Nketsia as acting principal of the university did not result in transformation. Conservative institutional cultures were hard to transform. Nkrumah himself contributed to delays in transformation because of his drive for international acceptance. For instance, in 1961 he appointed Conor Cruise O'Brien as vice-chancellor of the University of Ghana when the nation expected him to appoint a Ghanaian (O'Brien 1965: 240–251).

At the University of Ghana, an Institute of African Studies was viewed by the government as the vehicle of transformation, espousing ideas of fighting against neo-colonialism, construction of a socialist society and promoting a political union of African states. At the Institute's inaugural ceremony, Nkrumah articulated his vision for it:

> This Institute must surely ... study the history, culture and institutions, languages and arts of Ghana and of Africa in new African centred way

– in entire freedom from the propositions and pre-suppositions of the colonial epoch ... We must re-assess and assert the glories and achievements of our African past and inspire our generation, and succeeding generations, with a vision of a better future. (Nkrumah 1963: 2–3)

The problem was that the institute was embedded within a university which was very slow in undergoing transformation. Because of the slowness and reluctance of the University of Ghana to fully embrace Nkrumah's ideas and philosophies, the alternative was for him to establish a separate institute at Winneba that promoted Nkrumahism as an ideology. Before his departure from power in 1966, Nkrumah had also played a role in creating institutes of music and dance, as well as an institute for cultural studies, that were separate from the university. He had also created a new university of science and technology, where all the undergraduates irrespective of discipline were to study a course on African civilizations. Taken together, all these initiatives were meant to achieve cultural transformation of higher education in such a way that it reflected its African environment and cultural issues.

Cultural transformation of higher education in South Africa

South Africa was the last sub-Saharan country to attain freedom from apartheid in 1994. As such, it is engaged in attempts to culturally transform higher education to reflect constitutional democracy, on the one hand, and, on the other, to reflect African context and cultures. Both formerly black institutions and formerly white institutions need cultural transformation albeit in different directions. The challenge is that the formerly English institutions have perpetuated English cultures whereas the formerly Afrikaner institutions have perpetuated Afrikaner cultures. These challenges have to be transformed through simultaneous processes of de-racialization and decolonization to combat exclusion of blacks. For formerly black institutions, the transformation has to change the 'Bantustan cultures' that breed mediocrity, sluggishness and underperformance.

The cultural transformation has begun with such initiatives as renaming of buildings and increasing the number of black academics. Just as in Ghana, the conservative discourses of maintaining standards have surfaced as a justification to resist cultural transformation in South Africa. The challenges to cultural transformation of South African higher education are compounded by the tensions between forces of globalization and those of endogenization. This is manifest in some of the institutions' mission statements and mottos that combine the drive towards being 'African' and being 'world class' universities.

The Report Commissioned by the Minister of Higher Education and Training for the Charter for Humanities and Social Sciences: Final Report of 30 June

2011 is pushing for the establishment of five Virtual Schools that will be spread across Gauteng, KwaZulu-Natal, Western Cape, and Eastern Cape, with the mandate of dealing with issues of economy, race, culture, identity, literature, performance, creative arts, local languages and rural transformation (*Higher Education and Training Commission Report for Charter on Humanities and Social Sciences* 2011). As in Ghana, the cultural transformation agenda as reflected in the *Charter for Humanities and Social Sciences* seems to be indicating the use of Virtual Schools that are not directly embedded within existing universities as nodal points. But it is yet to be seen how these Virtual Schools would be able to facilitate cultural transformation of higher education from the margins. What is clear is that each Virtual School is dealing with those issues which existing universities have not been successful in achieving.

Conclusions

The theme of cultural transformation of higher education has a long pedigree in African studies and liberation histories. It even pre-dates the decolonization period. It is traceable to the period of colonial encounters. The early educated African elites like Blyden and Horton who began to imagine an African university and toyed with ideas of an African university in the nineteenth century already grappled with the difficult question of Eurocentrism and how such a university should be underpinned by African histories, cultures and arts. At the centre of early discourses of cultural transformation of higher education was the issue of reclaiming an African identity that was affected by colonial encounters and ploughed under by the introduction of Western knowledge and education. This chapter has tried to provide a historical as well as conceptual understanding of the problems and prospects of cultural transformation of higher education in Africa.

While it underscores the importance and accepts the logic of cultural transformation of higher education in Africa, the chapter also raised various warnings and conceptual pitfalls that need to be navigated carefully as African people struggle to culturally transform higher education. To back up its propositions and claims the chapter provided the empirical cases of Ghana and South Africa, the former to indicate the challenges faced during the first wave of higher education reform and the latter to demonstrate the continuation of these challenges during the third wave of higher education reform. Cultural transformation of higher education was also defined as falling within the broader liberation discourses and identity recovery processes, taking the form of sociology of knowledge and ideology of knowledge as a terrain to attain epistemological freedom and cognitive justice.

CHAPTER 8

The African National Project and National Question

Introduction

Indeed I believe that a real dilemma faces the pan-Africanist. On the one hand is the fact that pan-Africanism demands an African consciousness and an African loyalty; on the other hand is the fact that each pan-Africanist must also concern himself with the freedom and development of one of the nations of Africa. These things can conflict. Let us be honest and admit that they have already conflicted.
(Julius Nyerere 1966: 1)

The National Question therefore is the perennial debate as to how to order the relations between the different ethnic, linguistic and cultural groupings so that they have the same rights and privileges, access to power and equitable share of national resources; debate as to whether or not we are on the right course towards the goal of nationhood; debate as to whether our constitutions facilitate or inhibit our march to nationhood; or whether the goal itself is mistaken and we should seek other political arrangements to facilitate our search for legitimacy and development.
(J. F. Ade Ajayi 2000: 218)

What would an unsententious historiographical study of the nature and conflicted agendas of the national project(s) to inform future African political trajectories yield? This is a pertinent question today because the global crisis of modernity has ignited the need to re-launch national project(s) and rethink the national question at a time when neo-colonialism, which privileged market forces as central organizers of the modern world order, is failing. The neo-liberal assault backed up by postmodernist and cosmopolitanist discourses, which had submerged issues of national project(s) and the national question, has unraveled, opening the way for the return of the repressed issues of nationalism, the national project(s) and the national question (Moyo and Yeros 2011).

Therefore, this chapter begins by engaging with the definition of the African national project and delineation of its core national and social elements. The second section analyses how founding fathers understood and implemented the national project(s), including identifying the challenges they confronted. The focus is on what I have termed the Nkrumah-Nyerere debate that was introduced in Chapter Two of this book on how divergences on implementation of pan-Africanism ended up symbolizing a divided African house. This chapter elaborates on the challenges and links these to the initiatives of seeking to resolve the national question through implementation of national projects.

The third section analyses the factors that plunged the African national project into crisis in the early 1970s. The fourth section traces how some intellectuals and policy-makers defended the African national project from delegitimation by the Bretton Woods institutions and assaults by 'post-'s (postcolonialism, postmodernism, post-structuralism). This is important because in the 1980s and 1990s, national project(s) and nationalism itself became cornered by the Washington Consensus advocates of Structural Adjustment Programmes (SAPs) and by postmodernist discourses, only to be defended by a few committed African scholars who remained faithful to the redemptive and liberatory potentials of nationalism. In that sense, the national project also became an intellectual project and was sustained by intellectual discourses opposed to SAPs and postmodernist interventions. The fourth section builds on this tradition to argue for new national project(s) that are predicated on decoloniality, democracy and participation of the masses. The fifth concludes the chapter.

What is meant by national project(s) and the national question?

Three related concepts need to be defined because they underpin the whole discussion of this chapter. These are nationalism, national project(s) and the national question. While it is clear that these three concepts mean different things to different people partly because of their ideological nature and partly due to their dynamic nature, an attempt is made to explain what they mean in the context of this chapter. Nationalism is the broader identitarian and ideological framework and anchor for struggle that sought to create people-as-nation and people-as-state. This is why Michael Billig (1995: 24) argued that the term nation carried two interrelated meanings: first, there is nation as nation-state, and second, there is the nation as the people within the state. This definition is reinforced by Anthony D. Smith (1999: 18–19), who defined nationalism as 'an ideological movement for attaining and maintaining identity,

unity and autonomy of a social group whose members deem it to constitute an actual or potential nation'.

A national project grows from nationalism as an ideological blue-
print that is often named and written into such documents as the Arusha Declaration in Tanzania under Julius Nyerere, the Mulugushi Declaration in Zambia under Kaunda, the Freedom Charter in South Africa,
the Common Man's Charter in Uganda under Milton Obote, and many
other examples. National projects also carried various specific names
such as *Ujamaa* in Tanzania, *Harambee* in Kenya under Jomo Kenyatta,
Authenticité in Zaire under Mobutu Sese Seko, *Humanism* in Zambia, and
many other examples (Laakso and Olukoshi 1996: 14). In countries like
Zimbabwe under Robert Mugabe, the national project is not clearly articulated beyond the notion of *Chimurenga*, underpinned by the need to
achieve economic decolonization otherwise known as indigenization of
the economy (Ndlovu-Gatsheni 2009a; Ndlovu-Gatsheni 2011a).

Drawing from these examples, the national project(s) crystallizes as a
nationalist-inspired imagination of a postcolonial future. It also emerges
as an ideological guide that is at times shaped into national policy, as
was the case with *Ujamaa* in Tanzania and *Authenticité* in Zaire (Lumumba-Kasongo 1991). A national project can also assume the character of
a national developmental plan or agenda aimed at resolving particular
problems and transcending particular challenges such as poverty. As
such, a national project can be simply understood as an encapsulation of
plans, policies and actions aimed at resolving a national question. A national question in this sense becomes that which the national project(s)
sought to solve.

All political regimes irrespective of ideological differences developed forms of national project as foundations of their socio-economic
platforms for resolution of the national question (Lumumba-Kasongo
2011: 63). They need to be understood at a number of levels. They can
be defined as imaginary politico-ideological concepts, springing from
the minds of those political elites in charge of the state who intend to
facilitate the routinization of their power and control. At another level,
they are open to easy dismissal as simple tools of political domination evolved by the dominant nationalist elites. The way that national
projects are presented in documents, like the Arusha Declaration, can
also be seen as complex embodiments of the nationalist strategies aimed
at connecting the priorities of African political elites and the expectations of the masses as the foundation of postcolonial developmental
initiatives (Lumumba-Kasongo 2011: 63–64). These different interpretations are by no means exhaustive of the meaning and essence of the
national project(s).

Lumumba-Kasongo (2011: 85) defined a national project as 'a state
policy to address the political inadequacy, citizenship dislocation, and
social and structural dysfunctionality'. What must be admitted is that

national project(s) are open to different definitions. Their ontology is inherently dynamic and ever-changing in relation to ever-shifting internal and external imperatives and factors such as imperialism. In Africa, nationalism, national project(s), and national question(s) are also defined in relation to imperialism, colonialism, and neo-colonialism as those inimical processes that existed to deny and negate African liberation, economic progress and African identity. In the 1960s and 1970s, imperialism that had mutated into neo-colonialism as its highest stage, and tribalism, were understood as the greatest threats to the success of the African national project.

Tribalism was viewed as threatening from below while neo-colonialism was threatening from above. This is why Yash Tandon (2008: 66) presented a picture of a national project as a multifaceted nationalist strategy that incorporated quests for local, national, regional, and South-South self-determination, independence, dignity, solidarity and the means to end aid dependence. For him, it was the continuation of the struggle for independence, which needed to be revived during this era of globalization where imperialism was returning under disguise (Tandon 2008: 66). But this multifacetedness of the national project(s) makes it hard to define in precise terms because it is watered from different ideological springs and is a response to equally divergent contemporary problems that are often summarized as the national question. But Lumumba-Kasongo is able to provide this definition:

> The national project is one of the most important dimensions of the state building in Africa. This dimension is about creating new institutions and agencies, and defining new culture and citizenry in pragmatic manner. It includes formulating policies and political frameworks to address people's demands and their expectations to try to institutionalize, to a certain extent, the idea of sovereignty of the state. (Lumumba-Kasongo 2007: 5)

Defined this way, the national project is a discursive terrain within which the national question, as a totalization of the challenges of nation-building, building state institutions, and social issues of poverty, is located. But the national question is itself open to various definitions by scholars as the totality of the political, economic, territorial, legal, ideological and cultural relations among national groups (majorities around which nations often crystallize) and nationalities (minorities of different identities) in their various socio-economic and cultural formations. It encapsulates the entire network of problems arising from the co-existence of nations and nationalities (Stalin 1934 [2003]).

This traditional view has been revised and expanded to reflect the national and social dimensions of problems faced by postcolonial Africa in particular. The national dimension encompasses African people's assertions of their humanity and identity through acquisition of independence and building of sovereign nation-states. The social dimension entailed the initiatives aimed at raising the standard of living of citizens of the postcolonial nation-states and eradication of poverty (Nzongola-Ntalaja 1987; Mkandawire 2009).

But the old definition rooted in Stalin's analysis of the Soviet situation is noticeable in the way Ernest Wamba dia Wamba understood the core components of the national question. He thought of the national question in terms of a problematic of how leaders could exercise legitimate power over states inhabited by people of diverse identities, experiencing inequalities of underdevelopment and competing among each other over claims to self-determination (Wamba dia Wamba 1991: 57). While Stalin's definition was informed by the situation in the Soviet Union where people of different ethnic backgrounds were to be brought together into a bigger Union of Soviet Socialist Republics (USSR), Wamba dia Wamba came from the Democratic Republic of Congo (DRC) where forming a singular, national, and legitimate government has been a big challenge since the departure of Belgian colonialists and the assassination of Patrice Lumumba.

Postcolonial Africa as a whole has been deeply nervous about its internal unity to the extent that such cases as Biafra, and Katanga secessionist tendencies, were feared so much that the gospel became that of declaring death on the tribe if the nation were to survive. But at the centre of the national project(s) were also concerns about 'imagining a new society, new rules and new paradigms of change to satisfy people's expectations' as well as about African self-definition, building consensus between elite groups and other citizens, and cultivation of a national psychology of unity and spirit of innovation and hard work (Lumumba-Kasongo 2011: 74).

But controversies always surrounded the national project(s) as top-down mechanisms that were often imposed on society through a mixture of coercion and persuasion. Principles underpinning the national project(s) depended not only on the period and ideology, but also on regime typologies and styles of governance preferred by different founding fathers within their societies. For pan-Africanist leaders, like Julius Nyerere, the most problematic aspect of the national project(s) remained that of how to convert nationalism into pan-Africanism. Nyerere identified the problematic as taking the form of reconciling imperatives of narrow nation-building and wider pan-African unity (Nyerere 1966; Lumumba-Kasongo 1991; Lumumba-Kasongo 1994; Lumumba-Kasongo 2003). But for Nkrumah pan-Africanism was a superior form of nationalism informed by ideals of greater continental freedom, equality, independence, and social justice.

In countries like Nigeria, Ethiopia, Sudan, DRC, and South Africa, to name just a few big ones, with a kaleidoscope of ethnic, racial, cultural, linguistic, religious and other differences, the national question is often reduced to that of identity. The national project crystallizes around how to deal with identity issues, which are often identified as a hindrance to economic development, peace, and democracy. Where material inequalities and poverty were pervasive, as in Tanzania, the national question became defined as that of material inequality and the *Ujamaa* national project was meant to resolve it through the introduction if not recovery of a socialist ethos from the traditional society.

In South Africa, where the problem of race is rampant as the result of the apartheid regime, from the time of the adoption of the Freedom Charter by the African National Congress (ANC), the ongoing key initiatives have been aimed at dealing with racism. Besides the adoption of the Freedom Charter, South Africa has instituted the Truth and Reconciliation Commission (TRC) as an attempt to facilitate a smooth transition from apartheid to democracy (Chipkin 2007). South Africa also mobilized the power of *ubuntu* (humanism) and the imagery of the rainbow to try to bring about unity. The presidency of Thabo Mbeki introduced the concept of African Renaissance as a pivot around which the nation could crystallize since South Africa is part of Africa. But Mbeki's pronouncements and emphasis on African identity became interpreted as reverse racism and a departure from Nelson Mandela's non-racialism and Rainbowism (Glaser 2010: 3–39).

What is also becoming clear is that the architecture of the national project(s) and the content of the national question(s) have never been monolithic and static. Each historical epoch has imposed new issues on the national project's table and has changed the content of the national question. For instance, in the 1960s the concerns were with issues of how to deal with tribalism and neo-colonialism as African leaders pushed the agenda of development. In the 1960s and 1970s, development was more of a state and presidential project and the nation had to be silent while development was taking place. One-party state systems and executive presidencies were justified as solutions to divisive problems of ethnicity. Today, the one-party state system has been discredited beyond doubt. National projects must embrace multipartyism. Democracy and the element of popular participation have become so topical that any relevant national project(s) must fully embrace these issues.

As argued by Cynthia Enloe (1989: 44), nationalisms had typically sprung from 'masculinised memory, masculinised humiliation and masculinised hope'. This quality led Anne McClintock (1997: 89) to conclude that 'All nationalisms are gendered; all are invented; and all are dangerous'. Today such nationalism and its national project(s) cannot be considered progressive. Sensitivity to gender and commitment to the equality of men and women are now a major part of the national question and a national project that does not embrace these is doomed to fail.

Founding mothers have been unearthed from the archives and oral memory of the nationalist studies with the aim to demystify the impression that nationalist liberation struggles were masculine affairs. But in this chapter I use the term 'founding fathers' because in the 1960s all the presidents and prime ministers were male, reflecting Enloe's point of the emergence of nationalism within masculinized terrains. But relevant national project(s) and national questions in the twenty-first century must not only embrace topical issues of environment, ecology, and climate change but must also be amenable to conversion into pan-Africanism and be responsive to generational and global issues.

Crisis of implementation of national project(s)

Kwame Nkrumah and Julius Nyerere's thoughts on nationalism and pan-Africanism reminded one of the Stalin-Trotsky debates on socialism in the interwar years. Stalin and Trotsky were both committed socialists, with Stalin pushing the agenda of first building 'socialism in one country' then globalizing it. Trotsky favoured internationalization of socialism from the start. In the same manner, Nkrumah and Nyerere were both committed to the agenda of pan-Africanism but they differed on the methodology and route to be pursued towards realization of this goal. In the implementation and institutionalization of pan-Africanism, Nyerere favoured a cautious and gradualist approach and was equally preoccupied with transforming Tanzania into a socialist society. It would seem the Tanzanian national project(s) came first for Nyerere. Nkrumah's vision was for continental unity from the beginning and pan-Africanism came first for him. Shivji had this to say about Nkrumah and Nyerere as pan-Africanists:

> Mwalimu Nyerere was an ardent and militant African nationalist and an equally convinced and persuasive pan-Africanist. Unlike Nkrumah, though, Nyerere arrived at continental pan-Africanism through Tanganyikan nationalism. Nkrumah arrived at Ghanaian nationalism through pan-Africanism. Nyerere saw an irresolvable tension between nationalism and pan-Africanism. (Shivji 2012: 103–104)

Looking at how Nkrumah and Nyerere interpreted national project(s) and how they argued for the pan-African agenda provides a unique entry into further understanding the complexities of implementing the national project(s) while pushing forward the pan-African agenda. Their thinking and practical approaches to the national project(s), pan-Africanism and the national question converged and diverged in interesting ways that revealed the tensions in conceptualization and implementation. That the tensions created three groups – those of Casablanca, Monrovia and Brazzaville – confirmed the weaknesses of a divided African house that was easily susceptible to the destructive winds of neo-colonialism. It is clear from various historical records that former colonial powers like France and Britain played a role in influencing some of their former colonies to resist Nkrumah's grand plan for the continent.

Nkrumah and Nyerere operated within a complex postcolonial terrain. The immediate postcolonial period was dominated by popular expectations that needed to be fulfilled and political turmoil that needed to be avoided. The question of regime survival in the midst of the Cold War impinged on the national and social transformational agendas of the world's youngest states (Nkrumah 1965). Nkrumah considered continental political unity as the only means by which each African country could survive the onslaught of neo-colonialism and enjoy real freedom (Nkrumah 1963b; Nkrumah 1967). The contradictions and ambiguities between nationalism and pan-Africanism that ensued in the 1960s have continued to haunt postcolonial African initiatives towards achievement of pan-African unity.

Besides the contradictions and ambiguities between nationalism and pan-Africanism, the postcolonial African states were conceived and born into a world underpinned by imperialism. Sam Moyo and Paris Yeros (2011) mapped the evolution of the imperial world well into four broad epochs. The first epoch that is relevant for Africa was the mercantile period running from the years 1500 to 1800. It was marked by the slave trade, which provoked the racial nationalism strand of pan-Africanism. The slave trade is one of the major sins committed by imperialism against Africans. It manifested the beginning of primitive accumulation that became a key feature of colonialism and contributed to the genesis of underdevelopment. Dealing with underdevelopment and the scourge of poverty continues to be a core part of the agendas of the African national project.

The next epoch was industrial-monopoly capitalism running from 1800 to 1945. It enabled imperialism and colonialism. It was through these processes that Africa was conquered and brought into the nexus of the evolving and exploitative capitalist system. The third epoch was that of the ideological rivalry between the East and the West that was dubbed the Cold War (1945–1989). Africa became a theatre of some of the 'hottest' aspects of this rivalry. Angola and Mozambique's national projects were stifled at birth because of the conflicts linked to this global ideological rivalry as it was exported to Africa. Africa's decolonization unfolded within this context with nationalist leaders exploiting the ideological fissures to get armaments and other resources, including borrowing ideologies like Marxism, Leninism and Maoism. Africa's national projects were formulated and deployed within the context of this ideological war to the extent that founding fathers of the African states found themselves having to align with particular powers. Those leaders who openly aligned with the East, like Patrice Lumumba, Kwame Nkrumah, Amilcar Cabral, Eduardo Mondlane, Agostinho Neto and others, endured surveillance from the West that resulted in sponsored coups, assassinations and counter-revolutionary forces that depleted the stamina of their socialist-oriented national projects.

The current epoch unfolded from the 1990s, underpinned by the Washington Consensus and neo-liberalism. It has culminated in the age of globalization. Its slogan since the end of the Cold War had been that we are all now neo-liberals and that history, understood as propelled by ideological contestations, had come to an end. But since the 9/11 incident a new dimension emerged, known as the war against terror, spearheaded by the U.S.A. and its NATO allies. Ideologically informed by neo-liberalism and its rhetoric of democracy and human rights, the U.S.A. made it part of its foreign policy to spread neo-liberal values across the world while at the same time instituting regime changes in those peripheral areas constructed as the 'axis of evil' and as 'outposts of tyranny'. This move caused panic among African leaders who were committed to the preservation of hard-won national sovereignties (Moyo and Yeros 2011: vii–x). This is the broad terrain within which nationalists and pan-Africanists are operating.

Therefore, any historiographical critique of the national project(s) and the challenges facing African leaders as they tried to resolve the national question(s) must take into account the global imperial designs that have continued to entrap Africa since the time of colonial encounters. Decolonization did not result in a reversal of global imperial designs. It only resulted in changing the content of the language of engagement between Africa and the Western powers. Terms like sovereignty became popular as direct colonial administrations withdrew and opened the way for neo-colonialism. Within the African continent, there was a change in the content of the language used between African leaders and citizens. This is well captured by Tandon, who summarized some of the questions to which citizens demanded answers from their leaders:

> Where do we go from here? What now? What do we do with this hard won independence? ... Who are we as a 'nation'? How do we forge nationhood out of disparate ethnic, racial, linguistic, regional and sub-regional groups? (Tandon 2008: 67)

These critical questions have continued to this day without satisfactory responses. Nzongola-Ntalaja (1978: 48) alerted us to the foundational complexities of the national question to do with finding a template for the postcolonial nation-state. Founding fathers had three options. The first was to exhume the precolonial templates, which Nzongola-Ntalaja (1987: 48) described as 'the ethnic nation of ancient glory whose construction was arrested by colonialism'. The second was to embrace 'the colonially created territorial nation'. The third was to construct a pan-African nation that had never existed before (Nzongola-Ntalaja 1987: 48).

Building on precolonial template(s) meant trying to revive the various ethno-nations that had been destroyed by the Berlin consensus of

1884 to 1885. The pan-African nation was attractive to Nkrumah. Nzongola-Ntalaja (1987: 49), however, pointed out that the possible adoption of the pan-African nation 'was in flagrant contradiction with both the neo-colonialist strategy of imperialism and the class interests of the African petit-bourgeoisie'. Consequently, colonially created territorial states were accepted. This option did not disrupt global imperial designs. It went in tandem with imperatives of territorial nationalism.

But opting for colonially created territorial nations was the first step towards embracing neo-colonialism by the founding fathers. It also set the stage for betrayal of the pan-African vision. This led Nzongola-Ntalaja (1987: 50) to conclude that the political map of Africa of the 1960s represented a double failure: the failure of the pan-African ideal of a single nation under one continental state or several regional federations, and failure to harness precolonial histories and cultures in nation-state building. He explained this failure in terms of lack of well-organized class forces capable of championing these dreams (Nzongola-Ntalaja 1987: 50).

This double failure prompted scholars like Julius Ihonvbere to roundly blame African founding fathers for numerous betrayals of the national project(s). He blamed them for failure to restructure the state, to empower Africans, to challenge foreign domination and exploitation of Africans, and to challenge the cultural bastardization of the continent (Ihonvbere 1994: 5). But such reproaches do not answer or advance knowledge of these complex questions: what did the African leaders think about the national question, what went wrong with the national project(s), and why did they fail to improve the conditions of the ordinary people?

Nkrumah's national project(s) embodied both a nationalist and a pan-African vision. To him, there were complementarities rather than tensions between nationalism and pan-Africanism. This vision was clearly expressed in three of his widely quoted dicta: 'Seek ye first the political kingdom and all else shall be added unto it' (Mazrui 1999: 105). He also made it clear that 'The independence of Ghana is meaningless unless linked to the total liberation of the African continent'. He elaborated that 'The independence of Ghana was the first crack in the seemingly impregnable armour of imperialism in Africa. It created and furnished the bridgehead for organized assaults upon colonialism' (Nkrumah 1966: xiv).

Nkrumah interpreted the attainment of political independence by African states as the beginning of a political trajectory to real freedom predicated on pan-African unity. Territorial nationalism was for him a means to pan-Africanism. This is why he placed the independence of Ghana at the centre of the pan-African project, linking its sovereignty to the total liberation of the continent. Nkrumah identified neo-colonialism as the main threat to the independent states of Africa. To him imperialism was the common enemy of mankind. His view was that no African country stood a chance of pursuing an independent national project without inviting the wrath of neo-colonialism (Nkrumah 1965).

Therefore, to Nkrumah pan-African unity was a nationalist survival shield. It protected Africans from their vulnerability to neo-colonialism. Neo-colonialism could only be countered by a politically united Africa. Pan-African unity would enable Africans to own their natural resources and would be ideal for the pursuit of independent economic policies. What is problematic was Nkrumah's pan-African agenda interface with his national projectin Ghana. Such an understanding enables engagement with Nkrumahism in practice. When Ghana attained independence in 1957, Nkrumah pulled the pan-Africanist movement into the continent through hosting its conferences. He also accommodated liberation movements in Ghana and supported them materially to the extent that one of his critics accused him of 'sacrificing Ghana on the altar of pan-Africanism' (Omari 1970: 2).

At home Nkrumah promised his people an economic paradise to the extent that, in April 1957, he accepted an economic development challenge from Houphouët-Boigny, the leader of Côte d'Ivoire, over which country would be more developed in ten years time. The challenge was centred on who pursued the most effective developmental strategies. Nkrumah was against Côte d'Ivoire's choice to remain under the neo-colonial tutelage of France and its commitment to a free-market capitalist economy that he considered exploitative (Nugent 2004: 166–167).

Nkrumah channelled Ghana into a socialist path that was predicated on 'philosophical consciencism'. The philosophy was based on acknowledgement of a triple heritage: Afro-Islamic and Euro-Christian realities as well as the experience of the traditional African society. These heritages had to be blended into a harmonious national project aimed at stimulating the growth and development of Ghana (Nkrumah 1964: 70). To implement such a national project, Nkrumah need decolonized Ghanaian cadres who were socialist-oriented in their thinking. Logically, Ghana was among the 'first wave' of socialist experiments in Africa alongside Tanzania, Algeria, Guinea, Mali, Libya, Egypt and Tunisia. Nkrumah's socialism included the agenda of decolonizing the minds of Ghanaians and the cultivation of pan-African consciousness. He considered capitalism to be evil and alien to Africa. To him, socialism could be synchronized with an African humanism that was destroyed by colonialism (Nkrumah 1964: 70–71). The resolution of the national question was through creating an egalitarian society at home and creating pan-African unity at the continental level.

Nkrumah's economic vision, predicated on challenging neo-colonial relations between Ghana and the West, encountered serious structural constraints. His government depended on revenues from a weak monocrop (cocoa) economy. Nkrumah responded to this constraint through a policy of diversifying the economy. His biggest project was the Volta Dam and associated aluminium processing industry. But this venture needed new technology and finance. Fredrick Cooper (2002: 161) argued that the Volta Dam and the aluminium processing industry projects 'actually put much of the Ghana economy into the hands both of multinational aluminum companies, which had the needed technology, and of international financial institutions, which had the money'.

Nkrumah's implementation of the national project was not predicated on democracy. He turned Ghana into a one-party state. He believed that it was a remedy for political tribalism, particularly that of the Asante, which, according to him, had to disappear for Ghana to survive as a unitary nation-state. He used the Convention People's Party (CCP) as an instrument of power consolidation to the extent of conflating it with the people and the nation: making it the supreme institution in Ghana (Mazrui 2004). Added to this, Nkrumah himself became omnipotent to the extent of assuming the title of *Osagyefo* (Redeemer). His ideas became a national 'ism' called Nkrumahism, which Ghanaians had to learn (McRae 1966).

As alluded to in Chapter Two, in 1966, Nkrumah had to exit the political stage as the consequence of a military coup, which followed immediately after the publication of his *Neo-Colonialism: The Last Stage of Imperialism* (October 1965). It became clear that counter-revolutionary onslaught was unleashed on the leading father of pan-Africanism, confirming beyond doubt the operations of colonial matrices of power. Consequently, by 1966 Nkrumah's dream of continental political unity had not materialized together with his initiative to position Ghana in the forefront of the struggle for a free and united Africa.

The coup that removed Nkrumah from power was followed by many others, to the extent that the late 1960s and early 1970s became an age of military coups, many in West and East Africa, which opened the way for the rehabilitation of imperialism and entrenchment of coloniality. One can also say that Nkrumah's preoccupation with the idea of pan-Africanism did not allow him enough time to concentrate on recreating and decolonizing Ghana into an African state. For instance, the Ghanaian army remained a centre of power that carried coloniality. Nkrumah could have moved in the same manner as Nyerere and dismantled the colonially inherited army that was susceptible to infiltration by the U.S. Central Intelligence Agency (CIA), a major cog in the maintenance of global imperial designs and neo-colonialism.

Nyerere's ability to survive until he voluntarily retired from formal politics in 1985 is partly explained by the fact that he was less revolutionary than Nkrumah and partly because he managed to create an African state infused with his ideology. Nkrumah's approach towards resolution of the social question assumed what became known as 'developmental authoritarianism' pushed forward by a vanguardist party that imposed the development agenda on the society. This generated resistance and disillusionment. His choice of the one-party state, accompanied by the closing down of political spaces and intolerance of opposition, dented his legacy. But these approaches to the resolution of the social and national questions became ubiquitous across different regime types in the 1960s and 1970s (Zolberg 1966).

On the other hand, Nyerere's national project was built around the metaphor of traditional family that was informed by mutual respect, cooperative spirit, equality, and harmony. Like Nkrumah, Nyerere believed that socialism was the order of traditional African societies and that capitalism was foreign to Africa (Nyerere 1967: 162–171). Nyerere's socialism was predicated on principles of human equality (material equality); freedom (freedom from exploitation); self-reliance (freedom from neo-colonial dependency); and national unity (Nyerere 1967). Like Nkrumah and Kenneth Kaunda, he believed in an overarching humanism/communalism as a response to an alienating and exploiting capitalist system.

Nyerere tried to study the life of rural Tanzanians before implementing his national project. His first major action was to nationalize the commanding heights of the economy. The second was to establish the villagization scheme. In all this, promotion of rural development through agricultural development was central to the resolution of the national question. The aim was to transform rural society to create 'rural economic and social communities where people would live together for the good of all' (Nyerere 1968: 337). This was to be achieved through persuading peasants into collective villages where the government provided land and resources to enable cooperative farming.

The reasons for the failure of villagization as a resolution of the social question of poverty and inequality are given by many scholars (Shivji 1974; Hyden 1980). Suffice to say, the implementation of the national project became entangled in contradictions and coercion, prompting resistance from the rural people. Nyerere, just like Nkrumah, became a 'benevolent dictator' with his party (Chama Cha Mapinduzi (CCM)), just like CCP in Ghana, being elevated to the centre of nation, state, and society, issuing developmental decrees to the people, emanating from the president's desk.

But Nyerere achieved literacy in the area, raising it to the highest in Africa through building primary schools in every village. National unity and political stability were also achieved. Tanzania survived ethnic and regional conflicts that rocked its neighbours like Kenya, Rwanda, Uganda and others. Nyerere survived politically until he stepped down from presidency in 1985.

Nyerere, however, underestimated the colonial matrices of power that made it impossible for him to achieve self-reliance in one country. Nyerere had a tenuous relationship with the Bretton Woods institutions, critiquing their conditionalities and prescriptions, while seeking their funding. At retirement, Nyerere admitted his mistakes, including the nationalization programme, which destroyed thriving enterprises, and urged his successors to adopt a free market economy.

Nkrumah and Nyerere's examples reveal some core aspects of how the founding fathers thought about the national projects, how they tried to implement them, the challenges they encountered and how they tried to deal with them. It would seem the diagnosis of the core elements of the national question was correct but the implementation mechanism became very complicated for them, dominated by trials and errors, contradictions and authoritarianism.

The threat of imperialist interventions hovered over the heads of the African leaders as they tried to implement the national project(s). Occasionally, imperialist forces intervened to physically eliminate those committed pan-Africanists like Lumumba, dethroning others through sponsored military coups. Nkrumah and Lumumba were in agreement on territorial nationalism being just a momentary stage in the struggle for pan-Africanism. They both understood that imperialism was part of the political economy of capitalism and that it had to be resisted at a continental level.

Nyerere, on the other hand, had seemed not to have understood or appreciated the vastness of imperialism, not realizing it was in tension with sovereignty of the African state. He therefore articulated resistance to imperialism in terms of the sovereign right of people to make their own decisions (Shivji 2012: 104). The reality is that, from the beginning, Africa's national projects were conceived within the belly of colonial matrices of power and all the efforts at resolution of the national question remained hostage to imperial surveillance. The force of pan-Africanism was consistently diluted by imperial forces that wanted to keep Africa disunited in order for Western powers to continue fishing for economic resources in troubled situations like the one which obtained in the Democratic Republic of Congo after the assassination of Lumumba.

Inevitably, by the 1970s, the national project(s) fell into crisis of various intensities across the continent. It was during this period that ambitious soldiers, including the notorious Idi Amin Dada and Mobutu Sese Seko, toppled elected founding fathers, overturning the nationalist agenda. Most of these 'soldier-presidents' were beholden to foreign powers and inevitably became conduits for the rehabilitation of imperialism. The next section explores the crisis of the national project(s).

The crisis of the national project(s)

A combination of founding fathers' mistakes and structural factors explains the crisis. The birth of the postcolonial states was straight into the snares of neo-colonialism. Ramón Grosfoguel (2007: 219) correctly argued that the most powerful myth of the twentieth century was the notion that the end of direct colonialism amounted to decolonization of the ex-colonized world. This myth led to another myth of a 'postcolonial world' (Grosfoguel 2007: 219).

Independence euphoria and triumphalist speeches by some African leaders ignored the invisible and systemic operations of colonial matrices of power that underpinned 'global coloniality' (Grosfoguel 2007: 219; Ndlovu-Gatsheni 2012b). While Nkrumah was fully aware of this structural constraint, Nyerere seemed to downplay the threats of neo-colonialism. Nyerere even entertained the idea that freedom from dependence through self-reliance could be attained in one particular country. Nkrumah, who fully realized that imperialism and colonialism, operating on a global scale, had given birth to neo-colonial dependence, forcefully argued for a pan-African struggle waged at the pan-African level whereas Nyerere tried to fight it within a single country.

At another level, the crises of the national project(s) were linked to the crisis of the constitution of the postcolonial state itself. Basil Davidson (1992) located the roots of this in the mistaken imagination of, and actual predication of, the postcolonial state on a Western template by founding fathers. Basing the nation-state project on the European Westphalian model sharpened, rather than diminished, identity tensions. For Davidson (1992), the nation-state project was not informed by Africa's own rich, varied history and experiences. This approach to the postcolonial nation-state project allowed founding fathers to accept colonial boundaries as inviolable.

Ultimately, subjection was reproduced rather than liberation (Davidson 1992: 12). Samir Amin amplified this argument by noting that when the postcolonial nation-states were being constructed, the very notion of the nation-state 'was entering a crisis everywhere, even at its centres of origin, a crisis from which there seemed no escape' (Amin 1990a: 84). While the nation-state has survived many predictions of its imminent demise, in Africa it has not served the interests of the African people.

What has been perpetuated has been the colonial legacy of bifurcated colonial states of citizens and subjects permeated by divide and rule, which prevented the coalescence of different ethnicities and races into a national identity (Mamdani 1996). This manifested in various forms, such as weak internal identity, internal instability, dependency, and corruption (Lumumba-Kasongo 2011: 69). These structural constraints were compounded by the inherited weak and dependent economies characterized by internal economic disarticulation and reliance on an export sector dominated by raw materials, which ensured the subaltern position of Africa in the global hierarchy of power.

Across the Anglophone-Francophone divides, founding fathers held strong convictions on building centralized and interventionist states, capable of pushing forward the national project(s) and resolving the national question. Within this context, the imperative to democratize the inherited state, which had survived through the exclusion of black people from governance and popular participation, fell into the cracks. Eventually, inside the postcolonial states, the requisite organic connection between national projects and democracy became a missing link (Laakso and Olukoshi 1996: 9).

At another level, Africa's national projects were predicated on the flawed idea of a tight correspondence between the nation and the state. Even in situations where a kaleidoscope of multiple cultures, languages, religious, races, and ethnicities dictated a need for a different and flexible approach, the homogenization of identities and centralization of power was preferred as an essential pre-requisite for the success of the national project(s) (Laakso and Olukoshi 1996: 12–13). This resulted in the national project(s) unfolding as a state-driven, top-down and centralizing approach, premised on the false thinking that the existence of ethnic diversity was a major threat to the nation.

African leaders across the continent believed that for the nation to live the tribe had to die. Attempts to eradicate tribal identities became justifications for some forms of authoritarianism, including adoption of one-party systems. The apogee of this crisis was lopsided conceptions of the national project(s) and the national question, which Shivji (2003: 8) summarized as: 'Nation-building turns into state-building. Nation is substituted by party and party by leader, the father of the nation'. He added that 'The National Question is reduced to a race question or ethnic question or cultural question' (Shivji 2003: 8).

National project(s) ended up as presidential projects that were abstracted from people's struggles. The good example is Mobutu Sese Seko's 1971 *Authenticité* national project, which Lumumba-Kasongo (1991: 44–45) characterized 'as a counter-revolutionary ideology to protect his regime and system against any potential revolutionary tendencies that could emerge in Zaire. It was a cultural measure or tool consciously fabricated by the ruling class to discourage any revolutionary ideas that could develop of our Zaire's social and political conditions'. Under *Authenticité*, nationalism and African culture were fetishized to back up the idea of Mobutu's heroism, revolutionary claims, and to justify his centralization of power in his person. *Authenticité* became a typical nativist philosophy lacking any revolutionary features beyond the essentialization of African identity.

While this lopsided conception of the national project was deepening, the oil crisis broke out in 1973, worsening the situation. Within this context, the foreign development assistance of the 1960s that was relatively well meaning, consisting of large-scale infrastructure programmes, dried up (Bierschenk and Spies 2010: 4). The oil crisis heralded a global paradigmatic shift from Keynesianism with its notions of full employment and the role of the state in the economy to neo-liberalism with its emphasis on the free operation of market forces and its anti-statist philosophies. Bretton Woods institutions became active in Africa at this time when African states were already saddled by a heavy debt crisis and declining economies (Onimode 1989; Bangura and Beckman 1991).

African leaders had to look to the developed North for financial help. The prescription came in the form of the notorious Structural Adjustment Programmes (SAPs) (Bangura and Beckman 1991). The adoption of SAPs had a direct impact on the national project(s) as it led to loss of policy space and control by Africans. Shivji (2003: 8) argued that 'if the national question was distorted, truncated, and caricatured during the period of meta-nationalism, it completely disappears and is delegitimized in the current globalization phase of imperialism'. Fantu Cheru (2009: 277) added that 'So, policy making, an important aspect of sovereignty, has been wrenched out of the hands of the African state. This is recolonization, not development'. SAPs removed both the national and social questions from the centre of development. The market with its socially blind macroeconomics became a solution to African problems (Mkandawire 2009: 147).

Rita Abrahamsen (2001) also captured the double-bind that befell African leaders as they had to be answerable to African people, external agencies and donors simultaneously. Africa became a terrain of so many external policy interventions and political experiments. As public policy became directed from outside, postcolonial states lost their little remaining legitimacy (Laakso and Olukoshi 1996: 18–24). Pursuit of the SAPs' agenda entailed, on the one hand, authoritarian rule and, on the other, a less interventionist state for the economy. Africa has not fully recovered from SAPs' dismantling of the state and its removal from initiating national project(s). Inevitably, current resuscitation of the national project inevitably calls for reconstitution and democratization of the state, in Africa, as an agent of development.

African intellectuals and the defence of national project(s)

The agenda to redeem the national project(s) has never completely died. Scholars like Zeleza (2003), Mkandawire (2009), Shivji (2009) and Cheru (2009) kept it alive throughout the age of SAPs. They defended nationalism and its national project(s) from assaults by postmodernists and globalists who depicted nationalism as a shibboleth of discredited geographies and histories that should belong to the dustbins of history. Such scholars as Kwame Anthony Appiah (1992), Achille Mbembe (2002a, 2002b) and others, became very critical of nationalism and its national project(s), caricaturing them as nothing but nativism.

For postmodernists, national project(s) were based on flawed post-Enlightenment philosophies that enabled totalizing meta-narratives; essentialization of identities; and denial of contingency and diversity as a fact of human life. National project(s) were blamed for promoting 'metaphysics of difference', 'nativism', and other phobias that generated conflicts all over the world (Mbembe 2002a, 2002b). What they proposed as solutions to African problems included embracing cosmopolitanism and transnationalism while devising ways of tapping into the fruits of globalization. That globalization was in actual fact an outgrowth of imperialism and capitalism was not opened to critical analysis by postmodernists.

Nationalist-inspired scholars mounted strong counter-arguments to those who condemned nationalism and its projects. They argued that such wholesale condemnation was based on failure to distinguish between national projects: between progressive and repressive forms, reactionary and revolutionary ones, democratic and authoritarian types. To them, such a repudiation of nationalism, including its proudest moment (decolonization) was an act of disavowal of history, wilful amnesia of the past and ignoring the future (Zeleza 2003: vi–vii). They noted that postmodernists' and globalists' call for transcendence of nationalism had not resulted in any better future. The suggested post-nationalist alternatives have been disastrous, consisting of heightened ethnic subnationalisms, religious particularisms, global migration that provoked racism and xenophobia, and uncritical embracement of neo-liberal globalism (Mkandawire 2009: 133).

During the age of SAPs and globalization, the national project(s) became largely an intellectual project as African leaders had succumbed to the dictates of the Washington Consensus. What is significant about this is that committed African intellectuals made sure that nationalism and national project(s) were not completely effaced by SAPs' discourses and by postmodernist thought. Claude Ake was one of the defenders of the national project(s) while calling for the restructuring of the state to normalize its relationship with social classes, deal with the state's development/underdevelopment duo, embrace democracy, respond to dependent capitalism and open up epistemological change (Afemini 2000; Arowosegbe 2008; Arowosegbe 2011: 8).

These central roles could not be carried forward by a state that was not thoroughly decolonized, fully autonomous, and deeply indigenized (Ake 1981; Ake 1985a; Ake 1992a; Ake 1996; Ake 2000). Ake was also concerned about the political integration of Africa, arguing for the resolution of sources of political instability (Ake 1967a; Ake 1967b; Ake 1973). He preferred 'endogenous initiatives of rebuilding the state from below' to enable it to fulfill the popular demands of ex-colonized people. To Ake (1985b: 5), these structural changes were necessary because the state was 'burdened with onerous responsibilities which it is hardly in a position to fulfill'.

Ake's push for an epistemological paradigm shift, from using Euro-American knowledge systems to using indigenous knowledge as an anchor for the state, must be understood in the context of Davidson's critique of using Westphalian notions of a state for postcolonial Africa. The Euro-American models of power, state, nation and citizenship contributed to the alien-ness of the state (Ake 1979). One way of circumventing the colonial legacy and decolonizing the postcolonial state was to try and anchor it on African values and infuse its institutions with knowledge and values from precolonial Africa. At the same time, the inherited state needed to be thoroughly democratized if it were to be accepted as a legitimate drive of the national project. While it is true, as argued by Mkandawire (1997), that despite internal inconsistencies and contradictions, the national project(s) had noble objectives to build nations and kick-start economic development, those of the 1960s lacked commitment to democracy, gender equality, and popular participation. Questions were asked as to whose these projects were, and how national the projects were if they excluded women and other popular forces apart from those organized into ruling parties and those in charge of the state.

But Shivji (2003; 2009) argued that most of the negative analysis of the national project(s) ignored that they were largely 'work-in-progress' and a terrain of struggles that consistently underwent definition and redefinition even by those who were actively involved. He emphasized that some nationalists had a minimalist and reformist conception while others had a maximalist and revolutionary understanding of the projects as aspects of liberation. Amilcar Cabral had a maximalist and revolutionary conception whereby he articulated the foundation of the liberation struggle as lying 'in the inalienable right of every people to have their own history', adding that as long as imperialism existed 'an independent African state must be a liberation movement in power, or it will not be independent' (Cabral 1980: 116–117). One can add that as long as imperialism existed national project(s) remain relevant as sites for resisting it and charting alternative policies.

This is why Shivji (2003: 13) has argued for 'a new national democratic consensus in Africa that would be thoroughly popular, thoroughly anti-imperialist, and thoroughly anti-comprador'. This national project(s) should be constituted by three interrelated questions: the national question, the democratic question and the social question. Shivji elaborated on these issues in terms of popular livelihoods, popular participation and popular power (Shivji 2003: 13; Shivji 2009). His addition of the democratic question demonstrates a critical appraisal of previous national project(s) that were largely undemocratic. The addition of the democratic question has the potential to resolve the pertinent issue of popular participation that is essential for national project(s) to gain legitimacy as they shed the legacy of being presidential, rather than democratic, affairs.

Shivji articulated the concept of popular at four levels. First, popular entails anti-imperialism, which continues to be a negation of the national project(s). Second, it means translation of state sovereignty to people's

sovereignty. Third, popular entails identification of peasants and workers as social forces for the new national democratic consensus in alliance
with the lower middle classes. Finally, popular captures the 'grounded-
ness' of the national project(s) in African history and culture as the living terrain of struggles (Shivji 2003: 13; Shivji 2009). For Shivji (2011: 5),
the crisis that is threatening the capitalist/neo-liberal system currently
presents a strong case for re-launching the pan-African project as a way
of addressing the unfinished national, social, and democracy questions.
The challenge, which was identified by Nyerere long ago, is how to practically convert nationalism into pan-Africanism. The gradualists still pin
their hope on the Regional Economic Communities (RECs), such as the
Southern Africa Development Community (SADC) and others, as ideal
for conversion of nationalism to pan-Africanism. But the reality is that
the RECs seem to be failing to break imperatives of state sovereignties as
they advance the pan-African agenda through the introduction of common currencies and passports for example.

Fantu Cheru's entry into this debate was to point out that what failed
was an imperial project that disguised itself as an African project (Cheru
2009: 275). This imperial project unfolded, as an imposition on African
societies from outside, to the extent that it stifled peasant autonomy and
production, constrained people's creative energies for self-improvement,
denied space for participation in governance, and operated as a purely
elitist project that was far removed from ordinary people's lives. It provoked a cry from the poor which said 'Please don't develop us!' (Cheru
2009: 275). To Cheru, the resuscitation of the national project(s) should
involve adoption of key radical reforms at the national and regional levels informed by an imperative of 'strategic integration' of national economies into the international economy on the basis of African interests
(Cheru 2009: 277). But further work is needed in elaborating what 'strategic integration' entails in practical policy terms since Africa remains
in the subaltern position within a global power hierarchy with limited
policy options as long it relies on aid from the developed North. Perhaps
the rise of new centres of power crystallizing around emerging powers
of China, Brazil, India and others would provide Africa with a strategic
outlet to innovate ways in which its economies are integrated into the
global economy.

But national project(s) are not just an intellectual concern, they have
become a major practical concern for African policy-makers embedded in such institutions as the United Nations Economic Commission
for Africa (UNECA). UNECA has been concerned about the relevance
of SAPs and their potential to resolve African development problems
(Lumumba-Kasongo 1994; Agbese and Kieh 2007b; Mueni wa Muiu and
Martin 2009). UNECA began to think of alternatives to SAPs. It did this
as nationalism and pan-Africanism were being pushed to the sidelines
by neo-liberal forces and their agendas were being displaced by the

Washington Consensus. UNECA tried to deploy pan-Africanism as a basis for reviving the national project(s) and re-capturing development policy's lost centre-space. The Lagos Plan of Action of 1980 was one of these attempts to reclaim the development initiative that has been lost to the IMF and the World Bank (Adedeji 1999: 423).

Adebayo Adedeji (2002: 3–4), the Executive Secretary General of UN-ECA, identified five landmark initiatives, which together provide the continent's preferred development agenda for the 1980s and 1990s. These reports and policies were the Lagos Plan of Action, 1980–2000 (1980); Africa's Priority Programme for Economic Recovery, 1986–1990 (1986); the African Alternative Framework to Structural Adjustment Programme for Socio-Economic Recovery and Transformation (1989); the African Charter for Popular Participation for Development (1990); and the United Nations New Agenda for the Development of Africa in the 1990s (1991). But these initiatives 'were opposed, undermined, and jettisoned by the Bretton Woods institutions and Africans were impeded from exercising the basic and fundamental right to make decisions about their future' (Adedeji 2002: 4).

Gilbert Khadiagala (2010: 387) argued that the vacuum left by disciplined nationalism and pan-Africanism, as well as the actions of the 'captured' state that was subservient to the dictates of the IMF and World Bank, made it difficult to relaunch any successful African development agenda. Most of the African states were still busy implementing an imperial project imposed on them in the 1970s, as they asked for financial help from the developed North. It is this vacuum that UNECA, under Adedeji, fought to fill. In this endeavour, UNECA produced the *Revised Framework for Implementation of the New International Order in Africa* in 1976, which formed the intellectual and theoretical foundation of the Lagos Plan of Action.

Adedeji was convinced that without democratization of the existing world order, which was informed by the interests of the North, any developmental processes beneficial to Africa would be in vain (Adedeji 2002). While Adedeji was aware of some of the internal factors that prevented development in Africa, such as corruption and dictatorship, he also identified structural problems and asymmetrical power relations manifest in the global capitalist economic system that was hindering development in Africa. This is why Adedeji argued that the development process was dominated and operated by a 'development merchant system' (DMS) that drove and imposed an exogenous development agenda on Africa. This DMS was quick to fund exogenous economic reform policies regardless of the negative impact of such policies on African economies and polities (Adedeji 2002: 4).

In its fights against the Bretton Woods institutions in the 1980s, UN-ECA produced the *Alternative Framework to Structural Adjustment Programmes for Socio-Economic Recovery and Transformation* (AAF-SAP) in

1989. The report made it clear that there were fundamental structural bottlenecks that hindered development of Africa (UNECA 1989). While UNECA's struggles for alternative pan-African-oriented development agendas did not then succeed, they kept the pan-Africanist development alternative alive and challenged the hegemony of Bretton Woods. UNECA consistently exposed the dangers of SAPs for Africa. When Adedeji retired from UNECA in 1991 he made sure that the struggles to regain the lost policy space remained on course.

By 2000, Nkrumah's vision of pan-African unity received a new boost. The Nkrumahist position, which emphasized immediate pan-African political unity, became occupied by the late Libyan leader Colonel Gaddafi, while the Nyererian gradualist position was occupied by the former leaders of South Africa and Nigeria, Thabo Mbeki and Olusegun Obasanjo, respectively. These pushed for regional economic integration and democratization as prerequisites for later continental union government (Biney 2008b: 148). The revival of the drive to achieve pan-Africanism resulted in the conversion of the OAU into the African Union (AU), formulation of the New Partnership for Africa's Development (NEPAD) as the latest African development plan, the establishment of the pan-African Parliament (PAP) and the creation of the African Peer Review Mechanism (APRM) among other policies and institutions meant to underpin the new drive to realize pan-African unity. Unfortunately some of the initiatives such as NEPAD and APRM came under a barrage of criticism as imposed on Africa by the developed North.

For instance, for Jimi Adesina (2006), NEPAD is premised on the misreading of Africa's economic and social experiences. It replicates the evolving discourse of the Bretton Woods institutions. Its call for deeper integration of African economies into the global neo-liberal capitalist order creates a false idea that lack of development is due to the shallow integration of Africa into the world economy. Emphasis on the mobilization of external resources to finance African development is seen as reinforcing dependence that was long ago identified as a barrier to an autonomous development path. President Jammeh of Gambia (2002: 18) spoke for many critics of NEPAD when he said 'If it is an African project, why take it to the Westerners to approve it? Was it necessary to take it to the G8?' These contestations reveal the continuing problems in the search for a plausible future trajectory for Africa.

Conclusion

This chapter has tried to map out what went wrong with the national projects that were instituted by African leaders in the 1960s. It identified both structural and agency factors that combined to compromise the African projects while at the same time revealing that these projects were in fact hard to clearly define. The key limiting factor was that these African projects emerged from the belly of the beast of imperialism (at its highest stage), which Nkrumah correctly termed neo-colonialism. This chapter used the case study of Nkrumah and Nyerere to reflect on how the founding fathers of postcolonial states understood the postcolonial situation differently to the extent that this impinged on the prospects of a united front against neo-colonialism. Finding a clear and agreed pathway to be followed in pursuit of the agenda of pan-African unity became elusive.

The attempts by African leaders to implement their individual national project(s) revealed poor conceptualization, and preference for top-down and authoritarian approaches within postcolonial states that were not fully decolonized and indigenized. The acceptance of the Westphalian template for the postcolonial state reinforced the continued subjection of Africans to Euro-American global imperial designs, including using the same institutions they deployed to colonize Africa. What are needed are African institutions anchored in African histories, cultures and values that are not alienating to the African majority. It is clear from this study that some African intellectuals have kept the fort of nationalism and pan-Africanism protected while pushing for democratization.

The useful lesson from this chapter is that the twenty-first century requires national projects that are underpinned by new values of democracy as well as by gender equality. The previous national project(s) were premised on masculinized and patriarchal forms of nationalism that were deemed dangerous. Popular participation in the national project was not taken seriously to the extent that they became presidential projects that were imposed on society by coercion. Postmodernists took advantage of this to repudiate nationalism and its projects. But Craig Calhoun (2007) has warned that any attempts at pursuing a post-national politics were premature at best and at worst dangerous because nationalism was not inherently antagonistic to democracy. Nationalism offered a strong base to subvert imperialism and colonialism as well as contending with neo-colonialism. Nationalism still has the potential to contest neo-liberal versions of globalization that threaten the gains of the national liberation struggles.

The best way forward is to approach nationalism with critical attention 'to its limits, illusions, and potential for abuse, but we should not dismiss it' (Calhoun 2007: 1). Africa today needs nationalism that is easily convertible to pan-Africanism rather than one described by Nyerere as existing in tension with pan-Africanism. The future struggle should be about converting nationalism into pan-Africanism because Nkrumah's fears have been confirmed by history: without pan-African unity, Africa is doomed to remain in a subaltern position, failing to resist imperialism and neo-colonialism successfully.

PART 4

CONCLUSION

CHAPTER 9

Global Crisis and Africa Today

Introduction

We have to look directly at the terrifying reality of the world we live in. It is necessary to ask a series of questions on the basis of the risks and threats we face: why is the United States the only country that scatters the planet with military bases? What is it afraid of to allocate such a staggering budget for increasing its military power? Why has it unleashed so many wars, violating the sovereignty of other nations which have the same rights on their own fates? How can international law be enforced against its insensible aspiration to military hegemonizing of the world in order to ensure energy sources to sustain their predatory and consumer model? Why does the UN do nothing to stop Washington? If we answer these questions sincerely we would understand that the empire has awarded itself the role of judge of the world, without being granted this responsibility by anyone, and, therefore, imperialist war threatens us all. Washington knows that a multipolar world is already an irreversible reality. Its strategy consist of stopping, at any price, the sustained rise of a group of emerging countries, by negotiating great interests with its partners and followers in order to guide multipolarity along the path the empire wants. What is more, the goal is to configure the world so it is based on Yankee military hegemony. Mankind is facing the very real threat of a permanent war. The empire is ready to create political conditions for triggering a war anywhere, and the case of Libya proves it. Within the imperial view of the world, the well-known Clausewitz's axiom is being reversed: politics is the continuation of war by other means.

(Hugo Chavez, President of Venezuela, Speech to the UN, 26 September 2011)

The conditions that brought about the crisis of modernity have not yet become the conditions to overcome the crisis beyond modernity. Hence the complexity of our transitional period portrayed by oppositional postmodernism theory: we are facing modern problems for which there are no modern solutions. The search for a postmodern solution is what I call oppositional postmodernism ... What is necessary is to start from the disjunction between modernity of the problems and the postmodernity of the possible solutions, and turn disjunction into the urge to

> *ground theories and practices capable of reinventing social emancipation out of*
> *the wrecked emancipatory promises of modernity.*
>
> (Boaventura de Sousa Santos 2002: 18)

This book has been primarily concerned with three related themes of empire, global coloniality and African subjectivity. It demonstrated the intricate embeddedness of Africa within global power structures and how this embeddedness produced a particular kind of African subjectivity. The book unfolded as a major critique of how Western modernity, which was marketed as civilizational and emancipatory, was underpinned by complex technologies of subjectivation that continuously reproduced global coloniality. Since its expansion over the non-Western world, modernity became de-territorialized, hybridized, contested, uneven, multiple and universal. In the twenty-first century, this modernity plunged into multi-layered crisis/crises of which the current financial crisis is just one part. At least three broad arguments encompass the core of the global crisis, as well as the African predicament, capturing the dilemmas of current paradigms and the unsatisfactory imagination of alternatives. The first argument comes from Frantz Fanon, who advised peoples of the colonized world to avoid mimicry and begin to think of an alternative world inhabited by a new humanity free from violence and racism (Fanon 1968: 251).

The second argument is from Immanuel Wallerstein, who exposed the epistemological dimension of the global crisis when he argued for the overhaul of nineteenth-century social science, because many of its presumptions, previously considered 'liberating of the spirit, serve today as the central intellectual barrier to useful analysis of the social world' (Wallerstein 1991: 1). The third one comes from a leading Portuguese sociologist and committed decolonial thinker, Boaventura de Sousa Santos, who dealt with the issue of strategies of transformation as necessary components for resolving the global crisis. He stated that:

> In search for alternatives to domination and oppression, how can we distinguish between alternatives to the system of oppression and domination and alternatives within the system or, more specifically, how do we distinguish between alternatives to capitalism and alternatives within capitalism? In sum, how do we fight against the abyssal lines using conceptual and political instruments that don't reproduce them? (Santos 2007a: 78)

These three broad arguments speak to three pertinent issues that are at the core of the present crisis. Fanon was railing against 'nauseating mimicry' of European ways of doing things and urged his comrades, who were fighting against colonialism, to 'find something different'. Wallerstein pointed to the exhaustion of nineteenth-century social sciences which were useful then but today are found wanting in terms of enlightening the current state of the social world. He lamented how this exhausted social science continues to have 'far too strong a hold on our mentalities'. Wallerstein urges us to grow up epistemologically from the intellectual habit of 'rethinking' issues to consider the option of 'unthinking' some of the presumptions and worldviews that do not enable liberation and development. Santos speaks of a pervasive crisis that has bedeviled Africa ever since the time of colonialism: the crisis of seeking liberation and development within the same system of domination and oppression. Even once celebrated socialism was conceived within the belly of the beast of Euro-American modernity as a critique of the capitalist aspect of modernity as exploiting the workers, without challenging modernity itself.

This book sought to understand how empire, global coloniality and subjectivity reveal how Africans have remained ensnared within invisible global imperial designs and colonial matrices of power. It tried to make visible this African condition through deployment of three important conceptual resources, namely coloniality of power, coloniality of knowledge, and coloniality of being, as part of its modest attempt to provoke a new thinking about how to transform existing global asymmetrical power structures while at the same time revealing how these same power structures produced a particular African subjectivity and specific ideas on development. These concepts, which highlight coloniality, enabled a fresh reflection on issues of the current world order, particularly its underpinning by asymmetrical power relations that do not open enough space for Africa to take charge of its developmental trajectory and policy formulation. They also help to enlighten the magnitude of contemporary problems such as those of the crisis in global leadership; the global capitalist economic crisis; ecology, the environment, and climate change; the ongoing scramble for African natural resources; and epistemological and cognitive justice issues.

The three concepts constitute what is known as the decolonial epistemic perspective that has the potential to breathe fresh air on how epistemological and cultural issues should be harnessed to shape alternative development trajectories; critical reflections on current models of government and governance and their appropriateness or otherwise for Africa; and the role of education in contributing towards African economic resurgence. The three concepts also formed a basis for interrogation and a critique of current paradigms informed by modernization thought that have been deployed to understand global and African issues, without much success in enabling development in Africa.

At one level, the decolonial perspective indicates that the very exercise of identifying topical global issues is informed by one's locus of enunciation. The clearest example is that of Jean-François Rischard's book, *High Noon: 20 Global Problems, 20 Years to Solve Them* (2003), in which he identified twenty 'global problems'. He classified them into three broad groups: those to do with 'sharing our planet', 'sharing our humanity' and 'sharing our rulebook'. Table 1 provides the whole list of what, according to Rischard, constituted planetary problems.

Table 1: Jean-François Rischard's 20 Global Issues

1. SHARING OUR PLANET: ISSUES INVOLVING THE GLOBAL COMMONS
• Global warming
• Biodiversity and ecosystem losses
• Fisheries depletion
• Deforestation
• Water deficits
• Maritime safety and pollution
SHARING OUR HUMANITY: ISSUES REQUIRING A GLOBAL COMMIT-MENT
• Massive step-up in the fight against poverty
• Peacekeeping, conflict prevention, combating terrorism
• Education for all
• Global infectious diseases
• Digital divide
• Natural disaster prevention and mitigation
SHARING OUR RULEBOOK: ISSUES NEEDING A GLOBAL REGULATORY APPROACH
• Reinventing taxation for the twenty-first century
• Biotechnology rules
• Global financial architecture
• Illegal drugs
• Trade, investment and competition rules
• Intellectual property rights
• E-commerce rule
• International labour and migration rules

Jean-François Rischard, 2003. *High Noon: 20 Global Problems, 20 Years to Solve Them*. New York: Basic Books.

While there is no doubt that Rischard's list is comprehensive and well thought-out, it is clear that, as a World Bank economist based in Paris, his identification of the problems reflected his position and location in the centre of Europe. If the list were to be compiled by an African located in Africa and working for an African government, the content might be different. For instance, the issues of the scramble for African resources, underdevelopment, land grabbing, and the question of democratization of the global system of governance would have been added. The core discussion of this book is informed by Africa as an epistemic locus of enunciation, and, as such, it identified and discussed major global changes and issues as seen from an African scholar's eyes, whose thinking is driven by a strong belief in 'I am where I think' (Mignolo 2000: 91–126).

What the book tried to do was to offer a clear understanding of the architecture of the modern capitalist world order and explain the position of Africa within existing power structures. This was considered important because all the initiatives to understand Africa's development challenges are taking place within a specific global power that was put in place at the time of colonial encounters. This concluding chapter, therefore, reiterates the core arguments of the book as it projects into the future.

Africa inside the belly of empire

Without an accurate analysis of the technologies used to construct the present world order and how it is complicit in the generation of African problems including those of governance, institutional crisis and many others, there cannot be any correct strategy for mitigating and combating them. This book, therefore, endeavoured to trace the roots of the contemporary African problems to the centre of the constitution of the modern world order that has culminated in what Michael Hardt and Antonio Negri (2000) described simply as 'empire'. This empire can be best described as a capitalist, patriarchal, Euro-American-centric, Christian-centric, hetero-normative, and hegemonic world-system (Mignolo 1995b; Mignolo 2000; Quijano 2000a; Grosfoguel 2007; Grosfoguel 2011). Its roots are traceable to the dawn of modernity and the colonial encounters of the fifteenth century. During this period Europe intensified its imperial expansion into Latin America, Asia, Africa, and other parts of the world.

Africa is still acting and struggling inside the belly of the beast of empire. As such, it cannot be spared from the debilitating effects of the ongoing global financial crisis and other crises inherent in the operations of the capitalist system. Despite the fact that modernity is suffering a deep crisis and that the empire, which it has given birth to, is also riddled by crises, both continue to manifest two faces. One is seductive and beautiful. The other is fierce, ugly and violent. It is therefore an incomplete analysis to simply enumerate its horrific aspects, which commenced with the slave trade, fratricidal imperial and colonial wars, violent imposition of alien development and civilization, concentration camps and prisons, genocidal wars, nuclear weapons and apartheid. To complete the story, one needs to take into account that from that belly of modernity and empire emerged ideas of individual, civil, and political liberties; equality and fraternity; universal suffrage, democracy, socialism, modern and secular nation-states that liberated the masses from the tyranny of tradition and religion; rationality and the scientific spirit; popular education, economic progress and many other accomplishments (Baron 2005: 32).

But to experience either the positive or the negative aspects of modernity depended on which side of the 'abyssal lines' one was located. Santos (2007a: 45) introduced and defined 'abyssal thinking' as consisting of a 'system of visible and invisible distinctions, the visible ones being the foundation of the invisible ones'. The concept of abyssal thinking was used to capture two sides of the world, created by modernity and consolidated by empire, where one side was the colonial zone where the dark side of modernity was experienced and the other side was where the positives of modernity were reaped and enjoyed. Hence if one were fortunate, in Europe and America, then yes, the positives of modernity were available. If one were unfortunate, in Africa, the darker aspects of modernity and empire constituted one's reality.

What is disturbing is that since the time of decolonization and particularly the end of the Cold War, Africans have adopted a complacent and cavalier view of this empire, at a time when it was consolidating its global outreach and in the process continuing to subordinate the African continent, criminalizing all the initiatives aimed at liberation of the black people, and generating dispossessions and poverty. This complacency is explained by Ramón Grosfoguel as one of the 'most powerful myths of the twentieth century' (Grosfoguel 2007: 219). It is a myth of believing in the existence of a non-existent post-imperial and postcolonial world.

The African complacency in the face of empire led them to celebrate the myth of decolonization, which in reality 'obscures the continuities between the colonial past and current global colonial/racial hierarchies and contributes to the invisibility of "coloniality" today' (Grosfoguel 2007: 220). As Africans continue to struggle and search for alternative development paths and to take the unfinished decolonization process to the realm of economic and social justice, no illusion must be entertained of proceeding without a precise knowledge of the enormity of the antagonist and the broader terrain on which the major battles would be fought.

While it is true that today's imperialism is not the same as the one that existed thirty years ago, this change does not in any way imply that it is less dangerous and that it can be embraced and depoliticized into globalism. The reality is that 'it has not changed into its opposite, as neo-liberal mystification suggests, giving rise to a "global" economy in which we are all "interdependent"' (Boron 2005: 3). In this context, Hardt and Negri (2000) missed the point when they postulated a situation of existence of empire without imperialism. Empire remains underpinned by criminalization of social protest and militarization of international politics (Boron 2005: 19).

Unlike Africans, who were seized by complacency at the end of the Cold War, policy-makers in Europe and America did not rest on their laurels. They became active in imagining ways of keeping Africa within the exploitative ambit of global capitalism and maintaining it at the bottom level of power hierarchies within the empire. After the Cold War, global imperial designs coalesced around neo-liberal imperialism, which concealed the old habits of imperialism behind discourses of human rights, democracy, and cultures of good governance. Fighting against global terrorism also offered a justification for even military invasion, particularly of those countries endowed with strategic resources such as oil. Boron argued that:

> Oil constitutes, at this time, the central nervous system of the international capitalism, and its importance is even greater than that of the world of finance. The latter cannot function without the former: the entire edifice of what Susan Strange has correctly labeled 'casino capitalism' would collapse within minutes if oil disappeared. (Boron 2005: 13–14)

What needs to be dispelled is the confusion of celebration of wars of pillage and territorial occupation like the Iraq War, and the invasion of Libya, with altruistic/humanitarian operations aimed at dealing with outposts of tyranny in order to effect regime changes that would open the way for nation-building and the export of democracy. What must be noted is that discourses of democracy, human rights and good governance have now been added to the imperial arsenal of technologies of subjectivation. Behind their rhetoric lie imperial designs of scrambling for natural resources and latent discourses of re-colonization of those areas endowed with strategic resources in an age where even the multilateral order is in crisis.

The crisis of global leadership and the troubles of multilateral order

The empire's hypocrisy and double standards have been on display since it first came into existence and have now resulted in a crisis of global leadership. The sole superpower – the U.S.A. – has abused its position to the point where the world has lost confidence. G. John Ikenberry argued that 'the rise of America's unipolar position during the 1990s has complicated the old postwar logic of cooperation among allied democratic states. America's power advantages make it easier for it to say no to other countries or go it alone' (cited in Barry 1998: 144). The crisis of global leadership is manifest within the United Nations and other multilateral institutions.

Global governance is suffering a crisis of confidence. David Held (2006: 157) noted that 'the collective issues we must grapple with are of growing extensity and intensity and, yet, the means for addressing these are weak and incomplete'. This inability to deal with global problems is attributed to the fact that global and regional institutions and governance arrangements are very weak. The institutions suffering this crisis range from the United Nations (UN), the European Union (EU), the North Atlantic Treaty Organization (NATO), the African Union (AU) and many others. This situation led Ikenberry to note that 'today the machinery of the postwar era is in disrepair. No leader, international body or group of states speaks with authority or vision on global challenges' (Ikenberry 2005: 30).

Held (2006: 163) pointed out that 'the existing generation of leaders appears as much part of the growing impasses as its solution'. The crisis of global leadership is inextricably intertwined with the troubles of the multilateral order and international bodies. The present-day leadership crisis and the troubles of the multilateral order are partly linked to resurgence of nationalism in the peripheral areas, unilateralism of the U.S.A., disarray of the EU, and the growing confidence and power of China, India, Russia and Brazil (Held 2006: 164). Taken together, these developments are inaugurating power shifts in global decision-making.

The crisis of global leadership and troubles of the multilateral order are manifesting themselves as crises of approach and methodology and as a crisis of legitimacy. The former speaks of how global problems of governance, climate change, trade imbalances, resources and others have to be resolved. The question of the shifting meaning of sovereignty in a globalized world also presents itself as a topical global problem. For instance, one can question the appropriateness of military interventions and the taking of African leaders for trial by the International Criminal Court (ICC) at The Hague in the Netherlands (Mutua 2010). The African nationalist school of thought views these two approaches as part of global imperial designs aimed at violating African sovereignty.

The neo-liberal school of thought embraces the notions of the right to protect (R2P) and has no problem with interventions that target leaders who violate people's rights and do not adhere to democratic forms of government. What is at issue here is what Held (2006: 165) has termed 'intermestic', that is intermeshed international and domestic issues. The interventions in the Libyan conflict by the U.S.A. and NATO, while sidelining the AU, which argued for negotiations rather than military solutions, strengthened the position of nationalists who placed the action within the longstanding global imperial agenda, where violence and war were always ready when other means of getting to the resources such as oil had failed.

There is a third school of thought that views the ICC as pursuing retributive justice at the expense of constructive peace-making and reconciliation efforts (Mutua 2010: 3). This is one clear example where a crisis of approach is manifest. But the crisis of approach has made it difficult for agreements or consensus to be reached on a number of global issues that need urgent action. The crisis is manifest at many sites of global governance such as the Doha Trade 'Roundtable', when no agreement is reached, including attempts to deal with climate change, despite high profile meetings such as the recent COP17 held in South Africa in 2011.

The crisis of approach is linked to the crisis of legitimacy that is haunting even the UN. The racialized global hierarchy of power that has been in place since the dawn of modernity, and has been institutionalized into the UN system, is raising more disagreements than agreements. There are increasing voices from the Global South, in particular, that argue that the United Nations Security Council does not represent the world of today. Africa is campaigning for inclusion among permanent members of the UN. But within Africa, there is no consensus on which country or countries are well placed to represent the continent. The duel so far seems to be between the two main contenders, Nigeria and South Africa. The legitimacy crisis at the UN level has resulted in what Carlos Lopes termed 'elastic resolutions', that is resolutions that were easily denounced even by those who participated in and approved them. The example of the resolution over the Libyan conflict is a case in point.

The crisis of global leadership and the concomitant troubles of multilateral order are also manifesting themselves as a lack of clear division of labour among multilateral institutions. This is seen in overlapping functions and conflicting mandates. This also manifests itself as a crisis of 'difficulties of inter-agency cooperation' (Held 2006: 164). It is yet to be seen whether global leaders would be able to restore symmetry and congruence among key multilateral agencies dealing with global governance. The difficulty is compounded by the fact that some regional multilateral institutions were formed to oppose the unilateralism of others. This is why it is imperative that questions of approach to, and the legitimacy of, multilateral institutions must take into account the need for structural reform of the present global-power arrangements, which result from a long history of imperialism. The problems are deep-rooted in the hierarchical and asymmetrical organization of states, markets, and nations under the general direction of an international dominant bloc of the U.S.A. and its NATO partners. Because of this power imbalance, the UN is destined to support the interests of American imperialism.

It is within this context that Africans have to take bold steps at a number of levels. The most immediate terrain of the new struggles should be an epistemological one. Should Africans continue to have confidence in Euro-American epistemologies that are clearly failing to produce modern solutions to deal with modern problems? It is high time for Africans to desist from living a life imposed on them from elsewhere and from trying to use knowledge from elsewhere to resolve African problems. The slogan of African solutions to African problems must not remain a mere rhetoric. Indigenous and endogenous knowledge, which was pushed to the barbarian margins, must be mobilized and harnessed towards the resolution of African problems, including those of an environmental nature.

What the epistemological struggle should seek to attain is cognitive justice, which would enable everyone to benefit from ecologies of knowledge while enriching humanity. The horizon that is sought is pluriversality rather than universality because the latter is predicated on the Euro-American hegemonic drive that results in inequality rather than equality. The epistemological struggle lies at the base of re-imagination of another world not founded on racism. What continues to inhibit African creativity, innovation and imagination is epistemological colonization that dates back to the time of colonial encounters. A new struggle pitched at the epistemological level, and underpinned by decolonial epistemic perspective, not only reveals the truth about the continuation of colonialism but also entails the decolonization of the minds of the African people. Without mental decolonization, it is impossible to imagine another world.

What this book has done is to provide three concepts (coloniality of power, coloniality of knowledge, and coloniality of being, borrowed from Latin American decolonial thinkers) on which to mount a decolonial epistemic perspective, as a combative epistemology to enable Africans to pursue a redemptive epistemological struggle. Such a struggle entails engaging in a deep diagnostic understanding of those African social formations and African experiences that began at the dawn of modernity and culminated in the current form of African subjectivity. It also entails seeking a deeper diagnostic understanding of the global imperial technologies of subjectivation that created the modern world order in which Africa was subalternized. At the same time it entails deep appreciattion of the emerging discourses that indicate the different directions the world is taking, including re-westernization, de-westernization, building socialism of the twenty-first century and decoloniality.

Beyond Euro-American hegemony: towards a decolonial turn

The global crisis has stretched from the collapse of socialism to the present occupation of Wall Street. According to Zizek (2011: xi), there are five responses to this crisis, which he described as a 'forthcoming apocalypse'. He mapped the reactions as follows:

> The first reaction is one of ideological denial: there is no fundamental disorder; the second is exemplified by explosions of anger at the injustices of the new world order; the third involves attempts at bargaining ("if we change things here and there, life could perhaps go on as before");

when the bargaining fails, depression and withdrawal set in; finally, after passing through this zero-point, the subject no longer perceives the situation as a threat, but as the chance of a new beginning—or, as Mao Zedong put it: "There is great disorder under heaven, the situation is excellent". (Zizek 2011: xi–xii)

Attempts to move beyond the current crisis have involved calling into question a narrative of modernity, progress, civilization, and modernization, cascading from Euro-American epistemic sites. From inside Europe and America, a Eurocentred critique of 'modernity within modernity' commenced with Marxism and psychoanalysis (Mignolo 2011b). It involved Christian, liberal and socialist options. It has grown into post-structuralism, post-modernism, and postcolonialism as critical forms of critique of 'modernity within modernity'.

From outside of Europe and America, the longstanding critique has sought to reveal how the Euro-American human trajectory was entwined with overseas conquest of the non-Western zones. It also sought to reject the tendency of consignment of the 'non-Western world' to 'static backwardness regardless of how those regions' fates were shaped by interaction with Europe, including the side-tracking of other modes of change and interaction' (Cooper 2005: 6).

The Eurocentred critique of modernity resulted in a series of 'turns' such as the 'historical turn', the 'cultural turn' and 'linguistic turn', which failed to radically transform Euro-American hegemony as introduced in Chapter One of this book (Cooper 2005: 6–8). The critique of modernity from non-Western epistemic sites inaugurated the 'decolonial turn' which not only questions modernity but calls for the end of Euro-American hegemony that generates underdevelopment. As noted by Nelson Maldonado-Torres:

> The decolonial turn does not refer to a single theoretical school, but rather points to a family of diverse positions that share a view of coloniality as the fundamental problem in the modern (as well as postmodern and information age), and decolonization or decoloniality as a necessary task that remains unfinished. (Maldonado-Torres 2011: 2)

Broadly speaking, the decolonial turn involves many initiatives, including decoloniality and de-westernization, which have locked horns with re-westernization. Decoloniality originated as a response to the capitalist and communist imperial designs. The Bandung Conference of 1955 was one of the major decoloniality projects that sought to chart a new human trajectory beyond capitalism and communism, building on decolonization and Global South solidarity. Present-day decolonial options also include the Islamic option, the feminist option, the nationalist option and the Afrocentric option. Decoloniality became an epistemic and political project involving epistemic disobedience, decolonization of power, decolonization of being and decolonization of knowledge as those people who experienced the negative aspects of modernity continue the struggle for a new humanism (Fanon 1968).

What are emerging are four future-oriented global trajectories. The first is re-westernization which seeks to save and to re-imagine the 'future of capitalism' (Mignolo 2011b). The second is 'reorientations of the Left' with a view to build what is known as 'socialism of the twenty-first century' associated with some Latin American leaders such as Lula and others (Mignolo 2011). The third is 'de-westernization' which originated in East and Southeast Asia and has seen such countries as Malaysia, Indonesia, India and China appropriating and adapting modernity and shifting the centre of development from Europe into Asia. As Mignolo puts it:

> Dewesternization means the end of long history of Western hegemony and of racial global discrimination projecting the image and the idea that Asians are yellow and that yellow people cannot think. Like many others, East and Southeast Asians have come out of the closet, and in this regard dewesternization means economic autonomy of decision and negotiations in the international arena and affirmation in the sphere of knowledge, subjectivity. It means, above all deracialization. (Mignolo 2011b: 48)

The fourth trajectory is the decolonial option which is a longstanding and long-term liberatory process ranged against coloniality, which denied African humanity. It embraces de-westernization and envisages a pluriversal world in which Africa has a dignified space.

Within decoloniality, the African human trajectory is understood as a graduation from coloniality into liberation, and from 'objecthood' into 'subjecthood', which I introduced at the beginning of this book. At the power level, African realization of humanity is defined as a triumph over an unsustainable Euro-American-centric global status quo in place since the fifteenth century.

At the level of being, realization of African humanity entails graduation of African people from 'zone of non-being' to 'zone of being' (from objecthood to subjecthood) (Santos 2007a: 45–87). The efforts to realize humanity for African peoples have therefore become a consistent and persistent struggle for new humanism that was clearly defined by Frantz Fanon to mean liberation and self-determination (Fanon 1968). It is the same struggle that Marcus Garvey described as 'universal negro improvement', predicated on self-help principles (Hill 1983).

At the level of epistemology, the realization of African humanity means successful 'provincialization' of Euro-American epistemological hegemony and opening up ecologies of knowledges that reflect the plurality of human experience, including restoration of those knowledges that had been displaced and silenced (Santos 2007a: 80–87). It involves turning the previously colonized peoples who have been reduced to objects of Euro-American knowledge into participants and generators of knowledge from the vantage points of their geographical and biographical locus of enunciation.

References

Abraham, K. 2003. *The African Quest: The Transition from the OAU to AU and NE-PAD Imperatives: Political and Economic History of Modern Africa and the Drive for the African Renaissance.* Addis Ababa: The Ethiopian International Institute for Peace and Development.

Abrahamsen, R. 2001. *Disciplining Democracy: Development Discourse and Good Governance in Africa.* London: Zed Books.

Adebajo, A. 2010. *The Curse of Berlin: Africa after the Cold War.* Scottsville: University of KwaZulu-Natal Press.

Adedeji, A. 1999. 'Comparative Strategies of Economic Decolonization in Africa'. In A. A. Mazrui (ed.), *UNESCO General History of Africa: VIII Africa since 1935.* New York: UNESCO, pp. 393–431.

Adedeji, A. 2002. 'From the Lagos Plan of Action to the New Partnership for African Development and from the Final Act of Lagos to the Constitutive Act: Whither Africa?' Unpublished Keynote Address for Presentation at the African Forum for Envisioning Africa, Nairobi, Kenya, pp. 26–29.

Adedeji, A. 2007. 'Democracy and Development: A Complex Relationship'. In K. Matlosa, J. Elklit and B. Chiroro (eds), *Challenges of Conflict, Democracy and Development in Africa.* Johannesburg: Electoral Institute of Southern Africa, pp. 19–43.

Adejumobi, S.A. 2001. 'The Pan-African Congresses'. In N. Mjagkij (ed.), *Organizing Black America: An Encyclopedia of African-American Association.* New York: Garland Publishing, pp. 456–480.

Adejumobi, S. and Olukoshi, A. 2008. 'Introduction: Transition, Continuity, and Change'. In S. Adejumobi and A. Olukoshi (eds), *The African Union and New Strategies for Development in Africa.* New York: Cambria Press, pp. 3–19.

Adesina, J.O. 2006. 'Development and the Challenge of Poverty: NEPAD, Post-Washington-Consensus and Beyond'. In J.O. Adesina, Y. Graham and A. Olukoshi (eds), *Africa and Development: Challenges in the New Millennium: The NEPAD Debate.* Dakar/London/Pretoria: CODESRIA/Zed Books/UNISA Press, pp. 33–62.

Adhikari, M. 2010. *The Anatomy of a South African Genocide: The Extermination of the Cape San Peoples.* Cape Town: University of Cape Town Press.

Adibe, J. 2009. 'Introduction: Africa without Africans'. In J. Adibe (ed.), *Who is an African? Identity, Citizenship and the Making of the Africa-Nation.* London: Adonis and Abbey Publishers Ltd., pp. 16–25.

Afemini, A.O. 2000. *Claude Ake's Philosophy of Development: Implications for Nigeria.* Ibadan: Ibadan University Press.

African Union. 2006. *Study on an African Union Government: Towards the United States of Africa*. Addis Ababa: African Union.

African Union. 2007. *Declaration of the 9th Ordinary Summit of AU Heads of State and Government (Accra Declaration)*. Accra: African Union.

Afrifa, A.A. 1966. *The Ghana Coup*. London: Frank Cass.

Agbese, P.O. and Kieh, G.K. 2007a. 'Preface'. In P.O. Agbese and G.K. Kieh (eds), *Reconstituting the State in Africa*. New York: Palgrave Macmillan, pp. i–ix.

Agbese, P.O. and Kieh, G.K. 2007b. 'Introduction: Democratizing States and State Reconstitution in Africa'. In P.O. Agbese and G.K. Kieh (eds), *Reconstituting the State in Africa*. New York: Palgrave Macmillan, pp. 1–23.

Ahluwalia, P. 2001. *Politics and Post-Colonial Theory: African Inflections*. London and New York: Routledge.

Ahluwalia, P. 2003. 'The Struggle for African Identity: Thabo Mbeki's African Renaissance'. In A. Zegeye and R.L. Harris (eds), *Media, Identity and the Public Sphere in Post-Apartheid South Africa*. Leiden and Boston, MA: Brill, pp. 27–39.

Ahluwalia, P. 2005. 'Out of Africa: Post-Structuralism's Colonial Roots'. *Postcolonial Studies*, 8(2), pp. 137–154.

Ahluwalia, P. and Nursey-Bray, P. 1997. 'Introduction'. In P. Ahluwalia and P. Nursey-Bray (eds), *Post-Colonialism: Culture and Identity in Africa*. Commack, NY: Nova Science Publications, Inc., pp. 1–10.

Ajayi, J.F. Ade. 2000. 'The National Question in Nigeria in Historical Perspective'. In T. Falola (ed.), *Tradition and Change in Africa: The Essays of J. F. Ade Ajayi*. Trenton, NJ: Africa World Press, pp. 217–241.

Ake, C. 1967a. *A Theory of Political Integration*. Homewood, IL: Dorsey Press.

Ake, C. 1967b. 'Political Integration and Political Stability: A Hypothesis'. *World Politics*, 19(3), pp. 486–499.

Ake, C. 1973. 'Explaining Political Instability in New States'. *Journal of Modern African Studies*, 11(3), pp. 347–359.

Ake, C. 1979. *Social Science as Imperialism: The Theory of Political Development*. Ibadan. University of Ibadan Press.

Ake, C. 1981. *A Political Economy of Africa*. London: Longman.

Ake, C. 1985a. 'The Future of the State in Africa'. *International Political Science*, 6(1), pp. 105–114.

Ake, C. (ed.) 1985b. *The Political Economy of Nigeria*. Lagos and London: Longman.

Ake, C. 1992a. 'The Legitimacy Crisis of the State'. In D. Kennett and T. Lumumba Kasongo (eds), *Structural Adjustment and the Crisis in Africa*. New York: Edwin Mellen Press, pp. 29–47.

Ake, C. 1992b. *The New World Order: A View from the South*. Lagos: Malthouse Press Ltd.

Ake, C. 1996. *Democracy and Development in Africa*. Washington, DC: The Brookings.

Ake, C. 2000. *The Feasibility of Democracy in Africa*. Dakar: CODESRIA Books.

Alexander, J., McGregor, J. and Ranger, T. 2000. *Violence and Memory: One Hundred Years in the 'Dark Forests' of Matabeleland*. Oxford: James Currey.

Allen, A. 2006. 'Dependency, Subordination, and Recognition: On Judith Butler's Theory of Subjection'. *Continental Philosophy Review*, 38, pp. 199–222.

Amin, S. 1989. *Spectres of Capitalism: A Critique of Current Intellectual Fashions*. New York: Monthly Review.

Amin, S. 1990a. *Delinking: Towards a Polycentric World*. London: Zed Books.

Amin, S. 1990b. *Maldevelopment: Anatomy of a Global Failure*. London: Zed Books.

Amin, S. 1991. 'The Ancient World System versus Modern Capitalist World System'. *Review*, XIV(3), pp. 349–385.

Amin, S. 1992. *Empire of Chaos*. New York: Monthly Review.

Amin, S. 1997. *Capitalism in the Age of Globalization*. London: Zed.

Amin, S. 2000. 'Economic Globalisation and Political Universalism: Conflicting Issues?' *Journal of World-Systems Research*, 3(Fall/Winter), pp. 582–622.

Amin, S. 2006a. *Beyond U.S. Hegemony: Assessing the Prospects for a Multipolar World*. London and New York: Zed Books.

Amin, S. 2006b. The Political Economy of the Twentieth Century'. *Monthly Review*, 52(2) (June), pp. 1–28.

Amin, S. 2009. *Eurocentrism: Second Edition*. New York: Monthly Review Press.

Amin, S. 2010. *Ending the Crisis of Capitalism or Ending Capitalism?* Oxford: Fahamu Books.

Anderson, B. 1983. *Imagined Communities*. London: Verso.

Ankersmit, F. 2010. 'Preface'. In M.O. Eze, *The Politics of History in Contemporary Africa*. New York: Palgrave Macmillan, pp. ix–xii.

Appadurai, A. 1996. *Modernity at Large: Cultural Dimensions of Globalisation*. Minneapolis and Indianapolis: Indiana University Press.

Appiah, K.A. 1992. *In My Father's House: Africa in the Philosophy of Culture*. Cambridge: Cambridge University Press.

Asante, M.K. 2003. *Afrocentricity: The Theory of Social Change*. Chicago, IL: African American Images.

Asante, M.K. 2007. *An Afrocentric Manifesto: Towards an African Renaissance*. Cambridge: Cambridge University Press.

Ashby, E. 1966. *Universities: British, Indian, African*. London: Weidenfeld and Nicholson.

Ashcroft, B. 1997. 'Globalism, Post-Colonialism and African Studies'. In P. Ahluwalia and P. Nursey-Bray (eds), *Post-Colonialism: Culture and Identity in Africa*. Commack, NY: Nova Science Publishers, Inc., pp. 12–26.

Ashforth, A. 1990. *The Politics of Official Discourse in Twentieth-Century South Africa*. Oxford: Clarendon Press.

Asiwaju, A.I. (ed.). 1984. *Partitioned Africans*. Lagos: Lagos University Press.

Asmal, K. 2001. *Foreword to Manifesto on Values, Education and Democracy*. Pretoria: Department of Education.

Attwell, D. 2005. *Rewriting Modernity: Studies in Black South African Literary History*. Scottsville: University of KwaZulu-Natal Press.

Ayittey, G.B.N. 1994. *Africa Betrayed*. London: The Macmillan Press Ltd.

B'beri, B.E. de and Louw, E. 2011. 'Introduction: Afropessimism: A Genealogy of Discourse'. *Critical Arts*, 25(3), pp. 335–346.

Bangura, Y. and Beckman, B. 1991. 'African Workers and Structural Adjustment with a Nigerian Case- Study'. In D. Ghai (ed.), *IMF and the South: Social Impact of Crisis and Adjustment*. London: Zed Books.

Batsa, K. 1985. *The Spark from Kwame Nkrumah to Limann*. London: Bellew Publishing.

Bayart, J.-F. 2000. 'Africa in the World: A History of Extraversion'. *African Affairs*, 99, pp. 217–267.

Bayart, J-F. 2004. *Global Subjects: A Political Critique of Globalization*. Cambridge: Polity Press.

Beach, D.N. 1971. 'The Rising in South-Western Mashonaland, 1896–97'. Ph.D. thesis, University of London.

Beach, D.N. 1979. 'Chimurenga': The Shona Rising of 1896–7'. *Journal of African Historical Studies*, 13(1), pp. 107–112.

Beach, D.N. 1980. 'Review Article: Revolt in Southern Rhodesia'. *International Journal of African History*, 20(3), pp. 401–416.

Beach, D.N. 1986. *War and Politics in Zimbabwe, 1840–1900*. Gweru: Mambo Press.

Beach, D.N. 1998. 'An Innocent Woman, Unjustly Accused? Charwe, Medium of Nehanda Mhondoro Spirit, and the 1896–97 Central Shona Rising in Zimbabwe'. *History in Africa*, 25, pp. 27–54.

Bennett, T. 1995. *The Birth of the Museum: History, Theory, Politics*. London: Routledge.

Bhabha, H. 1994. *The Location of Culture*. London and New York: Routledge.

Biehl, J., Good, B. and Kleinman, A. 2007. 'Introduction: Rethinking Subjectivity'. In J. Biehl, B. Good and A. Kleinman (eds), *Subjectivity: Ethnographic Investigations*. Berkeley, CA: University of California Press, pp. 1–23.

Bierschenk, T. and Spies, E. 2010. 'Introduction: Continuities, Dislocations and Transformations, 50 Years of Independence in Africa'. *Africa Spectrum*, 3, pp. 3–10.

Biko, S. 1978. *I Write What I Want*. Harmondsworth: Penguin.

Billig, M. 1995. *Banal Nationalism*. London: Sage.

Biney, A. 2008a. 'Samir Amin: A Titan of Radical Thought'. *Pambazuka News*, Issue 546, pp. 1–4.

Biney, A. 2008b. 'The Legacy of Kwame Nkrumah in Retrospect'. *The Journal of Pan-African Studies*, 16(3), pp. 387–398.

Blair, D. 2000. *Degrees in Violence: Robert Mugabe and the Struggle for Power in Zimbabwe*. London: Continuum.

Blair, T. 2006. *A Global Alliance for Global Values*. London: The Foreign Policy Centre.

Blaut, J.M. 1993. *The Colonizer's Model of the World: Geographical and Eurocentric History*. New York: The Guilford Press.

Boron, A. 2005. *Empire and Imperialism: A Critical Reading of Michael Hardt and Antonio Negri*. London and New York: Zed Books.

Bozzoli, B. 1978. 'Capital and State in South Africa'. *Review of African Political Economy*, 5(11), pp. 34–58.

Bozzoli, B. 1981. *The Political Nature of a Ruling Class*. London and Boston, MA: Routledge and Kegan Paul.

Brickhill, J. 1995. 'Daring to Storm the Heavens: ZIPRA Strategy'. In N. Bhebe and T. Ranger (eds), *Soldiers in Zimbabwe's Liberation War*. Harare: University of Zimbabwe Publications.

Bundy, C. 2007. 'New Nation, New History? Constructing the Past in Post-Apartheid South Africa'. In E. Stolten (ed.), *History Making and Present Day Politics*. Uppsala: Nordic Africa Institute, pp. 73–97.

Bush, B. 2006. *Imperialism and Postcolonialism*. London: Pearson.

Butler, J. 1997. *The Psychic Life of Power: Theories in Subjection*. Stanford, CA: Stanford University Press.

Butler, J., Laclau, E., and Žižek, S. 2000. *Contingency, Hegemony, Universality: Contemporary Dialogues on the Left*. London: Verso.

Cabral, A. 1972. *Revolution in Guinea: Selected Texts by A. Cabral*. New York: Monthly Review Press.

Cabral, A. 1980. *Unity and Struggle: Speeches and Writings*. London: Heinemann.

Calderisi, R. 2007. *The Trouble with Africa: Why Foreign Aid Isn't Working*. New York: Palgrave Macmillan.

Calhoun, C. (ed.). 1994. *Social Theory and the Politics of Identity*. Oxford: Blackwell.

Calhoun, C. 2007. *Nations Matter: Culture, History, and the Cosmopolitan Dream*. London and New York: Zed Books.

Calpin, G.H. 1941. *There Are No South Africans*. London: Thomas Nelson and Sons Ltd.

Castells, M. 1997. *The Information Age: Volume II*. Oxford: Blackwell Publishers.

Castro-Gomez, S. 2002. 'The Social Sciences, Epistemic Violence, and the Problem of the 'Invention of the Other'. *Nepantla: Views from the South*, 3(2), pp. 269–285.

Catholic Commission for Justice and Peace (CCJP) and Legal Resources Foundation (LRF). 1997. *Breaking the Silence, Building True Peace: Report on the Disturbances in Matabeleland and the Midlands Regions, 1980–1989*. Harare: CCJP and LRF.

Césaire, A. 1955. *Discourse on Colonialism*. Translated by Joan Pinkham. New York and London: Monthly Review Press.

Chabal, P. and Daloz, J.P. 1999. *Africa Works: Disorder as Political Instrument*. London: James Currey.

Chakrabarty, D. 2000. *Provincialising Europe: Postcolonial and Historical Difference*. Princeton, NJ: Princeton University Press.

Chambers, R. 1995. 'Poverty and Livelihoods: Whose Reality Counts?' *Environment and Urbanization*, 7, pp. 173–204.

Chan, S. 2003. *Robert Mugabe: A Life of Power and Violence*. London and New York: I.B. Tauris.

Chavez, H. 2011. 'Venezuelan President Hugo Chavez's Speech to the UN', at http://venezuelanalysis.com/print/6521 (Accessed 28 March 2012).

Cheeseman, N. and Tendi, B.-M. 2010. 'Power-Sharing in Comparative Perspective: The Dynamics of "Unity Government" in Kenya and Zimbabwe'. *Journal of Modern African Studies*, 48(2), pp. 203–229.

Chen, K.-H. 1998. 'Introduction: The Decolonization Question'. In K.-H. Chen (ed.), *Trajectories: Inter-Asia Cultural Studies*. London: Routledge, pp. 1–38.

Cheru, F. 2009. 'Development in Africa: The Imperial Project versus the National Project and the Need for Policy Space'. *Review of African Political Economy*, 120, pp. 275–278.

Chikowero, M. 2008. 'Struggles over Culture: Zimbabwean Music and Power, 1930s-2007'. Unpublished Ph.D. thesis, University of Dalhousie.

Chinweizu, 1975. *The West and the Rest of Us*. New York: Random House.

Chinweizu, 1987. *Decolonizing the African Mind*. Lagos: Pero Press.

Chipkin, I. 2007. *Do South Africans Exist? Nationalism, Democracy and Identity of 'the People'*. Johannesburg: Wits University Press.

Chitando, E. 2002. '"Down with the Devil, Forward with Christ!" A Study of the Interface between Religious and Political Discourses in Zimbabwe'. *African Sociological Review*, 6(1), pp. 1–16.

Chitando, E. 2005. 'In the Beginning Was Land: The Appropriation of Religious Themes in Political Discourse in Zimbabwe'. *Africa*, 75(2), pp. 220–239.

Chung, F. 2006. *Re-Living the Second Chimurenga: Memories from Zimbabwe's Liberation Struggle*. Uppsala: Nordic Afrika Institute.

Cobbing, J. 1976. 'The Ndebele under the Khumalos, 1820–1896'. Unpublished Ph.D. thesis, University of Lancaster.

Cobbing, J. 1977. 'The Absent Priesthood: Another Look at the Rhodesia Risings of 1896–1897'. *Journal of African History*, 18, pp. 61–84.

Cobbing, J. 1988. 'The Mfecane as Alibi: Thoughts on Dithakong and Mbolompo'. *Journal of African History*, 29, pp. 487–519.

Cohen R. 1986. *Endgame in South Africa? The Changing Structures and Ideology of Apartheid*. London: James Currey.

Comaroff, J. 2002. 'Governmentality, Materiality, Legality, Modernity: On the Colonial State in Africa'. In J.-G.D.P. Probst and H. Schmidt (eds), *African Modernities: Entangled Meanings in Current Debate*. Oxford: James Currey, pp. 107–134.

Comaroff, J.L. and Comaroff, J. 1997. *Of Revelation and Revolution: The Dialectics of Modernity on a South African Frontier: Volume Two*. Chicago, IL and London: The University of Chicago Press.

Comaroff, J.L. and Comaroff, J. 2003. 'Reflections on Liberalism, Policulturalism, and ID-ology: Citizenship and Difference in South Africa'. *Social Identities*, 9(4), pp. 443–473.

Comaroff, J.L. and Comaroff, J. 2009. *Ethnicity, Inc.* Chicago, IL: University of Chicago Press.

Comaroff, J.L. and Comaroff, J. 2012. *Theory from the South or How Euro-America Is Evolving towards Africa*. Boulder and London: Paradigm Publishers.

Cooper, F. 2002. *Africa since 1940: The Past of the Present*. Cambridge: Cambridge University.

Cooper, F. 2005. *Colonialism in Question: Theory, Knowledge, History*. Berkeley, CA: University of California Press.

Cooper, R. 2000. *The Postmodern State and the World Order*. London: The Foreign Policy Centre.

Crais, C.C. 1992. *White Supremacy and Black Resistance*. Cambridge: Cambridge University Press.

Crossman, P. 2004. 'Perceptions of "Africanisation" or "Endogenisation" at African Universities: Issues and Recommendations'. In P.T. Zeleza and A. Olukoshi (eds), *African Universities in the Twenty-First Century, Volume Two: Knowledge and Society*. Dakar: CODESRIA Books, pp. 319–340.

Cugoano, Q.O. 1999 [1787]. *Thoughts on the Evils of Slavery and Other Writings*. New York: Penguin Books.

Curle, A. 1962. 'Nationalism and Higher Education in Ghana'. *Universities Quarterly*, 16(3), pp. 232–233.

Dagnini, J.K. 2008. 'Marcus Garvey: A Controversial Figure in the History of Pan-Africanism'. *Journal of Pan-African Studies*, 2(3) (March), pp. 198–208.

Dascal, M. 2009. 'Colonizing and Decolonizing Minds'. In I. Kucurandi (ed.), *Papers of 2007 World Philosophy*. Ankara: Philosophical Society of Turkey.

Davidson, B. 1992. *The Black Man's Burden*. London: James Currey.

De Vos, P. 2010. 'Looking Backward, Looking Forward: Race, Corrective Measures and the South African Constitutional Court'. Unpublished Paper Presented at the Revisiting Apartheid Race Categories: A Colloquium, University of the Witwatersrand, October.

Debord, G. 2002. *The Society of the Spectacle*. Canberra: Treason Press.

Delavignette, R. 1964. *Christianity and Colonialism*. New York: Hawthorn Books.

Dirlik, A. 2002. 'Rethinking Colonialism: Globalization, Postcolonialism, and the Nation'. *Interventions*, 4(3), pp. 428–448.

Dorman, S.R. 2001. 'Inclusion and Exclusion: NGOs and Politics in Zimbabwe'. Unpublished D.Phil. thesis, University of Oxford.

Dorman, S, Hammet, D. and Nugent, P. 2007. 'Introduction: Citizenship and Its Causalities in Africa: States and Citizenship in Africa.' In S. Dorman, D. Hammett and P. Nugent (eds.), *Making Nations, Creating Strangers: States and Citizenship in Africa*. Leiden and Boston, MA: Brill, pp. 3–26.

Du Bois, W.E.B. 1965. *The World and Africa: An Inquiry into the Part Which Africa Has Played in World History*. New York: International Publishers.

Du Bois, W.E.B. 1986. 'Dusk to Dawn: An Essay Towards an Autobiography of a Race Concept'. In W.E.B. Du Bois, *Writings*. New York: Library of America, pp. 634–686.

Dubow, S. 1987. 'Race, Civilization and Culture: The Elaboration of Segregationist Discourse in the Inter-War Years'. In S. Marks and S. Trapido (eds), *The Politics of Race, Class and Nationalism in Twentieth-Century Africa*. London and New York: Longman, pp. 71–94.

Dubow, S. 1997. 'Colonial Nationalism, the Milner Kindergarten and the Rise of "South Africanism", 1902–1910'. *History Workshop Journal*, 43, pp. 51–84.

Dubow, S. 2006. *A Commonwealth of Knowledge*. Oxford: Oxford University Press.

Dubow, S. 2007. 'Thoughts on South Africa: Some Preliminary Ideas'. In H. Erik Stolten (ed.), *History Making and Present-Day Politics*. Uppsala: Nordic Africa Institute, pp. 51–72.

Dussel, E. 1995a. 'Eurocentrism and Modernity (Introduction to the Frankfurt Lectures)'. In J. Beverley, J. Oviedo and M. Aronna (eds), *The Postmodernism Debate in Latin America*. Durham, NC: Duke University Press, pp. 65–77.

Dussel, E. 1995b. *The Invention of the Americas: The Eclipse of the 'Other' and the Myth of Modernity*. New York: Humanities.

Dussel, E. 1996. *The Underside of Modernity: Apel, Ricoeur, Rorty, Taylor, and the Rigorous Science of Philosophy*. Rutgers: Transactions Books.

Dussel, E. 2000. 'Europe, Modernity and Eurocentrism'. *Nepantla: Views from the South*, 1(3), pp. 465–478.

Edmondson, L. 1986. 'Pan-Africanism and the International System: Challenges and Opportunities'. In W. Ofuatey-Kodjoe (ed.), *Pan-Africanism: New Directions and Strategies*. Boston, MA and London: University Press of America, pp. 256–295.

Elliot Berg's Report. 1981. 'An Agenda for Accelerated Development in Africa'. New York: World Bank.

Engel, U. and Olsen, G.R. 2005. 'Introduction: The African Exception: Conceptual Notes on Governance in Africa in the New Millennium'. In U. Engel and G. R. Olsen (eds), *The African Exception*. London: Ashgate, pp. 1–25.

Enloe, C. 1989. *Bananas, Beaches, and Bases: Making Feminist Sense of International Politics*. Berkeley, CA: University of California Press.

Eno, M.A. and Eno, O.A. 2009. 'Surveying through the Narratives of Africanity'. In J. Adibe (ed.), *Who is an African? Identity, Citizenship and the Making of the Africa-Nation*. London: Adonis and Abbey Publishers Ltd., pp. 61–78.

Escobar, A. 1995. *Encountering Development: The Making and Unmaking of the Third World*. Princeton, NJ: Princeton University Press.

Escobar, A. 2004. 'Beyond the Third World: Imperial Globality, Global Coloniality and Anti-Globalization Social Movements'. *Third World Quarterly*, 25(1), pp. 207–230.

Escobar, A. 2005. 'An Ecology of Difference: A Latin American Approach to Sustainability'. Unpublished Paper Presented under the Panel on Ecological Threats and New Promises of Sustainability for the 21st Century at the Queen

Elizabeth House 50th Anniversary Conference on New Development, Threats and Promises, Oxford University, 3–5 July 2005.

Escobar, A. 2007. 'Worlds and Knowledges Otherwise: The Latin American Modernity/Coloniality Research Program'. *Cultural Studies*, 21(2/3) (March/May), pp. 197–210.

Etherington, N. 2001. *The Great Treks: Transformation of Southern Africa, 1815–1854*. London: Pearson Education Press.

Etherington, N. 2004. 'A False Emptiness: How Historians May Have Been Misled by Early Nineteenth-Century Maps of South-Eastern Africa'. *Imago Mundi*, 56(1), pp. 67–86.

Eze, M.O. 2010. *The Politics of History in Contemporary Africa*. New York: Palgrave Macmillan.

Falola, T. 2001. *Nationalism and African Intellectuals*. Rochester, NY: The University of Rochester Press.

Falola, T. 2005. 'Great Wings Beating Still: Africa and the Colonial Legacy'. In T. Falola (ed.), *The Dark Webs: Perspectives on Colonialism in Africa*. Durham, NC: Carolina Academic Press, pp. 3–21.

Fanon, F. 1952 [2008]. *Black Skins, White Masks*. New York: Grove Press.

Fanon, F. 1968. *The Wretched of the Earth*. New York: Grove Press.

Ferguson, J. 1990. *The Anti-Politics Machine: "Development'," Depoliticisation, and Bureaucratic Power in Lesotho*. Cambridge: Cambridge University Press.

Ferguson, N. 2003. *Empire: How Britain Made the Modern World*. London: Allen Lane/Penguin.

Fine, B. 2006. 'Debating the "New" Imperialism'. *Historical Materialism*, 14(4), pp. 133–156.

Foucault, M. 1972. *The Order of Things: An Archaeology of the Human Sciences*. London: Routledge.

Foucault, M. 1977. 'Nietzsche, Genealogy, History'. In D.F. Bouchard (ed.), *Language, Counter-Memory, Practice*. Ithaca, NY: Cornell University Press, pp. 135–182.

Foucault, M. 1982. 'The Subject and Power'. In H. L. Dreyfus and P. Rabinow (eds), *Michel Foucault: Beyond Structuralism and Hermeneutics*. Brighton: Harvester Press, pp. 212–221.

Freidman, S. 2009. 'Belonging of another Type: Whiteness and African Identity'. In J. Adibe (ed.), *Who Is an African? Identity, Citizenship and the Making of the Africa-Nation*. London: Adonis and Abbey Publishers Ltd., pp. 79–83.

Friedman, T. 2000. *The Lexus and the Olive Tree*. New York: Anchor Books.

Fukuyama, F. 1992. *The End of History and the Last Man*. New York: Avon Books.

Gallagher, J. and Robinson, R. 1968. *Africa and the Victorians: The Climax of Imperialism*. New York: Doubleday.

Garvey, A.J. 1970. *Garvey and Garveyism*. New York: Collier Books.

Geiss, I. 1969. 'Pan-Africanism'. *Journal of Contemporary History*, 4(1), pp. 145–197.

Geiss, I. 1974. *The Pan-African Movement*. London: Methuen.

Gelder, E. van. 2012. 'Inside the Kommando Camp that Turns Boys' Doubts to Hate'. *Mail and Guardian*, 24 February–1 March 2012, p. 24.

Geshiere, P. 2009. *The Perils of Belonging: Autochthony, Citizenship and Exclusion in Africa and Europe*. Chicago: University of Chicago Press.

Geshiere, P., Meyer, B. and Pels, P. (eds). 2008. *Readings in Modernity in Africa*. Bloomington, IN: Indiana University Press.

Giddens, A. 1990. *The Consequences of Modernity*. Stanford, CA: Stanford University Press.

Glaser, D. 2010. 'Mbeki and His Legacy: A Critical Introduction'. In D. Glaser (ed.), *Mbeki and After: Reflections on the Legacy of Thabo Mbeki*. Johannesburg: Wits University Press, pp. 1–39.

Glynos, J. and Stavrakakis, Y. 2008. 'Lacan and Political Subjectivity: Fantasy and Enjoyment in Psychoanalysis and Political Theory'. *Subjectivity*, 24, pp. 256–274.

Gobbon, P., Bangura, Y. and Ofstad, A. (eds). 1992. *Authoritarianism, Democracy and Adjustment: The Politics of Economic Reform in Africa*. Uppsala: SIAS.

Griffiths, M. 2007. 'Worldviews and IR Theory: Conquest or Coexistence?' In M. Griffiths (ed.), *International Relations Theory for the Twenty-First Century: An Introduction*. London and New York: Routledge, pp. 1–27.

Grosfoguel, R. 2004. 'Race and Ethnicity or Racialised Ethnicities: Identities Within Global Coloniality'. *Ethnicities*, 4(3), pp. 315–336.

Grosfoguel, R. 2007. 'The Epistemic Decolonial Turn: Beyond Political-Economy Paradigms'. *Cultural Studies*, 21(2–3) (March), pp. 211–223.

Grosfoguel, R. 2011. 'Decolonizing Post-Colonial Studies and Paradigms of Political Economy: Transmodernity, Decolonial Thinking, and Global Coloniality'. *Modernity: Journal of Peripheral Cultural Production of the Luso-Hispanic World*, 1(1), pp. 1–39.

Guevara, C. 1965. 'Speech by Che Guevara to the Second Economic Seminar on Afro-Asia Solidarity', Algiers, Algeria, 24 February 1965', at http://www.marxists/org/archive/guevara/1965/02/24.html (Accessed 1 January 2011).

Habermas, J. 1973. *Legitimation Crisis*. Boston, MA: Beacon Press.

Habermas, J. 1987. *The Philosophical Discourse of Modernity*. Cambridge, MA: MIT.

Hardt, M. and Negri, A. 2000. *Empire*. Cambridge, MA: Harvard University Press.

Harvey, D. 2003. *The New Imperialism*. Oxford: Oxford University Press.

Harvey, D. 2007. 'In What Ways Is "The New Imperialism" Really New?' *Historical Materialism*, 15, pp. 57–70.

Held, D. 2006. 'Reframing Global Governance: Apocalypse Soon or Reform!' *New Political Economy*, 11(2) (June), pp. 157–176.

Hensbroek, P.B. van. 1999. *Political Discourse in African Thought, 1860 to the Present*. Westport, CT: Praeger.

Higher Education and Training, 2011. *The Report Commissioned by the Minister of Higher Education and Training for Charter for Human and Social Sciences Final Report, 30 June 2011*. Pretoria: Higher Education and Training.

Hill, R.A. 1983. *The Marcus Garvey and Universal Negro Improvement Association Papers*. Berkeley, CA: University of California Press.

Hill, R.A. and Pirio, G. 1987. 'Africa for the Africans: The Garvey Movement in South Africa, 1920–1940'. In S. Marks and S. Trapido (eds), *The Politics of Race, Class and Nationalism in Twentieth-Century South Africa*. London and New York: Longman, pp. 209–253.

Hippler, J. 2005. 'Violent Conflicts, Conflict Prevention and Nation-Building – Terminology and Political Concepts'. In J. Hippler (ed.), *Nation-Building: A Key Concept for Peaceful Conflict Transformation?* London: Pluto Press, pp. 3–14.

Hobsbawn, E. and Ranger, T.O. 1983. *The Invention of Tradition*. Cambridge: Cambridge University Press.

Hofmeyr, I. 1987. 'Building a Nation from Words: Afrikaans Language, Literature and Ethnic Identity, 1902–1924'. In S. Marks and S. Trapido (eds), *The Politics of Race, Class and Nationalism*. London and New York: Longman, pp. 95–123.

Hook, D. and Neill, C. 2008. 'Perspectives on 'Lacanian Subjectivities'. *Subjectivity*, 24, pp. 247–255.

Howarth, D. and Stavrakakis, Y. 2000. 'Introducing Discourse Theory and Political Analysis'. In D. Howarth, A. Norval and Y. Stavrakakis (eds), *Discourse Theory and Political Analysis*. Manchester: Manchester University Press, pp. 1–24.

Hudson, M. 1981. *Triumph or Tragedy? Rhodesia to Zimbabwe*. London: Hamish Hamilton.

Hudson, P. 2006. 'The Concept of the Subject in Laclau'. *Politikon*, 33(3), pp. 299–312.

Hudson, P. 2012. 'The State and the Colonial Unconscious'. Lecture presented at Public Affairs Research Institute (PARI), Johannesburg, South Africa, 31 May.

Hugo, P. 1988. 'Towards Darkness and Death: Racial Demonology in South Africa'. *Journal of Modern African Studies*, 26(4), pp. 545–580.

Huntington, S.P. 1999. 'The Lonely Superpower'. *Foreign Affairs*, 78(2), pp. 28–59.

Hyden, G. 1980. *Beyond Ujamaa in Tanzania: Underdevelopment and an Uncaptured Peasantry*. Berkeley, CA: University of California Press.

Ihonvbere, J.O. 1994. 'Pan-Africanism: Agenda for African Unity in the 1990s'. Unpublished Keynote Address Delivered at The All-African Student's Conference, Peter Clark Hall, University of Guelph, Ontario, Canada, 27 May.

Ikenberry, G.J. 2005. 'A Weaker World'. *Prospect*, 16(October), pp. 18–39.

Iliffe, J. 1979. *A Modern History of Tanganyika*. New York: Cambridge University Press.

Inskeep, R.R. 1987. *The Peopling of Southern Africa*. Cape Town: David Philip.

Irene, A. 1991. 'The African Scholar: Is Black Africa Entering the Dark Ages of Scholarship'. *Transition*, 51, pp. 28–58.

Jammeh, J. 2002. *New Africa Magazine*, 410, September.

July, R.W. 1987. *An African Voice: The Role of Humanities in African Independence*. Durham, NC: Duke University Press.

Kaunda, K. and Morris, C.M. 1966. *A Humanist in Africa: Letters to Colin M. Morris from Kenneth D. Kaunda, President of Zambia*. New York: Abingdon Press.

Keating, M. 2000. *Nations against the State: The New Politics of Nationalism in Quebec, Catalonia and Scotland*. New York: Palgrave Macmillan.

Khadiagala, G.M. 2010. 'Two Moments in African Thought: Ideas in Africa's International Relations'. *South African Journal of International Affairs*, 17(3) (December), pp. 375–386.

Killingray, D. 2010. 'Origins of Pan-Africanism: Henry Sylvester Williams, Africa, and the African Diaspora'. *Journal of Imperial and Commonwealth History*, 39(2), pp. 348–351.

Kleinmen, A. and Fitz-Henry, E. 2007. 'The Experiential Basis of Subjectivity'. In J. Biehl, B. Good and A. Kleinman (eds), *Subjectivity: Ethnographic Investigations*. Berkeley, CA: University of California Press, pp. 52–65.

Kriger, N.J. 1995. 'The Politics of Creating National Heroes: The Search for Political Legitimacy and National Identity'. In N. Bhebe and T. Ranger (eds), *Soldiers in Zimbabwe's Liberation War*. London: James Currey, pp. 137–156.

Kriger, N.J. 2003. *Guerrilla Veterans in Post-War Zimbabwe: Symbolic and Violent Politics, 1980–1987*. Cambridge: Cambridge University Press.

Kriger, N.J. 2005. 'ZANU (PF) Strategies in General Elections, 1980–2000, Discourse and Coercion'. *African Affairs*, 104(414), pp. 1–34.

Kriger, N.J. 2006. 'From Patriotic Memories to "Patriotic History" in Zimbabwe, 1990–2005'. *Third World Quarterly*, 27(6), pp. 1151–1169.

Laakso, L. and Olukoshi, A. 1996. 'The Crisis of the Post-Colonial Nation-State Project in Africa'. In A.O. Olukoshi and L. Laakso (eds), *Challenges to the Nation-State in Africa*. Uppsala: Nordic Africa Institute, pp. 7–39.

Lacan, J. 1966. 'The Mirror Stage as Formative of the Function of the "I" as Revealed in Psychoanalytical Experience'. In *Ecrits: A Selection*. New York: W.W. Norton.

Lacan, J. 1973. *The Four Fundamental Concepts of Psycho-Analysis: Seminar XI*. New York: W.W. Norton and Co.

Laclau, E. (ed.). 1994. *The Making of Political Identities*. London and New York: Verso.

Laclau, E. 1996. *Emancipation(s)*. London: Verso.

Laclau, E. 2005. *On Populist Reason*. London and New York: Verso.

Laclau, E. and Mouffe, C. 1985. *Hegemony and Socialist Strategy*. London: Verso.

Laidi, Z. 1990. *The Superpowers and Africa: The Construction of a Rivalry*. Chicago, IL: University of Chicago Press.

Landau, P.S. 2010. *Popular Politics in the History of South Africa, 1400–1948*. Cambridge: Cambridge University Press.

Lander, E. 2002. 'Eurocentrism, Modern Knowledges, and the "Natural" Order of Global Knowledges'. *Review*, XXX(1), pp. 87–89.

Laremont, R.R. 2005. 'Borders, Nationalism and the African State'. In R.R. Laremont (ed.), *Borders, Nationalism, and the African State*. Boulder, CO and London: Lynne Rienner Publishers, pp. 1–24.

Lebakeng, J.T., Phalane, M.M. and Dalindjebo, N. 2006. 'Epistemicide, Institutional Cultures and the Imperative for the Africanisation of Universities in South Africa'. *Alternation*, 12(1), pp. 71–98.

Lecoutre, D. 2008. 'Reflections on the 2007 Accra Grand Debate on a Union Government for Africa'. In T. Murithi (ed.), *Towards A Union Government for Africa: Challenges and Opportunities*. Pretoria/Tshwane, Institute for Security Studies, pp. 45–59.

Lembede, A.M. 1972. 'Policy of the Congress Youth League'. In T. Karis and G.M. Carter (eds), *From Protest to Challenge: Volume 2*. Stanford, CA: Stanford University Press, pp. 313–317.

Lester, A. 2001. *Imperial Networks: Creating Identities in Nineteenth-Century South Africa and Britain*. London: Routledge.

LeVan, A.C. 2011. 'Power Sharing and Inclusive Politics in Africa's Uncertain Democracies'. *Governance: An International Journal of Policy, Administration, and Institutions*, 24(1), pp. 31–53.

Lewellen, T.C. 2002. *The Anthropology of Globalization: Cultural Anthropology Enters the 21st Century*. Connecticut: Bergin and Garvey.

Lewis, M.W. and Wigen, K.W. 1997. *The Myth of Continents: A Critique of Metageography*. Berkeley, CA: University of California Press.

Lindauer, D.L. and Pritchett, L. 2002. 'What's the Big Idea? The Third Generation of Policies for Economic Growth'. *Economia*, 3, pp. 1–25.

Lopes, C. 2010. 'Keynote Address'. Paper Presented at the International Conference *Fifty Years of African Independence – Continuities and Discontinuities*, University of Mainz, Germany, 8–10 April.

Lumumba-Kasongo, T. 1994. *Political Re-Mapping of Africa: Transnational Ideology and the Definition of Africa in World Politics*. Lanham, MD and New York: University Press of America.

Lumumba-Kasongo, T. 2003. 'Can A "Realist Pan-Africanism" Be a Relevant Tool Towards the Transformation of African and African Diaspora Politics? Imagining a Pan-African State'. *African Journal of International Affairs*, 6(1–2), pp. 13–38.

Lumumba-Kasongo, T. 2007. 'Rethinking the African State: A Background Paper on Building the Democratic Developmental State'. Unpublished Paper Written for the United Nations Development Programme, December, New York.

Lumumba-Kasongo, T. 2011. 'The National Project as a Public Administration Concept: The Problematic of State Building in the Search for New Development Paradigms in Africa'. *Africa Development*, XXXVI(2), pp. 63–96.

Mafeje, A. 2011. 'Africanity: A Combative Ontology'. In R. Devisch and F.B. Nyamnjoh (eds), *The Postcolonial Turn: Re-Imagining Anthropology and Africa*. Bamenda and Leiden: Langaa and African Studies Centre, pp. 31–44.

Magubane, B.M. 1996. *The Making of a Racist State: British Imperialism and the Union of South Africa 1870–1910*. Trenton, NJ: Africa World Press.

Magubane, B.M. 1997. *The Political Economy of Race and Class in South Africa*. New York: Monthly Review Press.

Magubane, B.M. 2007. *Race and the Construction of the Dispensable Other*. Pretoria: UNISA Press.

Makinda, S.M. and Okumu, F.W. 2008. *The African Union: Challenges of Globalisation, Security and Governance*. New York: Routledge.

Maldonado-Torres, N. 2004. 'The Topology of Being and the Geopolitics of Knowledge: Modernity, Empire, Coloniality'. *City*, 8(1) (April), pp. 29–56.

Maldonado-Torres, N. 2006. 'Post-Continental Philosophy: Its Definition, Contours, and Fundamental Sources'. *Worlds and Knowledge Otherwise*, Fall, pp. 1–29.

Maldonado-Torres, N. 2007. 'On the Coloniality of Being: Contributions to the Development of a Concept'. *Cultural Studies*, 21(2–3), pp. 240–270.

Maldonado-Torres, N. 2008. *Against War: Views from the Underside of Modernity*. Durham, NC: Duke University Press.

Maldonado-Torres, N. 2011. 'Thinking Through the Decolonial Turn: Post-Continental Interventions in Theory, Philosophy, and Critique—An Introduction'. *Transmodernity*, Fall, pp. 1–25.

Mamdani, M. 1996. *Citizen and Subject: Contemporary Africa and the Legacy of Late Colonialism*. Princeton, NJ: Princeton University Press.

Mamdani, M. 1991. 'Social Movements and Constitutionalism in the African Context'. In I.G. Shivji (ed.), *State and Constitutionalism: An African Debate on Democracy*. Harare: SAPES Books, pp. 224–246.

Mamdani, M. 2001a. 'When Does a Settler Become a Native? Citizenship and Identity in a Settler Society'. *Pretext: Literacy and Cultural Studies*, 10(1) (July), pp. 36–76.

Mamdani, M. 2001b. *When Victims Become Killers: Colonialism, Nativism, and the Genocide in Rwanda*. Oxford: James Currey.

Mamdani, M. 2007. 'Political Violence and State Formation in Post-Colonial Africa'. *International Development Centre Working Paper Series*, Paper No. 1, October, pp. 1–38.

Mamdani, M. 2011. 'The Importance of Research in a University'. *Pambazuka News*, 526, pp. 21–23.

Mandaza, I. and Sachikonye, L. (eds). 1991. *The One-Party State and Democracy: The Zimbabwe Debate*. Harare: SAPES Books.

Marks, S. 1980. 'South Africa: The Myth of the Empty Land'. *History Today*, January, pp. 5–12.

Marks, S. and Trapido, S. 1987. 'The Politics of Race, Class and Nationalism'. In S. Marks and S. Trapido (eds), *The Politics of Race, Class and Nationalism*. London and New York: Longman, pp. 1–70.

Martin, G. 1995. 'Francophone Africa in the Context of Franco-African Relations'. In J. W. Harbeson and D. Rothchild (eds), *Africa in World Politics: Post-Cold War Challenges*, 2nd edition. Boulder, CO: Westview Press, pp. 163–188.

Martin, G. 2002. *Africa in World Politics: A Pan-African Perspective*. Trenton, NJ: Africa World Press.

Marx, A.W. 1998. *Making Race and Nation*. Cambridge: University of Cambridge Press.

Marx, K. and Engels, F. 1848. 'Manifesto of the Communist Party'. In *Marx/Engels Selected Work: Volume 1*. Moscow: Progress Publishers, 1969, transcribed by Zodaic and Brian Baggins. Available at http://www.marxistsfr.org/archive/marx/works/download/manifest.pdf (Accessed 29 April 2012).

Masunungure, E.V. 2006. 'Nation-Building, State-Building and Power Configuration in Zimbabwe'. *Conflict Trends Magazine*, 1, pp. 3–8.

Mathews, K. 2009. 'Renaissance of Pan-Africanism: The AU and the New Pan-Africanists'. In J. Akokpari, A. Ngida-Muvumba and T. Murithi (eds), *The African Union and Its Institutions*. Johannesburg: Jacana Media, pp. 25–39.

Mazarire, G.C. 2011. 'Discipline and Punishment in ZANLA, 1964–1979'. *Journal of Southern African Studies*, 37(3), pp. 571–591.

Mazrui, A. 1982. 'Africa between Nationalism and Nationhood: A Political Survey'. *Journal of Black Studies*, 13(1), pp. 13–36.

Mazrui, A.A. 1999. 'Seek Ye First the Political Kingdom'. In A.A. Mazrui (ed.), *UNESCO General History of Africa*. New York: UNESCO, pp. 105–126.

Mazrui, A. 2004. *Nkrumah's Legacy and Africa's Triple Heritage between Globalization and Counter Terrorism*. Accra: University of Ghana Press.

Mazrui, A.A. 2009. 'Preface: Comparative Africanity: Blood, Soil and Ancestry'. In J. Adibe (ed.), *Who is an African? Identity, Citizenship and the Making of the Africa-Nation*. London: Adonis and Abbey Publishers Ltd., pp. xi–xv.

Mazrui, A. 2011. 'Using 50 Years of Independence to Judge 100 Years of Colonial Rule'. Unpublished paper presented at the Centre for African Studies, University of the Free State, June.

Mbeki, M. 2009. *Architects of Poverty: Why African Capitalism Needs Changing*. Johannesburg: Picador Africa.

Mbeki, T. 1996. Speech Delivered on the Occasion of the Adoption of Constitutional Assembly of the Republic of South Africa Constitutional Bill, Cape Town.

Mbeki, T. 2011. 'The Role of Africa's Student Leaders in Developing the African Continent: Carthage Must Be Rebuilt'. Address by Thabo Mbeki at the African Student Leaders Summit Meeting, University of Cape Town, 6 September 2010.

Mbeki, T. 2012. Address by Thabo Mbeki at Makerere University's Institute of Social Research Conference on the Architecture of Post-Cold War Africa – Between Internal Reform and External Intervention, Makerere University, Kampala, Uganda, 19 January.

Mbembe, A. 2000. *On Private Indirect Government*. State of the Literature Series No. 1–2000.

Mbembe, A. 2001a. *On the Postcolony*. Berkeley, CA: University of California Press.

Mbembe, A. 2001b. 'What is Postcolonial Thinking? An Interview with Achille Mbembe'. *Eurozine*, at www.eurozine.com.

Mbembe, A. 2002a. 'African Modes of Self-Writing'. *Public Culture*, 14(1), pp. 239–273.

Mbembe, A. 2002b. 'On the Power of the False'. *Public Culture*, 14(3), pp. 629–675.

Mbembe, A. 2006a. 'On the Postcolony: A Brief Response to Critics'. *African Identities*, 4(2), pp. 143–178.

Mbembe, A. 2006b. 'The Cultural Politics of South Africa's Foreign Policy: Between Black (inter)nationalism and Afropolitanism'. Paper presented at the Wits Institute of Economic and Social Research (WISER), University of the Witwatersrand.

Mbembe, A. 2011. 'Fifty Years of African Decolonization'. *Chimurenga Online*, at http://www.chimurenga.co.za/page-147.html (Accessed 26 August 2011).

Mbembe, A. 2012a. 'Roundtable Presentation and Discussion: Fanon on Blackness'. WISER Seminar Series, WISER Seminar Room, University of Witwatersrand, 31 May.

Mbembe, A. 2012b. 'Rule of Property versus Rule of the Poor'. *Mail and Guardian*, 15–21 June, pp. 34–35.

McClintock, A. 1997. '"No Longer in a Future Heaven": Gender, Race and Nationalism'. In A. McClintock, A. Mufti and E. Shohat (eds), *Dangerous Liaisons: Gender Nation, and Postcolonial Perspectives*. Minneapolis: University of Minnesota Press, pp. 89–112.

McEachern, D. 1997. 'Foucault, Governmentality, Apartheid and the "New" South Africa'. In P. Ahluwalia and P. Nursery-Bray (eds), *Post-Colonialism: Culture and Identity in Africa*. Commack, NY: Nova Science Publishers, Inc., pp. 111–133.

McKaiser, E. 2010. 'Towards a Common National Identity: Did Thabo Mbeki Help or Hinder?' In D. Glaser (ed.), *Mbeki and After*. Johannesburg: Wits University Press, pp. 187–208.

McRae, D.G. 1966. 'Nkrumahism: Past and Future of an Ideology'. *Government and Opposition*, 1(4) (July), pp. 535–546.

MDC. 2000. *MDC Election Manifesto*. Harare: Information and Publicity Department.

MDC. 2007. *A New Zimbabwe: A New Beginning*. Harare: Information and Publicity.

Memmi, A. 1974. *The Coloniser and the Colonised*. London: Earthscan.

Mhanda, W. 2011. *Dzino: Memories of a Freedom Fighter*. Harare: Weaver Press.

Mignolo, W.D. 1995. *The Darker Side of Renaissance: Literacy, Territory, and Colonization*. Ann Arbor, MI: University of Michigan Press.

Mignolo, W.D. 1999. 'I Am Where I Think: Epistemology and the Colonial Difference'. *Journal of Latin American Cultural Studies*, 8(2), pp. 235–245.

Mignolo, W.D. 2000. *Local Histories/Global Designs: Coloniality, Subaltern Knowledges, and Border Thinking*. Princeton, NJ: Princeton University Press.

Mignolo, W.D. 2005a. *The Idea of Latin America*. Oxford: Blackwell Publishing.

Mignolo, W.D. 2005b. 'Prophets Facing Sidewise: The Geopolitics of Knowledge and the Colonial Difference'. *Social Epistemology*, 19(1) (January–March), pp. 111–127.

Mignolo, W.D. 2007a. 'Introduction: Coloniality of Power and De-Colonial Thinking'. *Cultural Studies*, 21(2/3) (March/May), pp. 155–167.

Mignolo, W.D. 2007b. 'Delinking: The Rhetoric of Modernity, the Logic of Coloniality and the Grammar of De-Coloniality'. *Cultural Studies*, 21(2/3) (March/May), pp. 449–514.

Mignolo, W.D. 2008. 'Epistemic Disobedience, Independent Thought and De-Colonial Freedom'. *Theory, Culture and Society*, 26(7–8), pp. 1–23.

Mignolo, W.D. 2011a. 'Epistemic Disobedience and the Decolonial Option: A Manifesto'. *Transmodernity*, 1(2) (Fall), pp. 44–66.

Mignolo, W.D. 2011b. *The Darker Side of Western Modernity: Global Futures, Decolonial Options*. Durham, NC and London: Duke University Press.

Mirsepassi, A. 2000. *Intellectual Discourse and the Politics of Modernization: Negotiating Modernity in Iran*. Cambridge: Cambridge University Press.

Mkandawire, T. 1997. 'Globalisation and Africa's Unfinished Agenda'. *Macalester International*, 7, pp. 71–107.

Mkandawire, T. 2003. 'Institutions and Development in Africa'. Unpublished Paper Submitted to *Cambridge Journal of Economics* Conference on Economics for the Future, 17–19 September, pp. 1–30.

Mkandawire, T. 2005. 'African Intellectuals and Nationalism'. In T. Mkandawire (ed.), *African Intellectuals: Rethinking Politics, Language, Gender and Development*. London: Zed Books, pp. 1–34.

Mkandawire, T. 2009. 'From the National Question to the Social Question'. *Transformation*, 68, pp. 130–160.

Mkandawire, T. 2011. 'Running While Others Walk: Knowledge and the Challenge of Africa's Development'. *Africa Development*, XXXVI(2), pp. 1–36.

Mkandawire, T. 2012. 'Building the African State in the Age of Globalization: The Role of Social Compacts and Lessons for South Africa'. Inaugural Annual Lecture Delivered at Mapungubwe Institute of Strategic Reflections (MISTRA), University of Witwatersrand, Johannesburg, South Africa.

Molteno, P.A. 1986. *A Federal South Africa*. London: Juta.

Mookherjee, D. 2004. 'Is There Too Little Theory in Development Economics Today?' *Economic and Political Weekly*, 1, pp. 34–60.

Moore, D. 1995a. 'The Zimbabwe People's Army: Strategic Innovation or More of the Same?' In N. Bhebe and T. Ranger (eds), *Soldiers in Zimbabwe's Liberation War*. London: James Currey, pp. 73–103.

Moore, D. 1995b. 'Democracy, Violence, and Identity in the Zimbabwean War of National Liberation: Reflections from the Realm of Dissent'. *Canadian Journal of African Studies*, 29(3), pp. 387–390.

Moore, D. 2005. 'Investing the Past, Creating Hegemony: Deconstructing Ngwabi Bhebe's Simon Vengayi Muzenda: The Struggle for and Liberation of Zimbabwe'. Unpublished Paper Presented at the South African Historical Society Biennial Conference, *Southern Africa and the World: The Local, the Regional and the Global in Historical Perspective*, University of Cape Town, 26–29 June.

Moore, D. 2008. 'Coercion, Consent, Context: Operation Murambatsvina and ZANU-PF's Illusory Quest for Hegemony'. In M. Vambe (ed.), *The Hidden Dimensions of Operation Murambatsvina in Zimbabwe*. Harare and Pretoria: Weaver Press and Africa Institute of South Africa, pp. 25–39.

Moore-Gilbert, B. 1997. *Postcolonial Theory: Contexts, Practices, Politics*. London: Verso.

Moyo, S. and Yeros, P. 2011. 'Preface'. In S. Moyo and P. Yeros (eds), *Reclaiming the Nation*. London: Pluto Press, pp. vii–x.

Msindo, E. 2007. 'Ethnicity and Nationalism in Urban Colonial Zimbabwe: Bulawayo, 1950 to 1963'. *Journal of African History*, 48, pp. 245–373.

Mthwakazi People. 2011. 'Open Letter from the People of Mthwakazi to Head of State and Government of the Republic of Zimbabwe, President Robert Mugabe', 24 February.

Muchemwa, K.Z. 2010. 'Galas, Biras, State Funerals and the Necropolitan Imagination in Re-Construction of the Zimbabweans Nation, 1980–2008'. *Social Dynamics*, 36(3), pp. 504–514.

Mudenge, S.I.G. 1988. *A Political History of Munhumutapa c. 1400–1902*. Harare: Zimbabwe Publishing House.

Mudimbe, V.Y. 1988. *The Invention of Africa: Gnosis, Philosophy, and the Order of Knowledge*. London: James Currey.

Mudimbe, V.Y. 1994. *The Idea of Africa*. Bloomington, IN: Indiana University Press.

Mueni wa Muiu. 2008. *The Pitfalls of Liberal Democracy and Late Nationalism in South Africa*. New York: Palgrave.

Mueni wa Muiu and Martin, G. 2009. *A New Paradigm of the State: Fundi wa Afrika*. New York: Palgrave.

Mugabe, R.G. 1978. 'ZANU Carries the Burden of History'. *Zimbabwe News*, 10(2), 5–6.

Mugabe, R.G. 2001. *Inside the Third Chimurenga*. Harare: Ministry of Information and Publicity.

Mukherjee, B. 2006. 'Why Political Power-Sharing Agreements Lead to Enduring Peaceful Resolution of Some Civil Wars, but Not Others'. *International Studies Quarterly*, 50, pp. 479–504.

Mulder, P. 2012. 'Are Sexwale and Ramaphosa Really White Land Owners?', at http://www.politicsweb.co.za/politicsweb/view/po (Accessed 26 February 2012).

Murithi, T. 2008a. 'Introduction: Contextualizing the Debate on a Union Government for Africa'. In T. Murithi (ed.), *Towards a Union Government for Africa*. Pretoria/Tshwane: Institute for Security Studies, pp. 1–23.

Murithi, T. 2008b. 'Conclusion: The Prospects for a Union Government for Africa'. In T. Murithi (ed.), *Towards a Union Government for Africa*. Pretoria/Tshwane: Institute for Security Studies, pp. 183–189.

Mutua, M. 2010. *The International Criminal Court in Africa: Challenges and Opportunities*. Stockholm: Norwegian Peacebuilding Centre.

Muzondidya, J. 2007. 'Jambanja: Ideological Ambiguities in the Politics of Land and Resource Ownership in Zimbabwe'. *Journal of Southern African Studies*, 33(2), pp. 321–325.

Muzondidya, J. 2010. 'The Zimbabwe Crisis and the Unresolved Conundrum of Race in the Post-Colonial Period'. *Journal of Developing Societies*, 26(2), pp. 5–38.

Muzvidziwa, V.N. 2005. 'Globalisation and Higher Education in Africa: The Case of the African University'. *UNISWA Research Journal*, 19(December), pp. 67–98.

Nabudere, D.W. 2011. *Afrikology, Philosophy and Wholeness: An Epistemology*. Pretoria: Africa Institute of South Africa.

Ndlovu-Gatsheni, S.J. 2006. 'Puppets or Patriots: A Study of Nationalist Rivalry over the Spoils of Dying Settler Colonialism in Zimbabwe, 1977–1980'. In W.J. Burzta, T. Kamusella and S. Wojciechowski (eds), *Nationalisms Across the Globe: An Overview of Nationalisms in State-Endowed and Stateless Nations: Volume II: Third World*. Poznan: School of Humanities and Journalism, pp. 345–397.

Ndlovu-Gatsheni, S.J. 2007a. 'Fatherhood and Nationhood: Joshua Nkomo and Re-Imagination of the Zimbabwe Nation in the 21st Century'. In K. Muchemwa and R. Muponde (eds), *Manning the Nation: Father Figures in the Zimbabwean Literature and Society*. Harare and Johannesburg: Weaver Press and Jacana, pp. 73–87.

Ndlovu-Gatsheni, S.J. 2007b. *Tracking the Historical Roots of Post-Apartheid Citizenship Problems*. Leiden: ASC Working Paper 72.

Ndlovu-Gatsheni, S.J. 2008a. 'Black Republican Tradition, Nativism and Populist Politics in South Africa'. *Transformation*, 68, 53–85.

Ndlovu-Gatsheni, S.J. 2008b. 'Nation-Building in Zimbabwe and Challenges of Ndebele Particularism'. *African Journal on Conflict Resolution*, 8(3), pp. 27–55.

Ndlovu-Gatsheni, S.J. 2009a. *Do 'Zimbabweans' Exist? Trajectories of Nationalism, National Identity Formation and Crisis in a Postcolonial State*. Oxford: Peter Lang.

Ndlovu-Gatsheni, S.J. 2009b. 'Making Sense of Mugabeism in Local and Global Politics: "So Blair, Keep Your England and Let Me Keep My Zimbabwe"'. *Third World Quarterly*, 30(6), pp. 1139–1158.

Ndlovu-Gatsheni, S.J. 2009c. 'Africa for Africans or Africa for "Natives" Only? New Nationalism' and Nativism in Zimbabwe and South Africa'. *Africa Spectrum*, 1, pp. 61–78.

Ndlovu-Gatsheni, S.J. 2009d. *The Ndebele Nation: Reflections on Hegemony, Memory and Historiography*. Amsterdam and Pretoria: Rozenberg Publishers and UNISA Press.

Ndlovu-Gatsheni, S.J. 2011a. 'Beyond the Drama of War: Trajectories of Nationalism in Zimbabwe, the 1890s to 2010'. In S.J. Ndlovu-Gatsheni and J. Muzondidya (eds), *Redemptive or Grotesque Nationalism? Rethinking Contemporary Politics in Zimbabwe*. Oxford: Peter Lang, pp. 37–79.

Ndlovu-Gatsheni, S.J. 2011b. 'African, Know Thyself: Epistemic Awakening and the Creation of an Identity for a Pan-African University'. Plenary Presentation Delivered at the Pan-African University (PAU) Stakeholder Curriculum Validation Workshop, Organized by the African Union Commission's Department of Human Resources, Science and Technology, Addis Ababa, Ethiopia, 14–18 November.

Ndlovu-Gatsheni, S.J. 2011c. *The Zimbabwean Nation-State Project: A Historical Diagnosis of Identity and Power-Based Conflicts in a Postcolonial State*. Uppsala: Nordic Afrika Institute.

Ndlovu-Gatsheni, S.J. 2012a. *Coloniality of Power in Postcolonial Africa: Myths of Decolonization*. Dakar: CODESRIA Books.

Ndlovu-Gatsheni, S.J. 2012b. 'Fiftieth Anniversary of Decolonization in Africa: A Moment of Celebration or Critical Reflection?' *Third World Quarterly*, 33(1), pp. 71–89.

Ndlovu-Gatsheni, S.J. and Willems, W. 2009. 'Making Sense of Cultural Nationalism and the Politics of Commemoration under the Third Chimurenga in Zimbabwe'. *Journal of Southern African Studies*, 35(4), pp. 945–965.

Ndlovu-Gatsheni, S.J. and Willems, W. 2010. 'Reinvoking the Past in the Present: Changing Identities and Appropriations of Joshua Nkomo in Post-Colonial Zimbabwe'. *African Identities*, 8(3), pp. 191–208.

Negri, A. 2008. *Reflections on Empire*. London: Polity Press.

Neocosmos, M. 2008. 'The Politics of Fear and the Fear of Politics: Reflections on Xenophobic Violence in South Africa'. *Journal of Asian and African Studies*, 43(6), pp. 586–594.

Neocosmos, M. 2010. *From 'Foreign Natives' to 'Native Foreigners': Explaining Xenophobia in Post-Apartheid South Africa: Citizenship and Nationalism, Identity and Politics* (2nd edition). Dakar: CODESRIA Books.

Ngugi wa Thiong'o. 1986. *Decolonizing the Mind: The Politics of Language in African Literature*. Nairobi: Heinemann Education Publishing Ltd.

Ngugi wa Thiong'o. 2009. *Re-Membering Africa*. Nairobi: East African Education Publishers Ltd.

Nkrumah, K. 1963a. *Africa Must Unite*. London: Longman.

Nkrumah, K. 1963b. *The African Genius*. No Publisher Details.

Nkrumah, K. 1964. *Consciencism: Philosophy and Ideology for Decolonization*. New York: Monthly Review Press.

Nkrumah, K. 1965. *Neo-Colonialism: The Last Stage of Imperialism*. London: Thomas Nelson and Sons Ltd.

Nkrumah, K. 1966. *Challenge of the Congo*. New York: International Publishers.

Norval A.J. 1996. *Deconstructing Apartheid Discourse*. London and New York: Verso.

Nugent, P. 2004. *Africa since Independence: A Comparative History*. New York: Palgrave.

Nyamnjoh, F.B. 2001. 'Concluding Reflections on Beyond Identities: Rethinking Power in Africa'. In H. Melber (ed.), *Identity and Beyond: Rethinking Africanity: Discussion Paper 12*. Uppsala: Nordic Africa Institute, pp. 15–35.

Nyamnjoh, F.B. 2006a. *Insiders and Outsiders*. Dakar: CODESRIA Books.

Nyamnjoh, F.B. 2006b. 'Re-Thinking Communication Research and Development in Africa'. In Paul Tiyambe Zeleza (ed.), *The Study of Africa: Volume 1, Disciplinary and Interdisciplinary Encounters*. Dakar: CODESRIA Books, pp. 393–416.

Nyerere, J. 1966. 'The Dilemma of the Pan-Africanist'. Speech delivered at the University of Zambia, Marking the Inauguration of President Kenneth Kaunda as the First Chancellor of the University of Zambia, 13 July.

Nyerere, J. 1967. *Freedom and Unity: A Selection from Writings and Speeches, 1952–65*. Dar-es-Salaam: Oxford University Press.

Nyerere, J. 1968. *Freedom and Socialism*. New York: Oxford University Press.

Nzongola-Ntalaja, G. 1987. *Revolution and Counter-Revolution in Africa: Essays in Contemporary Politics*. London: Zed Books.

O'Brien, C.C. 1965. *Writers and Politics*. New York: Pantheon.

Odendaal, A. 1984. *Vukani Bantu! The Beginning of Black Protest Politics in South Africa to 1912*. Cape Town and Johannesburg: David Philip.

Ogot, B.A. 2002. 'The Role of a University in the Development of National Unity and Consciousness'. In T. Falola and A. Odhiambo (eds), *Essays of Bethwell Allan Ogot: The Challenges of History and Leadership in Africa*. Trenton, NJ: Africa World Press, pp. 593–598.

Olukoshi, A. and Zeleza, P.T. 2004. 'Introduction: The Struggle for African Universities and Knowledges'. In P.T. Zeleza and A. Olukoshi (eds), *African Universities in the Twenty-First Century: Volume 1*. Dakar: CODESRIA Books, pp. 1–18.

Omari, P. 1970. *Kwame Nkrumah: The Anatomy of an African Dictatorship*. London: C. Hurst.

Onimode, B. (ed.). 1989. *The IMF, the World Bank and the African Debt*. London: Zed Books.

Orowosegbe, J.O. 2008. *Decolonizing the Social Sciences in the Global South: Claude Ake and the Praxis of Knowledge Production in Africa*. Leiden: African Studies Centre Working Paper 79.

Orowosegbe, J.O. 2011. *Reflections on the Challenge of Reconstructing Post-Conflict States in West Africa: Insights from Claude Ake's Political Writings*. Uppsala: Nordic Africa Institute Discussion Paper 54.

Osha, S. 2005. *Kwasi Wiredu and Beyond: The Text, Writing and Thought in Africa*. Dakar: CODESRIA Book Series.

Paolini, A.J. 1999. *Navigating Modernity: Postcolonialism, Identity, and International Relations.* Boulder, CO and London: Lynne Rienner Publishers.

Parry, B. 2004. *Postcolonial Studies: A Materialist Critique.* London and New York: Routledge.

Pearse, M. 2004. *Why the Rest Hates the West: Understanding the Roots of Global Outrage.* Illinois: InterVarsity Press.

Pilger, J. 2008. 'Honouring the Unbreakable Promise'. Unpublished Address delivered at Rhodes University during a Ceremony to Receive an Honorary Doctorate in Literature, 6 April.

Pityana, N.B. (n.d.) 'Higher Education, Transformation and Africanisation: A Paradigm Shift?'

Planning Commission. 2011. *Nation Building Diagnostic.* Pretoria: Planning Commission of South Africa.

Prah, K.K. 2009a. 'A Pan-Africanist Reflection: Point and Counterpoint'. Unpublished Paper Presented at the Centre for Advanced Studies of African Society (CASAS), University of Cape Town.

Prah, K.K. 2009b. 'Who is an African?' in J. Adibe (ed.), *Who is an African? Identity, Citizenship and the Making of the Africa-Nation.* London: Adonis and Abbey Publishers Ltd., pp. 57–60.

Pratt, M.L. 1992. *Imperial Eyes: Travel Writing and Transculturalism.* London and New York: Routledge.

Quijano, A. 2000a. 'The Coloniality of Power and Social Classification'. *Journal of World Systems*, 6(2) (Summer–Fall), pp. 342–386.

Quijano, A. 2000b. 'Coloniality of Power, Eurocentrism, and Latin America'. *Nepantla: Views from the South*, 1(3), pp. 533–579.

Quijano, A. 2007. 'Coloniality and Modernity/Rationality'. *Cultural Studies*, 21(2–3) (March/May), pp. 168–178.

Raftopoulos, B. 1999. 'Problematising Nationalism in Zimbabwe: A Historiographical Review'. *Zambezia*, XXVI(ii), pp. 83–115.

Raftopoulos, B. 2007. 'Nation, Race and History in Zimbabwe'. In S. Dorman, D. Hammett and P. Nugent (eds), *Making Nations, Creating Strangers: States and Citizenship in Africa.* Leiden: Brill, pp. 145–189.

Raftopoulos, B. 2010. 'The Global Political Agreement as a 'Passive Revolution': Notes on Contemporary Politics in Zimbabwe'. *The Round Table*, 99(411), pp. 705–718.

Raftopoulos, B. and Phimister, I. (eds). 1997. *Keep on Knocking: A History of the Labour Movement in Zimbabwe 1900–1997.* Harare: Weaver Press.

Raftopoulos, B. and Sachikonye, L. (eds). 2001. *Striking Back: The Labour Movement and Post-Colonial State in Zimbabwe, 1980–2000.* Harare: Weaver Press.

Rahnema, M. 1991. 'Global Poverty: A Pauperizing Myth'. *Interculture*, 24(2), pp. 4–51.

Ramphalile, M. 2011. '"Patriotic Blackness"' and "Liberal/Anti-Patriotic" Whiteness: Charting the Emergence and Character of an Articulation of Black/White Racial Subjectivity Peculiar to Post-Apartheid South Africa'. Unpublished M.A. thesis, University of Witwatersrand.

Ranger, T. 1967. *Revolt in Southern Rhodesia 1896–7. A Study in African Resistance.* London: Heinemann.

Ranger, T. 1969. 'Connections between "Primary Resistance" Movements and Modern Mass Nationalism in East and Central Africa'. *Journal of African History*, 9(3/4), pp. 437–453.

Ranger, T. 1977. 'The People in African Resistance'. *Journal of Southern African Studies*, 4(1), pp. 125–146.

Ranger, T. 1985. *Peasant Consciousness and Guerrilla War in Zimbabwe*. London: James Currey.

Ranger, T. 1993. 'The Invention of Tradition Revisited: The Case of Colonial Africa'. In T. Ranger and O. Vaughan (eds), *Legitimacy and the State in Twentieth-Century Africa*. London: Macmillan, pp. 62–111.

Ranger, T. 1999. *Voices from the Rocks: Nature, Culture and History in the Matopos Hills of Zimbabwe*. Harare: Baobab.

Ranger, T. 2002. 'The Zimbabwe Elections: A Personal Experience'. *Transformation*, pp. 54–76.

Ranger, T. 2004. 'Nationalist Historiography, Patriotic History and History of the Nation: The Struggle over the Past in Zimbabwe'. *Journal of Southern African Studies*, 30(2), pp. 215–234.

Ranger, T. 2005a. 'The Uses and Abuses of History in Zimbabwe'. In M. Palmberg and R. Primorac (eds), *Skinning the Skunk – Facing Zimbabwean Futures*. Uppsala: Nordic Africa Institute, pp. 1–15.

Ranger, T. 2005b. 'Rule by Historiography: The Struggle Over the Past and Its Possible Implications'. In R. Muponde and R. Primorac (eds), *Versions of Zimbabwe: New Approaches to Literature and Culture*. Harare: Weaver Press, pp. 217–243.

Reddy, T. 2000. *Hegemony and Resistance*. London: Ashgate Publishing.

Ribeiro, G.L. 2011. 'Why (Post)colonialism and (De)coloniality Are Not Enough: A Post- Imperialist Perspective'. *Postcolonial Studies*, 14(3), pp. 285–297.

Rischard, Jean-François. 2003. *High Noon. Global Problems, 20 Years to Solve Them*. New York: Basic Books.

Rivkin, R. 1969. *Nation-Building in Africa: Problems and Prospects*. New Brunswick: Rutgers University Press.

Robertson, R. 1992. *Globalization: Social Theory and Global Culture*. London: Sage Publications.

Robins, S. 1996. 'Heroes, Heretics and Historians of the Zimbabwe Revolution: A Review Article of Norma Krieger's Peasant Voices'. *Zambezia*, XXIII(1), pp. 71–93.

Rodney, W. 1973. *How Europe Underdeveloped Africa*. London and Dar-es-salaam: Tanzania Publishing House and Bogle-L'Ouverture Publications.

Rorty, A.O. 2007. 'The Vanishing Subject: The Many Faces of Subjectivity'. In J. Biehl, B. Good and A. Kleinman (eds), *Subjectivity: Ethnographic Investigations*. Berkeley, CA: University of California Press, pp. 34–51.

Ross, R. 1999. *A Concise History of South Africa*. Cambridge: Cambridge University Press.

Sadomba, Z.W. 2011. *War Veterans in Zimbabwe's Revolution: Challenging Neo-Colonialism and Settler and International Capital*. Harare and London: Weaver Press and James Currey.

Said, E. 1978. *Orientalism*. New York: Vintage Books.

Santos, B. de S. 2002. *Towards a New Legal Common Sense*. London: Butterworth.

Santos, B. de S. 2005. 'General Introduction: Reinventing Social Emancipation: Towards New Manifestos'. In B. de S. Santos (ed.), *Democratizing Democracy: Beyond the Liberal Democratic Canon*. New York: Verso, pp. xvii–xxxiii.

Santos, B. de S. 2007a. 'Beyond Abyssal Thinking: From Global Lines to Ecologies of Knowledges'. *Review*, XXX(1), pp. 45–89.

Santos, B. de S. (ed.) 2007b. *Another Knowledge Is Possible: Beyond Northern Epistemologies*. London and New York: Verso.

Santos, B. de S., Nunes, J.N. and Meneses, M.P. 2007. 'Opening Up the Canon of Knowledge and Recognition of Difference'. In B. de S. Santos (ed.), *Another Knowledge Is Possible: Beyond Northern Epistemologies*. London and New York: Verso, pp. i–xix.

Sarkar, S. 1992. 'The Kalki-Avatar of Bikrampur: A Village Scandal in Early Twentieth Century Bengal'. In R. Guha (ed.), *Subaltern Studies* VI. Oxford: Oxford University Press, pp. 1–23.

Sartre, J.-P. 1976. *Black Orpheus*. Paris: Presence Africaine.

Scarnecchia, T. 2008. *The Roots of Urban Democracy and the Political Violence in Zimbabwe: Harare and Highfield, 1940–1964*. Rochester, NY: Rochester University Press.

Schreiner, O. 1923. *Thoughts on South Africa*. Johannesburg: Africana Book Society.

Senghor, L.S. 1998. 'Negritude: A Humanism of the Twentieth Century'. In R.R. Grinker and C.B. Steiner (eds), *Perspectives on Africa: A Reader in Culture, History, and Representation*. London: Blackwell Publishing, pp. 115–116.

Shaw, W.H. 1986. 'Towards the One-Party State in Zimbabwe: A Study in African Political Thought'. *Journal of Modern African Studies*, 24(3), pp. 373–394.

Shivji, I.G. 1974. *The Silent Class Struggle*. Dar-es-Salaam: Tanzania Publishing House.

Shivji, I.G. (ed.). 1991. *State and Constitutionalism: An African Debate on Democracy*. Harare: Sapes Books.

Shivji, I.G. 2003. The Rise, the Fall and the Insurrection of Nationalism in Africa. Unpublished Keynote Address to the CODESRIA East African Regional Conference held in Addis Ababa, Ethiopia, 29–31 October.

Shivji, I.G. 2009. *Where is Uhuru? Reflections on the Struggle for Democracy in Africa*. Oxford: Fahamu Books.

Shivji, I.G. 2011. 'The Struggle to Convert Nationalism to Pan-Africanism: Taking Stock of 50 Years of African Independence'. *Pambazuka News*, 544, pp. 1–6.

Shivji, I.G. 2012. 'Nationalism and Pan-Africanism: Decisive Moments in Nyerere's Intellectual and Political Thought'. *Review of African Political Economy*, 39(131), pp. 103–116.

Sithole, M. and Makumbe, J. 1997. 'Elections in Zimbabwe: The ZANU (PF) Hegemony and Its Incipient Decline'. *African Journal of Political Science*, 2(1), pp. 122–139.

Smith, A.D. 1999. *Myths and Memories of the Nation*. Oxford: Oxford University Press.

Smith, L.T. 1999. *Decolonizing Methodologies: Research and Indigenous Peoples*. London: Zed Books.

South African Communist Party (SACP). 1962. *The Road to South African Freedom*. London: Inkululeko Press.

Southern Africa Report. 2000. 'Interview with Morgan Tsvangirai'. *Southern Africa Report*, 15(3) (June), pp. 1–5.

Soyinka, W. 1976. *Myth, Literature, and the African World*. Cambridge: Cambridge University Press.

Soyinka, W. 1994. 'Interview with Nathan Gardels: Bloodsoaked Quilt of Africa'. *Mail and Guardian*, 20–26 May, p. 31.

Soyinka, W. 2004. *Climate of Fear*. London: Profile Books.

Spivak, G.C. 1988a. 'Can the Subaltern Speak?' In C. Nelson and L. Grossberg (eds), *Marxism and the Interpretation of Culture*. Basingstoke: Macmillan, pp. 24–28.

Spivak, G.C. 1988b. *In Other Worlds: Essays in Cultural Politics*. New York: Routledge.

Spivak, G.C. 1990. *The Post-Colonial Critic: Interviews, Strategies, Dialogues*. London: Routledge.

Spivak, G.C. 1991. 'Theory in the Margin: Coetzee's Reading Defoe of Crusoe/Roxana'. In J. Arac and B. Johnson (eds), *Consequences of Theory*. Baltimore, MD: The John Hopkins University Press, pp. 154–180.

Stalin, J. 1934. *Marxism and the National Question*. Moscow: Progress University Press.

Stewart, P. 2007. 'Re-envisioning the Academic Profession in the Shadow of Corporate Managerialism'. *Journal of Higher Education in Africa*, 5(1), pp. 123–146.

Stewart, P. 2011. 'Development and Good Change'. *Africanus: Journal of Development Studies*, 41(3), pp. 38–47.

Taiwo, O. 2010. *How Colonialism Preempted Modernity in Africa*. Bloomington, IN: Indiana University Press.

Tandon, Y. 2008. *Ending Aid Dependence*. London: Fahamu Books.

Tendi, B.-M. 2010. *Making History in Mugabe's Zimbabwe: Politics, Intellectuals and the Media*. Oxford: Peter Lang.

Thaver, B. 2002. 'Transforming the Culture of Higher Education in South Africa: Opening Up the Conversation About Institutional Culture and Race in South African Universities'. *Academe Online*, at http://www.aaup.org/AAUP/pubsres/academe/2009/JF/Feat/thav.html?PF=1 (Accessed 31 March 2012).

The Report Commissioned by the Minister of Higher Education and Training for the Charter for Humanities and Social Sciences, Final Report of 30 June 2011.

Theal, G.M. 1873. *A Compendium of South African History*. Lovedale: Institution Press.

Theron, M. and Swart, G. 2009. 'South Africa and the New Africa: Chasing African Rainbows'. In J. Adibe (ed.), *Who Is an African? Identity, Citizenship and the Making of the Africa-Nation*. London: Adonis and Abbey Publishers Ltd., pp. 153–177.

Thorbecke, E. 2006. 'The Evolution of Development Doctrine, 1950–2005'. In United Nations University World Institute for Development Economics Research (UNU-WIDER) Research Paper No. 155, pp. 1–34.

Tlostanova, M.V. and Mignolo, W.D. 2009. 'Global Coloniality and the Decolonial Option'. *Kult 6 – Special Issue: Epistemologies of Transformation: The Latin American Decolonial Option and Its Ramifications*, Fall, pp. 130–147.

Tobias, P. (ed.). 1978. *The Bushmen: San Hunters and Herders of Southern Africa*. Cape Town: Human and Rousseau.

Torfing, J. 1999. *New Theories of Discourse*. Oxford: Blackwell Publishers.

Tripathy, J. and Mohapatra, D. 2011. 'Does Development Exist Outside Representation'. *Journal of Developing Societies*, 27(2), pp. 93–118.

Trollope, A. 1973 [1878]. *South Africa: A Reprint of the 1878 Edition, with an Introduction and Notes by J. H. Davidson*. Cape Town: Juta.

Truman, H. 1949. *Public Papers of the Presidents of the United States: Harry S. Truman*. Washington, DC: US Government Printing Office.

Vambe, M.T. 2008. 'Introduction: Rethinking Citizen and Subject in Zimbabwe'. In M. Vambe (ed.), *The Hidden Dimensions of Operation Murambatsvina in Zimbabwe*. Harare: Weaver Press, pp. 1–13.

Vambe, M.T. 2009. 'Perspectives on Africanisation of Curriculum in Africa'. In J. Mitchell and A. le Roux (eds), *Curriculum Issues in Higher Education: Conference Proceedings*. Pretoria: UNISA Press, pp. 1–23.

Vansina, J. 2010. *Being Colonized: The Kuba Experience in Rural Congo, 1880–1960*. Madison, WI: University of Wisconsin Press.

Vilakazi, H.W. 1999. 'The Problem of African Universities', in M.W. Makgoba (ed.), *African Renaissance: The New Struggle*. Cape Town: Mafube Publishing Ltd, pp. 23–46.

Wallerstein, I. 1974. *The Modern World-System*. New York: Academic Press.

Wallerstein, I. 1991. 'Introduction: Why Unthink?' In I. Wallerstein (ed.), *Unthinking Social Science: The Limits of Nineteenth Century-Paradigms*. Cambridge: Polity Press, pp. 1–30.

Wamba dia Wamba, E. 1991. 'Discourse of the National Question'. In I.G. Shivji (ed.), *State and Constitutionalism*. Harare: SAPES Books, pp. 57–69.

Wiredu, K. 1995. *Conceptual Decolonization in African Philosophy: Four Essays*. Ibadan: Ibadan University Press.

Wiredu, K. 1996. *Cultural Universals and Particulars: An African Perspective*. Bloomington, IN: Indiana University Press.

Wise, D. and Ross, T.B. 1964. *The Invisible Government*. New York: Random House.

ZANU-PF Department of Information and Publicity. 2004. *Traitors Do Much Damage to National Goals*. Harare: ZANU-PF Department of Information and Publicity.

ZAPU. 2010. *ZAPU Manifesto*. Bulawayo: Information and Publicity Department.

Zartman, I.W. 2007. 'The African State'. In J.C. Senghor and N.K. Poku (eds), *Towards Africa's Renewal*. Aldershot: Ashgate Publishing Ltd., pp. 28–46.

Zeleza, P.T. 1997. *Manufacturing African Studies and Crises*. Dakar: CODESRIA Books.

Zeleza, P.T. 2003. *Rethinking Africa's Globalisation: Volume 1, The Intellectual Challenges*. Trenton, NJ: Africa World Press.

Zeleza, P.T. 2006 'The Inventions of African Identities and Languages: The Discursive and Developmental Implications'. In O.F. Arasanyin and M.A. Pemberton (eds), *Selected Proceedings of the 36th Annual Conference on African Linguistics: Shifting the Centre of Africanism in Languages and Economic Globalization*. Somerville, MA: Cascadilla Proceedings Project, pp. 15–26.

Zeleza, P.T. 2008. 'Introduction: The Causes and Costs of War in Africa: From Liberation Struggles to the "War on Terror"'. In A. Nhema and P.T. Zeleza (eds), *The Roots of African Conflicts: The Causes and Costs*. Oxford: James Currey, pp. 1–35.

Zillah, E. 2004. *Against Empire: Feminisms, Racism and the West*. London: Zed Books.

ZIPA. 1977. 'Chimurenga – A People's War'. *Zimbabwe News*, March/April, pp. 5–7.

Žižek, S. 1999. *The Ticklish Subject: The Absent Centre of Political Ontology*. London and New York: Verso.

Žižek, S. 2008. *In Defence of Lost Causes*. London and New York: Verso.

Žižek, S. 2009. *Violence: Six Sideways Reflections*. London: Profile Books.

Zizek, S. 2011. *Living in the End of Times*. London and New York: Verso.

Zolberg, A.R. 1966. *Creating Political Order*. Chicago and London: University of Chicago Press.

Zvobgo, E. 1984. 'The ZANU Idea'. In G. Baumhogger (compiler), *The Struggle for Zimbabwe: Documents of the Recent Developments of Zimbabwe, 1975–1980*, Volume IV. Hamburg, pp. 13–23.

Zvobgo, E. 1995. 'Agenda for Democracy, Peace and Sustainable Development in the SADC Region'. Unpublished Paper Delivered at Parliamentarians at the CPA/IPU Joint Dinner, Meikles Hotel, Harare, 14 November.

Index

CPSIA information can be obtained
at www.ICGtesting.com
Printed in the USA
LVHW01s0950010618
579242LV00007B/35/P